Critique of Cosmopolitan Reason

New Visions of the Cosmopolitan

Series Editors

PATRICK O'MAHONY
TRACEY SKILLINGTON
University College Cork, Ireland

Volume 2

PETER LANG
Oxford • Bern • Berlin • Bruxelles • Frankfurt am Main • New York • Wien

Critique of Cosmopolitan Reason

Timing and Spacing the Concept of World Citizenship

Edited by
Rebecka Lettevall and Kristian Petrov

PETER LANG
Oxford • Bern • Berlin • Bruxelles • Frankfurt am Main • New York • Wien

Bibliographic information published by Die Deutsche Nationalbibliothek
Die Deutsche Nationalbibliothek lists this publication in the Deutsche Nationalbibliografie; detailed bibliographic data is available on the Internet at http://dnb.d-nb.de.

A catalogue record for this book is available from the British Library.

Library of Congress Control Number: 2013948794

ISSN 1664-3380
ISBN 978-3-0343-0898-4

Hochfeldstrasse 32, CH-3012 Bern, Switzerland
info@peterlang.com, www.peterlang.com, www.peterlang.net

"Upon suffering beyond suffering [...] I see a time of seven generations when all the colors of mankind will gather under the sacred Tree of Life and the whole Earth will become a circle again. In that day there will be those among [my people] who will carry knowledge and understanding of unity among all living things, and the young white ones will come to those of my people and ask for this wisdom. I salute the light within your eyes where the whole universe dwells. For when you are at that center within you and I am [at] that place within me, we shall be as one."

— TȞAŠÚŊKE WITKÓ (Crazy Horse),
Oglala Sioux warrior and chief, 1877
(four days before he was killed)

Contents

Note on the Cover Image

Title

Star Trails, Oxfordshire © Mary Spicer, 2013.

Description

A star trail is a phenomenon conditioned by diurnal motion, in which an apparent motion of the stars in the sky, due to the rotation of the Earth, has been captured by long-time exposure photography. The image on the cover was taken close to midnight on 9 June 2013 in rural Oxfordshire, and is a single exposure of 40 minutes at ISO 100, focused manually. If the photographer (as here) focuses the North Celestial Pole, indicated by Polaris, the trails appear as concentric circles, reminiscent of rings created on water. As amazing as they are in their own right, they are also suggestive of the unity of time and space, the interdependency between the part and the whole, history's dialectic between continuity and discontinuity and the hermeneutical movement towards new horizons of understanding.

Introduction

REBECKA LETTEVALL AND KRISTIAN PETROV

Toward a Critique of Cosmopolitan Reason

Being a cosmopolitan literally means being a citizen of the world, implying an expansion of one's identity from the *polis* to the *cosmos*. This self-transformation occurs continuously through processes of mediation and interplay, having existential, hermeneutic, as well as political implications. As a cosmopolitan, developing sympathy toward humanity at large does not necessarily require detachment from particular affiliations, rather, in the words of Amanda Andersen (1998, 267), that one is creating a reflective distance from oneself, which enables a broader understanding that takes into account the culture and customs of the other. The cosmopolitan is thus inscribed in an increasingly inclusive global network of overlapping solidarities, in which individuals rather than collectives emerge as moral agents, inhabiting a new world community fostered by unprecedented universal challenges and conditioned by the declining authority of the nation-state. These are common imageries of cosmopolitanism.

However, one may ask, whose model of the *polis* fits the cosmopolitan vision that one ultimately has drawn upon? And, is a *cosmopolis*, that is, a universal "city-state" of equal citizens governed by reason, conceivable anyway for those who have traditionally lacked any particular *polis* to apply their "civic" ethos to in the first place?[1] To reverse the first question, *which* cosmos (if there is only a cosmos in the singular, that is) is implied in "cosmopolitanism" and how big is it? Is this cosmos, or indeed its delimited yet absolute approximation as the "globe" (cf. Jordheim and Sandmo

1 The complicated question about the relationship between statelessness and rights is, indeed, very central in the writings of Hannah Arendt (1951/1979, 31–45), e.g. in her discussions on the Rights of Man in interwar Europe where loss of citizenship meant loss of fundamental rights (as well as the very quality of being human).

2011), to be taken literally or figuratively? Is it natural or cultural? Is it always-already structured as a common reference point or an ideal order (the Greek *kósmos* being the logical opposite of *khaos*), or alternatively, is it essentially constructible, negotiable, divisible and, hence, contestable? The "cosmos" and the "*polis*", as well as the compound "cosmopolitanism", have each a long history, and, accordingly, have been mediated and conceptualized in numerous ways.

Scope and Problem

Academic interest in cosmopolitanism, or rather what in the literature has emerged as "new cosmopolitanism" (Strand 2010), to which the philosopher Immanuel Kant, though in a quite selective representation, has been retroactively credited as its spiritual ancestor, has since the end of the Cold War been growing dramatically. Ironically, socio-political currents outside academia have simultaneously, if one omits the revival of humanitarian intervention and (quasi-imperialist) *mission civilisatrice*, to a significant extent been characterized by increased emphases on particulars—the "fundamentals" of religion, culture and ethnicity. Some of these did undeniably legitimize the infamous atrocities committed during the bloody closing of the old millennium (and the virtually equally violent opening of the new one). It is as if the fall of the Berlin wall ushered us into an intellectual and political vacuum that has been filled by a new dialectic, if not plain antagonism, between sheer universalistic interests and perspectives on the one hand and downright particularistic counterparts on the other, in which cosmopolitanism has appeared trying to legitimize itself as a compromise solution. What comes to mind in a European context, is the inexhaustible talking about, and the relentless efforts to create, in recent years, a borderless integration and unification, while the structural possibilities for a cosmopolitan citizenship have become all the less evident to identify—conditioned by the accelerating monetary crisis of the eurozone. In this respect, the universalistic project of Europeanization[2] has ironically contributed to evoking a revival of ethnocentric nationalism, that is, the very antithesis of the European project, the combating of which constitutes its *raison d'être*.

Historically, Europe has perhaps more than any other area in the world, internally as well as externally, been conceptualized as a universalistic civilization—the birthplace of Reason, Science, Democracy, Human Rights and Economic Globalization. Paradoxically, however, it has all along been dependent upon archaic patterns of essentialist dichotomization. In the shadow of contemporary Europe's search for a cosmopolitan identity (see European Commission 2012), implicitly in contradistinction to anti-democratic and traditionalist "others" in Europe's near and far abroad, there reside neglected human rights' problems, associated with marginalized groups, *sans-papiers*, national minorities and even indigenous peoples, also *within* Europe. One is tempted to ask whether cosmopolitanism has turned out to be the "false consciousness" of an essentially Eurocentric or neoliberal process of globalization, which, although formally pertaining to universality, contrary to its articulated ideals reproduces hierarchical structures of domination and segregation, disrespect for human rights and a modernity still essentially *colonial*? This is certainly the charge against new cosmopolitanism[3] laid by theorists such as Peter van der Veer (2002, 166), David Chandler (2003, 25) and Chantal Mouffe (2005, 100–101). Or is cosmopolitanism yet to be interpreted in the opposite way, as a historically-evolved possibility of ultimately recognizing all humans, including the *in-between* individuals and collectives of post-territorial spaces, as well as actually overcoming the xenophobia and antagonism, including the constant risk of a "war of all against all" on the international stage, imposed by the early-modern and modern nation-state paradigm? Accordingly,

2 "Europeanization" has come to refer to the adoption by member states of the European Union to the convergence criteria of the union. However, it must be remembered that the European Union is not the same as Europe. The term is thus misleading.

3 Among the protagonists of "new cosmopolitanism" are included David Held (1995), Daniele Archibugi (Archibugi and Held 1995), Arjun Appadurai (1996), Jürgen Habermas (1997), Ulrich Beck (2002/2005), and also, although taking a less optimistic stance, Mary Kaldor (2003), Kwame Anthony Appiah (2006) and Seyla Benhabib (2006).

cosmopolitanism in the twenty-first century may refer to several different, if not contradictory, notions. The way its contexts fluctuate, so does its meanings. One might, however, say that it was not until the late 1990s that cosmopolitanism developed towards the more political idea, which, at least occasionally, is referred to as new cosmopolitanism.

In order to approach the questions posed above reflexively one needs to re-think cosmopolitanism in the context of its historical and geographical conceptualization, which is suggested by this volume's subtitle: *Timing and Spacing the Concept of World Citizenship*.[4] The first aim of this book is to display new historically oriented perspectives and insights on a discourse rather dominated by *ahistorical* presumptions. A critical contextualization of cosmopolitanism, not only as an empirical concept but also as an analytical tool, might contribute with an understanding of cosmopolitanism's explicit and implicit meanings and its significance and potential within contemporary political and social thought. In post-communist scholarship, cosmopolitanism is often treated as a universal in order to describe, explain, justify or criticize processes of, or responses to, "globalization". Here, the effort is to look at cosmopolitanism more as an historically contingent concept. A guiding question is how our perception of the notion of "cosmopolitanism" has changed during different historical periods.

4 In the words of Peter Burke, "[Contexts] are not found but selected or even constructed, sometimes consciously, by a process of abstracting from situations and isolating certain phenomena in order to understand them better. What counts as a context depends on what one wishes to explain" (Burke 2002, 172). A "context"—etymologically a metaphor from weaving, one of its denotations being the *circumstances* enabling the understanding of the meaning of a text, an utterance, an act or an artefact—is always relative to other contexts (in principle the number of possible contexts is infinite). But even though a contextual analysis must be based on a delimitation of contexts (the relevant context, usually in the singular, being defined by the particular research question rather than by the research topic itself), one should never stop asking what an object of study *might* mean in a totally different context. In this volume this hypothetical plurality is reflected by the diversified selection of disparate contexts of cosmopolitanism, taking into account the "contextuality" of time as well as space, in both diachronic and synchronic respects.

The second objective of the volume is to critically explore alternative trajectories beyond the Western imagination, by redefining the Enlightenment legacy and the role of the periphery vis-à-vis the centre. Most notably, Eastern Europe and the Arab world are included in the analysis of cosmopolitanism. Human rights thought, as an integral part of cosmopolitanism, has during different periods of history received strong impulses from these particular regions, for example in the form of ideas mediated by the Islamic theological *Muʿtazilah* school of the eighth to the tenth centuries AD, as well as by the *Charter 77* initiative in Czechoslovakia in the late twentieth century, even though these areas are often remarkably neglected in contemporary cosmopolitanism research.[5] By highlighting the function of the outside world as Europe's, or the "West's", dialectical *other*, the risk of unconsciously giving oneself to a perspective that is not able to see its own contingency may be reduced. From a *European* horizon, representations such as "Russia", "Byzantium", "Northern Africa" and "the Orient" have since the Enlightenment functioned as what Reinhart Koselleck (1979, 211–212) characterized as asymmetric "counter-concepts", which have continuously reproduced a spirit of Europeanness, in contrast to its externally located alien and problematic shadows (see Petrov 2013, 340; cf. Petrov 2014, 32).[6] A wider geographic focus may enable a deeper understanding of the European as well as the global integration process.

5 More broadly, one could also, i.a., consider the significance of North American Iroquois culture for European eighteenth- and nineteenth-century critiques of social and sexual inequality (e.g. Engels 1884/2010, 129) and, albeit controversially hypothesized, its virtual influence on Euro-American ideas of constitutionalism and federalism (see e.g. Wilson 1960, 47; cf. Snow 1994, 154).

6 One could also mention, in relation to Europe, the case of America, having been occasionally presented as a deterrent example of cultural shallowness and vulgarity. Notwithstanding, strong representations of the country as a logical extension of Europe, a true "Euro-American" civilization, indeed, Europe's very foundation (in the character of *saviour* from fascism and communism), have prevailed. Regarding the dialectic between Europe and its "others" one should also bear in mind that "Western Europe", which is really the underlying hero of this narrative, is more a product of the Cold War than an historical constant. "Europe", as such, since the eighteenth century, has not always constituted a *centre*. Not least during the interwar era and

Actual development within Europe's "others", for example the Arab Spring in 2011, might be instructive in order to more "cosmopolitically" facilitate coming to terms dialectically with universalism and particularism. However, as the sceptically inclined reader might object, can the cosmopolitan project ever be released from its original Enlightenment impulses of so-called Eurocentrism and Occidentalism? We agree with Kant that even if an ideal is beyond human reach and thus unattainable, this fact does not undermine the moral validity of *striving* for its realization (Denis 2013, 169). The challenge thus consists in trying to reconstruct a horizon of intelligibility in which cosmopolitanism is *approximated* to transcend rather than reproduce its traditional implications of East/West- and North/South dichotomization, while simultaneously recognizing the Enlightenment legacy as constitutive, in both positive and negative respects.

Cosmopolitanism and Conceptual History

Theoretical and Methodological Remarks

Although this volume is essentially a multi-disciplinary endeavour, a historical perspective is salient. If it could be said to have a common methodological framework, one of the candidates would probably be the German sub-discipline of *Begriffsgeschichte* (conceptual history), emerging in post-war West Germany though having roots in German philosophical idealism of the early nineteenth century (Hampsher-Monk *et al.* 1998).[7]

the Cold War, it was obvious that "Europe" was radically marginalized, ideologically as well as politically.

7 There is also an Anglo-Saxon equivalent to German conceptual history, sometimes referred to as "Linguistic Contextualism"—Quentin Skinner (e.g. 1999) being its foremost practitioner. Skinner's work is actor-centric and draws upon analytical philosophy of language in emphasizing the rhetorical and polemical context of the *speech act*, while *Begriffsgeschichte* rather informs its analyses with consideration to social structures and problems of hermeneutics and the philosophy of history.

Symptomatically, the reader will notice the preoccupation with the etymology and semantics of words, concepts, synonyms, antonyms, prefixes and suffixes, as well as with the pragmatics of linguistic accommodation, appropriation and translation, throughout the volume, although explicit references to *Begriffsgeschichte* or to an equivalent occurs only in some of the contributions.

From the point of view of conceptual history, cosmopolitanism can be treated as a controversial concept that dialectically indicates as well as constructs the world, or the "global" (cf. Koselleck 1972; 2002). As Andrew Vincent, the author of the concluding chapter in this volume, points out, even a seemingly innocent *distinction* like what differentiates old from new cosmopolitanism may become an arena for contestation—political or philosophical. Concepts that are essentially political, that is, controversial, acquire new, sometimes irreconcilable, meanings by virtue of the ways they are used in specific situations. Correspondingly, a conceptual practice can also re-define its socio-contextual framework, which conditions its meaning, consequently unleashing new horizons of expectation for acting and thinking; although there always, at least according to Koselleck, one of the founders of *Begriffsgeschichte*, exist social and material pre-conditions that escape language and discourse. Only since Kant, and particularly his paradigmatic 1795 work *Zum ewigen Frieden* (*Perpetual Peace*), have the notions of human nature, citizen, city, nation, state, sovereignty, politics, border, asylum, migration, Europe and humanity fluctuated. When Kant re-discovered and transformed the Stoic idea of world citizenship, he did so in the light of the theories of natural law current in the seventeenth and eighteenth centuries—even while his limited claims suggest that he also tried to distance himself from this tradition and such metaphysical premises it presupposed. The concept of world citizenship today is internally linked to *human* rights which are ontologically different from *natural* rights as understood during Kant's time. (It must be pointed out, however, that Kant implicitly does include a kind of *human* rights in *Perpetual Peace*.) Contemporary human rights are not justified by the positing of a natural state, neither are humans supposed to share an eternal or common nature, and rights are granted by a collective act of human will, rather than seen as an expression of a divine plan or a natural law. These are important considerations when discussing contemporary problems of globalization from a "cosmopolitan" perspective. How, when and why, asks the conceptual historian, do the semantic transformations and pragmatic appropriations of cosmopolitanism occur, and how are these linked to other "histories"—of the cultural, political, social and economic?[8] Yet, whilst several contributions in this volume do not explicitly address "*Begriffsgeschichte*", it is still symptomatic that many of them do try to explore alternative paths in relation to what could be considered as the royal road of conventional intellectual history or political philosophy and theory. A *conceptual* historian should preferably not only consult the canonized classics but perhaps delve more so into relatively marginal sources, in this volume represented by "atypical" cosmopolitan thinkers, like Plato, Rousseau, Cloots, Herder and to some extent even Kant, in the role of a "pre-political" rather than political philosopher.

The history of a particular concept is, however, difficult to distillate, since it is so sophistically embedded in its context. It is proposed here that the philosopher Hans Georg Gadamer's concept of *Wirkungsgeschichte* is constructive for understanding concepts and their historicity. The Gadamerian perspective implies that the hermeneutic effort fluctuates between the whole and the part and back again. The "effective history" means that historical interest does not just concern a particular historical event or phenomenon, but also their effects. This includes also the history of research. From this it might be assumed that several effects or meanings do not disappear but prevail, so that in the conceptual history of cosmopolitanism, several meanings of the concept are being used at the same period, and sometimes the actors do not seem to be totally aware about this. For example, it is appropriate to talk about a cosmopolitan as an elite traveller even today while also several other meanings prevail. And even so, cosmopolitanism existed also in the nineteenth century, or perhaps one should say between Kant and the end of the Cold War, even if it was not talked about as such.

8 For a case study that approximates a *conceptual history* of cosmopolitanism, see Frijhoff (1998).

From Cosmopolitanism to New Cosmopolitanism

It is clearly indicated in the library catalogues that academic interest in cosmopolitanism increased after the end of the Cold War. In so far as cosmopolitanism was an issue at all during the Cold War era, it was being discussed very differently from today. For example, even within academic disciplines it was mostly used as an image of the upper-class travelling cosmopolitan (Lettevall 2007), not least within literature. The proponents of new cosmopolitanism usually write the current's own history as starting with Immanuel Kant, even though the sage from Königsberg developed his theories on cosmopolitanism in a different context and perhaps would not recognize his own philosophy in today's discussions. Kant in his turn referred to the Stoics and the Stoic tradition. Since the end of the Cold War, academic interest in other parts of Kant's political philosophy has increased, and now there exists a field of experts in this area. Pauline Kleingeld, for example, suggests that cosmopolitanism for Kant was "an attitude taken up in acting" and thus has nothing to do with rootlessness that was a common view of cosmopolitans during Kant's time (Kleingeld 2012, 1).

The broad spectrum of meanings owing to cosmopolitanism has widened much further during the past decade, and its linguistic form as an -ism might tempt readers to see it as a coherent theory, which it absolutely is not. It is even difficult to see any hard core in it at all: versions of cosmopolitanism cannot be reduced to one central meaning or thesis, even if several scholars have tried to do so.

The starting point of Western thinking is usually placed in ancient Greece. That is also the case in *Historisches Wörterbuch der Philosophie* (Horstmann 1976, 1155), according to which there are traces of a cosmopolitan perspective already in some of the oldest remains of Greek philosophy, that is, in the Ionian philosophy of nature, which is seen in relation to the changing political and social situation with a new colonial horizon. Heraclitus proposed a world order that was common for all. Within the earlier history of the concept of cosmopolitanism, as described in this particular and impressive work, it is supplementary to a law that deals with the state, with a cosmic law. In the narrative, cosmopolitanism, if one may call it so, deals with a law beyond the law in the *polis*. Cosmopolitanism is thus understood as a system of rights, which are justified by Nature. Even if it is unclear whether Socrates saw himself as a world citizen, it is through Plato's spokesperson Socrates argued that the philosopher's body is situated within the *polis*, while his soul transcends its limitations.

In the authoritative *Historisches Wörterbuch*-article, cosmopolitanism is understood as a kind of humanism. Therefore, the quotation from Terence, "I am a human being, I consider nothing that is human alien to me", is interesting as it points toward one particular understanding of humanism. Starting with Terence, the story ends with the United Nations as an institutionalization of the Kantian idea of a rational world order.

Historically, the term supposedly was first used by Diogenes from Sinope when he called himself a cosmopolitan. This has been interpreted, or travestied, as a statement that a cosmopolitan is a person who is beyond such temporal political boundaries as geopolitical units, that is, city-states, or today's nation-states. Independent from the fact whether this is true, the interpretation is a part of the conceptual history of cosmopolitanism.

However, since the remaining source of this conceptual use was conceived several hundred years later, by Diogenes Laertius, one cannot be sure about the validity of truth in this utterance. But from the perspective of the history of ideas or concepts, that does not matter so much since even ideas that are not true, so to speak, still are valid as having an impact on what comes afterwards. An approximation of the Cynic Diogenes' kind of cosmopolitanism is actually quite common in contemporary discussions on the concept. According to the sources, he appears as an individualist who did not seem to care so much about humanity as a whole or its related conceptions. His goal seemingly was more about criticizing the prevailing system of norms. This cosmopolitanism resembles what Fougeret de Monbron, the French eighteenth-century writer and traveller, had connected to during his travelling, caring more about oneself than about anyone or anything else, hence a rather selfish cosmopolitanism. Such a description has been associated with the elite cosmopolitan traveller of the eighteenth century (Lettevall 2008). It is, then, more an individualist understanding of the concept, one with closer connections to the elite cosmopolitanism that prevailed during the eighteenth century among the elite nobility.

The stoic kind of cosmopolitanism is, however, a bit different. The legacy from Stoic philosophy, founded in ancient Greece and later developed in Roman antiquity, perhaps in Kant in particular, has engaged with problems associated with universal natural rights and thus rather dealt with the universal than the individual perspective.

If in the Western tradition the conceptual history of cosmopolitanism before Kant is closely connected to the history of Christianity,[9] the history from Kant onwards is more secularized, even if it is still universalistic. Kant focuses on cosmopolitanism as a secular right of man, by which the individual is guaranteed what he calls the right of hospitality. What should become obvious by the end of this introduction is that this right is rather complicated. For example, it entails an obligation of the states and includes a sophisticated structure between the general and the particular that tends to be justified through the global argument, which Kant develops in *Perpetual Peace*. According to this, every human being has originally equal right to everything on earth—the globe, but historical circumstances have created a situation that implies a factual difference in rights. Thus, the equality in rights becomes restricted to situations when there is a danger of someone's life.

Kant developed a cosmopolitan theory that has political implications. However, the nineteenth century was not a fertile ground for cosmopolitan ideas, even if the ideas prevailed in other ways and under different labels. For one thing, in the period from ca 1850 until the First World War, it was quite easy to travel in Europe without a passport. However, not surprisingly that situation changed during the war. The articulation of nationalism during the so-called long nineteenth century was accompanied by internationalism and several official as well as grass roots level efforts were made to increase the amount and quality of internationalism. Several social and political movements were very important in this respect, including the peace movement, the socialist and worker's movements. It can be claimed that within many of them the idea of cosmopolitanism had surfaced even if it was not called as such. The word cosmopolitan had been used in the

9 For a development and discussion on this, see Jacobsen (2011) and Cheneval (2002).

Russian pogroms to classify Jews. It had also been defined as signifying an arrogant person, evoking the Cynic, or as with the Fougeret de Monbron, a characteristic selfishness that goes before human rights and compassion. However, a strong sense of internationalism and care for a common world might still be endorsed among writers who define cosmopolitanism in that respect.[10] Arguing like this, certain kinds of internationalism have carried cosmopolitanism over some time, and later on they turned into "transnationalism", by which traditional institutions have lost much of their former power.

In the conceptual history of cosmopolitanism, as in all histories, it is easy to be caught in the trap of cumulativity. It is then interesting that cosmopolitanism is presumed to have two quite different roots. For how is the Stoic natural rights universalism to be combined with the Cynic individualism? Reacted from this perspective, the criticism of cosmopolitanism becomes quite understandable: The overreaching universalism might actually hide the majority, essentially supporting only a small minority of individuals.

The contemporary cosmopolitanism that took shape shortly after the decline of the Soviet empire, in the hands of Ulrich Beck, Jürgen Habermas, David Held and James Bohman, among others, is characterized by normativity and universalism, which in many ways theoretically seem hard to escape. At the same time, Kant's legacy is crucial, and shows one of the difficulties with cosmopolitanism. It turns out that "new cosmopolitanism" is not so *new* in the twenty-first century. Since Kant's time, the role and strength of the nation-state as well as that of the citizen have changed and developed. One kind of cosmopolitanism is characterized by mobility, movement and fluidity, and having encounters with diaspora, for example. Such cosmopolitanism is even "newer" than new cosmopolitanism. Even though the meaning of the categories "new" and "old" can be more absolute, rather than strictly relative or modifying (such as in the case of the "New World"), calling something "new" is dangerous because sooner

10 Swedish philosopher and pedagogue, Ellen Key (1849–1926), presents cosmopolitan ideas in her writings on peace and internationalism (Lettevall 2011).

or later it might likely turn old. Perhaps a critical cosmopolitanism, such as proposed in this volume, would be more descriptive.

A critique of cosmopolitanism includes the critique of the Enlightenment where focus is brought on the invisibilization of the other. Kant's legacy seems to make this an unavoidable part of cosmopolitanism. The starting point is always a situation in time and place, and from that perspective we do not see what is in the shadow or beyond the horizon and unawareness of this causes problems. The fact that the Enlightenment perspective invisibilizes the other is absurd just as inclusion and human rights are at the same time at the centre of cosmopolitanism. This is the problem with all kinds of "cosmopolitanisms". In this respect cosmopolitanism argues against itself. Even if this volume aims to widen the Enlightenment universalistic cum Western-biased perspective, in this case by including Eastern Europe and postcolonial theory, the Western context is still dominant. It is, however, important to remember that in principle, cosmopolitan ideas could be traced back as well to Indian (Ashoka), Chinese (Confucius) and Babylonian (Hammurabi) tradition, among others, such as is partly reflected in Micheline Ishay's (2004/2008) monumental work on Human Rights.

Cosmopolitanism seems to have encountered a change in value during the last decade. While broadly across academia writers loved to project an image of themselves as cosmopolitans at the last turn of the century, that has now changed. Cosmopolitanism has come to embrace different kinds of multiculturalism, globetrotter travelling and migration. Cosmopolitanism has also become the label for naïveté and oyster mentality.

The Ethos and Structure of the Book

The idea of this book emerged during an international conference, "Cosmopolitanism in a Wider Context: Conceptualizing Past and Present", which was organized in 2011 with support by the Swedish Baltic

Sea Foundation, which funded a research project, "East of Cosmopolis: The World Citizen and the Paradox of the *sans-papiers*". The conference took place at Södertörn University and the Nobel Museum in Stockholm and attracted participants from some twenty countries around the world. As conference organizers we decided to select the most original contributions, written by various scholars that attended the conference (although two of the contributions were especially written for this publication by the participants in retrospect). Academically, the authors have their background in the *humanities* and, hence, can add historical and contextual depth on cosmopolitanism, whose theories, methods, concepts and empirical indicators have become increasingly topical, especially within the *social sciences*. The book is thus an attempt at inter-disciplinary dialogue, aspiring to serve to preliminarily correct prevalent tendencies of anachronism, essentialism and ethnocentrism, in which cosmopolitanism tends to appear as a timeless (and thus depoliticized) universal.

The structure of this book is, despite its historical ethos, essentially thematic. Its respective thematic parts, however, including more empirical as well as more theoretical pieces, are organized in separate chronological order (although not entirely consistently), and generally moves forward in time throughout the book. Before reading the detailed overview in this volume, one might dwell momentarily on its title. *Critique of Cosmopolitan Reason* is, of course, a reflective allusion to Kant and his three *Critiques* (1781–1790), and, especially, his project to analyse the characteristics and limits of human reason—in a context of (envisioned) modernization and globalization. Analogously, we set out to assess the critical possibilities and limits of what, since the Enlightenment—particularly in the wake of Kant's influential 1795 "post-critical" essay *Perpetual Peace*—could be seen as a projected *cosmopolitan* reason, tentatively instigated in Kant but also developed in other thinkers. The reference reflects our intention to radically reconstruct the Kantian matrix of modern cosmopolitanism in its historicity, although our endeavour is perhaps more sympathetic to Kant than those writers who subject the Kantian project to punning in a more polemical, ironic or tongue-in-cheek manner.[11] Indeed, "critique" is here taken not in its lexical meaning of negative fault-seeking, but in its etymological sense, which Kant himself seems to have presupposed, of carefully *judging* and *discriminating*, between what is necessary and contingent, spontaneous and determinate, internal and external, conditioning and conditioned, founded and unfounded, and thereby reaching for (or even crossing) an object's or concept's transcendental limit, beyond what is given in pure experience. This form of analytical "discrimination" is characteristic in the writings of Tania Espinoza and Andrew Vincent, which will be presented below. These authors, alongside, however, almost all of the other contributors, also propose a more critical cosmopolitanism, which is less optimistic, more cautious, de-romanticized, non-ideal and non-foundational. This implies recognition of "dissensus", divergence, incompleteness, finitude, contingency, conditionality and intrinsic "problematicity". In the light of the thesis vehemently pursued by Jamil Khader in the volume's final section, somebody might even ask whether cosmopolitanism, as we know it, is possible to reform at all. More specifically, the relation between *reason* and cosmopolitanism is explicitly addressed in the first part of the volume, the structure of which now will be assessed.

11 Examples of such writings include: "critiques" of *Dialectical Reason*, *Cynical Reason*, *Modern Reason*, and, not surprisingly, *Postcolonial* and *Postmodern Reason* (Sartre 1960; Sloterdijk 1983/1987; Kremer-Marietti 1999; Spivak 1999; Salleh 2009). These authors, if they engage with Kant at all, mostly aim to reckon with certain aspects of his philosophy, in an essentially negative manner, Spivak (1999), however, perhaps coming close to an exception. In this context one should also mention Chea (2006), who illustrates the above tendency as well. He entitled a section of one of his books "Critique of Cosmopolitan Reason". In that passage Chea returns to Kant and Marx, and draws upon postcolonial experiences in Asia in order to criticize theorists of new cosmopolitanism for neglecting the "cosmopolitan" impulse mediated by progressive nationalism outside Europe. Chea also chooses to criticize new cosmopolitanism theorists for positing a global consciousness, the imagery of which conceals factual consequences of *uneven development*. Cheah proposes a reflexive approach towards human rights vis-à-vis their *contexts*, in order to deal with veritably inhuman conditions during globalization.

The book consists of ten individual contributions and is divided into four thematic parts. In the first section, the authors set out to rethink cosmopolitanism and reason philosophically, doing so by dislocating the concept of cosmopolitanism from its canonical centre, not unlike the way Martin Heidegger once attempted to create a *beginning anew* for Western thinking, from within its own history, although with a different aim in mind.

In the opening chapter, AARON C. VLASAK contextualizes the concept of cosmopolitanism in Greek antiquity, albeit not primarily among Stoics or Cynics as one would expect, but in Plato—who sometimes has been regarded as the archenemy of cosmopolitan values like individualism, egalitarianism, tolerance, openness and hospitality (e.g. Popper 1966). Although many modern cosmopolitans have retrospectively attributed cosmopolitan principles of justice to *Socrates* (e.g. Brown 2006), Plato's mentor and literary spokesperson, Vlasak carefully tries to distinguish between what might be the "Platonic" and "Socratic" voices of the dialogues, by reading different dialogues against each other, in order to present evidence for an authentic *Platonic* cosmopolitanism. Vlasak uses a variety of dialogues and persuasively reconstructs a cosmopolitanism of "the estranged", which might also have some value for the understanding of the genealogy of the concept in Cynic and Stoic thought. Cosmopolitanism has, indeed, its origin in this very ancient context of philosophy that Vlasak tries to reconstruct. His attempt, however, is exemplary, in that it indicates that the meaning that the concept eventually acquired during the course of history, only represents a limited aspect of how it originally was used and defined.

What could we expect if the concept of cosmopolitanism were incarnated in the world as a real person and, as such, put on the psychoanalyst's couch? Perhaps in caricature we would find revealed the individual's suppressed libidinal energies, fuelling the narcissistic self-satisfaction of an immature and inferior individual, compensated with a grandiose but faulty self-image, prone to an attitude of "superiority", knowing it had projected a "grand narrative" of universal emancipation onto the world, in which Cosmopolitanism itself, self-servingly, appeared as the vanguard of civilization, located at the centre of all human progress? Similar, although not so simplistic, far-fetched and probably tendentious, questions are provocatively raised by TANIA ESPINOZA in the volume's second essay. In analysing

Kantian cosmopolitanism, she takes her point of departure in a re-reading of Kant's critical *theoretical* philosophy, hence turning, so to speak, Kant against Kant, with the help of concepts developed in Lacanian psychoanalytic thought. Espinoza does, hence, not use cosmopolitanism as an analytical tool in order to rationalize or criticize aspects of globalization, but the essay's originality is achieved by the manner in which she succeeds to diagnose the pathologies of cosmopolitan reason, and prescribe a cure for its recovery—aiming for a cosmopolitanism of the "not-all". (Although Espinoza remains deliberately ambivalent whether Kant is the patient or the analyst!)

The second part of the volume presents four historically oriented studies that revolve around cosmopolitanism as it was articulated in connection to the Enlightenment.

When a representative from the Enlightenment is sought for cosmopolitanism, Kant usually is found to be the sole candidate. Although today being a virtually forgotten figure of the French revolution, Anacharsis Cloots (1755–1794) was during the nineteenth century still regarded as the archetype of cosmopolitanism: a cosmopolitan either gone wrong or mad; or successfully incarnating humankind in its unity and diversity. FRANK EJBY POULSEN makes an important contribution to the conceptual history of cosmopolitanism by bringing the neglected Cloots to the fore. Although Poulsen's subject chronologically post-dates Nina Lex's focus on Rousseau, which will be presented shortly, his essay opens the section since it exemplarily illustrates as well as problematizes what a *conceptual history* approach to cosmopolitanism might look like. According to Poulsen, the contradictions in Cloots' work are also our own today, which could make his work a vantage point of historical reflection for contemporary cosmopolitan theory: How to conciliate in a global polity the need for local self-determination with universal law? If sovereignty, as Cloots argues, is too dangerous to be left in the hands of a particular group of people, would it not risk universal tyranny in the hands of humankind (conceptualized as a totality)? Still Poulsen asks, could Cloots' ideas about the "sovereignty of humankind", and with it, the conversion of the social contract into a global contract, form a better basis upon which to apply the 1948 Universal Declaration of Human Rights?

Jean-Jacques Rousseau is probably one of the greatest thinkers to appear in the history of Western moral and political philosophy, and he has, accordingly, been most influential on subsequent philosophers, not least, Immanuel Kant. Rousseau is, however, also generally described as a fierce critic of Enlightenment cosmopolitanism (e.g. Rosenblatt 2008; Kleingeld and Brown 2011), if not a plain proto-nationalist. In her essay, NINA LEX portrays Rousseau differently, as a cosmopolitan, although an ambivalent one. When initially faced with Rousseau's theory of the subject, we seem to encounter an absolute confrontation between what is denoted by the terms "man" and "citizen", which seems to contradict the current theories of cosmopolitanism. However, as Lex maintains, drawing on recent reviews, Rousseau's aim was not only to characterize the human condition as a diremption, but he also outlined a *third way* open to man, in which the individual is not only inhabiting the city state but also the *world*. Lex's contribution is valuable particularly in this respect, since Rousseau's theory, partly reformulated from a viewpoint of contemporary cosmopolitanism, allows for the opportunity to comprehend the individual as oscillating between diversification and commonality, solitude and commitment, impulse and reflection, and, therefore, Rousseau might offer a path to togetherness beyond political extremism, existential isolation and Stoic renunciation, which also reaches beyond the universalistic yet relativistic levelling of multiculturalism. One should, however, note that Lex uses the terms nationalism and nationalist, which, in this context, prior to the American and French revolutions, do not necessarily locate actual concepts in the sources, but rather are analytical constructs, used by the author in order to conceptualize Rousseau's philosophy for comparative purpose.

In the following essay, GEORG CAVALLAR attempts to contextualize Kant's concept of cosmopolitan right. He convincingly illustrates how this law of the world citizens relates to other conceptions of hospitality rights developed and contained in international legal theory from Francisco de Vitoria up to Kant's time. Kant understands *Nature* "reflectively" as a "moral facilitator" of the education of the human species. Here there is, as Cavallar notes, a tension, between the human species *propelled* by Nature towards legal and moral ends, on the one hand, and on the other, an understanding of human history as a collective learning process, whereby humans are seen as more or less autonomous agents *not* manipulated by Nature. By contextualizing Kant's cosmopolitanism historically Cavallar exposes its possibilities and limitations for contemporary thought. As Cavallar indicates, a remarkable asymmetry resides in Kant, which is played out in various forms. One way to exemplify this could be to point to Kant's approach toward man and his neighbour. The principle of treating fellow human beings as ends in themselves evidently opposes the request to *force* those who are presumed to live in a primitive natural state to move into the superior state of rights. This problem will be further addressed by the end of this introduction.

Herder is often credited as the originator of modern nationalism (e.g. Berlin 1976, 145), although he paradoxically questioned the need for the state altogether. In his *Letters* (1792), Herder, nonetheless, seemed to welcome the French revolutionary and universalistic attempts of creating a law-governed republic based on citizens' active participation. From a viewpoint of moral particularism, if not sheer cultural relativism, Herder rejected the cosmopolitan theories of his time. Yet he also, as EVA PIIRIMÄE convincingly makes the case, sharply criticized modern imperialism and national chauvinism. In fact, his "nationalism" is intertwined with a theory of republican patriotism. Herder explicitly embraced the latter as a distinct kind of cosmopolitanism, a *patriotic* cosmopolitanism. Piirimäe goes on to scrutinize the nature of this seemingly oxymoronic cosmopolitanism, and searches for what meaning it might have today, doing so in the light of contemporary discussions on universalism, particularism and imperialism. Interestingly, Herder's "patriotic cosmopolitanism" presupposes an alternative "enlightenment" of the sentiments. In emphasizing the role of sentiments and passions, Herder shares with not only Rousseau but also with a contemporary cosmopolitanism critic like Chantal Mouffe (2000), the denunciation of democratic or republican politics as an essentially rational and deliberative activity, freed from human emotions.

In Part III the theme of exile, which was originally framed and addressed in the volume's first part, is taken up again, now set in the context of interwar and post-war Eastern Europe.

Does exile, or border-crossing, produce cosmopolitan attitudes? So goes conventional wisdom. GALIN TIHANOV'S essay is an attempt to critically historicize and theorize about the relationship between cosmopolitanism and exile. Exile is found here to be a cultural construct from the age of Romanticism. The author demonstrates, with cited cases from interwar Eastern Europe, that exile cannot be reduced to an effect of asymmetric force but is also, and perhaps more importantly, a negotiation between the state and the individual. Analysing the foundations that form the basis for narratives about exile, as both suffering and creativity, Tihanov's arguments stimulate the critical examination of the liberal consensus on mobility (of goods, services, money, and *people*, if we take the European Union as an example). Rather than imagining exile on the plane of individual creativity or suffering, victory or failure, and thus also binding the project of cosmopolitanism to individual capacities, the author urges the possibility of contemplating a different cosmopolitanism, one that breaks the spell of the liberal imagination, on the one hand, and the romanticized notion of exile, on the other, and thus goes beyond the idea of fixed attainment. From a viewpoint of the humanities, Tihanov in that manner demonstrates the danger present in the social sciences of trading off the paradigm of methodological nationalism for one of methodological individualism or cosmopolitanism, without genuine historical reflexivity.

How should the cosmopolitan project be conceived in a post-metaphysical, if not post-universalistic, theoretical framework? Given the universality and utopianism of contemporary cosmopolitan principles, a partial shadow of totalitarianism seems to fall on any attempt to formulate cosmopolitanism anew, risking that a new master narrative is created. Does the East European post-war experience of intellectual, cultural and political dissent provide any lessons for contemporary debates on cosmopolitanism, and for the possibility of formulating, in Espinoza's words, a cosmopolitanism of the "not-all"? In her essay, TAMARA CARAUS focuses on *Charter 77*, the human rights movement in socialist Czechoslovakia, and the writings of the philosopher Jan Patočka (1907–1997), its cofounder and spokesperson. Caraus' hypothesis is that Patočka's thought, although presupposing a belief in human rights and the individual as the centre of all ethics, provides a minimalist framework for conceiving a non-totalizing and post-universalistic cosmopolitan theory, congruent, one might add, with the resurgent academic interest in local subjectivities and micro-narratives, and which avoids the Habermasian postulation of global "consensus", instead embracing the dynamics of contestability and disagreement, aiming at, in Patočka's words, "permanent questioning" and a "living in problematicity". From this perspective, the practice of Eastern European dissidence and its non-violent resistance provide, as Caraus contends, a valuable resource for thinking a self-critical cosmopolitan political theory, which is reflective upon its own temptations of totalitarianism.

The final part of the book is in many respects also the most critical one. The two contributors each imagine and reflect upon a state of things beyond the horizon of current cosmopolitanism(s), although several of their appraisals, such as regarding postcolonial theory, go in opposite directions. The point of departure is no longer cosmopolitanism as we know it, but rather a situation, agency, discourse or reason, in which a redefined cosmopolitan vision might have a legitimate and constructive role to play.

In JAMIL KHADER'S critical, at times intransigent, settlement with cosmopolitanism, he relocates the concept to the context of anti-colonial struggle for national liberation, as well as tries to redefine it within the *internationalist* tradition. Even though Khader is seeking to rehabilitate "the nation" as a living site for struggle and resistance within the globalized world order, one should understand that he is not attacking cosmopolitanism, *per se* (characteristically, he terms his target "cosmopolitics"), but rather confronts the logic and implications of a neoliberal order in which, one could add, the imagery of the cosmopolite has come to serve as the discursive justification of the "Global Entrepreneur" (e.g. Williams 2011, 25–26), who seductively fuses together global narratives with middle-class consumer desires (cf. Bookman 2012, 68). Instead of the above cited reflective distance, in relation to one's own particular affiliation, the cosmopolitan-as-the-global-entrepreneur, surrounded by an aura of "cosmopolitan cool", risks, at least in the worst scenario, implementing a mono-cultural "business as usual", embracing everyone, everywhere asymmetrically, whatever the possible social costs or human (or environmental) sacrifices. What might seem as a rather difficult and controversial intellectual enterprise, Khader tries to extract "the postcolonial impetus" of the revolutionary thought of Vladimir Lenin, taken as a resource for a politically reformed cosmopolitanism. If cosmopolitanism is not to be replaced all together, presumably by its more radical cousin internationalism,[12] it seems imperative for Khader to upgrade cosmopolitanism into a more powerful version that is rebuilt "from the margins". Inspired by Slavoj Žižek, Khader thus applies Lenin's anti-imperialist perspective on current globalization. The "world revolution" of the title is not as such the keyword of a Lenin or a Trotsky, denoting what in retrospect appears as a rather naïve expectation of a bygone era, but comprises the wider, on-going project of *decolonization*. In so doing, Khader is essentially critiquing cosmopolitan reason from a post-Marxist viewpoint, even though, as has been suggested, this critique does not affect all forms of cosmopolitan theory. Possibly, one might object, Khader may to some extent be over-emphasizing the significance of anti-colonialism for Lenin. The latter was probably less interested in the anti-colonial movements in Asia than he was of the immanent contradictions of the imperialist system, which ultimately were conditioned by intra-European conflicts. But even if one might question the validity and ethos of the Leninist perspective, Khader succeeds in actualizing the historical lines up to the postcolonial movements and theories of the present, as well as the global revolutionary wave (emblematized in the Arab Spring) that we have been witnessing. And this question that Khader arrives at is very crucial: How can cosmopolitan theory, inclusive of its efforts to renew and internationalize democracy, explain, encompass and even promote this revolutionary wave? As such a contribution of the essay is to fill a gap in current theoretical literature by connecting cosmopolitanism with agency and global activism.

How should we conceive of cosmopolitanism after the alleged failure of the grand narratives of modern political ideologies? By trying to formulate a "bottom-up", minimal or thin cosmopolitanism, ANDREW VINCENT readily accepts the challenge proposed by Caraus in the previous section. In the light of cosmopolitanism's intellectual and conceptual history, Vincent's intention is to gather the threads of discussion on cosmopolitanism together

12 Khader tries to redefine cosmopolitanism within the internationalist tradition, or rather what he calls "postcolonial revolutionary experimentation", hence committing to the ideals of internationalism in a manner not dissimilar from Micheline R. Ishay (1995, 129), albeit viewing their present potential much more optimistically.

by reflecting upon some of the latter's constitutive assumptions, several of them already being presented earlier in the volume, as well as more particularly revisiting the question of (cosmopolitan) reason, originally addressed in the first section. In doing so he tries out the concept in different contexts and traditions, as well as applies several analytical distinctions to it, from the viewpoint of the history of moral, political and legal philosophy (resulting in the most analytical, but probably also most self-reflective chapter in this book). Vincent is seeking a *via media*, between the universalistic overtones of cosmopolitanism on the one hand and its relativistic implications of multiculturalism on the other. In criticizing the various accounts of cosmopolitanism he also raises some difficulties with the standard critiques of cosmopolitanism. Finally, Vincent turns to what he sees as a relatively neglected component of cosmopolitanism, namely its political rendition (although in a quite different sense from how the concept is used by "cosmopolitan democracy"-advocates). The political conceptualization of cosmopolitanism harbours a clue to what Vincent characterizes as a sceptical or outrightly *reluctant* cosmopolitan point of view.

New Cosmopolitanism—and Beyond

As many scholars have already observed, including several contributors to this volume, the wider conceptual history of cosmopolitanism is Janus-faced, containing tensions and contradictions, the polarities of which are perhaps more mutually constitutive than exclusive. Perplex is, accordingly, the historical conceptualization of hospitality, which was earlier addressed in this introduction. Hospitality right is not only modelled upon honourable ancient practices found in most cultures of the world. It has also, as Cavallar indicates, a darker side to it, reflected ever since the advent of modernity in debates over natural rights and their applicability to non-Europeans, especially indigenous peoples, from which, as Cavallar also explicates, Kant himself was unable to successfully release himself. Besides, as will now become apparent, the conceptualization of hospitality has an evident spatial dimension. This is of course also the case with cosmopolitanism, and the spatiality of this concept is a crucial ground for a critique of cosmopolitan reason, as is shown throughout this book.

Eighteenth- and nineteenth-century North America, perceived by Europeans of the time both as an approximation of the natural state of the past and as a projection of the future progress of civilization (cf. Tocqueville 1835–1840/1899, especially Vol. I, Ch. XVIII), is taken here as an example of cosmopolitanism's "negative" dialectic. The natural rights to travel, visit, engage in commerce, settle and preach the gospel, as well as the reciprocal obligation of indigenous "Indians" to treat the millions of European "visitors" with *hospitality*, undoubtedly justified not only the white man's exploration but also his *expansion*. Nearly from the start, this demanded the building of permanent houses, fencing-in of sensitive hunting places (for the sake of intensive agriculture), and the digging for gold in the heart of sacred lands. However, by exercising this set of individual rights, the most fundamental of all rights was denied on behalf of "the other", namely, the right to life or self-preservation. In the wake of the constant westward expansion, driven by the hunger for fertile soil and valuable minerals, uncountable foreign menaces followed: Plagues, wars, massacres, "pro-active" military protection of settlers and gold-diggers, militia initiated "retributions", a lucrative fur trade and thereby, eventually, the near-extinction of the buffalo with the help of large-calibre, long-range rifles, not to mention the forced removal of Indians to reservations with cramped housing and malnutritious rationing, were all together factors that contributed immensely to the post-Columbian extermination of more than approximately 95 per cent of all Amerindians north of the Rio Grande River.[13]

13 By the end of the nineteenth century, the population of indigenous peoples in the United States had fallen to some 250,000. In a much politicized contemporary debate, scholars are divided on how many people that actually inhabited the corresponding area at the time of the first contact with the Europeans. Figures range from between 1 and 18 million. Russell Thornton (1987, 36), the author of a most credible and diligent demographic overview, estimated that the population might well have been as much as 7 million.

A catalyst in this context was truly the misguided beneficence of many a forced universalistic campaign, be it of mission or civilizing or education or pacification, where pastors, ethnographers, philanthropists, school teachers, government bureaucrats and military officers enthusiastically set out, and thereby unreflectively sped the negative demographic tendency, to make the collective of barbarians into the white man's universal image (e.g. Brown 1970, 372; cf. Wilson 1998, 152, 301–302). The "other" was to be remodelled, ultimately, that is, into an ideal—a Christianized and individualized property owning commercial farmer, while ironically, virtually never being admitted to the white man's law and his privileges (cf. Brown 1970, 232, 366; Wilson 1998, 151, 157). But would the Indians, counter-factually speaking, have been benefitted if they had been granted the rights and attributed with agency as moral persons? Although collective rights, with their particularistic implication, seem to be theoretically opposed to individual rights and thus undermine cosmopolitanism's sense of equity, it would seem presumptuous to reduce the destruction of entire tribes, peoples, cultures and nations, to matters of "individual" moral concern. Individual rights, at least *negative* individual rights, are constitutively designed to secure individual ownership. So what if "the other", from a European horizon, had elusively escaped any authoritative definition of ownership in the first place?

The assaults on the Native Americans accelerated during the second half of the nineteenth century, infamously marked in perpetuity when General Sheridan supposedly said that "The only good Indian is a dead Indian", or, if one fancies "civilizing" over warfare, in Captain Richard H. Pratt's flagrant motto: "Kill the Indian [...], and save the man" (Pratt 1892/1973, 261). These aphorisms, and the campaigns about which they are emblematic, could not only be explained in relation to an emerging biological racism, or what Marx would view as antagonism between incompatible modes of production.[14] Such expression of hatred and hostility

14 Cf. chapter by Cavallar in this volume, and his reference to the eighteenth century's so-called four-stage theory, according to which the modern business-engaged farmer in this context was endowed with history's highest morality, and in relation to which

could perhaps also be viewed within Freudian psychoanalysis as a repetition compulsion of patricidal fantasy, indeed, echoing an already committed, albeit suppressed, father-murder in one's own past (cf. chapter by Espinoza in this volume). The encounter with the diversified cultures of the "savages" in America, sometimes appearing as more "advanced", not least when it came to supplying and distributing food and organizing a cohesive yet non-hierarchical and peaceful society, likewise indicated that the absolute truth claims of the Judeo-Christian revelation were not valid, despite that one did one's best to project one's own initial helplessness and sense of metaphysical awkwardness onto the savage (cf. Burke's critique of colonialism in the chapter by Cavallar). Consequently, in the name of universalism, the Amerindians, as well as so many other original inhabitants across the world, were either to be assimilated or annihilated, forced to choose "civilization" or war.

Analogously to the paradigm of the Christian mission in Western history, one might ask whether the *reluctant* "other" in our contemporary world is going to be politically "converted" to cosmopolitanism? The discourse surrounding cosmopolitanism has traditionally reflected what has here been referred to rather vaguely as a Eurocentric impulse, but also one that is metaphysically *anthropocentric* (characteristically expressed, e.g., in the philosophy of Cloots), according to which universal humanity, guided by reason, has been endowed with the absolute sovereignty (and superiority) originally attributed to God (and thus, it seems, also having inherited the Almighty's alienation towards the rest of His creation), and whose implementations have had profound, many times devastating, cultural and ecological consequences (cf. Jonge 2011, 307). How can one formulate a more open-ended and symmetric cosmopolitanism that is not dismissive of currents of "dissensus" because of allegiance to an ideal "consensus"? To begin with, such a cosmopolitanism cannot privilege those voices already included in a *polis*, that is, with access to advanced modernity, and confessing only to a monotheistic (mostly, but not necessarily, Christian)

---

the "hunter-gatherer", a nomad, simply appeared as a barbarian, who should be treated accordingly, i.e., like a wild beast (cf. Wilson, 1998, 64).

worldview, or alternatively, to its "rational" and secular equivalent, that is, a post-monotheistic view. Perhaps then a global *cosmopolis* might be approximated, in which "the others" are granted substantial equal autonomy, and their expressions are not reduced to objects of correction or convergence (and, consequently, in which alternative production relations are not conceptualized as "primitive", "barbaric" or "antagonistic"). In a world where pre-urban and pre- or even proto-agrarian ways of life have virtually been modernized out of existence, a cosmopolitan reconciliation between abstract ideas of universal rights and the concrete respect for diversity can certainly be a prospect worth striving for, not least as a challenge to the really existing "globalism" of economic determinism, or to "multiculturalism", the latter which is nominally committed to pluralism but also induces a self-segregating retreat into particularism and essentialism.

According to the French philosopher of science, Bruno Latour, whose position in this context escapes any attempt to categorize it with reference to the new–old distinction of cosmopolitanism, "[t]here are more ways to be other, and vastly more others, than the most tolerant soul alive can conceive" (Latour 2004, 453). If one takes his argument seriously and accepts its validity for the intents and purposes of our discussion, the class of "others" would include not only traditionally silenced humans of the peripheries but all *nonhuman* entities, that in different ways exhibit activity and unarguably make humans act (Latour 2004, 454), including animals, plants, minerals and artefacts (and even imagined spirits and deities). Figuratively speaking, these "entities" could be seen knocking on the door to mutual recognition as well, that in itself being a challenge to the anthropocentric conception of man as intrinsically rational, moral, autonomous and exceptional. Even the wider physical environment, which for centuries has been defined apart from humans as a controllable object, could be seen to "insist" on being included in our very own "cosmos". This insight, which symptomatically is probably congruent with most "animistic" worldviews of "primitive" peoples, certainly points to a blind spot of cosmopolitanism, both in its "old" and "new" forms. According to Latour, this cosmos can, with the help of "a politics of the cosmos" (Latour 2004, 453, n. 4) rather than a traditional "cosmopolitanism", be reinterpreted, negotiated and *constructed* anew, and as such would embrace everyone and *everything* (although Latour should perhaps consider the lesson drawn by Espinoza that "wholeness" and "totality" can never be anything but *regulative* ideas of reason!), while recognizing, and not trying to eliminate, inherent tensions, differences and "intersectionalities".[15] The question thus arises: can human dignity really be maintained if all other *nonhuman* things are denied intrinsic meaning and worth? Whether to use the term for this project, cosmopolitan or cosmopolitical, does not really matter. However utopian (or dystopian) Latour's remarks may sound, it is exactly a study of the conceptual history of cosmopolitanism, indicating an open space of plural, contingent and contestable meanings, that enables a reflexive analysis of cosmopolitan reason's propensity to totality, idealistic normativity and captivity within the subject-object dualism (to which the authors of this introduction also seem unwillingly liable). A conceptual-historical approach is, however, not only deconstructive but also reconstructive. Besides being corrective, it allows us to linguistically (and thereby also practically) imagine our very own present and future differently, a disposition which is always inherent in human existence, although which is peculiarly often hidden to us. This is a critique of cosmopolitan reason.

References

Anderson, Amanda, 1998. "Cosmopolitanism, universalism, and the divided legacies of modernity". In: Pheng Cheah and Bruce Robbins (eds.), 1998. *Cosmopolitics: Thinking and feeling beyond the nation*. Minneapolis: University of Minnesota Press, 265–289.

Appadurai, Arjun, 1996. *Modernity at large: Cultural dimensions of globalization*. Minneapolis: University of Minnesota Press.

15 The thesis of this project overlaps that of what is increasingly referred to as "posthumanism" (e.g. Butterfield 2012, 18–19), which, although it is rarely mentioned in discussions on cosmopolitanism, also aims to deconstruct or abandon the anthropocentrism inherent in any humanism.

Archibugi, Daniele and David Held (eds.), 1995. *Cosmopolitan democracy: An agenda for a new world order*. Cambridge: Polity Press.

Arendt, Hannah, 1951/1979. *The origins of totalitarianism*. London: Harcourt Brace.

Benhabib, Seyla, 2006. *Another cosmopolitanism (the Berkeley Tanner lectures)*. Ed. Robert Post. Oxford: Oxford University Press.

Berlin, Isaiah, 1976. *Vico and Herder: Two studies in the history of ideas*. London: Chatto & Windus Ltd.

Bookman, Sonia, 2012. "Branded cosmopolitanisms: 'Global' coffee brands and the co-creation of 'cosmopolitan cool'". *Cultural Sociology*, 7(1), 56–72.

Brown, Dee, 1970. *Bury my heart at Wounded Knee: An Indian history of the American West*. New York: Holt, Rinehart & Winston.

Brown, Eric, 2006. "Hellenistic cosmopolitanism". In: Mary Louise Gill and Pierre Pellegrin (eds.), 2009. *A companion to ancient philosophy: Blackwell companions to philosophy*. Malden, MA and Oxford: Blackwell Publishing Ltd, 549–559.

Burke, Peter, 2002. "Context in context". *Common Knowledge*, 8(1), 152–177.

Butterfield, Elizabeth, 2012. *Sartre and posthumanist humanism*. Frankfurt am Main: Peter Lang.

Chandler, David, 2003. "The cosmopolitan paradox: Response to Robbins". *Radical Philosophy*, (118), 25–30.

Cheah, Pheng, 2006. *Inhuman conditions: On cosmopolitanism and human rights*. Cambridge, MA and London: Harvard University Press.

Cheneval, Francis, 2002. *Philosophie in weltbürgerlicher Bedeutung*. Basel: Schwabe & Co.

Denis, Lara, 2013. "Virtue and its ends". In: Andreas Trampota, Oliver Sensen and Jens Timmermann (eds.), 2013. *Kant's "Tugendlehre"*. Berlin: de Gruyter, 159–182.

Engels, Friedrich, 1884/2010. *The origin of the family, private property and the state*. London: Penguin Books.

European Commission, 2012. *The development of European identity/identities: Unfinished business: A policy review*. Brussels: Directorate-General for Research and Innovation, Socio-economic Sciences and Humanities.

Frijhoff, Willem, 1998. "Conceptual history, social history and cultural history: The test of 'cosmopolitanism'". In: Iain Hampsher-Monk, Karin Tilmans and Frank van Vree (eds.), 1998. *History of concepts: Comparative perspectives*. Amsterdam: Amsterdam University Press, 103–114.

Hampsher-Monk, Iain, Karin Tilmans and Frank van Vree, 1998. "A comparative perspective on conceptual history—an introduction". In: Iain Hampsher-Monk, Karin Tilmans and Frank van Vree (eds.), 1998. *History of concepts: Comparative perspectives*. Amsterdam: Amsterdam University Press, 1–9.

Held, David, 1995. *Democracy and the global order: From the modern state to cosmopolitan governance*. London: Open University.

Horstmann, A., 1976. "Kosmopolit, Kosmopolitismus". In: Joachim Ritter and Karlfried Gründer (eds.), 1976. *Historisches Wörterbuch der Philosophie*. Vol. 4. Basel and Stuttgart: Schwabe & Co, 1155–1167.

Ishay, Micheline, 1995. *Internationalism and its betrayal*. Minneapolis: University of Minnesota Press.

Ishay, Micheline, 2004/2008. *The history of human rights: From ancient times to the globalization era*. 2nd ed. Berkeley, CA: University of California Press.

Jacobsen, Mogens Chrom, 2011. *Three conceptions of human rights*. Århus: NSU Press.

Jonge, Eccy de, 2011. "An alternative to anthropocentrism: Deep ecology and the metaphysical turn". In: Rob Boddice (ed.), 2011. *Anthropocenrism: Humans, animals, environments*. Leiden: Brill.

Jordheim, Helge and Erling Sverdrup Sandmo, 2011. "Hva verden var: En forfallshistorie". In: Helge Jordheim, Erling Sverdrup Sandmo and Herman Braun (eds.), 2011. *Verden: Begreper i historien*. Oslo: Unipub forlag.

Kaldor, Mary, 2003. *Global civil society: An answer to war*. Cambridge: Polity Press.

Kant, Immanuel, 1781/1998. *Critique of pure reason*. Ed. and trans. Paul Guyer and Allen W. Wood. Cambridge: Cambridge University Press.

Kant, Immanuel, 1788/1997. *Critique of practical reason*. Ed. and trans. Mary Gregor. Cambridge: Cambridge University Press.

Kant, Immanuel, 1790/2000. *Critique of the power of judgement*. Ed. Paul Guyer and trans. Paul Guyer and Eric Matthews. Cambridge: Cambridge University Press.

Kant, Immanuel, 1795/2003. *To perpetual peace: A philosophical sketch*. Trans. Ted Humphrey. Indianapolis: Hackett Publishing Company, Inc.

Kleingeld, Pauline and Eric Brown, 2011. "Cosmopolitanism". *The Stanford Encyclopedia of Philosophy* (Spring 2011 Edition). Available at: http://plato.stanford.edu/archives/spr2011/entries/cosmopolitanism/. Accessed 5 April 2013.

Koselleck, Reinhart, 1972. "Einleitung". In: Otto Brunner, Werner Conze and Reinhart Koselleck (eds.), 1972. *Geschichtliche Grundbegriffe: Historisches Lexikon zur politisch-sozialen Sprache in Deutschland*. Vol. 1. Stuttgart: Ernst Klett Verlag, xiii–xxvii.

Koselleck, Reinhart, 1979. *Vergangene Zukunft: Zur Semantik geschichtlicher Zeiten*. Frankfurt am Main: Suhrkamp.

Koselleck, Reinhart, 2002. *The practice of conceptual history: Timing history, spacing concepts*. Trans. Todd Samuel Presner *et al.* Stanford, CA: Stanford University Press.

Kremer-Marietti, Angèle, 1999. "Nietzsche's critique of modern reason". In: Babette Babich and Robert S. Cohen (eds.), 1999. *Nietzsche, theories of knowledge, and critical theory: Nietzsche and the sciences I.* Dordrecht: Kluwer Academic Publishers, 87–102.

Latour, Bruno, 2004. "Whose cosmos, which cosmopolitics? Comments on the peace terms of Ulrich Beck". *Common Knowledge,* 10(3), 450–462.

Lettevall, Rebecka, 2007. "Kosmopolitens gränser". In: Gunnar Broberg (ed.), 2007. *Europas gränser.* Nora: Nya Doxa, 181–206.

Lettevall, Rebecka, 2008. "The idea of Kosmopolis: Two kinds of cosmopolitanism". In: Rebecka Letteval and My Klockar Linder (eds.), 2008. *The idea of Kosmopolis: History, philosophy and politics of World Citizenship*. Stockholm: Södertörn University, 13–30.

Lettevall, Rebecka, 2011. "On the historicity of concepts: The examples of patriotism and cosmopolitanism in Ellen Key". In: Hans Ruin and Andrus Ers (eds.), 2011. *Rethinking time: Essays on history, memory and representation.* Stockholm: Södertörn Philosophical Studies, 179–189.

Mouffe, Chantal, 2000. "Deliberative democracy or agonistic pluralism". *Reihe Politikwissenschaft: Political Science Series*, 72 (December). Vienna: Institute for Advanced Studies. Available at: http://www.ihs.ac.at/publications/pol/pw_72.pdf. Accessed 22 June 2013.

Mouffe, Chantal, 2005. *On the political.* London: Routledge.

Petrov, Kristian, 2013. "Russia in the European home? Convergence, cosmopolitanism and cosmism in late Soviet Europeanisation". *Europe-Asia Studies*, 65(2), 321–346.

Petrov, Kristian, 2014. "The concept of transition in transition: Comparing the post-communist use of the concept of transition with that found in Soviet ideology". *Baltic Worlds*, 7(1), 29–41.

Popper, Karl R., 1945/1966. *The open society and its enemies: The spell of Plato*. Vol. 1. 5th ed. Princeton, NJ: Princeton University Press.

Pratt, Richard H., 1892. "The advantages of mingling Indians with whites". In: Francis Paul Prucha (ed.), 1973. *Americanizing the American Indians: Writings by the "Friends of the Indian" 1880–1900*. Cambridge, MA: Harvard University Press, 260–271.

Rosenblatt, Helena, 2008. "Rousseau, the anticosmopolitan?". *Daedalus*, 137(3), 59–67.

Salleh, Ariel, 2009. "The dystopia of technoscience: An ecofeminist critique of post-modern reason". *Futures*, 41(4), 201–209.

Sartre, Jean-Paul, 1960/1991. *Critique of dialectical reason*. Rev. ed. London: Verso.

Skinner, Quentin, 1999. "Rhetoric and conceptual change". *Finnish Yearbook of Political Thought*, 3, 60–73.

Sloterdijk, Peter, 1983/1987. *Critique of cynical reason*. Minneapolis and London: University of Minnesota Press.

Snow, Dean R., 1994. *The Iroquois*. Oxford: Blackwell.

Spivak, Gayatri Chakravorty, 1999. *A critique of postcolonial reason: Toward a history of the vanishing present*. Cambridge, MA: Harvard University Press.
Strand, Torill, 2010. "The making of a new cosmopolitanism". *Studies in Philosophy and Education*, 29(2), 229–242.
Tocqueville, Alexis de, 1835–1840/1899. *Democracy in America,* vol. 1. Trans. Henry Reeve. New York: D. Appleton and company.
Thornton, Russell, 1987. *American Indian Holocaust and survival: A population history since 1492*. Norman: University of Oklahoma Press.
Veer, Peter van der, 2002. "Colonial cosmopolitanism". In: Robin Cohen and Steve Vertovec (eds.), 2002. *Conceiving cosmopolitanism: Theory, context, and practice*. Oxford: Oxford University Press, 165–180.
Wilson, Edmund, 1960. *Apologies to the Iroquois: With a study of the Mohawks in high steel by Joseph Mitchell*. London: W.H. Allen.
Wilson, James, 1998. *The earth shall weep: A history of native America*. New York: Grove Press.
Williams, Ervin, 2005/2011. *The global entrepreneur: How to create maximum personal wealth in the new global economic era*. 2nd ed. Bloomington, IN: iUniverse.

PART I

Rethinking Cosmopolitanism

AARON C. VLASAK

Philosophic Exile: Plato's Care for the Self as Cosmopolitanism

The Greek cynic, Diogenes, who called himself a *kosmopolitēs*, was literally in exile from Sinope.[1] Legend has it that when someone reminded him that the people of Sinope condemned him to exile, he responded by saying that he condemned them all to Sinope. Exile, he claimed, let him become a philosopher (*Diogenes Laertius*, VI, 2, 49). Diogenes' suggestion is that philosophers, as philosophers, are in exile from the *polis* and belong instead to the *kosmos*. According to Diogenes, philosophers are basically cosmopolitan, and to be cosmopolitan is to be defiant of social convention and without a home.[2]

Plato reportedly called the infamous cosmopolitan "a Socrates gone mad" (*Diogenes Laertius*, VI, 2, 54). We might take this as an expression of disapproval, which it partially is, or as high praise, for, in Plato's mind, to be like Socrates (in respect to philosophical ability anyway) is surely worthy of admiration. With this remark, then, we are left to imagine the ways in which Diogenes and Plato's Socrates are alike.

1 An early, substantially different version of this chapter was published with the title "Plato's *Kunikos kosmopolitēs*" (Vlasak 2012).

2 Diogenes' biography shows that he certainly walked the hard-edged subversive talk. He is known to have masturbated in public and urinated on others (*Diogenes Laertius*, VI, 2, 46). Though Diogenes' version of the cosmopolitan itself deserves careful study, it seems safe to say that his emphasis is on the negative—that is, on what the cosmopolitan is not, a domesticated and provincial man. As we proceed, we should keep in mind a contemporary, fuller, general positive character of the cosmopolitan: one with a moral commitment and who demands that political institutions conform to certain moral standards.

Many would argue that Socrates is to some extent cosmopolitan.[3] In a work fittingly titled *On Exile*, the stoic Plutarch claims that Socrates called himself a *kosmios*, a man of the *kosmos* (*Mor*. 600f–601a). Similarly, Cicero, while considering whether exile is an evil, says that Socrates claimed to belong to the *mundanum*, the world (*Tusc. disp*. V.37.108). Whether or not Socrates ever said these things, the historical link from Socrates to stoicism, which inherited cosmopolitanism, is easy to trace.[4]

More to the point, Socrates' philosophic commitment is basically cosmopolitan in its orientation. Socrates' ethical/political authority was not derived from the state; it guided his relationships within the state; it brought him into discord with the state; and, ultimately, it got him killed by the state. In the "*Apology*" Socrates is openly defiant. He is thoroughly unapologetic as he exposes his true allegiance and his willingness to disobey the authority of the *polis*. There are two examples. On the prospect of quitting philosophy, Socrates is clear and direct:

> [...] if you said to me in this regard: "Socrates, we do not believe Anytus now; we acquit you, but only on condition that you spend no more time on this investigation and do not practice philosophy, and if you are caught doing so you will die;" [...] I would say to you: "Gentlemen of the jury, I am grateful and I am your friend, but I will obey the god rather than you, and as long as I draw breath and am able, I shall not cease to practice philosophy [...]" (*Apology*, 29c–d)[5]

The second example comes up shortly after Socrates divulges the cryptic source of discord between himself and the city: "This [the *daimonion*] is what has prevented me from taking part in public affairs" (31d). Socrates trusts and obeys the daemonic intervention, but he also subjects it to retroactive rational scrutiny: "[...] I think it [the daemonic] was quite right to prevent

3 Eric Brown (2000) makes a strong case for this.

4 Antisthenes (not a citizen of Athens by the way), was an associate of Socrates and the teacher of the cynic, Diogenes of Sinope. And it was a cynic, Crates, who influenced Zeno, the first stoic.

5 With the exception of *Republic* references, Plato references are to the John Cooper (1997) collection.

me".[6] Turning to the reasons why it is right, he says, "[...] if I had long ago attempted to take part in politics, I should have died long ago, and benefited neither you nor myself" (31d–e). And here we have our second example:

> When the oligarchy was established, the Thirty summoned me [...] along with four others, and ordered us to bring Leon from Salamis, that he might be executed [...] Then I showed again, not in words but in action, that, if it were not rather vulgar to say so, death is something I couldn't care less about, but that my whole concern is not to do anything unjust or impious. That government, powerful as it was, did not frighten me into any wrongdoing [...] the other four went to Salamis and brought in Leon, but I went home. (32c–d)

There is an authoritarian interpretation of the *Crito* that is inconsistent with Socrates' civil disobedience in the *Apology*.[7] Socrates believes, the interpretation goes, that the laws of the state require strict compliance, whether or not they are just.[8] Indeed one must reckon with the fact that unlike Diogenes, Plutarch and Cicero, Socrates, at first glance, appears to see exile as an evil.[9] In the *Apology* Socrates explicitly rejects exile as possible punishment (37c–e), and in the *Crito* Socrates recalls what was said in the *Apology*, that death is preferable to exile, to refuse Crito's invitation to escape from prison (*Crito*, 52c). However, when one attends to the reasons Socrates rejects exile and escape, one sees that there is nothing wrong with exile *per se*, and there may be good reason not to obey the authority of the city.

A word about Athenian law is necessary for understanding Socrates' rejection of exile in the *Apology*. If the jury were to find the defendant guilty, it would have to choose between the proposed penalty of the prosecutor and that of the defendant (Kraut 1984, 14). The jury has found Socrates guilty.

6 Aware of the tension between Socrates' dedication to rationality and his pre-rational authority, commentators have been observant to point this out. The influential Gregory Vlastos (1991, 280–287) is a good example.

7 On the reconciliation of Socrates' civil disobedience with his indebtedness to the state, I agree with Richard Kraut (1984).

8 Kraut (1984, 5) reviews the commentary and cites Romily, Dybikowski, A. Barker, Grote, Greenberg, Martin, Adkins and A.E. Taylor as proponents of this view.

9 Carl Cederberg, who is the editor of the volume *Att läsa Platon* (Reading Plato) (2010), deserves credit for encouraging me to engage the *Crito*.

Meletus has proposed death (*Apology*, 36b). And as a counter-assessment, Socrates provocatively proposes that he be honoured like an Olympic victor (36b–37a). There is reason to believe that if Socrates had chosen a realistic alternative to death (such as exile), the jury would have opted for it. Many did not even think Socrates guilty. He would have been acquitted if a mere thirty votes had gone the other way (36a–b). Surely the 221 jurists who voted for Socrates' acquittal do not want to see an innocent man now die.[10] Socrates himself thinks that the jury might accept exile (37c), but he is the one who rejects it.[11]

When Socrates chooses death over exile, he is choosing a possible good over a certain evil. Death might be a blessing (40c), and the unexamined life is not worth living (38a). Since Socrates believes that men of other cities would be no more likely to tolerate his ways than the men of Athens (37c–e), accepting exile would inevitably amount to abandoning philosophy. Thus the evil that Socrates avoids in favour of death is not exile from the *polis*, but exile from philosophy.

Turning to the *Crito*, the reason Socrates refuses to escape from prison is that long ago he effectively chose to live in Athens, and since he chose Athens over other cities, he must either obey the laws of Athens or persuade the city of its injustice (*Crito*, 51d–52a). Reading this conditional logically, initially Socrates had no special obligation to remain in Athens. Upon choosing Athens however, at that point he is obliged to either obey the laws or show the city it is wrong. Blind allegiance to the authority of the city regardless of its injustice is in no way required. Insofar as Socrates attempts to persuade the city of its injustice, which he does, his disobedient behaviour is consistent with the reason he gives Crito for not escaping. Seeking to persuade, he is not required to obey; failing to persuade, he must now obey. Why does Socrates choose Athens over other cities in the first place? The answer to this goes back to the reason exile is not

10 There were 501 jurists in total.

11 Socrates is quite close to being a suicide. His defence tactic sounds like what we sometimes call "suicide by cop". It is as if Socrates turns a metaphorical gun on the law with the expectation that he will be killed.

a suitable punishment: Socrates would expect the same (mis)treatment from men in any other city. The reason for choosing Athens is that there is no other city that better supports what he must do: practise philosophy. Despite its injustice, Athens appears relatively tolerant of unconventional philosophers. Recall the eccentric and subversive behaviour of Diogenes.[12] Or recall that the verdict of conviction was won only by a narrow margin, and the jury seemed not to want the death penalty. Socrates refuses exile because Athens is a decent place for a philosopher in exile.

Thus far we have engaged dialogues that are presumed to approximate the historical Socrates and lack a strong Platonic voice. Though the idea of a cosmopolitan Socrates is widely regarded as tenable, the role that the cosmopolitan Socrates plays in Plato's *Republic* (a presumed middle dialogue) remains undeveloped or underappreciated.[13] *The Open Society and its Enemies*, by philosopher Sir Karl Popper (1945/1957), provides an extreme case in point.

Popper has done much to vilify Plato, characterizing him as an enemy of open society. Popper does not deny that there are humanistic expressions in Plato, but, he argues, these expressions come only under Socratic influence, while Plato's *Republic* endorses this view of morality: "Good is what is in the interest of my group; or my tribe; or my state" (quoted in Popper 1945/1957, 107). Of course Popper (p. 107) is well aware of the implications of this view for both domestic and international relations: the state can do no wrong as long as it is strong. In fact, in Popper's mind this is what makes Plato an enemy.

One would have to agree that Plato has Socrates say things in the *Republic* that seem out of sorts for the Socrates of, say, the *Apology*, but, clearly it is another claim altogether to say that Plato's fiction amounts to

12 Keep in mind, though, that the obligations and entitlements of a citizen applied to Socrates but not to Diogenes. Being literally in exile in Athens may have been easier than being only figuratively in exile.

13 We are not dealing with a simple oversight here. There are reasons not to attribute a cosmopolitan concept of justice to Plato, perhaps the best known of which involves the discussion of war and barbarians at *Republic* 469b–471b. We will come around to this problem at the close of this chapter.

a radical subversion of Socrates' cosmopolitan outlook. My view is that the *Republic* is Plato's continued attempt to come to rational terms with the trial and death of Socrates, and, far from justifying the mistreatment of both citizens and strangers alike (as Popper thinks), it, like the *Apology*, indicts the city for its un-philosophic ways.

Appreciating Socrates' role as cosmopolitan philosopher in the *Republic* is requisite for grasping one of the central and most important paradoxes there. Plato's fictional prospect of appointing someone like Socrates to rule the *polis*, after the *polis* has executed Socrates, is absurd, no doubt. This paradox is captured in the *Republic* by the name "philosophic exile". The primary sense of "philosophic exile" is that philosophers who become of service to politicians are exiled from the practice of philosophy (*Republic*, 495a).[14] But we can also take the term to designate philosophy's exile from politics. It is the cosmopolitan character of true philosophy that accounts for its historical exclusion from domestic politics. The mere suggestion of the coincidence of philosophy and political power in the ideal state is already a challenge to state sovereignty. Far from a justification of parochial, exclusionary politics, the *Republic* can be read as a cosmopolitan critique of domestic politics. In the next section, I look more closely at the philosopher-ruler paradox and exhibit the Platonic model of cosmopolitan virtue. The subsequent and final section examines the consequences of cosmopolitan virtue relating to the organization of the *polis*.

The City and the Philosopher

The Paradox

Plato's *Republic* is an attempt at dialogue on justice against the threat of force. This is how the dialogue begins. Polemarchus (whose name means "war-starter"), after having Socrates and Glaucon physically detained,

14 All *Republic* translations are from Bloom (1966/1991).

presents them with two options: either prove stronger or stay put. Socrates wants a third option, to persuade Polemarchus and gang to let them go, but to this Polemarchus responds, "Could you really persuade [...] if we don't listen?" (327c). The consideration of the (im)possibility of persuasion by (even true, just) speech against unwilling conversational partners who threaten force foreshadows the notion of philosophical exile, the paradoxical coincidence of philosophy and political power.

As Plato introduces it, a basic problem in political philosophy concerns the cultivation of the political will to moralize politics.[15] This problem is articulated theoretically and played out dramatically. At nearly the beginning of the dialogue, when Socrates says, "[...] it is not the work of the just man to harm either a friend or anyone else [...] but of his opposite, the unjust man" (335d), Thrasymachus (meaning "bold-in-battle"), Plato writes, hunches up like an angry wolf and pounces on Socrates (336b). Thrasymachus' challenge to justice, that "[...] the just is nothing other than the advantage of the stronger" (338c), frames the dialogue for its duration. Much later (at 499b–502a) we learn that this is one of the most difficult impediments to the realization of the ideal regime, to persuade the multitude to accept the philosopher. The reason this is difficult is that philosophers are just, whereas conventional politicians are like Thrasymachus, a wild beast who only looks after his own. The work of the *Republic* is the gradual rational taming of the spirited, wolf-like Thrasymachus.

15 In Kant's (1784) Sixth Thesis in the *Idea for a Universal History with a Cosmopolitan Intent* he states that the most difficult and last problem for human beings is that "Man is an animal that [...] has need of a master". What we need, Kant explains, is a guarantor of justice, who will remain just (not abuse his freedom like men) and yet be man. That this problem is the last to be solved, Kant continues, "[...] follows from this: it requires the correct concept of the nature of a possible constitution, great experience during much of the world's course, and above all else a good will prepared to accept that constitution; but it is hard to find three factors such as these together all at once; when it happens, it will only be very late, and after many futile attempts". Plato is certainly Kant's forerunner here. While Kant appears to locate the "master" in a constitution and Plato, in a philosopher-ruler, the two are alike in their assessment of the task of cultivating the political will to accept the "master".

Speaking of wolves, when the notion of a philosopher-guard first appears in book two of the *Republic*, he ironically appears in the image of the domesticated wolf, the dog (375e). The dog as image of the guard is selected because it exhibits a combination of characteristics not frequently found in human beings: great spirit and gentleness. It is friendly with the familiar. Unlike the wolf, the domesticated dog does not prey on a flock of sheep (416a). Clearly sheep here are analogous to citizens, and the distinction is between guards who look after the good of the citizens and guards who look after only their private advantage. The dog is already a tamer creature than Thrasymachus, who supposes that rulers do nothing for the benefit of the ruled (343b–c), but the dog, next to the just philosopher who would harm no one, still appears wild.

Plato's dog is an image of an exclusionary political leader whose moral concern extends only to his own citizens. While friendly with the familiar, the dog is hostile with the strange:

> When it sees someone it doesn't know, it's angry, although it never had any bad experience with him. And when it sees someone it knows, it greets him warmly, even if it never had a good experience with him. (376a)

This leads Plato to call the dog a lover of learning, a *philomathēs*, and philosophic. We are puzzled as to why loving learning is here equated with loving that which one has learned. We are further puzzled as to how the dog could ever learn and thus love. In order to learn, indeed, one would have to "love learning", but we think the true lover of learning is curious about the unknown. A non-prejudicial posture toward the unknown seems a precondition for getting-to-know. Insofar as the dog learns and loves, it must love learning in this sense. Yet we are told that the dog gets angry at the unknown.

If this irrational guard dog were Plato's ideal, indeed he would not be cosmopolitan, but maintaining an affective disposition (whether of hate or love) toward the unknown must be irrational on Platonic grounds. Outside of the *Republic*, there is ample evidence for this. Socrates, in the *Apology*, characterizes himself as a stranger in court (*Apology*, 17d), and says that his philosophic vocation requires that he seek out strangers as well as citizens (23b). Further, the philosophic vocation itself is fundamentally opposed to making assumptions about the unknown. Socrates' remarks on death (29a) are noteworthy and may be generalized: it is irrational to hate what one knows nothing about. It is equally irrational, one may add, to love what one knows nothing about. This is patently clear from what Socrates says in the *Phaedo* about misology and misanthropy (*Phaedo*, 89d–90d).[16] The mistake of misologues and misanthropes is basically the same. Misologues grow to hate ideas after their unwarranted beliefs are continually debunked. Similarly, misanthropes grow to hate people after their unwarranted trust in people is continually betrayed. Both misologues and misanthropes precisely make the mistake of the *Republic* dog. They are friendly with the familiar even without a good experience. In a dog-like way, they make claims and trust people without good reason. Such a disposition is bound to be upset and tend toward the other dog-like disposition, that of believing in nothing and hating people for no good reason. Along these lines, to say the *Republic* dog is philosophic is to make the philosopher out to be a fool or a nihilist. The true philosopher, of course, is neither. The rational way to respond to the unknown is with curiosity and scrutiny, not with hostility or with trust. For the dog to be truly philosophic on Platonic grounds, it would have to love only after learning and refuse to hate in ignorance. Rational loving is based on getting-to-know, and getting-to-know is only possible on non-prejudicial terms. Now a dog that loves rationally would be a cosmopolitan. The question is whether the guard dog of the *Republic* is subject to the same rational standards evinced in the *Apology* and the *Phaedo*.

Concerning the explanation of the discord between politics and philosophy, the similarities between the *Apology* and the *Republic* are unmistakable.

16 The *Phaedo* is, of course, the dialogue in which Socrates dies. Looking toward death, Socrates is serene, while he aims to put his companions at ease. The centrally positioned discussion about misology, called the greatest evil (89d), arises in response to the cynical challenges brought by Simmias and Cebes regarding the deathlessness of the soul (84c–88b). The account of misology is given with its analogue, misanthropy, but true philosophy is as hostile to misanthropy as it is to misology. Philosophy seems to require a certain disposition toward the three sites: death, ideas and people. The full character of that disposition and its precise relationship to the three sites are topics rich for reflection.

In the *Republic*, Socrates, along with Theages, is a candidate for the philosopher-ruler (496c). After Glaucon and Socrates conclude that they would only turn the city over to men of philosophic nature (487a), Adeimantus interjects, pointing out that many disparage the philosopher for being vicious or useless (487d).[17] Socrates does not deny that the philosophic nature often becomes useless and often becomes vicious. Instead he gives an explanation of how the decent ones in philosophy become useless,[18] and of how many other philosophic natures become vicious. The latter occurs when citizens recognize greatness in the philosophic nature, and they want to use it for their own affairs (494b). In this way, "[...] the very elements of the philosophic nature, when they get a bad rearing, are, after all, in a way the cause of its being exiled from the practice" (495a).[19] The band of true philosophers has a way of becoming exceedingly small. The few that remain are useless (490e). It seems that Socrates and Theages are among the useless few. Both Theages and Socrates escape corruption in his own way:

> And the bridle of our comrade Theages might be such as to restrain him. For in Theages' case all the other conditions for an exile from philosophy were present, but the sickliness of his body, shutting him out of politics, restrains him. My case—the demonic sign [*daimonion sēmeion*]—isn't worth mentioning, for it has perhaps occurred in some one other man, or no other, before. (496c)

Were it not for Theages' frail physical condition, called his "bridle", he surely would have fallen into corruption.[20] Like Theages, Socrates too has a sort of bridle, the *daimonion*, which shuts him out of politics.[21]

17 It is worth noting that the philosophic nature at this point is: "[...] a rememberer, a good learner, magnificent, charming, and a friend and kinsman of truth, justice, courage, and moderation" (487a).

18 This explanation is given in the image of the ship at 488a.

19 Here we hit upon the centrally positioned notion of philosophic exile, which, so I claim, has cosmopolitan import.

20 On the one hand, Socrates is paying Theages a great compliment, basically saying that he has a philosophic nature. Yet on the other hand, Socrates is drawing attention to the fact that Theages' escape was due to no credit of his own but to circumstances beyond his control.

21 It is significant that in the only two cited examples of escape from exile, the escapees, in some sense, got lucky. The fortuitous presence of sickness in Theages and the

Immediately following the reference to Theages' and Socrates' escape from an exile from philosophy, Socrates says:

> Now the men who have become members of this small band have tasted how sweet and blessed a possession it is. At the same time, they have seen sufficiently the madness of the many, and that no one who minds the business of the cities does virtually anything sound, and that there is no ally with whom one could go to the aid of justice and be preserved. Rather—just like a human being who has fallen in with wild beasts and is neither willing to join them in doing injustice nor sufficient as one man to resist all the savage animals—one would perish before he has been of any use to city or friends and be of no profit to himself or others. Taking all this into calculation [*logismō*], he keeps quiet and minds his own business—as a man in a storm, when dust and rain are blown about by the wind, stands aside under a little wall. Seeing others filled full of lawlessness, he is content if somehow he himself can live his life here pure of injustice and unholy deeds, and take his leave from it graciously and cheerfully with fair hope. (*Republic*, 496c–e)

Here, in the *Republic*, if Socrates were to keep bad company, against the opposition of the *daimonion*, he would have two options: either join in injustice or perish. There, in the *Apology*: "[…] no man will survive who genuinely opposes you or any other crowd" (31e). And if the philosopher were to die, as it is put in both dialogues, he would be of service to no one. Along these lines, as the *Republic* has it, one would choose to keep quiet and mind one's own business. And again in the *Apology*: "A man who really fights for justice must lead a private, not a public, life if he is to survive for even a short time" (32a).

---

daemonic in Socrates cannot be replicated in others. This speaks to the likelihood of fulfilling an important condition for the possibility of the perfect regime. That is, it speaks to the probability of the coincidence of political power and philosophy (473d). The perfect regime requires that the philosopher have political power, yet the imperfect, actual regime regularly destroys philosophers who meddle in politics. It seems that nothing short of divine assistance is required to breed a philosopher in a base regime (*Republic* 492a and 493a). Not coincidentally, the name "Theages" could mean "revered by god", and Socrates hears a voice which purports to have a daemonic source. We are told in the *Apology* that demons are either gods or children of the gods (27d).

In the *Republic* and the *Apology*, it is the *daimonion* that repels Socrates from the depravity of the multitude, thereby encouraging a private existence, preserving both his life and his moral/philosophic integrity.[22] Also common to both dialogues, reasoning speech confirms the prudence of the daemonic opposition. A reasonable member of the small band thus keeps to himself, and so in the *Republic* he is likened to a man in a storm, standing beside a wall. In the dialogues one often witnesses Socrates standing out of harm's way, as if seeking shelter from a political storm.[23] The *Apology* on the other hand is squarely positioned in the public sphere. It is here that he falls in with beasts, and, rather than perpetrate injustice, he chooses to perish graciously.

The idea of the philosopher that Socrates, Diogenes and Plato all seem to share is that the true philosopher is a stranger at home and at home with the strange. This idea is encapsulated in the term "philosophic exile". Philosophic integrity requires the condemnation of the business of the city. Plato could not be more direct about this: he has Socrates say that philosophers despise the business of the city (*Republic*, 496b). The theme articulated by Socrates in the *Apology*, that the philosopher is not permitted to take part in public affairs, is continued into the heart of the *Republic*,

22 One might argue that the pre-critical authority, the *daimonion*, is not a true authority, given Socrates' view that reason is the final arbiter. The argument would go that since the *daimonion* is a blind guide and would not await the arbitration of reason before passing judgment on strangers, it is bound to produce a man like the *Republic* dog, a person capable of loving someone untrustworthy and hating someone trustworthy. The proper response to this is that though the *daimonion* does prohibit Socrates from even associating with certain people, the judgment about them is not made in utter ignorance. *Theaetetus* (151a) tells us that the *daimonion* forbids certain associations. The same idea is in *Theages* (129e) and *Alcibiades* (103a). Though the authenticity of the latter two dialogues has been contested, on this point they agree with genuine Plato. Potentially, the daemonic does provide Socrates aid in the discrimination of "strangers", but the daemonic would neither greet warmly without any good experience nor get angry without any bad experience. This is what the parochial dog does; he growls and barks at the strange without using his nose. The *daimonion* is like a good nose on Socrates the dog. It lets him sense good and bad qualities in the strange.

23 For instance, the *Republic* itself is set in the port of Piraeus, located ten kilometres out of town.

where the philosopher is presumed useless and, at best, compelled to live aside the vulgar and base business of the city.

Estrangement and Cosmopolitan Resignation

When the "philosophic" dog first appears as the image of the guard, he resembles the conventional politician, the philosopher in exile, the philosopher, who, having fallen in with beasts, has become himself a beast. The explanation for this is that the guardian class at this point is not yet bifurcated into auxiliaries and rulers. The attributes of the guard prior to the introduction of the so-called "philosophic" dog are sharp senses, speed, strength, courage and spirit. Conspicuously absent from this list is justice. Yet the philosophic nature is virtuous, that is "[...] a friend and kinsman of truth, justice, courage, and moderation" (487a). The dog, without justice, is wholly unfit to rule.

After the rulers become their own class at 414b, they take on the role of rational shepherds who lay down the law for the spirited dogs. Later still, the just individual appears in isomorphic relation to the just city:

> And what about when a man believes he's being done injustice? Doesn't his spirit in this case boil and become harsh and form an alliance for battle with what sees just; and, even if it suffers in hunger, cold and everything of the sort, doesn't it stand firm and conquer, and not cease from its noble efforts before it has succeeded, or death intervenes, or before it becomes gentle, having been called in by the speech [*logou*] within him like a dog by a herdsman? (440c–d)

The dog here is not the same unfettered, pre-critical beast that gets angry without any bad experience. This tamed animal knows exactly what he is mad about and why. Speech demands anger's justification and permits only indignation. In the just soul, speech makes spirit gentle. Plato has defended dialogue, Socrates and philosophy against the menacing Thrasymachus and conventional domestic politics.[24]

24 Of course Plato justifies Socrates and philosophy by invoking an ontology that may only be fictionally attributed to Socrates.

The ground for the justification of the philosopher in exile is revealed as ontological. Fundamentally, being cosmopolitan is not about refusing to love or hate in ignorance—although this is what the cosmopolitan does. *Being* cosmopolitan is a way of being in the world. This involves the rational reconfiguration of the self, which cannot occur without the re-evaluation of ambition. Ultimately, cosmopolitanism is a call for self-knowledge (or perhaps a hermeneutics of self). It is a call to figure out who we are and what we have become. It is a call to re-assess the importance of what we care about.[25]

There is perhaps no clearer illustration of the basic difference between the conventional politician and the philosopher than that offered near the beginning of the interchange between Callicles and Socrates in the *Gorgias*. The passage reads as follows. Socrates explains to Callicles that they each love two objects: Callicles loves the *demos* and a boy named Demos; and Socrates loves philosophy and a boy named Alcibiades. Socrates accuses Callicles of in each case being unable to oppose what his beloved says, even if what his beloved says is absurd. The only way to get Callicles to stop saying what he says is to stop his beloved. Socrates is the same way with respect to philosophy. He will not stop saying what philosophy says until someone stops her. Callicles' job is to refute philosophy, and if he chooses instead to ignore her and please the *demos*, he will be out of tune with himself. Socrates, on the other hand, would rather be dissonant with the majority of men than be out of tune with himself (*Gorgias*, 481c–482c).

It appears that Socrates is accusing Callicles of being a demagogue and offering a representation of the demagogue's psyche. In pursuit of his private ambitions, Callicles shuns certain normative constraints on speech (rational discourse and the concern for truth) and instead says what people want to hear. This is the picture of a particular type of unjust soul—the particular type whose spirit has gotten out of rational bounds. The psyche of the conventional politician, in other words, suffers from misplaced enthusiasm.

25 I am here borrowing Harry Frankfurt's title, *The Importance of What We Care About* (1988).

Plato fashions Callicles' response (484c–486d) to pick up the theme of philosophic exile in the *Republic*, which in turn goes back to the *Apology*. Specifically, Callicles represents the view advocated by Adeimantus in the *Republic* (487d), that those who dwell in philosophy become strange, vicious or useless:

> When I see an older man still engaging in philosophy and not giving it up, I think such a man by this time needs a flogging. For, as I was just now saying, it's typical that such a man, even if he's naturally very well favored, becomes unmanly and avoids the centers of his city and the marketplaces—in which, according to the poet, men attain "preeminence"—and, instead, lives the rest of his life in hiding, whispering in a corner with three or four boys, never uttering anything well-bred, important, or apt. (*Gorgias*, 485d–e)

And then Plato contrives a bit of prophecy:

> [...] if someone got hold of you or of anyone else like you and took you off to prison on the charge that you're doing something unjust when in fact you aren't, be assured that you wouldn't have any use for yourself. You'd get dizzy, your mouth would hang open and you wouldn't know what to say. You'd come up for trial and face some no good wretch of an accuser and be put to death, if death is what he'd want to condemn you to. (486a–b)

There is of course truth in what Callicles is saying. Remaining true to philosophy into old age, Socrates has fallen into ill-repute. He is allowed to carry on his philosophic ways only out of the way and at low volume. And when he is brought into court and made to defend himself, he seems ridiculous. He becomes the caricature of himself that Aristophanes gives in the *Clouds*, gaping up toward heaven when a gecko shat on him (lines 170–175).

But in terms of the allegory of the cave in the *Republic* (and here the account parallels the *Gorgias*), he is the extra-ordinary cave-dweller who sees only darkness because he has just come in from the light (516e). By prefacing Callicles' ridicule of philosophy with Socrates' interpretation of soul, Plato lets us see who Callicles really is: a talented, enthusiastic and practical man. He is a man of the people, judged useful, with a good reputation, but his psyche needs work. Callicles' love of the *demos* exiles him from justice. Contrariwise, Socrates' love of justice exiles him from the *demos*. Avoiding psychic dissonance makes him a political dissident.[26]

In the final analysis, the cynic/stoic evaluation of exile is consistent with the Platonic point of view. As Cicero claims, honour should not be coveted, and anonymity should not be feared:

> [...] neither is popular glory to be coveted for its own sake nor is obscurity to be sorely feared. "I came to Athens", said Democritus, "and no one there knew me". What dignified firmness for a man to glory in having no glory! (*Tusc. disp.* V.36.104–108)

To be cosmopolitan in Platonic terms practically entails the refusal to seek out reputation for its own sake, and, relatedly, the willingness to accept obscurity or even infamy. Cosmopolitan virtue is neither a loving embrace of universal humanity, nor is it a multicultural celebration. It is the serene resignation of the estranged.

(Im)practical (Re)organization of the City

This newfound ethical perspective has political ramifications. It regulates the state's internal practices in how it treats its own citizens, and it regulates the state's external practices in how it treats citizens of other states.

Internal

In the ideal regime, women are included in the band of guardians. When Socrates creates the mental picture of women exercising naked alongside the men it seems ridiculous to Glaucon (*Republic*, 352a–b). But Socrates is quick to correct him:

26 Cf. chapter by Caraus in this volume, especially subsection "The individual's preeminence over collectivity and the state".

> [...] he is empty who believes anything is ridiculous other than the bad, and who tries to produce laughter looking to any sight as ridiculous other than the sight of the foolish and the bad; or, again, he who looks seriously to any standard of beauty he sets up other than the good. (352d)

As with the presence of anger, ridicule should not precede just cause. Unwarranted ridicule exposes empty carelessness in the ridiculer, thus rendering him the truly ridiculous.

Perhaps the laughter of Glaucon is unfounded, but Socrates has yet to prove it. Socrates and Glaucon agree that men and women have different natures, and different natures should practise different things (453e). And yet Socrates asserts that men and women should do the same things (452a–b). We readers may be as puzzled as Glaucon. But Socrates' solution is as simple as it is edifying: saying that men and women should have different roles in the *polis* based on their different natures is like saying that bald men and longhairs should have different occupations (454c). The natural reproductive difference between men and women (454d–e) is irrelevant when it comes to assigning a woman her role in the *polis*. The relevant consideration is whether an individual is naturally given to her practice—whether she is a quick learner, whether she excels in her practice and advances her art. There is simply no practice relevant to the government of the *polis* that is peculiar to women (455d–e).

External

The allegiance to justice also functions to regulate the state's practices externally, in the way it deals with other states and their members. The example here involves the soldier's treatment of the enemy. Enslaving the enemy, plundering corpses and ravaging and burning houses are off limits (469b–471c).

With respect to enslaving the enemy, not only is it prohibited for the ideal regime but the ideal regime should not allow other states to enslave their enemies. In terms of what today we would call *jus ad bellum*, coming to the aid of a weak and threatened party in another state may constitute just cause for war.[27]

In regard to plundering corpses, Socrates asks, "[…] do you suppose that the men who do this are any different from the dogs who are harsh with stones thrown at them but don't touch the one who is throwing them?" (469d–e). The spirited dog does not realize that the stone is the instrument of the enemy rather than the enemy himself. The dog obedient to the justice of the shepherd would properly distinguish instrument from enemy. The corpse is an inanimate, harmless instrument, and so it should be left alone. In today's terms this rule falls under the category of *jus in bello*, justice in combat. We might add that even live enemy soldiers are instruments. They are instruments of the enemy state. This means they are political, not personal, enemies, and so if they pose no threat, they should not be harmed.

With respect to ravaging the countryside and burning houses, Socrates says that soldiers will not "[…] agree that in any city all are their enemies—men, women and children—but that there are always a few enemies who are to blame for the differences. And, on all these grounds, they won't be willing to ravage lands or tear down houses, since the many are friendly […]" (471a–b). Again, this can be classified in terms of *jus in bello*. Plato created something like a principle of discrimination meant to regulate the spirited dog-like guards, who get angry without a bad experience.

The sphere of ethical concern expands beyond the state, and this has political implications concerning the treatment of members of other states. This sounds all well and cosmopolitan, but one cannot, with a clear intellectual conscience, overlook the limited application of justice. The rules of just war extend to Greek states only, not to barbarians (471b). Socrates explains the limited application of justice through the distinction between war and faction. "War", he says, is the name for the hatred of the alien, and "faction" is the name for the hatred of one's own. Where Greeks and

27 James Childress (1978) provides a useful sketch of the traditional conditions of just war. I am not claiming that Plato's just war conditions are evidence for his cosmopolitanism. There are other notions of justice which support such conditions. I am claiming that in Plato's case, the conditions follow closely from the conception of the rational re-ordering of self, the cosmopolitan taming of the spirited, provincial dog.

barbarians are in conflict, they are enemies by nature. Where Greeks and Greeks are fighting, they are, through it all, friends by nature (470b–d). This passage supplies the principal counter-evidence to the thesis of this chapter. Plato is here extremely close to making Socrates say that the philosopher-ruler hates barbarians because they are alien. We've seen that such a posture toward the alien early on is mirrored by the "philosophic" dog, but, as we've also seen, the "philosophic" dog is not Plato's ideal. Can these claims be reconciled?

In setting up the polarizing Hellene/barbarian distinction, it seems as though Plato is reflecting a popular view of his time. According to classicist Edith Hall in *Inventing the Barbarian*, prior to the fifth century BC, the plural noun *barbaroi* (designating the entire non-Greek world) was not used. The word *barbaros* was in use, but it did not designate an inferior ethnic group. The term was originally onomatopoeic, signifying unintelligible speech—what we might call babbling. Hall (1989, 3–13) argues that during the fifth century, as Greek states were threatened by Persia, there was a growing sense of panhellenic identity which made possible the invention of the barbarian as the inferior ethnic kind. Although the *Republic* passage in question appears to follow this fifth-century trend, it would be rash and inaccurate to assume that Plato simply adopts the popular posture of prejudice toward the barbarian.

We have seen that with regard to the treatment of women, Plato explicitly rejects the view that the nature of woman justifies her exclusion from politics. There is no reason a woman cannot be a philosopher-ruler. The question worth asking is why didn't Plato construct a similar argument with regard to barbarians? (Baldry 1965, 72–87). Why did he not claim that the supposed "natural" differences between Greeks and barbarians are irrelevant when it comes to the consideration of how they should be treated in armed conflict?

There are at least three noteworthy points for consideration. First, the *Republic* never explicitly states that barbarians should be hated because they are alien. Nor does it state that the natural composition of the barbarian warrants the hatred and the violence toward him. What the *Republic* does state is that in a conflict, the name for the hatred of the alien is "war". The discussion is situated within a fictional already commenced armed conflict. We readers imagine the Greek to confront the barbarian at the limit of understanding. Without a shared language or culture, the conflict between Greeks and barbarians would be unlike a dispute between family members or close friends, who perhaps mutually understand that, even throughout the dispute, certain things are forbidden. Should Greeks and barbarians fight, they would fight tooth and nail. Along these lines, perhaps we understand the neglect of justice in the Greek/barbarian conflict, yet clearly understanding is not justification. Prior to the eruption of conflict, we would expect Plato to promote the cosmopolitan virtue of not hating and harming the alien.

This leads to the second consideration. Outside of the *Republic* there is evidence to suggest that the differences between Greeks and barbarians are non-essential and barbarians are potentially excellent and wise, just like Greeks. I will give only four brief examples.[28] First, the dialogue on the language, the *Cratylus*, effectively challenges the notion that Greek speech is basically different from and superior to the barbarian. On the topic of determining the correctness of names, Socrates introduces the position that a given thing has a natural name, which is neither identical to the Greek nor to the foreign name. Just as different blacksmiths may make tools for the same job out of different materials, he suggests, in the same way different language users may use different syllables for the same form: "Provided they give each thing the form of name suited to it, no matter what syllables it is embodied in, they are equally good rule-setters, whether they are in Greece or abroad" (390a). The discussion of language is especially interesting because the Greek believed that language is the primary criterion for determining ethnic belonging (Hall 1989, 3–5). Whatever problems we may have with the particularities of this position in the *Cratylus*, we can glean from it an instructional message: one's native language does not indicate one's worth in the natural order of things.

28 Baldry (1965, 80–84) adopts a similar course of argument. The place to begin an exhaustive study on Plato's view of the barbarian would be with Vourveris' (1938) collection of Plato's barbarian passages.

In a second example from the *Statesman*, the Eleatic stranger takes issue with the assumption that the appellation "barbarian" designates a particular natural kind. In truth, countless dissimilar kinds are inappropriately subsumed under the single name (262c–263a).

The *Laws* provides a third striking counter-example to the view that barbarians are naturally inferior. In a discussion of policies restricting the travel of citizens abroad and entrance of aliens at home, the central preoccupation seems to be the preservation of virtue in the *polis*. With this aim the community should beware that corrupt characters are not produced as the state comes into contact with other states. Since corruption potentially results when "the unfamiliar customs of the visitors rub off on to their hosts" (949e–950a), steps should be taken to keep a state and its citizens away from vicious characters. On the other hand,

> If any citizen would like to spend rather longer surveying at his leisure the life lived by foreigners, no law should prevent him, because no state will ever be able to live at a properly advanced level of civilization if it keeps itself to itself and never comes into contact with all the vices and virtues of mankind [...] In the mass of mankind you'll invariably find a number—though only a small number—of geniuses [*theioi*] with whom it is worth anything to associate, and they crop up just as often in badly-ruled states as in the well-ruled. So the citizen of a well-run state, provided he's incorruptible, should go out and range over land and sea to track them down [...] (951a–c)

This example functions to repudiate the presumption that cultural difference indicates natural worth. Since it is possible to find an excellent/virtuous barbarian, the Greek, seeking excellence, may do well ranging into barbarian lands.

Likewise in the *Phaedo*, we find Socrates recommending that his friends associate with barbarians. The men are in need of a good singer of incantations, capable of driving away their fear of death, and Socrates says that such a person may found among the many races of *barbaroi* (77e–78a). Taken together, these passages from the *Cratylus*, *Statesman*, *Laws* and *Phaedo* give us cause to suspect that the barbarian passage of the *Republic* is a remnant of the Greek *ethos* that does not necessarily reflect Plato's view.

The final consideration is that the barbarian passage in the *Republic* seems foremost a call to cease the mistreatment of foreign Greeks. Despite the growing sense of pan-Hellenism, Greeks continued to mistreat each other. During the Peloponnesian War, it was common practice to kill off the men of military age and enslave the women and children.[29] Shortly after Plato's plea, Philip of Macedon enslaved entire populations of other Greek states (Baldry 1965, 87).[30] The plea to expand the sphere of ethical consideration to non-citizens is a cosmopolitan plea. However, undeniably and problematically, Plato issues the plea by invoking the perception of the normalized ill-treatment of strangers. In the *Republic*, Plato, by expanding the sphere of ethical concern while simultaneously preserving its arbitrary limit, is letting the fifth-century *ethos* eclipse the cosmopolitan ideal.

Let me conclude by offering a few general speculative remarks. From an historical point of view, cosmopolitanism seems to be about the ethical response to changes brought about by processes of globalization. The scope and limits of cosmopolitan virtue are defined by the world-historical condition. New ways of life and forms of social interaction set the conditions for new obligations and spheres of identification. The world of Plato's time was basically the Greek speaking world, which stretched from Sicily to the Black Sea. For most in his context it would have made little practical sense to extend cosmopolitan virtue to other peoples with whom the Greeks had less frequent contact—Egyptians, Phoenicians, Phrygians, Thracians … Then, the world was small, however vast and mysterious a Greek imagined it to be. Conversely, the world in our proverb "it's a small world" has expanded to the size of the globe. We call the world small because we might go to the other side of it and find someone we know. Certainly "cosmopolitan" practically means something different to us than it would have to the Greeks 2,500 years ago. We have outgrown the limited scope in which the exercise of cosmopolitan virtue was encouraged. What we have not outgrown, and what we might learn from, is the notion of cosmopolitan virtue itself.

29 Vincent J. Rosivach (1999, 133–136) scrutinizes the source of Greek slaves in the fifth and fourth centuries.

30 One can question the relevance of this, as Philip was from Macedonia, a borderline area in between Hellas and Thrace. Where one draws the boundaries of barbarian belonging seems to depend on whether one believes Macedonians spoke a non-Greek language or some regional variation of Greek (Hall 1989, 179).

Acknowledgement

The scholar Christopher Ward deserves recognition for his insightful comments. I also thank my students, friends and colleagues at Syracuse University and the Humanities Center.

References

Aristophanes [see Henderson].

Baldry, H.C., 1965. *The unity of mankind in Greek thought*. Cambridge: Cambridge University Press.

Bloom, Alan (trans.), 1968/1991. *The Republic of Plato*, 2nd ed. New York: Basic Books.

Brown, Eric, 2000. "Socrates the cosmopolitan". *Stanford Agora: An Online Journal of Legal Perspectives*, 1(1). Available at: http://agora.stanford.edu/agora/libArticles/brown/brown.pdf. Accessed 20 June 2012.

Childress, James, 1978. "Just-war theories". *Theological Studies,* 39, 427–445.

Cicero [see King].

Cooper, John (ed.), 1997. *Plato: Complete works*. Indianapolis, IN: Hackett.

Diogenes Laertius [see Hicks].

De Lacy, Phillip H. and Benedict Einarson (eds. and trans.), 1959. *Plutarch's Moralia*, vol. 7. Cambridge: Harvard University Press.

Frankfurt, Harry, 1988. *The importance of what we care about: Philosophical essays.* New York: Cambridge University Press.

Hall, Edith, 1989. *Inventing the barbarian: Greek self-definition through tragedy*. New York: Oxford University Press.

Henderson, Jeffrey (ed. and trans.), 1998. *Aristophanes*, vol. 2. Cambridge, MA: Harvard University Press.

Hicks, R.D. (ed. and trans.), 1925/2005. *Diogenes Laertius: Lives of eminent philosophers*, vol. 2. Cambridge: Harvard University Press.

Kant, Immanuel, 1784. "Idea for a universal history with a cosmopolitan intent". In: Ted Humphrey (ed. and trans.), 1983. *Perpetual peace and other essays.* Indianapolis: Hackett.

King, J.E. (ed. and trans.), 1927/1971. *Tusculan disputations*. Cambridge: Harvard University Press.

Kraut, Richard, 1984. *Socrates and the state*. Princeton, NJ: Princeton University Press.

Plato [see Bloom and Cooper].

Popper, Karl, 1945/1957. *The open society and its enemies: The spell of Plato*, vol. 1. London: Routledge.

Rosivach, Vincent, 1999. "Enslaving *barbaroi* and the Athenian ideology of slavery". *Historia: Zeitschrift für Alte Geschichte*, 48(2), 129–157.

Vlasak, Aaron, 2012. "Plato's *Kunikos kosmopolitēs*". *Agathos: An International Review of the Humanities and Social Sciences*, 3(1), 49–60.

Vlastos, Gregory, 1991. *Socrates, ironist and moral philosopher*. Ithaca, NY: Cornell University Press.

Vourveris, K.J., 1938. *Hai historikai gnōseis tou Platōnos: A. Varvarika*. En Athenais: [s.n.].

TANIA ESPINOZA

Cosmopolitanism of the Not-All, from a Psychoanalytic Point of View

If cosmopolitanism were put under psychoanalysis, we would perhaps expect a process of disenchantment and reduction to be set in motion; a process, for example, revealing the extent to which the cosmopolitan ideal corresponded to a childhood wish. Or, having seen that Freud's psychoanalysis of monotheism resulted in the provocative thesis that religion is the childhood neurosis of civilization and the disguised memory of a true historical event—the murder of the father by the brothers of a primal horde—we might hope for or dread a similar outcome. There are reasons to fear that cosmopolitanism would turn out to be nothing more than an illusion, or perhaps even a delusion at the service of philosophical systems, political ideologies or global designs.

Whatever the outcome of such an analysis would actually be, it is true that to expose an ideal to the psychoanalytic gaze is to risk its destruction. From the "psychical assets of a culture" that help men reconcile to civilization, namely art and cultural ideals, Freud holds the latter to be based on projections of particular and partly contingent achievements of a cultural unit, thus giving it the sort of narcissistic satisfaction that leads to nationalism (Freud 1927, 13). The view that "cosmopolitanism", or at least the cosmopolitan aim articulated by Immanuel Kant (1724–1804), occasionally canonized as an early thinker of Western liberalism (cf. chapter by Cavallar in this volume), is simply one of these ideals arising from a specific history of colonial domination by the West, would seem to be in line with this observation. Combining the two would destroy the notion of cosmopolitanism by making it into a logical contradiction. For if, as Freud held, "cultural ideals become a source of discord and enmity" between nations

(Freud 1927, 13), the cultural ideal of doing away with this enmity would inevitably have to fail.

Certainly, today's globalized capitalism, as the perversion of "the spirit of commerce" on which Kant placed his hopes of perpetual peace, and more than a decade of wars fought by liberal democracies under the cosmopolitan banner (notably in Iraq and Afghanistan), seem to confirm this hypothesis. The postcolonial scholar Walter Mignolo has pointed to the "need to conceive cosmopolitanism from the perspective of coloniality" namely, of those excluded from the project of modernity although having been, as the argument goes, its condition of possibility (Mignolo 2000, 723). And yet, the sources for a "critical cosmopolitanism", as Mignolo calls the latter, may also lie in the very legacy of Kantian thought. This essay will sketch the outlines of a "critical cosmopolitanism", thought not from the perspective of coloniality, but from the perspective of what Kant called theory, in the form it appeared after Freud and Lacan.

To return to psychoanalysis, this act of offering our ideals to scrutiny is not free of dogmatism. We enter, voluntarily, into a coercive contract that asks us to sacrifice all that has held the promise of meaning. Do we then not do this for another, therefore higher, ideal? Freud's imaginary interlocutor, in the text that unmasked the narcissistic structure of the cultural ideal, "The Future of an Illusion", calls the "psychological ideal"—capturing with certain mockery the Enlightenment spirit in which this text is written— "the primacy of intelligence" (Freud 1927, 371). We could go all the way to terming it, with Kant, "the ideal of pure reason" (A574/B602, 554).[1] However lofty all this may sound, there is a real danger that the process will nevertheless leave us empty handed. Yet this loss in belief might be a gain in maturity, and thus still a necessary "forward step" (Freud 1927, 372). We naturally come to the question of what would happen if the ideal of psychoanalysis, or the "ideal of intelligence" as Freud put it, were itself to be exposed to psychoanalytic study. And here again, we might turn to

1 All references to Kant's *Critique of Pure Reason* will be given in the standard "A" and "B" notation, corresponding to the first and second editions respectively. The page numbers refer to the Paul Guyer and Allen W. Wood translation (1998).

Kant for an answer, for this is precisely the operation of the *Critique of Pure Reason* (1781/1787); namely to submit reason to this self-referential examination. The result might then be, in the words of Kant himself, "an euthanasia of pure reason" (B434, 460), which again leaves us with nothing, unless, performing another translation, we with the help of clinical psychoanalysis called it the "end of analysis".

Not all in Enlightenment thought, however, involves this destruction of idols. There is the famous moment in the first *Critique* in which reason avows the need to sacrifice knowledge in order to leave room for faith (BXXX, 117); the moment, at the end of Freud's life, where psychoanalysis shows its vocation is not to destroy but to construct, in "Constructions in Analysis" (1937). Psychoanalysis does indeed construct fantastical histories for the individual and the species, models of the psyche, alternative logics, formulas of sexuation, myths and interpretations. These opposing tendencies—dissecting/destructive and fictional/constructive—might be seen as conflicting, producing an incessant oscillation, or as following one another sequentially, or even, combining the two possibilities, as producing a forward movement. The cosmopolitan ideal is, in fact, for Kant, equivalent to the ideal of reason, so that placing it under a psychoanalytic/critical gaze will retain the above structure of self-referentiality and reveal the dialectical conflict that grounds it. Rather than "nothing", I will suggest that the operation yields an ideal that has been made "not-whole/not-every", a cosmopolitanism that is—to use the expression with which Jacques Lacan qualified Truth, Woman and Being—*pastout*.

The Antinomy of the Cosmopolitan Ideal

Although Lacan's logic of the *pastout*, which he uses in his 1972–1973 seminar *Encore* to describe the female side of his formulas of sexuation, will here only serve as a point of entry into Kant's logic of the not-all/not-whole which precedes it, we can elucidate it briefly. Soon after having drawn these formulas on the board during the seminar on "A Love Letter", Lacan begins his commentary by asserting that while psychoanalytic discourse aims at meaning, meaning is conditioned for us by what we know already. "That has a limit, a limit provided by the meaning in which you live [...] What analytic discourse brings out is precisely the idea that that meaning is semblance" (Lacan 1975/1998, 79 [translation modified]). Thus, psychoanalysis shows that the world that constitutes our horizon of meaning is rather limited; it is not-all. If we substituted the word "semblance" with "appearance", we would obtain a reflection very close in spirit to Kantian philosophy, where the distinction between appearances and things in themselves is a way of limiting the arrogance of thought in two different senses. On the one hand, it prevents thought from venturing beyond what constitutes possible experience for us, which is sensible experience (although this is very difficult for the tendency to overlook this boundary is natural in reason), and, more importantly, the distinction prevents thought from imagining that there is nothing but the objects of our sensible experience. Importantly for ethics, the *phainomenon/noumenon* duality acts as a limit to the universality of natural causality or determinism, for we can conceive of causality in two different relations: as determined with respect to appearances and as free with respect to things in themselves. Thus Kant says:

> The human being himself is an appearance. His power of choice has an empirical character, which is the (empirical) cause of all his actions. There is not one of these conditions determining human beings according to this character which is not contained in the series of natural effects and does not obey the laws of nature. (A553/B581, 543)

However, he continues, this "dynamical law of nature" does not apply to everything, namely, it does not apply to reason "since reason itself is not an appearance and is not subject at all to any conditions of sensibility"(A553/B581, 543). Because there is reason, the power of choice of the human being also has an "intelligible character", as "we know that actions could be free, i.e., that they could be determined independently of sensibility" (A557/B585, 545). Or, to put it differently, not-all the power of choice of the human being is subject to the law of nature. This limitation of the universality of natural, deterministic causality, is necessary for the transition from theoretical to practical philosophy, for if it cannot prove the reality of freedom, it at least makes its possibility compatible with nature and the world of appearance.

If we take the law of nature, which is universal in regard to appearances, to be the equivalent of the phallic function in Lacan, we could write this representation of the duality as the logical formulas that correspond to the female side of Lacan's tables:[2]

$\sim(\exists x)\sim\Phi x$	There is no x which does not belong to the phallic function
$\sim(\forall x)\Phi x$	Not all x belong to the phallic function

This is why any speaking being who would inscribe itself on this side of the formulas "will not allow any universality—it will be not-whole, insofar as it has the choice of positing itself in Φx or of not being there (*de n'en pas être*)" (Lacan 1975/1998, 80). This *choice* of the power of choice between an empirical and an intelligible character is the only ground of freedom in the first *Critique*; one that, says Kant, proves neither the reality of freedom, nor even its possibility. All that this proves, as we said, is that "nature does not conflict with causality through freedom", where the latter remains a transcendental idea (A558/B586, 546). We could interpret Lacan's statement that woman unfolds/doubles herself (*se dédouble*) by being in relation both to the Other—that "locus in which truth stammers" (Lacan 1975/1998, 81)—and to the phallic function, as being equivalent to the doubling of the human being with respect to an intelligible and an empirical character; that is, its being in relation both to *noumena* and to sensibility.

The two formulations from Kant that I have just presented constitute the solution to the "Third Conflict of the Transcendental Ideas" in "The Antinomy of Pure Reason", whose relationship to cosmopolitanism will be outlined below. They also constitute the point of departure of Kant's

2 This step, as the approximation of Kant and Lacan through the question of the antinomies, is indebted to Joan Copjec's reading of Lacan's formulas in "Sex and the Euthanasia of Reason" (Copjec 1994). However, I am suggesting that the "Third Conflict of the Transcendental Ideas", which is dynamic, corresponds to the female side of the formulas, whereas Copjec aligned it with the male side.

1784 essay "Idea for a Universal History from a Cosmopolitan Point of View", a text that attempts to write a history of humanity without regard to the possibility of freedom but which, however, would not conflict with an intelligible causality or the ends of reason. This Universal History goes beyond the solution to the third conflict, in that it adds the coincidence of the ends of nature with the ends of reason. However, the condition for this coincidence is that we first allow that these two characters of causality can coexist. The essay begins precisely with the description of the "empirical character" of human action, with respect to which the law of nature applies universally: "Whatever concept we may hold, from a metaphysical point of view, concerning the freedom of the will, certainly its appearances, which are human actions, like every other natural event are determined by universal laws" (Kant 1784a, 17). And it continues with the "hope" that, from a different perspective, these laws could be seen to lead to the "original endowment" of the human race which is to fulfil the end of reason. Although this hope is to ultimately be able to eliminate the duality that we just held to be so important, this could only be achieved from the point of view of reason, which for us is transcendent, leading back into an antinomy—the antinomy of cosmopolitanism to which we now turn.

For Kant all ideas that imply a sensibly existing totality engage reason in an antinomy, for no absolute totality can be apprehended empirically. This is because apprehension involves a "synthesis of appearances", a necessary progression from the condition to the conditioned that can never be completed, as this would entail the experience of the unconditioned which is a contradiction in terms. In other words, since apprehension has a temporal structure, it transforms aggregates—potential wholes if they could be grasped all at once—into infinite or indefinite series of coordinated elements that can only be grasped in this progression, thus becoming radically not-whole. Kant calls these ideas "cosmological" or world-concepts, and classifies them according to his table of the categories into four kinds: the first two have to do with the magnitude of the world, its boundedness in time and space and its complete division; and the second two with the causality in the world, the possibility of a causality through freedom and of a necessary being (A406/B433–A420/B448, 460–467).

Many totalities are at stake in the concept of cosmopolitanism: "the human race as a whole", "the series of generations of all future times" (Kant 1793, 8:278, 281), but also "all natural capacities of a creature", which are, according to the first thesis in Kant's "Idea for a Universal History", "destined to evolve completely to their natural end" (Kant 1784, 18). These transcendental ideas could be called cosmological in that they seem to lay claim to an empirically existing reality, and should therefore receive a similar treatment to those discussed in the *Critique of Pure Reason*. In fact, the structure of the antinomy is crucial for understanding Kantian cosmopolitanism, and can even be read as the theoretical prototype of perpetual peace, for it is the model of a rational conflict in which there is hope that the parts "perhaps after they have exhausted rather than injured each other, [...] will see on their own that their dispute is nugatory, and part as good friends" (B45, 468).

This conflict, which Kant here calls "dialectical" and which is modelled on what he earlier considered a "real conflict" of opposing forces in nature, is one in which no side can win because once we venture beyond the phenomenal world, any assertion that is not self-contradictory can be made without the possibility that anything from experience could refute it. The only limitation that these assertions, which Kant calls "sophistical ideas", can encounter is another sophistical idea of equal weight that would come to oppose it. Assertions about human nature, for example, would necessarily enter into this type of conflict, so that Kant's often criticized moral optimism could be defended precisely on the grounds that a moral pessimism, as a posture towards life, is no more realistic than the former, for the inherent "goodness" or "badness" of the human being are both sophistical ideas.

The "skeptical method" of transcendental philosophy consists in allowing this type of conflict to take place in an level playing field. The role of the philosopher is here that of an instigating and yet impartial observer of the dispute, who lets the parts "settle the matter themselves" and probes only into whether the object of the same is not a mere "mirage" (*Blendwerk*) (B451, 468). Thus the ultimate hope of reason is placed on an enlightened public sphere, which does not destroy the illusions in which reason unavoidably gets entangled but renders them "harmless" (B450, 468), by ensuring that they will meet opposition. Kant's ungrounding of reason both from experience and from dogmatic theology leaves it no other mode of proceeding. This sober, minimal, role for the philosopher is a direct consequence of reason's newly found autonomy: "Transcendental reason [...] permits no touchstone other than its own attempt to bring internal unification to its assertions, and this requires a free and unhindered contest of these assertions among themselves" (B453, 469).

The unity of reason, which implies that it is ultimately equivalent to nature, will translate this trust in the "dialectical conflict" of reason into a trust in the "real conflict" of forces taking place constantly in nature, to bring humanity towards perpetual peace: "The very opposition of inclinations to one another, from which evil arises, furnishes reason a free play to subjugate them all and, in place of evil, which destroys itself, to establish the rule of good, which, once it exists, continues to maintain itself of its own accord" (Kant 1793, 8:312, 309).

The presentation of the "skeptical method", as transcendental reason's most appropriate mode of proceeding, opens the way for Kant's impartial exposition of the theses and antitheses of the four antinomies of pure reason. Consistent with the method of identifying the "mirage" that might be producing the dispute, the antinomies are then shown to rest on a transcendental illusion, namely the illusion that the world is a whole existing absolutely in itself, a transcendental object, rather than merely an appearance. Dissolving the illusion would mean accepting that the phenomenal world is not-whole and therefore, that any cosmopolitan project would not be able to overcome this structural incompleteness. That is, that it would have to remain a cosmopolitanism of the not-all. Not a cosmopolitanism that is not for all, but one that confronts its antinomic nature. As paradoxical as the notion may sound, my argument in what follows will be that this limitation on totality is inherent in Kant's treatment of the cosmopolitan and is also what makes it subversive and, on the other hand, indistinguishable from the practice of philosophy.[3]

To recapitulate, to say that the phenomenal world is not-all, is for Kant also a way to say that phenomena is not all there is. There is the Other, *il y*

3 I thank Tamara Caraus, the author of the chapter on East European dissidence in this volume, for indicating this inherent indistinguishability.

a de l'Autre, as Lacan would say, even though it may not exist. That is, it is a way to limit the power of empiricism, and its presumed incompatibility with the possibility of freedom. The not-whole of world-concepts opposes the universality of natural causality—that is, the fact that all empirical phenomena have a cause that is also empirical and therefore determined by the mechanism of nature—yet it does so in a peculiar manner, namely through two different strategies depending on whether the conflict is seen from the perspective of speculative reason or of practical reason. From the perspective of speculative reason, or theory, all that can be affirmed is the incompleteness in the synthesis of appearances, without, however, it being possible to pose anything beyond it. Freedom, seen from this point of view, has no positive "consistency"; it is only a *noumenon* in the negative sense. However, the postulate of freedom is still compatible with natural causality since we can never comprehend the totality of nature's indefinite chain of causes and effects. From the perspective of practical reason, on the other hand, the strategy is to pose not only the compatibility of intelligible and natural causality, but also the necessity of freedom. Kant's solution to the antinomy of cosmopolitanism fluctuates between these perspectives, yet the one we have attempted to show has been the one corresponding to the "Third Conflict of the Transcendental Ideas", which constitutes the tipping point between speculative and practical reason, and yields a cosmopolitanism of the not-all. However, as we will now see, even if the totality upon which the concept of the cosmopolitan is based is a transcendental idea, nothing forbids us to pose it as the necessary horizon of a philosophy, as did Kant, or of a science, as did Freud.

Cosmopolitanism and the Ideal of Pure Reason

Although Kantian cosmopolitanism is usually studied in the context of Kant's practical (moral), political and aesthetic writings, cosmopolitanism of the not-all would, as we have seen, necessitate the wider context provided by Kant's theoretical writings, and more specifically, Kant's first *Critique*.

Indeed, what I have called "cosmopolitanism of the not-all" could also be called *cosmopolitanism from a theoretical point of view*. This would also yield a "critical cosmopolitanism". Following Beatrice Longuenesse's "critical interpretation" of the "principle of complete determination" (Longuenesse 2005, 223), a critical interpretation of the cosmopolitan ideal would take it to be a natural illusion of reason that results from the substitution of the (legitimate) "distributive unity" of the will of all with an (illegitimate) "collective unity". If this substitution is justified, from a practical point of view, by the duty of perpetual peace—for duty alone allows this *passage à l'acte* from theory to practice—a critical perspective would render us more attentive to the potentially coercive and necessarily "fictive" dimension of such a passage. Any such substitution would demand a supplement that could not come from theoretical sources, and would therefore entail a moment of dogmatism. As it would be subject to the imperfections of the empirical philosopher or legislator (not the archetypical, absolutely just one) who would perform this addition, it would be simply a *provisional* step in the progress of humankind, always subject to the possibility of being modified by future generations.

While all of this is said explicitly in Kant's so called practical and political writings, the theoretical rendering of the cosmopolitan ideal shows its dependence on the "dialectical conflict" of reason or the logic of illusion, and thus, its affinity to the twentieth-century science that set out to explore such logic. What the psychoanalytic perspective perhaps adds to the critical one, is the idea that this "transcendental dialectic" is the ultimate horizon of reason. Namely, that the Ideal of Pure Reason which Kant situates beyond the antinomies is simply a reiteration of their solution. This reflection follows from the very ambiguity of the cosmopolitan ideal in Kant, which is both a cosmological idea, leading to an antinomy, and the Ideal of Pure Reason. In fact, when Kant says that the latter are not identical but related, I would like to propose that their relation is contained in the idea of a cosmopolitan condition, which refers both to a sensible idea and an ideal, and about which, furthermore, it has to be said that it can be realized here on earth, even if in an infinitely distant future. Once Kant leaves the island of the Transcendental Analytic, which he names "the land of Truth" (A 236, 354), finding another continent of certainty will be as illusory as Columbus' belief in having found another route to the Indies, to cite an example from Freud (1927, 30), for the stormy ocean of the dialectic is where truth can only be half-spoken. However, the cosmopolitan condition is the necessary fiction that humanity has to presuppose in order to trace its moral progress.

Cosmopolitanism does not feature explicitly in the *Critique of Pure Reason* until the very end. Only in the second to last chapter, "The Architectonic of Pure Reason", does Kant mention the "cosmopolitan concept (*conceptus cosmicus* [*Weltbegriff*])" defining it in a note as "one that concerns that which necessarily interests everyone", and opposing it to "scholastic concepts" which regard "the skills for certain arbitrary ends". Thought of as scholastic, philosophy would be "a system of cognition that is sought only as a science without having as its end anything more than the systematic unity of this knowledge, thus the logical perfection of cognition". From the perspective of the cosmopolitan concept, on the other hand, "philosophy is the science of the relation of all cognition to the essential ends of human reason (*teleologia rationis humanae*)". It is the latter concept, which makes philosophy essentially moral philosophy, which Kant clearly privileges and which is "represented as an archetype in the ideal of the philosopher" (A839/B867, 694–695). In Kant's dualistic system, this would roughly make scholastic concepts correspond to formal logic, which Kant criticizes for not concerning itself with the content of propositions, while the cosmopolitan concept would correspond to transcendental logic, where propositions are analysed also with respect to their content.

Furthermore, the two forms of universality that the different concepts express, namely the "systematic unity of knowledge" of a scholastic philosophy, and the "everyone" that constitutes the interest of a cosmopolitan philosophy, can be mapped onto the distinction Kant had made earlier between the purely formal principle of universality (*universalitas*) and all-ness (*universitas*) (A572/B600, 554). This distinction is introduced in the chapter on the Ideal of Pure Reason, in order to differentiate between the determinability of a concept and the determination of a thing. Every concept, Kant says, is specified by adding to it an affirmative or a negative predicate, since, given two contradictorily opposed predicates, either one or the other will necessarily apply to it. The problem with this form of specification is that it does not get at the reality of the object. In order to say something about the "content" or object of a concept, we would have to compare the predicate, not only with its contradictory opposite, but with its opposite within all possible predicates. This form of specification that would determine a thing with respect to "the sum total of all predicates of things in general" is the "principle of thoroughgoing determination" and it presupposes a "whole of possibility" that is not merely formal (A572/B600, 553).

This whole of possibility, says Kant, is then hypostatized into the idea of an original being (*ens originarium*) or a highest being (*ens summum*) and personified as God (A579/B607, 557 and A583/B611, 559). In fact, this idea cannot even be thought of as a "sum total" of possibility, as he had expressed earlier, "for then the original being would be regarded as a mere aggregate of derivative beings". Rather, it is thought of as "ground", where the manifoldness of experience would be "the complete consequences" of this original being (A579/B607, 557). This is to say, that this whole is thought of dynamically as the whole of causes and effects, including of a first cause, and not merely mathematically in regard to magnitude. However, when Kant gives the explanation of the source of this dialectical illusion, he says that it lies in the confusion of an "empirical principle of our concepts of the possibility of things as appearances" with "a transcendental principle of the possibility of things in general" (A583/B611, 559). Namely, the illusion follows from our taking "the sum total of all empirical reality", which is the condition of possibility of our experience of objects of sense, to be the sum total of possible things in general. What Kant seems to accept as a valid presupposition is a whole of empirical reality, taken as an aggregate, whereas the Ideal of Reason would be the result of a dialectical illusion:

> That we subsequently hypostatize this idea of the sum total of all reality, however, comes about because we dialectically transform the *distributive* unity of the use of the understanding in experience, into the *collective* unity of a whole of experience; and from this whole of appearance we think up an individual thing containing in itself all empirical reality, which then—by means of the transcendental subreption we have already thought—is confused with the concept of a thing that stands at

> the summit of the possibility of all things, providing the real conditions for their thoroughgoing determination. (A583/B611, 559)

In a commentary on this passage, the philosopher Paul W. Franks wonders "why Kant should take this dim view of the idea of an *omnitudo realitatis* [...] [s]ince it does not appear to lead to any antinomy" (Franks 2005, 68). However, its relationship to the cosmopolitan concept shows that although the Ideal might not *lead* into an antinomy, it nevertheless *arises* from one, namely, the cosmological idea of the whole world. This hypostatization is, furthermore, equivalent to the solution of the fourth conflict of the transcendental ideas regarding the existence of an "absolutely necessary being" (A452/B480–A460). As we will see later, the proximity of the cosmopolitan ideal and the Ideal of Pure Reason, and of the "dialectical conflict" that grounds it, will be crucial for Kant's treatment of cosmopolitanism in his practical philosophy.

More than a decade later, in *Perpetual Peace* (1795), Kant will return to this idea of the substitution of a collective for a distributive unity, which in the earlier example is at the source of a dialectical illusion, yet now it will be what is required for the achievement of perpetual peace:

> Admittedly, the volitions of *all individuals* to live in a lawful constitution in accordance to principles of freedom (the *distributive* unity of the will *of all*) is not adequate to this end [perpetual peace]; but there is still required for it this solution of a difficult problem, that *all together* will this condition (the *collective* unity of the united will), so that a whole of civil society comes to be [...]. (Kant 1795, 8:371, 339)

Here, the dialectical transformation of one version of unity into the other is a necessary step in the progress towards the cosmopolitan ideal, and constitutes "a difficult problem", the solution of which will require a supplement, namely, "a uniting cause must be added to this variety of the particular volitions of all, in order to produce from them a common will" (Kant 1795, 8:371, 339). This addition is formally equivalent to what Kant had called in the first *Critique* a "practical addition", which alone can tip "the indecisiveness of speculation out of balance" to bring reason to a decision "under the pressure of an urgent cause" (A589/B617, 562), in this case, the cause of peace. However, an addition of this nature, which shifts the use of reason from being merely negative (skeptical) to being positive (dogmatic), involves a risk, which Kant does not hide in this text. As in the case of a civil constitution which coerces individuals into a nation, Kant continues,

> [...] the only beginning of the rightful condition to be counted upon is that by *power*, on the coercion of which public right is afterward based; and (since we can scarcely allow for a moral disposition of the legislator such that, after the disorderly multitude has been united into a people, he will now leave the people to bring about a rightful constitution by its common will) it can be anticipated that in actual experience there will be great deviations from that idea (in theory). (Kant 1795, 8:371, 339)

The relationship between the "disorderly multitude" and "a people" is that between the sum of the parts and the whole; or a will that is not-all and a will that is made all through the addition of power. Maintaining that there is a fundamental discontinuity between the two—and this is why the passage from the former to the latter always entails a substitution—has crucial ethico-political consequences. In a short paper from 1958, the philosopher Sidney Axinn illustrates the logical fallacies that result from overlooking this discontinuity, using examples from social theory. The individualism of early liberal thought, or, we could add, Thatcherism, for which the interest of the community is simply the sum of the interests of its members, commits the fallacy of composition. Namely, it takes what is true of a part to be true of the whole. Conversely, Axinn observes, "fascism and communism are certainly examples of the fallacy of assuming that the parts are nothing but divisions of the whole" (Axinn 1958, 287), which consequently justifies the sacrifice of the welfare of individuals for the welfare of the State. To acknowledge the practical supplement (either of power or of illusion) that accompanies the transformation of a multitude into a people is Kant's attempt not to yield into either of these fallacies.[4]

4 However, the explanation that Kant gives in the section on the Ideal in the *Critique of Pure Reason* for the transcendental illusion of complete determination seems to be that it is the result of the fallacy of composition. Similarly, we could cite the question "is it reasonable to assume purposiveness in all the parts of nature and to deny it to the whole?" (Kant 1784, 20), whose negative answer justifies Kant's project of a "Universal History" and yet makes it into a reiteration of this fallacy.

The chasm between the distributive and the collective unity of the will is justified anthropologically by the opposition of the self-interested individual and a society that requires the limitation of the individual's lawless freedom. This is the opposition that organizes all of Freud's writings about culture, namely that between the individual and a civilization that demands from him the sacrifice of his instincts. The "difficult problem" of cosmopolitanism, or its antinomy, is precisely how this transformation is achieved, or, in the terms of Freud, how man is to be reconciled to civilization. None of the solutions based on the free will of individuals to bring about a rightful constitution—the people uniting in violent revolution, or the actions of a legislator—presented by Kant in *Perpetual Peace* seem satisfactory from the point of view of theoretical reason.[5] In fact, just a couple of years earlier, in the text "On the Common Saying: That May be Correct in Theory but it is of No Use in Practice", published in the *Berlinische Monatsschrift* in 1793, Kant's "solution" to the cosmopolitan antinomy looks rather similar to the dialectical transformation that produces the idea of a highest reality, hypostatized into the idea of a supreme wisdom or providence:

> Only from nature, or rather from *providence* (since supreme wisdom is required for the complete fulfilment of this end), can we expect an outcome that is directed to the whole and from it to the parts, whereas people in their *schemes* set out only from the parts and may well remain with them, and may be able to reach the whole, as something too great for them, in their ideas but not in their influence, especially since, with their mutually adverse schemes, they would hardly unite for it by their own free resolution. (Kant 1793, 8:311, 307)

Now this "dim view" of the possibility of ever reaching a cosmopolitan condition is consistent with the passage from the first *Critique*, in which the substitution of the whole for the sum of the parts is the result of a natural illusion of reason. However, this solution seems to be dangerously close to

5 Although Kant does state that if a (in itself illegitimate) revolution, "engendered by a bad constitution" would achieve a constitution that is "more in conformity with law", "it would then not be permissible to lead people back into the old one" (Kant 1793, 8:373, 340).

the eschatological idea that a kingdom of ends can only follow our terrenal existence. If the cosmopolitan condition depends solely on the existence of a "supreme wisdom", a critical interpretation of the Ideal of Reason would render the hope in human progress nugatory. Indeed, the following year, Kant will go on to criticize precisely this religious narrative in his humorous commentary on the Apocalypse, "The End of All Things". What is key in this formulation, however, is the equation between nature and providence, a move that could be seen as secularizing the latter.

Already in 1784's "Idea for a Universal History", Kant had made use of this analogy to justify his "philosophical history", yet, as we have said, the idea of this coincidence is a practical supplement, something that we "can and must *add in thought*" and which, from the point of view of theory is not incompatible with truth, while from the point of view of practical philosophy or ethics, is necessary:

> [T]he representation of their [the laws of nature's] relationship to and harmony with the end that reason prescribes immediately to us (the moral end) is an idea, which is indeed transcendent for *theoretical* purposes but for practical purposes (e.g., with respect to the concept of the duty of *perpetual peace* and putting that mechanism of nature to use for it) is dogmatic and well founded as to its reality. (Kant 1795, 8:362, 332)

The cunning of this move consists in "putting that mechanism of nature" which is all that exists from the point of view of theory, at the service of practice. This allows Kant to maintain the theoretically sound position of regarding human action only in relation to appearance while also affirming the cause of reason. This practical use of natural causality rests on the belief, again, in that peace could come from the mutual exhaustion of opposing forces in nature, namely, in the illusion that the "real conflict" of nature is capable of cancelling out evil, if not of posing good (Kant 1795, 8:362, 335).

Paradoxically, while Kant's hopes for perpetual peace lie more on the mutual exhaustion of the conflicting parts rather than on a rationally conceived cosmopolitan constitution (thus on nature and not on the work of civilization), it is Freud (1927, 53) who will place his hopes for the future in the soft voice of the intellect.

Cosmopolitanism and the Therapeutic of Pure Reason

Let us now then not dismiss entirely the idea of analysing cosmopolitanism from the point of view of psychology. Let us look at the mood in these texts and their peculiar movement. Is there not a certain melancholy in Kant's writings which comes forth especially in his "Idea for a Universal History", a desperate wish to find order where everything seems to be in chaos, purpose where everything seems to be purposeless, an intelligence in nature to redeem the idiocy in man? This could be what perhaps led Kant to place his hopes in an illusion that seems to side with empiricism, namely, in that nature reaches an equilibrium of forces that can cancel out evil. As we had noted, the most striking characteristic of this text, published in the *Berlinische Monattschrift* in the same year as the famous "An Answer to the Question: What is Enlightenment?" is the complete reversal of roles between man and nature. Whereas Kant's critical philosophy does not tire of affirming the possibility that man raises above sensibility through reason, deriving the moral principle completely independently of pathological considerations, here reason is on the side of nature. Seen from a broader perspective, it appears that it is nature and not man who has autonomy and decides always for the best. However, this apparent naiveté, which is many times as ironic and humorous as Voltaire's *Candide* (1759), hides a radical message.

Man's irrational tendency to "follow his own purpose, often in opposition to others" is precisely what makes him free (Kant 1784, 11–12). If we were all able to act as rational world citizens, we would simply be automatons. The fact that there is an unbridgeable gap between what man wills individually and what should be willed collectively leaves the cosmopolitan condition radically open. The crooked wood man is made of is also the guarantee of his inherent capacity for autonomy. In short, conflict will not be done away with, and, furthermore, it is nature that wills it. Nature, says Kant, wills discord, while man wishes concord. Thus, the equation of "brutish freedom", which is lawless, and blind chance is what provides the necessary opposition to a "lawful civil constitution" or any principle of coercion that would believe itself to be concluded and just, and therefore closed to the questioning of future generations. The problem of the ultimate master of humankind—be it a person or a constitution—is, says Kant in the sixth thesis, the "last to be solved" because its solution is impossible: man is an animal who needs a master, but the master is also an animal who needs a master, and so on indefinitely. In the absence of divine rule, an absence that Kant affirms, no body—human or institutional—can legitimately claim the position of absolute rule. As in the antinomy of the *Critique of Pure Reason*, where the problem of the limits of the world has no solution, so does, necessarily, the question of a perfect civil constitution. This is, I contend, why Kant ultimately opts for the "negative" version of cosmopolitanism, a cosmopolitanism of the not-all, rather than a positive one: "So (if all is not to be lost) in place of the positive idea *of a world republic* only the negative surrogate of a *league* that averts war, endures, and always expands can hold back the stream of hostile inclination that shies away from right, though with constant danger of its breaking out" (1795, 8:357, 328).

Freud's 1927 "The Future of an Illusion" speaks to Kant's text from the future, from the aftermath of the French and Russian revolutions, after Hegel and Marx, but also by adopting the perspective that was lacking in the "Idea". Whereas Kant's "Idea for a Universal History" being told from the standpoint of nature, which reveals itself, in the end, to be equal to Providence, Freud tells the story from the point of view of culture. I want to suggest that cosmopolitanism needs to be apprehended as a multi-stable figure, oscillating between these two perspectives.

"The Future of an Illusion" reformulates the antinomy of cosmopolitanism and adds to it the content of class conflict. Freud, like Kant, departs from the observation of a double tendency in man. What Kant calls "unsocial sociability" Freud explains through the opposition of instinct and rationality. Civilization demands from the individual enormous instinctual sacrifices, while at the same time it is necessary for his survival and development. "Every individual" says Freud, "is virtually an enemy of civilization though civilization is supposed to be an object of universal human interest" (Freud 1927, 6). Along this line of analysis, he makes the further observation that the lower classes in society have a particularly unequal share in the benefits of civilization, which only extracts their labour, giving very little back in terms of opportunities to participate in forms of sophisticated sublimation. Thus, they are perfectly justified in manifesting the unsocial tendency of man and attacking a civilization that, in short, does not educate them. The amorality of the masses and their readiness to overlook the prohibitions on which civilization is founded is what produces revolutions and destroys civilization. Yet Freud (1927, 7) even adds that a civilization that distributes its fruits so unevenly as to produce this state of affairs does not deserve to last.

Freud's critical view of the relative benefits of Western culture is in line with Kant's, who holds that far from being enlightened, what his civilization calls culture is often a form of empty sophistication, and even adds that until this enlightened condition arrives, the state of savagery is even preferable. However, as Freud points out, the discontent of the masses does not always result in the overthrow of the ruling classes, who are also the keepers of the beneficial part of civilization, namely art; nor does it result in a better distribution of wealth, but is easily directed outwards, towards other nations or cultures. Here, Kant's negative idea of the cosmopolitan as a "*league* that averts war" rather than of a world republic seems to be the rational solution for preventing this type of conflict; but this league, internationalist rather than cosmopolitan, would have to be endlessly reconfigured in order to benefit each of its members equally.

Rather than as contradictory, "cosmopolitanism of the not-all" should be understood as a concept that contains within itself a "real opposition" of forces which, if they entered into a rational conflict like the arguments in Kant's antinomies, would advance the cause of reason. The tendency towards a unified government conflicts with a nation's self-determination in the same way that an individual's gregariousness conflicts with their asocial tendency. It is only in this conflict and oscillation that human capacity has any chance to develop. Thus, an interlocutor appears in section IV of Freud's text and accompanies him through to the end. The movement of reason needs this dialogic structure. The same applies to the "uses" of reason employed in the essays, always balancing the critical or negative use with the practical or positive use. Both Kant and Freud abstain greatly from making any positive recommendations and in both cases, these have little to do with what we usually connect with cosmopolitanism, namely political forms of association between states or nations, what humanity shares, what is common, greater integration, etc. Kant limits himself to the recommendation that European states devote less resources to accumulating the means to go to war and internally administer them to improve the general education of its citizens while not censoring the efforts of those who work hard for upholding some of the gains of civilization; Freud also places his hopes on an enlightened non-religious education for the lower strata of society, since the upper strata has already exchanged religion for science. Both have a humble approach to cosmopolitanism, one which maintains that only a gradual advancement towards the "greatest revolution" that the enlightenment of mankind would entail is desirable.

In "The Future of an Illusion" Freud distinguishes between illusions and delusions in that the former, unlike the latter, do not necessarily conflict with reality. Religion here is an illusion in the process of being challenged by science. At the end of his life, however, this distinction dissolves and religion becomes a powerful delusion of mankind, although only after delusion itself is declared to be equivalent to psychoanalytic construction. Both the patient's delusions and the analyst's constructions "attempt at explanation and cure" and carry within themselves an element of "historical truth" (Freud 1937, 12). From a theoretical perspective, Kant's cosmopolitan ideal appears as a natural illusion of reason, as does Kant's "strange and apparently silly […] wish to write a history in accordance with an Idea" where "it seems that with such an idea only a romance could be written"(Kant 1784, 24). Kant's "Universal History" is indeed very similar to an analytic construction aiming to quench the philosopher's despair in witnessing "this idiotic course of things human"(Kant 1784, 12). Whether Kant is the patient or the analyst in this drama does not seem, after Freud, to be a valid question. He is probably both. What the truth element in the illusion/delusion/construction of cosmopolitanism is, remains to be seen.

To sketch out the direction of an answer, let us return to the notion of totality that we maintained cannot be completed. What is the totality that matters in cosmopolitanism? In Kant's "Idea for a Universal History", it seems to be the whole of human capacity, which is infinite and therefore cannot be accomplished in the individual but only in the entire race. The first and most important thesis of this text is that "All natural capacities of a creature are destined to evolve completely to their natural end" (Kant 1784, 12). This whole of human determination and moral perfectibility is equivalent to the *totum realitatis* in the *Critique of Pure Reason*, or the Highest Good. The realization of this end would thus amount to the complete determination of the concept of the human, and therefore needs to be deferred endlessly into the future. A "Universal History" would thus be the accomplishment of the highest ideal of reason.

What I have suggested is that this notion of the Ideal, of the "all" in "all natural capacities" has to be understood critically as a regulative and not a constitutive principle, namely, as a rule given by reason for the synthesis of concepts, and not as a totality that could be experienced by the senses. As Beatrice Longuenesse puts it, commenting on Kant's first *Critique*,

> From the standpoint of the Transcendental Analytic, the representation of a *totum realitatis* as the complete whole of positive determinations of things can only be a goal which reason sets to the understanding for the improvement of its knowledge, not an actually given whole. The illusion of rational metaphysics is precisely to think that such a whole is actually given in pure intellect alone, rather than having to be generated by the sensibly conditioned understanding. (Longuenesse 2005, 234)

Similarly, to believe that cosmopolitanism consists in the affirmation of universal values or rights shared by all cultures and humans as if "given in pure intellect alone" is also an illusion of rational metaphysics. The cosmopolitan condition has to be generated by the "sensibly conditioned understanding", in the same way that the "universal history" also has to be generated in part by the practical intervention of the philosopher who poses a certain teleology in nature. As Freud confesses, regardless of their optimism or pessimism about the course of human history, all the thinker can do is to "point out the necessity of a forward step" (Freud 1927, 49). To do otherwise would be to relinquish all possibility of agency to a metaphysical belief in an evil spirit directing nature or to the idea that a better world can only await us beyond the empirical one.

To finish with a psychoanalytic construction, let us say that the cosmopolitan ideal is a wish of returning to the womb in which the human but also nature is undetermined. This is how, after all, Kant explains the "universal cosmopolitan condition" in 1784, as the "womb [*Schoss*] wherein all the original capacities of the human race can develop" (Kant 1784, 23). This lost place of origin where the human potential has not yet atrophied becomes the image of the millenarian future. Kant conceives of the "human race" therefore as something unborn, undetermined, whose potential both for construction and destruction is infinite. In the same way, Freud based his hope on education in the "psychological discovery that man is equipped with the most varied instinctual dispositions, whose ultimate course is determined by the experiences of early childhood" (Freud 1927, 9). Freud's "hope for the future" is that there is "perhaps a treasure to be dug up capable of enriching civilization" (48), one that makes the experiment of an irreligious, enlightened education worth making. Similarly, he compares the intelligence of the child to the hermeticism of the adult. Growth is thus not only the steady path to maturity but also the determination of these capacities and the atrophy of other ones. There is no need to find a common denominator for the species or to imagine cosmopolitanism as a process of convergence, where the human race would become more homogeneous. Rather, this inclusiveness should be understood dialectically, where the more enlightened a society is, the more diverse. In this version of cosmopolitanism, the human as well as the cosmos would be radically not-all, always to be invented anew, with a rationality in perpetual formation through the conflict of *Logos* and *Ananke*, lawful and lawless freedom.

References

Axinn, Sidney, 1958. "Kant, logic, and the concept of mankind". *Ethics*, 68(4), 286–291.

Copjec, Joan, 1994. "Sex and the euthanasia of reason." In: Joan Copjec (ed.), 1994. *Supposing the subject*. London: Verso, 16–44.

Franks, Paul W., 2005. *All or nothing: Systematicity, transcendental arguments, and skepticism in German idealism*. Cambridge, Mass: Harvard University Press.

Freud, Sigmund, 1927. "The future of an illusion". In: James Stratchey (ed.), 1961. *The standard edition of the complete psychological works of Sigmund Freud: The future of an illusion, Civilization and its discontents, and other works,* vol. 21 (1927–1931). London: Hogarth Press, 1–56.

Freud, Sigmund, 1937. "Constructions in analysis". In: James Stratchey (ed.), 1966. *The standard edition of the complete psychological works of Sigmund Freud: Moses and monotheism, An outline of psycho-analysis and other works,* vol. 23 (1937–1939). London: Hogarth Press, 255–270.

Kant, Immanuel, 1781/1998. *Critique of pure reason.* Ed. and trans. Paul Guyer and Allen W. Wood. Cambridge: Cambridge University Press.

Kant, Immanuel, 1784. "Idea for a universal history from a cosmopolitan point of view". In: Lewis White Beck (ed.), 1963. *On history,* Indianapolis: Bobbs-Merrill, 11–26.

Kant, Immanuel, 1793. "On the common saying: That may be correct in theory but is of no use in practice". In: Immanuel Kant, 1996. *Practical philosophy.* Ed. and trans. Mary J. Gregor. Cambridge: Cambridge University Press, 273–311.

Kant, Immanuel, 1795. "Toward perpetual peace". In: Immanuel Kant, 1996. *Practical philosophy.* Ed. and trans. Mary J. Gregor. Cambridge: Cambridge University Press, 311–353.

Lacan, Jacques, 1998. *Seminar xx: On feminine sexuality, the limits of love and knowledge.* Ed. Jacques Alain and trans. Bruce Fink. New York and London: W.W. Norton.

Longuenesse, Béatrice, 2005. *Kant on the human standpoint.* Cambridge: Cambridge University Press.

Mignolo, Walter D., 2000. "The many faces of cosmopolis: Border thinking and critical cosmopolitanism". *Public Culture,* 12(3), 721–748.

PART II

Enlightenment Cosmopolitanism Revisited

FRANK EJBY POULSEN

Anacharsis Cloots and the Birth of Modern Cosmopolitanism

Introduction

In our current quest for a "*retour à l'origine*" or "*redécouverte*" of modern cosmopolitanism, we are naturally looking for the "*fondateur de discursivité*" (Foucault 1969–1970).[1] This founder is often identified as Kant, although there are disputes over whether he is a cosmopolitan, an internationalist, or even a nationalist or a plain Eurocentric racist (see e.g. Cavallar 2011, 65–66, and chapter by Cavallar in this volume). His cosmopolitan credentials are undoubtedly linked to his use of the word "*Weltbürger*" and his development of a "*Weltbürgerrecht*".[2] However, cosmopolitanism cannot be reduced to the study of the concepts of *world citizenship*, the *cosmopolitan*, or even of the occurrences of the word "cosmopolitanism"; it is a vast and diverse philosophy.

Before I go on to reconstruct the cosmopolitanism of another Enlightenment thinker, Anacharsis Cloots (1755–1794), I would like to continue reflecting upon the possibilities of the historiography of "isms" in general and cosmopolitanism in particular.

When writing a history of cosmopolitanism, it is essential to understand what cosmopolitanism is in order to account for genuine versions of cosmopolitanism, and not of universalism, federalism, imperialism, or a study of educated globetrotters without any practical idea about how

1 "return to the origin"; "rediscovery"; "founder of discursivity".
2 "citizen of the world"; "law of world citizenship".

to improve the world. But inversely, it is exactly the point of a history of cosmopolitanism to inform us about what cosmopolitanism is, by understanding where it comes from. And moreover, defining cosmopolitanism may well turn into "an un-cosmopolitan thing to do", and, instead, one ought to talk of "cosmopolitanism*s*" in the plural (Pollock *et al.* 2000).

One can agree or disagree with the "un-cosmopolitan" endeavour of defining essentially cosmopolitanism, but it is certain that cosmopolitanism remains difficult to define precisely because it is its very essence to remain at the point of tension between universalism and particularism. It is useful to "define" cosmopolitanism by what it is not: not universalism, not nationalism, but somewhere in between. Cosmopolitanism aims at finding universal values, principles, laws, which are respected and can be virtually agreed upon by the vast diversity of humanity.

This raises questions as to the method for writing a history of cosmopolitanism and the figures that ought to be included or not. There are several methods in intellectual history that can be applied to the study of cosmopolitanism: *Begriffsgeschichte* or the history of concepts with for example Reinhardt Koselleck (2002); the so-called "Cambridge school" and its focus on contexts with for example Quentin Skinner (2002); the study of political ideologies with Michael Freeden (1998); or the analysis of discourses with Michel Foucault (1969).

However, cosmopolitanism is different from other "isms", not only because of the above-mentioned status that cosmopolitanism ought to be understood as a perpetual tension between universalism and local particularisms, but because it simply does not exist.

Cosmopolitanism does not exist and it never has. It is yet to be invented (or is a perpetual re-invention as Pollock *et al.* (2000) argue). There has never been any successful philosophy combining universally agreed upon principles respecting local particularities. However, it is possible to study the history of attempts, according to the languages, the *epistemes* or paradigms or meta-discourses, and the political, economic and social settings of a particular time and place.

For this reason, I find it difficult to apply in full any of the above-mentioned methods in intellectual history. Cosmopolitanism is not a genuine concept,[3] but rather regroups various concepts under one philosophy. Cosmopolitanism could be considered under the angle of ideology, but that would equate essentializing it as to what its core is and what its periphery is. Considering cosmopolitanism as a discourse (Tihanov 2011) could bypass this issue, but according to Foucault, a discourse is equally a rigid structure with rules and "laws" structuring the "enunciative field", and including "objects", "concepts" and "strategies" (Foucault 1969). Moreover, it seems to apply to greater units than cosmopolitanism.

One could instead consider cosmopolitanism under the angle of linguistics as an "ism". The suffix -ism, according to the *Oxford English Dictionary*, refers to, firstly, "forming a simple noun of action", and, secondly, "forming the name of a system of theory or practice [...]" (OED 1989). Most of the existing literature on the history of cosmopolitanism focuses on the "cosmopolitan" or the "citizen of the world" (Heater 2004; van den Heuvel 1986; Hazard 1930; Coulmas 1990; Frijhoff 1998). It is thereby taking the -ism in cosmopolitanism in its first sense—the action of the cosmopolitan.

There is no obvious reason and justification as to why the study of cosmopolitanism should be about the words "cosmopolite" or "citizen of the world". Does that mean that one needs to be a "cosmopolite"—as the term is understood during the author's time—to be able to express cosmopolitanism? Is the philosophy of cosmopolitanism only applicable to the group of individuals possessing a high level of education, economic means to travel the world, and polyglotism to understand it? While it is certain that these qualities do help anyone in formulating a philosophy of cosmopolitanism, it does not mean that cosmopolitanism must be solely

3 Cosmopolitanism could indeed be compared with what Koselleck (1979, 345, cf. 340) terms a "Vorgriff", in analogy to other concepts of *movement* such as communism. Cosmopolitanism is, from this viewpoint, in a certain sense not a proper concept (*Begriff*), since it is not empirically *grasping* (*begreifen*) "after" something in an experientially given space but is rather theoretically or hypothetically *anticipating* (*vorgreifen*) a horizon of things presumed to come, given the appropriate political circumstances and actions.

understood as the philosophy of the cosmopolitans, by the cosmopolitans, for the cosmopolitans.

By the same token, why are the concepts of "nation" and "*patrie*" (Fatherland) so tightly and exclusively linked to nationalism and patriotism? After all, these ideas were just as abstract and utopian to anyone before 1789 as some claim a *cosmopolis* is. Delon (1987, 127–128) cites the example of Valentin Jamerey-Duval, former peasant from Yonne, who became a librarian and historian at the court of Lorraine, during the first half of the eighteenth century. In his memoirs he evokes his sentimental attachment to the landscape of his childhood. The simple thought of leaving his native village makes him burst into tears. His love is attached to a very local territory: the land of the prince who made it possible for him to study and to achieve the position he held. The *patrie*, on the other hand, was for him too remote to evoke any feeling of love and attachment.

An ism is both a *signifiant* (signifier)—the phonetic picture of the word—and a *signifié* (signified)—the mental representation of the word. This entails that the *signifiant* may change among languages, while the *signifié* may remain the same. And inversely, the *signifié* of an ism changes through time, and also sometimes synchronically, while the *signifiant* remains.

An ism requires a reflective component: the need to name an existing *signifié* with a *signifiant*. Thus, the appearance of an ism is symptomatic of the existence and the taking into consideration of the existence of a *signifié*. The appearance of the word "cosmopolitanism" is therefore crucial in understanding when there is a reflected-upon movement. This also means that the *signifié* pre-existed the *signifiant*; or, as Skinner puts it, although many a word historically has predated the emergence of its eventual concept (cf. Koselleck 1972, xxii), a concept does not need to be named so to exist (Skinner 2002b, 160). What triggers this reflective consciousness and the following ism is equally of historical interest.

It is therefore important to date the appearance of the word "cosmopolitanism". In French, "*cosmopolitisme*" appeared in 1802, according to van den Heuvel (1986), while Dédéyan placed it in 1863 (Dédéyan 1976, 3). But, they do not differentiate between the first and second meaning of the ism. While van den Heuvel focuses solely on cosmopolitanism as the action of a cosmopolitan, Dédéyan is more interested in the philosophy of cosmopolitanism. Perhaps that would explain why Dédéyan considers its appearance so late. It is certain that the word "cosmopolitanism" understood as a political idea to unite humankind—and not the action of the cosmopolites—is contemporary to nationalism.

Moreover, one can note that the mention of "*cosmopolitisme*" already appeared as early as 1756 in an answer to Rousseau's *Discourse*:

> I will not stop in order to detail the advantages of the community of goods. This subject has been treated by several estimable authors, whom man corrupted by wealth reproached only a virtuous poverty and a cosmopolitanism too deeply reasoned. (Castillon 1756)[4]

It is however difficult to understand the meaning, probably because there is a typo in the sentence which obscures its meaning.

I am here interested in the second meaning of the ism, that is, the philosophy of cosmopolitanism, and more specially its political philosophy.

Now, a book of history always tells two histories—the history it studies, and the history of the time when it is written. When we, today, write a history of Enlightenment cosmopolitanism, we write a history of Enlightenment cosmopolitanism in a time of globalization and a search for a new world-narrative after the end of the bipolar order. The way we conceive of cosmopolitanism at the time when these words are being written is very different from even some one and a half decade ago, when O'Brien wrote:

> "Cosmopolitanism" is no longer a term much favoured by intellectual historians: as an idea, it seems to lack intellectual content; as a category of political thought, it has no referent. (O'Brien 1997, 2)

Since the 1990s, the literature on the philosophy of cosmopolitanism has grown substantially. Cosmopolitanism can no longer be solely equated with the highly educated citizen of the world, or with plain universalist views; nor is it longer possible to simply oppose cosmopolitanism to nationalism.

4 All translations from French in this chapter are the author's.

Curiously enough, Meinecke already stated this at the beginning of the last century:

> The current view is that an epoch of cosmopolitan thinking preceded the awakening of the national idea and of the idea of the national state in our country also. If we should demonstrate no more than that in this study, we shall have said nothing new. However, this same view also sees cosmopolitanism and national feeling as two modes of thought that mutually exclude each other, that do battle with each other, and that supplant each other. Such a view cannot satisfy the historical mind that has a deeper awareness of circumstances and that insists on a thoroughly detailed demonstration of every stage in the evolution of ideas. (Meinecke 1908/1970, 21)

One needs to understand the philosophy of cosmopolitanism in order to write its history. However, in the "second age of modernity", reflectively speaking, this also implies that the history of cosmopolitanism informs the philosophy of cosmopolitanism. Nonetheless, delineating what needs to be understood by cosmopolitanism to write its history does not mean to define it in essential terms. Nor does it mean considering it as a "perennial idea" (Skinner 2002a). It simply means that writing a history cannot be done while making an abstraction of the present, and it is necessarily a history of then and now at the same time. Cosmopolitanism changed over time because its concepts, ideas and structuring paradigm changed. It is still cosmopolitanism because of its general values and ideas placed in between the universal and the local.

I am therefore here positioning this essay as an intellectual history of Enlightenment cosmopolitanism from the reflexive perspective of "second modernity". I am not looking at the social history behind the emergence and demise of Enlightenment cosmopolitanism. Not because it is not important or interesting, but simply because there is no space here.

Anacharsis Cloots is a good example of eighteenth-century cosmopolitanism. Firstly, because one needs to have a clear methodology of the history of cosmopolitanism in order to include him into such a study. Secondly, because Cloots's political thought represents many of the aspects debated in modern cosmopolitanism.

Cloots posed the 1789 *Universal Declaration* as a basis for understanding a republic, which declared each individual free and equal by birth, as a philosophical result of metaphysical natural law theory. Cloots expanded the individualistic logic of the *Declaration* to include the whole of humanity—or rather the "human race"—as sole sovereign on earth, forming the "unique nation of the human race" into a "Republic of united individuals" (Cloots 1792; 1793).

All the elements of modern cosmopolitanism are present in Cloots's thought. In this essay, I will expound them in their context. But first, I will explain what I mean by "modern cosmopolitanism", in order to sketch a clear method for investigating the history of cosmopolitanism. Secondly, I will introduce Cloots and the main events of his life. I will then move to consider several aspects of his thought and what I think constitutes the birth of modern cosmopolitanism. Finally, I will place his political thought as a culmination of eighteenth-century natural law theory, in an atheist version, and his concept of "nation" as a cosmopolitan one.

Modern Cosmopolitanism

By modernity, I mean here the period that spans roughly from the mid-eighteenth century until the late twentieth century. What characterizes the "first age of modernity" has been described by for example Beck (1986; 2008) as opposed to a "second age of modernity", or "reflexive modernity". I will here call modernity what Beck describes as the "first age of modernity". It is characterized by being non-reflexive, based on rationality from the Enlightenment, in which modern societies are equated with bounded states and fixed identities. The present "second age of modernity" is characterized by reflexivity and globalization; second-modern societies are porous, with identities being reflectively individualized.

Cosmopolitanism had a modern period and developed during this modern period alongside nationalism. It would be a mistake to oppose the two as a prerequisite to study either the one or the other (cf. chapter by Piirimäe in this volume). Rather, the opposition should be studied as a particular moment in history, mainly set in the nineteenth century.

Cosmopolitanism should be understood as the philosophy, and in particular the political philosophy, that posits universal principles for a united humankind, whilst recognizing the diversity of humankind, and, hence, the need for protecting and respecting these particularities. As such, it is situated in between sheer universalism and sheer localism. We would nowadays consider universalism to be globalization, and localism to be nationalism. But these are temporary ideas of our time, replacing others such as universal Christianism and local monarchism.

However, this is not specific enough. One needs a philosophical probing of what ideas and ideals form this middle ground. Otherwise, one could consider imperialism as part of cosmopolitanism, as long as local particularities are preserved. This, however, does not mean that there is not a thin line, or that there is not a paradox, tension or debate inside cosmopolitanism for spreading normative values, especially human rights.

One question remains: whether one should then also differentiate cosmopolitanism from internationalism, or inter-statism. Cosmopolitanism is more than the mere sum of (nation-) states into a "system". Certainly, cosmopolitanism has in common with internationalism the aspiration to peace and the rule of law on the global scale. However, cosmopolitanism goes further by claiming the ultimate source of moral preoccupation to be the individual, and not the nation-state, and this includes the global scale as well.

This leads then into fleshing out what elements form the specific *ism* named cosmopolitanism. Turning to Western contemporary cosmopolitanism, one can identify a sort of trinity among all the existing theories: a universal metaphysics (or God), humanity and individuality.

Several examples illustrate this claim. For Pogge (2002, 169), "[t]hree elements are shared by all cosmopolitan positions"—namely: individuality, universality and generality. Caney (2006, 4) writes similarly that "[c]osmopolitans [...] affirm three principles: the worth of individuals, equality, and the existence of obligations binding on all".

This trinity can be understood as individuality, God and humanity, since God is originally the element claiming universality, with equality being a consequence of a general and common humanity. In the glossary of the international relations textbook *The Globalization of World Politics*, one can read under "cosmopolitanism":

> The ultimate source of meaning and value in human life resides with the individual (or perhaps with God). Cosmopolitans are disposed to favour very extensive accounts of universal human rights. (Baylis *et al.* 2008, 579)

In this definition of cosmopolitanism the emphasis is put on the individual, human life and God (or any metaphysical position).

Cosmopolitanism differs through time because of the different understandings that one has of the metaphysical universal, of humanity and of individuality. Moreover, different concepts of community and identity are superimposed to form various types of cosmopolitanism. In the following sections I will describe the beginning of modern cosmopolitanism through the thought of Anacharsis Cloots. But first, Cloots should be introduced.

The Life of Anacharsis Cloots (1755–1794)

Unlike Kant, Cloots does need an introduction. As the American poet Randall Jarrell wrote in the 1940s, Cloots "live[s] in footnotes" (quoted in Burt 2002). This poem—like many nineteenth-century biographies—is not sympathetic to Cloots, who is often considered "mad" (see Laurent 1869; Aurevilly 1898). Throughout his life, and his posterity, he triggered passions between either admiration from his followers or hatred from his detractors. He was popular during his lifetime, and remained known throughout the nineteenth century (see Avenel 1865/1977)—Melville notably mentions "an Anacharsis Clootz deputation" in for example *Moby Dick*.

I will here briefly sketch the most important events in Cloots's life, in order to situate him better in history. I am mainly using the two contemporary biographies, which are the most researched and accurate ones currently existing, as well as an album from an exhibition on Cloots in Cleves (Labbé 1999; Mortier 1995; Schminnes 1988).

Cloots was born on 24 June 1755 in the family castle of Gnadenthal (Val-de-Grâce in French) near Cleves, and baptised Joannes Baptista Hermannus Maria—or Jean-Baptiste. His family is of Dutch origins, his father having made a fortune as a merchant in Amsterdam, and then sought social recognition in Prussia and managed to get the title of baron after becoming adviser to Frederic the Great, and to acquire a castle and lands near Cleves, a town near the Dutch border. His mother's brother was none other than the renowned philosopher Cornelius de Pauw (1735–1799), who became canon in the nearby town Xanten when Cloots was a child.

Cloots had a typical aristocratic education, entirely in French, which remained the language for his writings. He certainly also knew German and Dutch, as his correspondence in these languages show, even if he never wrote in these languages. He was sent at nine to a Catholic boarding school in Brussels, together with his brother, who died two years later. Cloots was sent to the Jesuits in Mons, before asking to be educated at the Jesuit collège du Pléssis-Sorbonne in Paris as eleven years old, and studied at the same benches as other future revolutionaries like La Fayette. He would proudly recall later in his writings an episode when he ate a bacon omelette on a Friday, defying authorities. He then went to the prestigious and elitist *Académie militaire de Berlin*, where he was notably taught by Professor Sulzer (1720–1779), a disciple of Christian Wolff, and read Grotius and other works on the law of nations.

At twenty-five, Cloots published *Les Certitudes des preuves du mahométisme* (1780/1979), a thick book expanding a theist argument against religions. Cloots then moved to Paris with his book as credential, to enter intellectual clubs and salons. He published other works, such as *Les vœux d'un Gallophile* (1786), mixing personal biography, geopolitical analysis on the political economy of France and the theme of "natural frontiers", and *Lettres sur les juifs* (1783), a rare defence of the Jews in the eighteenth century, as well as a short play celebrating Voltaire against *"l'infâme"* religion, with *Voltaire triomphant* (1784).

In the summer of 1784, Cloots left, *nolens volens*, his beloved France to carry out the traditional *Grand Tour*. He would notably reside in London and befriend Edmund Burke and Lord Shelburne. In 1789, after travelling in North Africa, Spain and Portugal, the news of the storm of the Bastille reached him. He returned immediately to Paris, and never left.

It is then that Cloots started a public career. The abolition of censorship permitted many newspapers to appear. Cloots started to write as a journalist and disseminate his ideas to many various newspapers, depending on the audience he wanted to reach. Condorcet, who supported Cloots in his anti-monarchism, was among his colleagues at the newspaper *Chronique de Paris*.

The "PR" *coup* that made him instantly (in)famous—then and for posterity—was entering the Parliament in June 1790 leading a delegation of individuals representing various nationalities, some of them in traditional costumes. He claimed to be the "ambassador of the human race", pointing out that the French revolution was universal, and asking therefore to have the whole of humankind represented at the first celebration of the Bastille Day, 14 July 1790. This request was granted, and Cloots managed to hammer home his view that individuals, free and equal, forming the peoples, were the true representatives of their country, rather than the official ambassadors equally present at the "*fête de la fédération*",[5] representing their monarchs.

During this time in Paris, Cloots sided more and more with the common people, the *sans-culottes*. It was them, after all, that he wanted to convince with his pamphlets and articles. As a result, he stripped himself of his title of baron. He also started to term himself as "orator of the human race". Finally, following his atheist convictions, he abandoned his Christian name to choose the one of Anacharsis. "Anacharsis" was the object of a biography by the Jesuit scholar Barthélemy (1788) that told the story of this Scythian philosopher, Anacharsis, who travelled South from his native North to Athens to discover philosophy. Cloots identified himself with Anacharsis: coming from the Northern Cleves to the Southern contemporary centre of philosophy that was Paris to his eyes.

After war was declared to the king of Hungary, Cloots appeared at the National Assembly and stated:

> It is the crisis of the universe: the lot of the human race is in France's hands. We fight for the rights of man, and our victories will add a new spark to human dignity; we will strike the despots and we will set men free. (Quoted in Mortier 1995, 275)

5 "Celebration of the federation".

Cloots declared himself in favour of the use of military force, changing his opinion from what he expressed previously concerning the strength of the pen against the sword. He also donated an important amount of money and a copy of his new book *La république universelle* to the soldiers.

This provoked a violent critique against Cloots, who was accused of sending French soldiers to their death, starting the paranoid suspicion that he was a double agent for Prussia, in charge of sabotaging the French revolution. This suspicion would become even more virulent under Robespierre's regime.

On 26 August 1792, Cloots was among the foreigners who were granted French citizenship by decree. However, this was not only an honorific title for him and Thomas Paine, as it allowed them to run for election at the *Convention*. Cloots was elected in two circumscriptions, but he chose to represent his own in Oise, where he had propriety and lands. He was not interested in the local preoccupations of his constituency.

Cloots proved to be an opinionated and adamant philosopher but only a mediocre politician. He took responsibility for the events of 10 August 1792,[6] and the massacres in September 1792, even though he had no part in them, aside from his writings. Even if this was a genuine and frank position, it also placed blame on him—in his time and in historical posterity—for crimes committed when he had no political authority. Moreover, he would often change parties, following his own convictions rather than political strategy. First Jacobin, then Girondin, he then turned Montagnard, before becoming Sans-culotte. This drew even more criticism and enemies.

Cloots also opposed Robespierre and his men, firstly, on the question of war in 1792, and secondly on the question of secularization in 1793. Robespierre was in the beginning sympathetic to Cloots and his ideas, and according to Cloots would have told him that he was the only one to raise adequately the question of sovereignty. Reading Robespierre's writings and project of constitution in 1793, one cannot but draw a parallel to Cloots's own ideas. The only difference is that Robespierre is a theist where Cloots is a fierce atheist favouring the separation of the Church and the state.

6 These events of August 1792 refer to the insurrection of the Paris commune, and the attack of the Tuileries, which put an end to the monarchy in France.

Robespierre managed to get an important position with the institution of the Committee of Public Safety in December 1793. On 25 December 1793, Robespierre violently attacked the foreigners present in Paris in a speech at the Convention. Cloots was then arrested during the night between the 27 and 28 December from his residence, and was sent to prison. He was guillotined on 24 March 1794.

Cloots, the Cosmopolite Without the Name

One of the difficulties in formulating a cosmopolitan philosophy is the position of the speaking subject. When one claims a principle to be universally applicable, is one not merely imposing one's view on others?

Inside modernity, reason is above all what distinguishes the human race from the animal. Therefore, any human through the use of reason can claim universality. As a matter of fact, the word "cosmopolite", especially in the eighteenth century, developed into signifying "philosophe" (Hazard 1930; van den Heuvel 1986). It was used by many authors not only to avoid censorship, but also to claim a point of view beyond any local identity. In other words, it was a claim of universal truth.

Explaining this general phenomenon of cosmopolitan monikers, Rosenfeld argues that the Republic of Letters enabled the existence of some "transnational space" for expression, in which authors deliberately placed themselves in an unrooted position:

> [...] the idea of political engagement was not yet necessarily dependent on one's sense of belonging to a distinctive subgroup of humanity. Rather [...] public action often depended upon the opposite: deliberate deracination and namelessness on the part of the individual subject. (Rosenfeld 2002, 27)

Oddly enough, Cloots did not call himself a cosmopolitan, and only rarely used this word. When he used it, it was to refer to other individuals than himself, in the sense of travellers, or in the literal sense of citizens of the world in his universal republic. However, one would not think of Cloots as not being a cosmopolitan (Cloots 1792, 265). He understood at least three languages, travelled across Europe and North Africa, and moved from his native country to a foreign country and adopted it as his own. He even quoted as epigraph for *Les vœux d'un gallophile* "*ubi bene ibi patria*", the motto of the self-proclaimed citizens of the world, based on Cicero's "*Patria est, ubicunque est bene*" in *Tusculanæ Disputationes*. Moreover, Cloots aspired to become one of the *philosophes* of the Republic of Letters.

So why did he not call himself a cosmopolite? It is not very clear, but before the revolution, he had always claimed to be proud of his Prussian origins, seeing Frederic the Great as a leading example of an enlightened monarch. He had also always declared openly his love for France and its philosophers. In this sense, he does not really place himself beyond any particular identity, but instead actively claims two of them.

Even after the revolution, as well as when he called himself "ambassador" or "orator of the human race", he would remain ambiguous compared to this definition of cosmopolite. For instance, he would call for the French republic to be dubbed the German republic, in reference to the root of the name "German" of "having the same parents, closely connected" (Labbé 1999, 118).

But even if Cloots did not call himself "cosmopolite", he nonetheless expressed what any person claiming to theorize a universal principle has to justify: how can one claim to speak for the entire human race? To Cloots, and to modernity, reason was the answer. As reason was universal, any individual using reason could establish laws and principles that are universal.

Universal Reason and the "Orator of the Human Race"

On 22 August 1795, the Convention created the *Académie des sciences morales et politiques*, which still exists today under the same name. It marked the culmination of Enlightenment thought concerning morality and politics, considered as sciences to be developed, the same way natural sciences such as physics developed. Holbach, whom Cloots admired, wrote on developing a moral science based on "Nature", in an atheist version of morality.

Nature, uncreated and eternal, sets the rules of justice for the whole human race. The interest in respecting the laws of nature is therefore based on physical and psychological well-being. Any vice is sanctioned by a suffering of a kind. And these are universal laws, true for everyone.

> The motive which the morality of nature employs, is the self-evident interest of each individual, of each community, of the whole human species, in all times, in every country, under all circumstances. Its worship is the sacrifice of vice, the practise of real virtues; its object is the conservation of the human race, the happiness of the individual, the peace of mankind [...] (Holbach 1770, 451)

Nations must therefore educate the people in this religion of nature, this morality, in order to thrive; otherwise they will suffer and march to their own ruin.

Holbach aims at destroying the accepted contention that religion is the obvious path to morality, and that it is thereby of political usefulness. Instead of a supra-natural religion, it is a natural religion that should serve this political utility. It is a duty towards mankind moreover, to fight religion, this "superstition", this "imposture of morality", this "crime against truth", this "homicidal mask" that committed "hideous crimes", everywhere around the world (Holbach 1770, 452). Only then can man be truly free, freed from the slavery of outrageous laws. And only then can men love one another and do good for one another, thus rendering possible the unity of humankind. There is however no difference in content with the theist version.

When Cloots, equally a strong atheist, writes about his "system" of the sovereignty of the human race and the "unique nation", he compares himself to Newton, who united philosophers with his discoveries: Cloots will instead unite men with his political discoveries (Cloots 1979, 477). There is no doubt in Cloots's mind that these are "eternal laws". He discovered these eternal laws of the sovereignty of the human race and the unique nation by reasoning.

As such, any man using reason is capable of uncovering "eternal" and "universal" laws that apply to all humankind. Doing so, one can legitimately claim to speak on its behalf. Cloots considers himself the "orator of the human race" because he is speaking for the oppressed human race, which has not yet been freed by philosophy: the 1789 *Declaration*, and the coming 1792 republic.

This belief in "eternal laws" must now be explained, using the metaphysical universal paradigm of eighteenth-century Europe: natural law theory.

The Sovereignty of the Human Race: A Secularized Natural Law Theory

In order to understand Cloots's concept of the sovereignty of the human race, it is necessary to recast it against the backdrop of the main theoretical paradigm of the time—natural law theory. I argue here that Cloots's "sovereignty of the human race" is nothing but a secularized version of natural law theory, with the added context of the French revolution.

During his time at the Military Academy in Berlin, Cloots read, as we have seen, Grotius and other works on *ius gentium* (the law of nations), which were on the curriculum (Labbé 1999, 45). He also had as professor Johann Georg Sulzer (1720–1779), who was a disciple of Christian Wolff, and certainly had an influence on Cloots (Labbé 1999, 47). Several intellectual historians (Cassirer 1932; Renaut and Tavoillot 1999) have shown the influence of natural law theory, and its German origins from Leibnitz, Wolff and Pufendorf, on the 1789 *Declaration of the Rights of Man*.

Wolff, as translated by Formey, has had arguably a great influence on French natural law theories and the *Declaration of the Rights of Man* (Renaut and Tavoillot 1999, 71). Wolff posits the universality of humankind since the essence or nature of man is the same everywhere. Man is determined by his freedom that gives him will. This free will entails moral obligations. The individual will is to look for happiness, which forms the basic moral obligation of man, or law of nature since it applies to every man. From this,

Wolff deduces universal obligations and rights that all men are subjected to: human rights are deduced from the natural law that man seeks happiness through his individual will. Hence, the natural right to have the means to fulfil happiness: natural equality, natural freedom, right of security, property, etc. (Renaut and Tavoillot 1999, 73–75).

This reasoning is introduced in France by Barbeyrac's refutation of Leibnitz, to whom he must admit, nevertheless, that God necessarily has to be the power that establishes natural law (Hochstrasser 1993). Reason is what makes humans free and equal individuals, and freedom leads man to seek happiness, which forms the Laws of Nature. Barbeyrac introduces the concept of a moral community in French natural law theory, which is the "*communauté de Droite Raison*":[7]

> [...] the first Society that Men have, is with GOD, because of this community of Right Reason, out of which a Law is born, which they have in common; in such a way that the Universe is like a great Body of State, composed of Gods and Men. (Quoted in French in Hochstrasser 1993, 298)

Burlamaqui builds even more systematically on Barbeyrac. Natural law is God's law, superior in that to civil law (Burlamaqui 1756, 1). God placed us in a universal primitive state on this earth, hence society is God's will; and this natural society is thus a society of equality and liberty.

The problem for Burlamaqui is that between a sovereign and his subjects there is necessarily a society of inequality since one is governing the others (Burlamaqui 1756, 72). And men in the state of nature are essentially equal. So if man is the basis for political theory, how is it possible to justify power among them? Burlamaqui's reasoning is that there must be a superior and an inferior. Rejecting Hobbes and Pufendorf, he argues that

> [...] the right of Sovereignty derives from a Superior Power, accompanied by Wisdom and Kindness. (Burlamaqui 1756, 81)

Since God is a superior power and is wise and kind, Burlamaqui states that God is the universal sovereign of mankind ruling through natural laws.

7 "Community of Right Reason".

There are thus two societies, since sociability is universal: the civil society and the natural society. Civil societies must respect natural laws within, and also between each other's societies. This is the law of nation. God is the only sovereign in natural society and there is a hierarchical predominance of natural laws over any other as such. However, the only sanction of these laws for Burlamaqui lies in the afterworld, since men have a soul (Burlamaqui 1756, 246).

This is the issue that is at stake in all conceptions of natural law: the proper sovereign authority to enforce natural law. The same problem lies in atheist versions of natural law. God is replaced with Nature, and any breach of the natural laws leads to moral sufferings: a guilty conscience, sleepless nights and other psychological traumas.

Holbach wants to replace the religious metaphysics behind natural law with a science of the laws of nature, both physical and moral. This move is very much in line with the question of how natural law became a parallel of the laws of nature, that is, morality as a science obeying laws in par with the natural world (Daston and Stolleis 2008). The very basis of his system is that man is the work of nature and cannot escape this fact; nature is the only foundation for any knowledge on man (Holbach 1770, 2). Nature is a superior power to anything else, since no one can escape its sanctions: the voluptuous will be sanctioned by infirmities; and indulging in food and wine will shorten one's life etc. These laws are universal (Holbach 1770, 448).

From this *System of nature* one can induce the principles of *Natural politics* (Holbach 1773). "Nature" is organized into nations, and these nations were formed with a "social pact". This "social pact" is, for Holbach, a constant judgement on man's part of the good and the bad that society brings to him (1773, 13).

In this atheist account of natural laws, sovereignty is based on a human source: one man was stronger than others and hold a certain influence, yet only influence, since one man cannot be stronger than all the others. However, the only foundation of the constitutive sovereign power is the faculty to protect and do good (Holbach 1773, 20).

Nations are submitted to natural laws and they must apply to each other the same duties of "justice, good faith, humanity and help" (Holbach

1773, 31). Holbach concedes that there is a "supreme Law" that applies to all nations, and hence justice, but this law is not expressed and its sole existence is to be "felt by all nations". There is no superior power applying this "supreme Law", aside from the "balance of power" between nations, and the "general will" that "obliges them to observe the laws of fairness" (Holbach 1773, 30).

In the atheist versions of natural law, the "general will" is what constitutes the sovereign power imposing natural law on humans. It is reminiscent of the "individual will" that is present in the metaphysical side of natural law. It makes sense only in a state of society where the sum of individual wills would create this general one. God is thus "replaced" with the "general will" as the source of sovereign power constituting natural law and human rights.

In his article on natural law in the *Encyclopédie*, Diderot considers that the individual must look at the "general will" to find the limits of natural rights, and this limit is to do only what is not contested by the rest of humankind (Diderot 1755). General will is deduced from the pure act of reason of any individual stifling his passions. Since only the general will is always right, and individual will can be wrong, legislative power must belong to the general will. The general will also exists between individual societies for Diderot, but he does not stress explicitly the existence of a legislative power above the nations.

Rousseau responded in the first version of his *Social Contract* to Diderot's conception of "general will", which reflects his views well, even if it was unpublished. Like Holbach, Rousseau rejects the idea of a "golden age" of the state of nature (Rousseau 1887).[8] There is no social contract dictated by nature that establishes such a society as humankind for Rousseau. He observes that any other conception is necessarily basing the need for an external sovereign on God, and this is what he rejects, since morals should be established for political societies out of religion's reach, as there will always be senseless gods (Rousseau 1887, 285–286).

8 This first version of the *Social Contract* was only discovered and published in 1887.

If there is no natural society, if there is no natural state of freedom, equality and peace, and if man actually turns sad and wicked by being social, there is however still the possibility to take him out of moral depravation by correcting this social association with a new one: this is the object of the social contract. By means of a fundamental pact, a social contract, every individual's will create a public moral person with a common will. There is an original convention for Rousseau that we need to unveil, according to which a people is a people.

The sovereign can only be the general will, since it is the only force that can govern a state for the benefit of the "common good" (Rousseau 1762, 395). This makes sovereignty inalienable and indivisible. From this, Rousseau departs from natural law theory to state his own contribution to the theory of the social contract, which founds an absolute sovereignty—the state—without anything above it (Cassirer 1932).

Humankind, however, is separated into societies. Through the concept of "general will", Rousseau introduces the fact that a society forms a "political body", that is, a moral person with a will of its own, which always aims at the conservation of its members. This principle stops at other "political bodies" because for them, this general will is then a particular will. However, justice is still applied because it finds its source in natural law:

> [...] for then the big city of the human race becomes the political body of which the law of nature is always the general will, and of which the states and the peoples are but individual members. (Rousseau 1755, 245)

Rousseau's system of particular society defined by a social contract is not unsympathetic to the idea of a more general society (cf. chapter by Lex in this volume). Rousseau defended Saint-Pierre's (1713) project. He believed in the existence of a "European society", established by a common history and culture since the Greek and Roman time, making all European nations mutually dependent (Rousseau 1761). A "coercive force" must then be set in place to complete this state of unfledged society. This can only be done through a union between the most important sovereigns in the form of a *Diète* or Senate. However, Voltaire (1761) would sarcastically note that the Chinese emperor was not invited to this "universal" assembly.

Cloots in a letter to his cousin directly mentions his admiration for Barbeyrac's preface to his translation of Pufendorf. Burlamaqui is not directly mentioned in any of Cloots work, but his continuation of Barbeyrac's thought is directly relevant to the whole natural law tradition in France.

I argue that an atheist and materialist or, if not metaphysical, then simply physical versant of natural law developed in the second half of the century in France. Diderot and Holbach are important figures, but also Rousseau to a certain extent. Cloots was a great admirer of Rousseau, and even went on a pilgrimage to his tomb with a friend.

All these authors form the basis for Cloots's conception of sovereignty. Cloots's political system can be traced in three of his major post-revolutionary political writings: *L'Orateur du genre humain, ou dépêche du prussien Cloots au prussien Hertzberg*, March 1791; *La République universelle, ou adresse aux tyrannicides*, February 1792; *Bases constitutionnelles de la république du genre humain*, April 1793.

The 1789 *Declaration* is the founding pillar of all of Cloots's political thought (Cloots 1791, 160). The reasoning is as follows. If all men are born free and equal, then no one can claim authority over another. Following his most prominent intellectual mentor Jean-Jacques Rousseau, there must be an agreement between individuals to form a legitimate sovereign authority.

Here two arguments are mixed. On the one hand, recent French history is constantly evoked by Cloots, against Montesquieu's analysis of a separation of powers, to argue that no sub-national "corporation" should ever exist without having the possibility to gather sufficient power to create violent conflicts. And obviously, no multiple national powers should ever exist, as armies and wars are the only way they can solve conflicts. Only the "perfect fusion" of a "Confederation of individuals" can exist for Cloots.

Cloots expressed his atheism previously on diverse occasions. All metaphysical discussion for him is vain. To the natural law theorists discussing if God is sovereign because he created man, or if it is man who ought to respect God's power through reason, one could consider his answer to be what he writes about God: "The study of man makes us careful and lenient. Let us see nature as she is and not as we imagine it to be" (Cloots 1792,

257); "Does the chicken come before the egg or the egg before the chicken?" (p. 251); for "We belong to earth and not to the heavens" (p. 258).

So if God is out of the equation, it is the people that represent the only possible source of power. The only truth comes from the people: "The people is my oracle; truth does not come down the heavens, but down the rostrum" (Cloots 1793, 475). Cloots is here even more explicit in replacing the sovereign God of natural law. "[...] the human race is God [...]" (p. 476), or "[...] the human race, the supreme Being [...]" (p. 476).

In other words, the cosmos is complicated enough, without adding suppositions about a possible *theos*. One should just examine nature, because humankind is subject to primitive laws just as animals are (Cloots 1793, 494). And this natural state is the same as the civil state.

> The human species is subjected to primitive laws, like the family of bees or beavers. Let us rise to animal instinct, let us subject ourselves to the invariable laws. Natural laws are not distinct from civil and political laws because the social state is as natural to man as it is to bees or aunts. (Cloots 1793, 497)

And if nature is one, society is equally one. It is by consulting nature, claims Cloots (1793, 476), that he discovered his political system. The goal of a society is the conservation of natural rights (Cloots 1793, 497). What are natural rights? Natural rights are expressed in the 1789 *Declaration*. Cloots ascribed thereby a special status to this *Declaration*. It is the one and definitive expression of natural law. A curious position, when one considers the debates that surrounded the *Declaration*, its provisory character due to the compromises made, as well as its apparent division, at least implicitly, between civil and pre-civil (natural) rights.

The *Declaration* states that all men are born free and equal. Cloots's reasoning is twofold. If all men are free, then none can claim power over another. Anyone claiming sovereignty would be in contradiction with the "eternal principle" of the *Declaration*, on which Cloots bases his reflection. No individual or any group of individuals can claim sovereignty over a territory without being in contradiction with the eternal principle of freedom and equality. Only one community can exist in cohesion with human freedom: the whole of humankind.

Secondly, this freedom does not mean anything if it is limited, if others represent a constant threat to it, if barriers are needed to contain this threat, if military expenses for safety drive society into financial crisis, if the borders are a limit to the freedom of movement of persons and freedom of trade, or if they confine industries within limited territories.

This is why only the whole of humankind can hold sovereignty. Moreover, sovereignty is so despotic that no other power than humankind should hold it (Cloots 1793, 495).

In fact, Cloots would use French history, and the privileges and Machiavellian intrigues of the "corporations", to illustrate his system. Thanks to its unification, France managed to crush the corporations, not only professional ones, but also provincial or local ones. Therefore, the same principle ought to apply to the whole globe.

One more argument evokes the most fundamental principle of politics: that it ought to be founded on the general interest. The general will, as Cloots underlines, is the first principle of politics. In that, Cloots is faithful to Rousseau or Diderot. However, Cloots posits that Rousseau was wrong in delimiting this general will to tiny republics. If Rousseau would have lived in Cloots's own time, Cloots condescends, Rousseau would have agreed with him that the general will is in fact the universal will for all humankind.

Individuals are the foundation on which legitimate power is ascribed. Their rights are enshrined in the *Declaration*. Together they all form what Cloots calls a "confederation of individuals". Only collectively can individuals achieve something greater. Alone, they are pathetic creatures. United in a nation, like France, they are able to create great things. With a bit of imagination, Cloots argues that the whole nation of humankind could achieve even greater marvels.

The concepts of nation or *patrie* are not limited to France for Cloots. There is not space here for a *Begriffsgeschichte* of these two concepts (studied by e.g. Dann 1997; Delon 1987; Fehrenbach 1986), but one should indicate along with Koselleck that they were highly contested, together with the concept of sovereignty, especially between 1750 and 1850. The nation was not only used to describe a specific type of people, but also became—and Sieyès is the most famous example—the new concept replacing the King as the holder of sovereignty. Philosophers ascribed an idealist and abstract content to nation and *patrie*, as a collective of free and equal individuals, and a "*civitas*" in which these individuals would be citizens and not subjects. There is thus no contradiction in speaking of a nation of humankind, and of being patriotic in defending the nation. A patriot fights for the universality of the rights of man and the citizen.[9]

As nature is the model, Cloots considers his system in a highly positivist manner: "Liberty has only one form" (Cloots 1793, 477).

In line with the dominating conception of sovereignty, Cloots defines it as follow:

> Sovereignty resides essentially in the whole human race; it is one, indivisible, imprescriptible, immutable, inalienable, imperishable, unlimited, absolute, without boundaries and all mighty; consequently two peoples could not be sovereigns, because, by reuniting, there would only be one indivisible sovereign; thus no partial reunion, no individual can grant oneself sovereignty. (Cloots 1793, 476–477)

This immutable model based on nature and reason, as scientific as physics, admits therefore no division of power. For that reason, Cloots rejects any proposition for a federal constitution, and heavily criticizes the American constitution for being weak in that respect, and for necessarily leading to future conflicts among the thirteen states. Cloots distrusted any separation of powers for two reasons. Firstly, because of the French experience of various corporations with their privileges and powers, leading to the paralysis of the country and the creating of obstacles to the general will. Secondly, Cloots notices that in a united country like France, provinces do not engage in wars against each others, unlike Italian or German polities. To Cloots any provincial or national division is a barbarian political model, absurd and feudal. The division of humankind on the globe is nothing but a global feudalism in a barbaric time.

Therefore, and contrary to what Kleingeld argues (2011, 63–65), Cloots's argument is not entirely ahistorical and merely philosophical,

9 Kymlicka (2001) has equally—among others—argued that liberal nationalism was close to cosmopolitanism in its Enlightenment roots and Conversi (2000) discussed the complexity of such an antagonism.

but rather semi-historical and semi-philosophical. Cloots does not merely claim that the only nation possible is all humankind solely based on extending Rousseau's contract theory to the whole world—200 years before Beitz's extension of Rawls's revival of the contract theory (Beitz 1979; Rawls 1999). He also observes that it is in the world's interest, and puts forward historical evidence. When France started to form only one political body, the peoples inhabiting its territory stopped engaging in wars against one another, and instead engaged in peaceful judicial litigation. In comparison, Cloots notes that this is not the case for instance in Italy, or with the German countries (Cloots 1792, 8). This leads Cloots to think that sovereignty should not be divided. By the same token, Cloots is strongly opposed to any federation of states.

This historical observation of the peaceful effect of uniting peoples under one modern political body named the "nation", coupled with the philosophical argument of the nation as the abstract entity of free and equal men, leads Cloots to present his "system" of the unique sovereign nation of the human race.

The French revolution represents this hope, and is therefore a universal revolution. The French national assembly is in fact a representative and embryonic assembly of all humankind because the revolution was based on the *Declaration of the Rights of Man*. The new constitution should protect this fact and take into consideration the very likely future adhesion of other members to the French constitution.

However, Cloots negates all French imperialism. These principles are not French; they are universal. The declaration is not French but for everyone: "Liberty, never mind what Montesquieu says, is a plant that becomes acclimatized everywhere" (Cloots 1792, 249). Cloots even suggests, as we have seen earlier, that France drop its "beautiful name" for the one of Germany, the German Republic, as in the original meaning of German, that is, *brotherhood*.

In short, the universal republic is a minimal state in charge of protecting human rights. All collectivities in the universal republic are free to decide on the use of taxes, as long as universal taxes are collected.

Cloots thereby concludes his project for the 1793 constitution:

> Article 1: There is no other sovereign than the human race. (Cloots 1793, 498)

Conclusion

As Gauthier (1998) or Conversi (2000) show in their studies, the ideals of natural law disappeared during the revolution. The idea of social law without any further reference to the "Supreme Being" imposed itself. As I tried to argue, Cloots could be considered one of them, yet maintaining the universal ideals of natural law, and taking them to their logical conclusion when thinking about replacing a divine sovereign protector of natural rights with a human one.

Cloots thought that his system of the sovereignty of the human race and universal republic would solve the problem of violent conflicts among peoples and of the division of humankind. It is far from certain that such a system would ever be politically implementable, but Cloots represents the transition between one abstract divine sovereignty of natural law to a human abstract sovereignty of civil law. He was arguing for a way to universally apply the principles of natural law in society, without the original religious metaphysics.

Cloots took contradictory political positions for the implementation of his system. These contradictions are still very actual. On the one hand, he believed that tyrants should not be killed even though they would oppress and refuse human rights to their people. The fight ought to be taken on the ground of argumentation and persuasion: propaganda for human rights. On the other, he agreed for wars of extension to deliver these people and bring freedom to them.

Cloots symbolizes the tensions and contradictions within modern cosmopolitanism: between the imperialistic universal temptation and the respect for local diversity. In his model of a universal republic, Cloots is both arguing that all societies ought to retain their autonomy for deciding on how to organize life, but also argues that none other than Paris can know better what is the right thing to do: "Paris is the Vatican of reason" (Cloots 1792, 261).

I did not wish to argue here that Cloots had all the answers, nor that they are correct. His answers were the ones of his time. But certainly, his ideas and the contradictions in his thought represent the contradictions for reaching a working theory of cosmopolitanism in modernity, between universality and respect for local diversity, the general and the local. Reason, natural law theory, and social contract theory are still the premises of modern political philosophy, not only for nationalist theories, but also for cosmopolitan ones.

The distinction between cosmopolitanism and nationalism should be rethought within second-modern cosmopolitanism. Already, Habermas and his followers (Delanty 2009) have placed the dominance of reason as the foundational element in question. A cosmopolitan understanding of the concept of nation may bring cosmopolitanism and nationalism closer together. In any case, Cloots should be of interest to anyone working on cosmopolitanism as his work is beneficial to understanding its origins.

References

Aurevilly, Jules-Amédée Barbey d', 1898. *Portraits politiques et littéraires*. Paris: Alphonse Lemerre Éditeur.

Avenel, Georges, 1865/1977. *Anacharsis Cloots, l'orateur du genre humain*. Paris: Éditions Champ Libre.

Barthélemy, Jean-Jacques, dit l'abbé Barthélemy, 1788. *Voyage du jeune Anacharsis en Grèce, dans le milieu du quatrième siècle avant l'ère vulgaire*, 4 vols. Paris: DeBure.

Baylis, John, Steve Smith, and Patricia Owens (eds.), 2008. *The globalization of world politics*, 4th ed. Oxford: Oxford University Press.

Beck, Ulrich, 1986. *Risikogesellschaft: Auf dem Weg in eine andere Moderne*. Frankfurt am Main: Suhrkamp Verlag.

Beck, Ulrich, 2008. "The cosmopolitan perspective: Sociology of the second age of modernity". *The British Journal of Sociology*, 51(1), 79–105.

Beitz, Charles R., 1979. *Political theory and international relations*. Princeton, NJ: Princeton University Press.

Burlamaqui, Jean-Jacques, 1756. *Principes du Droit naturel.* Geneva and Copenhagen: Chez Cl. & Ant. Philibert.

Burt, Stephen, 2002. "Two poems by Randall Jarrell". *The New York Review of Books*, 19 December. Available at: http://www.nybooks.com/articles/archives/2002/dec/19/two-poems-by-randall-jarrell/. Accessed 7 July 2010.

Caney, Simon, 2006. *Justice beyond borders: A global political theory*. Oxford: Oxford University Press.

Cassirer, Ernst, 1932. *Die Philosophie der Aufklärung.* Tübingen: Mohr.

Castillon, Johann von, 1756. *Discours sur l'origine de l'inegalité parmi les hommes: Pour servir de réponse au Discours que M. Rousseau, citoyen de Géneve, a pub. sur le même sujet*. Amsterdam: Chez J.F. Jolly.

Cavallar, Georg, 2011. *Imperfect cosmopolis: Studies in the history of international legal theory and cosmopolitan ideas*. Cardiff: University of Wales.

Cloots, Anacharsis, 1780. *La certitude des preuves du Mahométisme, ou réfutation de l'examen critique des apologistes de la religion mahométane: Par Ali-Gier-Ber, Alfaki, ou Docteur en Théologie, Principal du Collége D'Andrinople, Associé à L'Académie des Sciences, Belles Lettres & Arts de Samarcandes*. London: n.p. [in reality published in Amsterdam in 1779, but labelled London 1780].

Cloots, Anacharsis, 1783. *Lettre sur les Juifs à un ecclésiastique de mes amis*, lue dans la séance publique du musée de Paris, le XXI novembre 1782 par M. le B[aron] d[e] C[loots D[u] V[al] D[e] G[râce]. Berlin: s.n.

Cloots, Anacharsis, 1784. *Voltaire triomphant, ou Les prêtres déçus: drame*, n.p. Available at: http://gallica.bnf.fr/ark:/12148/bpt6k72297n. Accessed March 9 2012.

Cloots, Anacharsis, 1786. *Voeux d'un gallophile*. Amsterdam: n.p.

Cloots, Anacharsis, 1791. "Dépêche du prussien Cloots au prussien Hertzberg". In: Anacharsis Cloots, 1979. *Écrits révolutionnaires 1790–1794*. Paris: Éditions Champ Libre, 101–170.

Cloots, Anacharsis, 1792. "La république universelle; ou, Adresse aux tyrannicides". In: Anacharsis Cloots, 1979. *Écrits révolutionnaires 1790–1794*. Paris: Éditions Champ Libre, 243–318.

Cloots, Anacharsis, 1793. "Bases constitutionnelles de la République du genre humain". In: Anacharsis Cloots, 1979. *Écrits révolutionnaires 1790–1794*. Paris: Éditions Champ Libre, 473–502.

Conversi, Daniele, 2000. "Cosmopolitanism and nationalism". In: Athena Leoussi (ed.), 2000. *Encyclopaedia of nationalism*. Oxford: Transaction Books, 34–39.

Coulmas, Peter, 1990. *Weltbürger: Geschichte einer Menschheitssehnsucht*. Reinbek: Rowohlt.

Dann, Otto, 1997. "Nation". In Michel Delon (ed.), 1997. *Dictionnaire européen des Lumières*. Paris: Presses Universitaires de France, 761–765.
Daston, Lorraine and Stolleis, Michael (eds.), 2008. *Natural law and laws of nature in early modern Europe: Jurisprudence, theology, moral and natural philosophy*. Farnham: Ashgate.
Dédéyan, Charles, 1976. *Le cosmopolitisme européen sous la Révolution et l'Empire*. Paris: Société d'édition d'enseignement supérieur.
Delanty, Gerard, 2009. *The cosmopolitan imagination: The renewal of critical social theory*. Cambridge: Cambridge University Press.
Delon, Michel, 1987. "Nation". In: Pascal Ory (ed.), 1987. *Nouvelle histoire des idées politiques*. Paris: Hachette, 127–135.
Diderot, Denis, 1755. "Natural rights". In: *The encyclopedia of Diderot & d'Alembert: Collaborative translation project*, 2009. Transl. Stephen J. Gendzier. Ann Arbor: M Publishing, University of Michigan Library. Available at: http://hdl.handle.net/2027/spo.did2222.0001.313. Accessed 17 June 2012. [Trans. of "Droit naturel", *Encyclopédie ou Dictionnaire raisonné des sciences, des arts et des metiers*, vol. 5. Paris, 1755.]
Fehrenbach, Elisabeth, 1986. "Nation". In: Gerd van den Heuvel and Anette Höfer (eds), 1986. *Handbuch politisch-sozialer Grundbegriffe in Frankreich 1680–1820*, vol. 7. Munich: Oldenbourg, 75–107.
Foucault, Michel, 1969. *L'archéologie du savoir*. Paris: Gallimard.
Foucault, Michel, 1969–1970. "Qu'est-ce qu'un auteur?". In: Daniel Defert and François Ewald (eds.), 1994. *Dits et écrits 1954–1988 par Michel Foucault*, vol. 1 (1954–1969), 789–821. Paris: NRF Gallimard.
Freeden, Michael, 1998. *Ideologies and political theory: A conceptual approach*. Oxford: Oxford University Press.
Frijhoff, Willem, 1998. "Conceptual history, social history and cultural history: The test of 'cosmopolitanism'". In: Iain Hampsher-Monk, Karin Tilmans and Frank van Vree (eds.), 1998. *History of concepts: Comparative perspectives*. Amsterdam: Amsterdam University Press, 103–114.
Gauthier, Florence, 1992. *Triomphe et mort du droit naturel en Révolution 1789 –1795 – 1802*. Paris: Presses Universitaires de France –PUF.
Hazard, Pierre, 1930. "Cosmopolite". In: Fernand Baldensperger, 1930, *Mélanges d'histoire littéraire générale et comparée offerts à Fernand Baldensperger*. Paris: Libraire ancienne Honoré Champion, 354–364.
Heater, Derek, 2004. *World citizenship: Cosmopolitan thinking and its opponents*. London and New York: Continuum.

Heuvel, Gerd van den, 1986. "Cosmopolite, cosmopoli(ti)sme". In: Rolf Reichardt and Hans-Jürgen Lüsebrink (eds.), 1986. *Handbuch politisch-sozialer Grundbegriffe in Frankreich 1680–1820*. München: Oldenbourg, 41–55.

Hochstrasser, Tim, 1993. "Conscience and reason: The natural law theory of Jean Barbeyrac". *The Historical Journal*, 36(2), 289–308.

Holbach, Paul Henri Thiry baron d', 1770. *Système de la nature; ou, Les loix du monde physique, & du monde moral* [...]. London: Slatkine.

Holbach, Paul Henri Thiry baron d', 1773. *La politique naturelle, ou, Discours sur les vrais principes du gouvernement, par un ancien magistrat*. Londres [i.e. Amsterdam]: n.p.

Kleingeld, Pauline, 2011. *Kant and cosmopolitanism: The philosophical ideal of world citizenship*. Cambridge: Cambridge University Press.

Koselleck, Reinhart, 1972. "Einleitung". In: Otto Brunner, Werner Conze and Reinhart Koselleck (eds.), 1972. *Geschichtliche Grundbegriffe: Historisches Lexikon zur politisch-sozialen Sprache in Deutschland*, vol. 1. Stuttgart: Ernst Klett Verlag, xiii–xxvii.

Koselleck, Reinhart, 1979. *Vergangene Zukunft: Zur Semantik geschichtlicher Zeiten*. Frankfurt am Main: Suhrkamp.

Koselleck, Reinhart, 2002. *The practice of conceptual history: Timing history, spacing concepts*. Trans. Todd Samuel Presner. Stanford, CA: Stanford University Press.

Kymlicka, Will, 2001. "From Enlightenment cosmopolitanism to liberal nationalism". In: Will Kymlicka, 2001. *Politics in the vernacular: Nationalism, multiculturalism and citizenship*. Oxford: Oxford University Press, 203–221(19).

Labbé, François, 1999. *Anacharsis Cloots, le Prussien Francophile*. Paris: L'Harmattan.

Laurent, François, 1869. *Histoire du droit des gens et des relations internationals*, vol. 15. Paris: Librairie Internationale.

Meinecke, Friedrich, 1908/1970. *Cosmopolitanism and the national state*. Princeton, NJ: Princeton University Press.

Mortier, Roland, 1995. *Anacharsis Cloots, ou, L'utopie foudroyée*. Paris: Stock.

O'Brien, Karen, 1997. *Narratives of Enlightenment*. Cambridge: Cambridge University Press. Available at: http://dx.doi.org/10.1017/CBO9780511519079. Accessed 28 June 2013.

OED, 1989. "-ism, *suffix*". *Oxford English Dictionary Online*. 2nd ed. Available at: http://www.oed.com/view/Entry/100006. Accessed 12 June 2012.

Pogge, Thomas W., 2002. *World poverty and human Rights: Cosmopolitan responsibilities and reforms*. Cambridge: Polity.

Pollock, Sheldon, Carol A. Breckenridge, Dipesh Chakrabarty, and Homi Bhabha, 2000. "Cosmopolitanism*s*". *Public Culture*, 12(3), 577–589.

Rawls, John, 1999. *A theory of justice*. Cambridge, MA: Belknap Press of Harvard University Press.

Renaut, Alain, and Pierre-Henri Tavoillot, 1999. "La pensée politique des lumières". In: Alain Renaut (ed.), 1999. *Histoire de la philosophie politique*, vol. 3. Paris: Calmann-Lévy, 50–101.

Rosenfeld, Sophia, 2002. "Citizens of nowhere in particular: Cosmopolitanism, writing and political engagement in eighteenth-century Europe". *National Identities*, 4(1), 25–43.

Rousseau, Jean-Jacques, 1755. "Discours sur l'économie politique". In: Jean-Jacques Rousseau, 1964. *Œuvres complètes*, vol. 3. Paris: Gallimard, 239–278.

Rousseau, Jean-Jacques, 1761. "Extrait du projet de paix perpétuelle de monsieur l'Abbé de Saint-Pierre". In: Jean-Jacques Rousseau, 1964. *Œuvres complètes*, vol. 3. Paris: Gallimard, 563–589.

Rousseau, Jean-Jacques, 1762. "Du contrat social ou principes de droit politique". In: Jean-Jacques Rousseau, 1964. *Œuvres complètes*, vol. 3. Paris: Gallimard, 347–470.

Rousseau, Jean-Jacques, 1887. "Du contrat social ou essai sur la forme de la république (Première version, manuscrit de genève)". In: Jean-Jacques Rousseau, 1964. *Œuvres complètes*, vol. 3. Paris: Gallimard, 279–346.

Saint-Pierre, Charles-Iréné Castel de, 1713. *Projet pour rendre la paix perpétuelle en Europe*. Autrecht: chez Antoine Schouten.

Schminnes, Bernd (ed.), 1988. *Anacharsis Cloots: Der Redner des Menschengeschlechts*. Kleve: Boss.

Skinner, Quentin, 2002a. "Meaning and understanding in the history of ideas". In: Quentin Skinner, 2002. *Visions of politics: Regarding method*, vol 1. Cambridge: Cambridge University Press, 57–89.

Skinner, Quentin, 2002b. "The idea of a cultural lexicon". In: Quentin Skinner, 2002, 158–174.

Tihanov, Galin, 2011. "Cosmopolitanism in the discursive landscape of modernity: Two Enlightenment articulations". In: David Adams and Galin Tihanov (eds.), 2011. *Enlightenment cosmopolitanism*. London: Legenda, 133–152.

Voltaire, François de, 1761. "Rescrit de l'empereur de chine à l'occasion du projet de paix perpétuelle". In: Jacques van den Heuvel (ed.), 1961. *Voltaire: Mélanges*. Paris: Gallimard, 157–202.

NINA LEX

Exemplary Universality: Jean-Jacques Rousseau and Global Citizenship

Regarding the long yet disparate history of the term cosmopolitanism, the time of the Enlightenment is surely considered an era that provides key sources to today's discourse on cosmopolitan philosophy. However, Jean-Jacques Rousseau, often referred to as an intellectual extremist or political radical, is scarcely seen in the line of thinkers that formed the notion of a world citizen. Reading *Émile, ou de l'éducation*: "Distrust those cosmopolitans who search out remote duties in their books and neglect those that lie nearest" (Rousseau 1762/1921, 10) one would even strongly doubt that the author is an advocate of cosmopolitanism and universal values. And indeed, as indicated in the quotation above, Rousseau held a view of cosmopolitanism that was far more negative than those of many of his contemporaries.

In the mid-eighteenth century the French philosopher Diderot stated that cosmopolitans are "strangers nowhere in the world" (quoted in Laertius 1925, 63), pointing towards the question of strangeness and nationality. This was a step towards questioning the tension contained in the term "cosmopolitanism", yet its critical potential was still not sufficiently present to a great number of eighteenth-century thinkers. While the Encyclopaedists still had a basically conflict-free view of the relationship between patriotic loyalty and universalistic human morals, as it is expressed in Enlightenment cosmopolitan thought, Rousseau breaks with this idea and articulates a much more problematic conceptual relationship.

My aim in this contribution is to show that despite the enhancement of proto-nationalistic ideas and the encapsulation of the individual that Rousseau is often accused of, he argues for an identity that allows for universal self-understanding and therefore a cosmopolitan or even *cosmopolitical* conception of socio-cultural togetherness. Accordingly, my concern is to correspondingly define Rousseau's approach as a form of a fundamentally ethical cosmopolitanism and to discuss this by means of a *subject theory* which is primarily developed in the context of Rousseau's work *Émile*, but also includes the so-called *Discourses* as well as selected political treatises and fragments. The particular significance of *Émile*, the work that Rousseau himself designated as his most important, finds in my opinion its justification in that the modern conflict potential of patriotism and cosmopolitanism is explicitly described for the first time, at least as far as I can see, and, at the same time, questions are generated that determine the discourse without having to necessarily revert to a simple assumption stemming from the prehistory of the French Revolution.

What is brought to light by the notion of cosmopolitanism that is characterized by the tension between nationalism and universal values is a debate that splits into two aspects with respect to Rousseau. Yet, these cannot be regarded as entirely independent of one another, but rather represent a mutually conditioned reciprocal relationship. For one, the thesis regarding identity therefore must be addressed, and second, the meaning and effect of normativity has to be taken into account. The former I mainly conceptualize through the notion of personhood and self-conception while the latter, the aspect of normativity, can be represented by focusing on the role of otherness, respectively strangeness, which is also present in the historical—and still not overcome—contrast between "barbarism" and "civilization". I therefore consider these key aspects with a view to a moral position in terms of a cosmopolitan identity. Since both aspects are connected or even determined by the conflict between patriotism and universalism and identification and demarcation, as well as inwardness and de-personalization, it also contains the overriding question about the constitution of the self and the formation of identity with respect to, or due to, the foreign. In relation to this, both aspects are closely linked to a discussion about the principles of justice with respect to a moral cosmopolitanism, although not in the strict sense of a normative cosmopolitanism. In this regard, however, freedom, equality and recognition are moments of central significance, in terms of giving expression to a global order.

My contribution thus attempts to briefly discuss how both theses of the cosmopolitanism debate in Rousseau find a fruitful connection. Hereby it must be demonstrated that Rousseau, although lacking the systematic stringency of Kant or Hegel, represents a consistently fundamental cosmopolitan position. In my opinion, he presents through *Émile* an exemplary universality which is due to cosmopolitan demands in contrast to mere individualism as well as dogmatic nationalism. Nevertheless, this understanding attempts neither to disclose the individual to a rootless existence nor to a universal levelling of multiculturalism, and thus provides a valuable contribution with respect to the interlacing of individuality and universality. Reflecting on these issues in my opinion allows for a review of the heritage of the history of cosmopolitan ideas that is still relevant for today's claims. Still, in view of the given frame I will have to restrict myself in terms of merely sketching the general outlines, and, at least for now, refrain from presenting a sufficiently precise definition concerning the cosmopolitan content of Rousseau's doctrine.

A Cosmopolitan Identity

So that cosmopolitanism does not remain only an empty construct, a merely relativistic viewpoint, the concept of personhood and therefore of identity has to necessarily be addressed. Montaigne's central sceptical question "Que sais-je?" (What do I know?) therewith finds in Rousseau's "Que suis-je moi-même?" (What am I myself?) (Rousseau 1782/1959, 994) from the *Reveries* a subject-specific equivalent, and as a result a complex formation of the relation between the individual and society. It is only through the basic question "what am I" that the tensions and the problematic areas of a cosmopolitan self-concept crystallize. By discussing identity—and Rousseau does this concerning various aspects, starting with the anthropological claim and spelling it out into a deeply psychological dialogue—a political as well as a personal facet of the concept of cosmopolitanism is addressed. The question of nationality and along with that a broader, yet more specific (since it concerns the individual person) question of belonging in terms of identification is also apparent. The latter, the aspect of identification respectively demarcation, is obviously central, since this very self-localization is necessary in order to speak at all about subjectivity; to refer to a subject who corresponds to, acts and performs a self-directed opinion, who is practicing self-mastery and who is an active counterpart. Yet an underlying aim will be to show that despite the claim of selflocalization or identification in a broader sense, Rousseau's argument is not that only citizenship as a collective concept meets the condition described above, but rather that the concept of personhood is sufficient for the understanding referred to here. When addressing the ideal political order and therewith the ideal citizenship, the reception often points to Rousseau's depiction of Sparta, ancient Rome or citizenship as Plato depicts it. Against those interpretations, it can be stated, in my opinion, that Rousseau not only argues against the idealization of those concepts but also that citizenship as a collective concept is not necessarily or perhaps not at all generating an identity that is in line with the primacy of his cosmopolitan claim.

The problematic tension Rousseau indicates is demonstrated in *Émile* already on the first page: "Forced to combat either nature or society, you must make your choice between the man and the citizen, you cannot train both" (Rousseau 1762/1921, 10). Obviously, Rousseau's juxtaposition of the terms man and citizen appears to imply an irreconcilable opposition. But what is it that seems to make both ideals mutually exclusive? In brief, the goal of the so depicted ancient citizen consists in becoming a patriot. Limited to his polity, the citizen is merely a fragment of his respective city and therefore dependent on his own kind. The good of the citizen is inseparable from the good of his state. And as the citizen earns his merits only through the reputation of others, he depends on their recognition as well as on their opinion. The underscored characteristic that Rousseau hereby evokes quite clearly is that the citizen only exists for others and is determined by the tyranny of their opinion. Man, in contrast, is conceived as a solitary being. He is a numerical unity and follows only his own principles. Also, the good of man is independent of his membership in a political association. Thus, he is self-sufficient as well as self-affirmative.

Traditional interpretation assumes that Rousseau merely argues that a decision can only be made between those two ideals. Despite this, my attempt in this contribution will be to show that none of these concepts allow the individual to develop the characteristics that a cosmopolitan identity requires and that, according to Rousseau, a *third way* therefore has to be considered (cf. Todorov 2001, 18). Regarding man, it means that the absolute existence man is striving for makes him isolated. Being guided by instincts and hence adopting a rather passive and non-reflexive stance, the solitary individual renounces almost every ethical claim instead of being a conscious or tolerant being. Therefore, the solitary being might be characterized as good but not as virtuous. His spontaneous and direct access to sensation vouches for an innocence that is at the expense of responsibility as well as acting according to the will in general.[1] This is why Jean Starobinski (1958/2003, 290) understands the solitary individual as a being, reduced to a mere aesthetic and biological existence that finally leads to fatality. The problem of a moral responsibility is eluded by self-sufficiency, but without any interaction the solitary being is driven only by necessities, whereas his asceticism verges on an inhuman existence, or respectively, a non-existence.[2]

The solitary being is not the "stupid and unimaginative animal" (Rousseau 1762, 47) any longer, like the natural man used to be, since he is self-conscious, and able to compare. Yet his self-centrism maintains a chimera, which not only effaces an adjustment with the exterior world, but prevents him from developing all the human traits that are developed in society and by interacting with others. This state would make it impossible to speak about order or morality, as there is no interaction at all that could search for order or morality. Furthermore, this solitude can be understood as accepting inequality, rather than avoiding it. One can say, according to Starobinski (cf. 1958/2003, 48), that there is a certain equality obtained but it is more a result of considering the others as not existing at all than of

1 In his self-understanding he is a natural man, yet he is not virtuous. However, it must be added that this depiction remains diffuse since in the same book also contrary statements are found (cf. Rousseau 1959, 823).

2 Rousseau credits only God with complete happiness, since it is only he who is endued with absolute self-sufficiency.

considering them to be equal. Starobinski's fatalistic interpretation might be harsh but even Rousseau himself concludes:

> [...] complete solitude is a sad state that contradicts nature: passionate sensation animates the soul, exchange of thoughts stimulates the mind. Our sweetest existence is relative and collective, and our true self is not completely within us. In brief, man in this life can never really enjoy himself without the cooperation of others. (Rousseau 1772–1776, 813 [author's translation])

Rousseau therefore clearly suggests being open to others, that the limitation to one's self would only prevent becoming oneself. But does that mean that the otherness he has in mind ends at the country's frontier or is limited to the respective *polis*? Thus, is a national concept sufficient regarding his ideas on autonomy, freedom and equality?

Looking at the depiction of citizenship, it becomes obvious that the citizen has a merely relative existence because of his dependence on his polity (Neuhouser 2010, 33). Thus, the citizen's viewpoint can hardly be separated from a local loyalty or a strict subjectivism formed by the collective good. Being a patriot therefore does not only include a strong repugnance against foreigners; a dependence on others also poses a standing threat to freedom. The citizen, as understood here, is governed by patriotism, and therefore a mistrust or repugnance against foreigners is essential to this concept. Regarding this Rousseau concludes: "Every patriot hates foreigners; they are only men, and nothing to him" (Rousseau 1762/1921, 10). Obviously the principle of equality, so much promoted by Rousseau, is revoked within this perspective of the citizen. Instead, a national or monologic perspective is fostered, where the individual reflects critically on his action only according to the claim of his *polis*. Otherness, and respectively, the other, therefore is excluded from the ethical judgments or is not even recognized as an existence with a moral significance. With the collective claim of the *polis* the single citizen therefore not only forgoes his self-awareness as an individual but also limits his view to a monotonous perspective insofar as a merely one-dimensional self-understanding is maintained instead of a multi-facetted conception of the self, where the subject conceives of himself as belonging to different identity forming groups at the same time, for example belonging to a religious group, being a lover or being left-handed.

With what Amartya Sen called the "Fallacy of Singular Affiliation" (Sen 2006, 20), the individual therefore neglects diversity in favour of a fictive unity that embraces all areas of life.

When taking into account Rousseau's depiction of the modern citizen, the bourgeois, the tension is only prolonged or even increased. The de-personalization in which the identity of the citizen constitutes itself, also determines the self of the bourgeois, though in a very different respect. Both fall victim to the irrevocable dependence on others. What both types of the self have in common is the tyranny of the opinion of others. Yet due to a developed self-reflection this contains a much more problematic tension for the bourgeois. Since the bourgeois consider the judgment of others to make their own decisions but also to generate a moral concept, the bourgeois find themselves confronted with the contradiction of their interests and those of their respective society. Thus, the dilemma of modern society consists in educating humans with two souls, who are "[...] always professing to live for others, while thinking of themselves alone" (Rousseau 1762/1921, 12). Thus, the bourgeois too is determined by a relative existence. The central factor here is the inflamed *amour-propre*. By making comparisons, and by being restless in seeking the first and best rank, it is the inflamed *amour-propre* that leads to a human's immaturity. The dependence that was addressed when discussing the model of the ancient citizen becomes evident for the bourgeois as well, in two respects. First, *amour-propre* forms a relative self-concept in the sense that the individuals judge their moral values only in relation to others. Second, the recognition the individuals are seeking depends completely on the judgement of others (Neuhouser 2008, 33). Therefore it becomes obvious that *amour-propre* must be observed critically. Frederick Neuhouser thus makes clear that it is the inflamed *amour-propre* that provokes this very dependence, and in consequence, poses a standing threat to freedom. The bourgeois possesses a certain level of reflexivity, yet:

> [...] he who would preserve the supremacy of natural feelings in social life knows not what he asks. Ever at war with himself, hesitating between his wishes and his duties, he will be neither a man nor a citizen. He will be of no use to himself nor to others.

> He will be a man of our day, a Frenchman, an Englishman, one of the great middle class. (Rousseau 1762/1921, 11)

Insofar as the imagined judgement of others becomes the guideline for the individual's acts, the *amour-propre* can be conceived as the problem of the internalized other. To satisfy their interests, the bourgeois are forced to neglect them and to adjust themselves to the claims society imposes on them. According to Rousseau, this can only lead to failure in both endeavours. Yet the citizen or patriot as well as the solitary being have something in common insofar as the individual is both times characterized by a certain transparency.[3] This is also expressed by an abandonment, in the sense of whether a similar inflated contemplation is the case regarding the solitary individual or complete identification with his kind regarding the patriot. In both moments, the self alienates itself in favour of, on the one hand, a complete objectification or, on the other hand, being a mere fragment of the crowd. Even though the bourgeois seems to represent the missing link between both extremes, he does not succeed in taking advantage of his reflexivity. Rather the contrary is the case; he is caught up in contradictions regarding the divergence of his interests and his duties.

The types of identity discussed above are dominated by fundamental prejudices, and provoke a rudimentary de-personalization, although in completely different respects. Moreover, in contrast to man, governed by *amour de soi* which serves self-preservation, the citizen becomes governed by an inflamed *amour-propre*, which leads to vanity and to seeking pride. Both are goods which in modern society directly advance alienation and inequality, which Rousseau locates as the main reasons for the decline of humanity. Complete solitude as well as, or specifically, modern citizenship turn out to be not only false ideals, but also undesirable forms of existence for beings like us. As shown above, it becomes evident that both concepts not only appear to be incompatible with the needs and the

3 Jean Starobinski (2004) assesses this in a positive manner but dissociates himself therewith from Rousseau in my opinion, since the latter categorically defends the maxim of autonomy and therewith also a certain objectivity or at least an objective angle.

form of happiness available to humans but also with the development of distinctively human potentials. More recent receptions therefore rather suggest that Rousseau must be understood in terms of looking through the citizen's as well as the solitary individual's lenses, although still not approving of what is seen.

It is undisputed, however, that both concepts display not only the challenges man has to face, but also the needs he has to satisfy. According to this, Rousseau in my opinion transcends this respective problematic of the bourgeois as well as the one of the solitary being regarding Émile with respect to the formation of an identity that is guided by an authentic, heartfelt cosmopolitanism. The efforts of mainly current receptions, to which I will subscribe my exposition as much as possible, attempted to demonstrate that Rousseau was not only held up in revealing an inconsistency in human existence, but was rather particularly able to comprehend the "conditio humana" *in* this ambivalence without capitulating before the attempt to reveal a practicable path where man and citizen are united in terms of becoming intimately entwined within the individual, rather than being two opposing identities.

How does one locate an identity beyond patriotism tied to the respective society, and at the same time beyond a life in complete solitude, without falling victim to either a "plural monoculturalism" (Amartya Sen) or a sheer "view from nowhere" (Thomas Nagel)? The moral individual in cosmopolitan terms, described by Rousseau, shall therefore be briefly outlined in the following. Cosmopolitan understanding in accordance with Rousseau is primarily based on two fundamental principles: the principle of autonomy and the principle of objective judgment. While the former stands for the individual, who can be understood in relation to open political structures but is, however, regarded as a free and equal person, the latter stands for the moral frame of reference, the basis on which the rules and principles are created, and which are of universal character. In order to tie together these two considerations, Rousseau takes account of nature as the overall reference point, and he emphasizes a strictly practical orientation in terms of a life-immanent experience. That is, instead of fleeing the world through contemplation, Émile's education consists of learning by doing and therefore is mainly concerned with the practical matters surrounding him, or with direct commerce, and not so much with remote theoretical or metaphysical issues. Rousseau bases the potentiality of the moral individual on the characteristics provided in a natural state, namely self-love (*amour de soi*), pity and perfectibility. With that Rousseau wants to foil the depravation of the individual living in society. In other words, the negative influence of inflamed *amour-propre*, that is, its contribution to the fragmentation and instrumentalization of the individual, is to be balanced by the recognition of the other as equal. Rousseau's aim is not to remove characteristics developed within society but to transform them, to extract from the ill itself the remedy which can cure it (cf. Rousseau 1882, 288).

The Programmatic Education

In the first step, the so-called negative education, the aim of Émile's mentoring therefore is to experience the limits of freedom in a self-directed manner and to limit the individual's egocentrism. This experience then constitutes the basis for building up a rational order of life which activates reason. The second stage is concerned with moral issues and virtue. Freedom and autonomy are only restrained insofar as Rousseau constitutes that only through becoming aware of the existence of others as well as through the gaze of others, does one discover one's own existence.[4] At this point, the central significance of *amour-propre*, and the inherent problems of moral togetherness, become apparent. Thus:

> [...] natural compassion, which lost, when applied to societies, almost all the influence it had over individuals, [and] survived no longer except in some great cosmopolitan spirits, who, breaking down the imaginary barriers that separate different peoples, [...] include the whole human race in their benevolence. (Rousseau 1755, 192)

4 The dependence on others must not be confused with a limitation of freedom in the strict sense, because considering the human condition according to Rousseau it becomes a path to real freedom.

With particular respect to natural compassion, the ambivalent role of *amour-propre* is demonstrated here. If it is, on the one hand, the foundation with which one identifies oneself with others, it is, on the other hand, the source of vanity and dissimilation. This ambivalence can be resolved, however, when the properly habituated *amour-propre* is considered. Let us therefore broadly summarize where *amour-propre's* strength lies and what Rousseau suggests to avoid its dangers, while still not defending one of the *radical* ideals mentioned above.

For Émile, who is, according to Nicholas Dent, embodying a successful identity, the remedy to inflamed, misled *amour-propre* is "being a 'man'" and "occupying 'man's estate'" (Dent 1998, 66). Having insight into common human experience and therefore accepting a fundamental equality or, as Dent puts it, supporting an immediate *affectionate union* (Dent 1998, 69) is the central lesson for Émile to learn that addresses our point here. Recognition as well as respect therefore mark the notion of being a man and "knowing one's station in society" (Rousseau 1762/1921, 11). With the reciprocity expressed by that, the constitution of the self becomes something bipolar—on the one hand, it has to be understood as a turn inwards, and on the other hand self-awareness is a result of the responses of others and intersubjective interaction. Instead of ending up in a state of "the epiphany of love" (Gauthier 1997, 14) like Gauthier concludes from reading Rousseau, the emphasis remains here on a more general social exchange based on an egalitarian understanding.[5]

Emphasizing reciprocity as well as mutuality requires to focus again on the role of *amour-propre*. Main goals of Rousseau's doctrine therefore must be seen in the abolishment of the constant endeavour for domination and the infinite regress of competition for so-called zero sum goods, like for example vainglory. Considering this, the most outstanding aim must be to avoid that every crime is considered as a personal affront or insult. If

5 Cohen (1997) supports this view as well when arguing against the prevailing view that inflamed *amour-propre* results in the insatiable desire for superior standing. Therefore his argument is based on the understanding that *amour-propre* can be cultivated in terms of an egalitarian *amour-propre*.

this is successful, *amour-propre* provides the capacity to take an external evaluative stance towards oneself and one's actions, but also towards the judgements regarding others. Thus, a further aspect comes in with regard to *amour-propre* and its relation to reason, spelled out by Neuhouser. Besides the crystallization of the need of "moral presence" (Dent 1988, 21–26, 49–50, 56–58), that is the criterion of standing and worth as a human being and therefore the capacity of affecting others, Neuhouser points out that Rousseau's account of *amour-propre* was much more ambitious in the sense that *amour-propre* as a capacity of mutually perspective-taking becomes the pre-condition of human rationality and thus the landmark for togetherness (Neuhouser 2008, 265). With respect to Neuhouser's distinction between esteem and respect he goes beyond the claim for the cultivation of *amour-propre* in terms of an equal standing, but shows with referring to the diversion of humankind how *amour-propre* still can be satisfied in accordance with Rousseau's doctrine.

Cultivating *amour-propre*

How then to admit a certain superiority that is not inflamed in a negative manner? The crucial benchmark therefore is universalizability, Neuhouser argues. The rational authority of the community that arises from the agent's autonomous self-legislation sketches the contours of a political order in which mutual recognition becomes a universal maxim. The core element is to foster an understanding of the moral equality of the other, that is, to see the other as an equal being. Included here is the internalization of the other's view which consequently implies a certain removal from one's self. This in particular makes it possible to also grant strangers—including the so-called "barbarians"—an equal moral significance, with which Rousseau makes his appeal for a simultaneous understanding of unity and plurality. The universality established here therefore must not be understood as an abstract cosmopolitan trait like Rousseau describes in the quotation I cited at the beginning of this essay. What Rousseau wants to support is a motivation by universal values so that the other is—at least in theoretical terms—involved in our actions or that we are somehow aware of the other's significance. Coming therewith to the second part of my contribution, which attempts to deal with the theme of normativity, my concern is less to figure out a precise normative structure of cosmopolitanism according to Rousseau, but instead to trace the primacy of a moral cosmopolitan disposition described by Rousseau, which must be seen as a basis for developing the former. In reference to the other, respectively the stranger, the aim is to give at least a rough idea of the immense relevance a counterpart has; not only regarding one's own actions but also in terms of defining the self.

Normativity in the Light of World Citizenship

The relational concept, and how it appears in Rousseau's depiction of identity, shows how important resemblance but also distinction are for generating identity. Identity, rootedness and national fencing off can of course be seen as contradictory to any cosmopolitan idea, yet although knowing one's station in society, Rousseau wants to foster in the individual a viewpoint that contains universal maxims. To avoid becoming a mere hostage of the other, Rousseau wants to support the autonomous individual. This also actualizes a meaning of reciprocity within his concept which embraces a moral claim that is regardless of national borders. When referring to Rousseau's account of personal autonomy, Neuhouser makes clear that the different aspects of freedom Rousseau indicates, do not lead to an encapsulation of individuals, but to "[…] associating themselves with others as members of a larger social organisation who think of their social membership as essential, not merely accidental, to who they are" (Neuhouser 2011, 480). While normative authority remains with the individual, so that speaking of a mere collective must be rejected, self-determined judgement is the result of the reasoning accomplished by intersubjectivity. In this respect, the general will is the expression of obeying one's own law, while conceiving of oneself as part of a cooperative social order to realize the fundamental interests of each social member. The "collective project" (Dent 1988, 490) is not necessarily or even not at all tied to a nation state since it has at its core individuals who expanded their own identity without being dispensed from being their own sovereign. The notion of recognition, discussed above therefore is meant to fulfil the necessary condition for both individuation and social inclusion. Regarding the essence of cosmopolitanism, to rise above one's self and to make the other's world accessible, cosmopolitanism must also be seen as a moral regard for difference.

Rousseau educates Émile "to bear the buffets of fortune [...] to live at need among the snows of Iceland or on the scorching rocks of Malta" (Rousseau 1762/1921, 13). With that Rousseau fosters in Émile a bodily constitution that is prepared for being not limited to just one country or one climate. When Émile travels in the world and encounters foreign people and cultural differences, he is not only characterized by his being open to otherness, but also by his being involved with otherness. Being a stranger himself when travelling, Émile is encouraged to adopt an objective point of view that allows for a critical examination of the host culture as well as his own:

> The belief that strangers perceive the host's practices, customs and values from a less subjective perspective than the host allows them to critically reflect on those practices, customs and values. As a consequence of this experience strangers are also able to reevaluate and reflect upon their own group's traditions and world-view. (Marotta 2011, 109)

Thus, a culture of critical discourse and of intellectual mobility is fostered in Émile, marked by reflectivity and critical analysis. Reflectivity, distance in terms of objectivity, openness, comparison and a critical viewpoint can be seen as genuine cosmopolitan dispositions that Émile is to adopt to develop a meaningful dialogic insight in terms of an ethical judgement. In that Émile is encouraged to limit his needs, on the one hand (with which Rousseau attempts to lay the foundation for autonomous living), and, on the other hand, that *amour-propre* is sensitized in terms of becoming aware of the moral equality of the counterpart, meaning strangers as well,

Rousseau tries in particular to anchor in the self a cosmopolitan respect for individual differences. The questionable ideal of a solid, permanent identity that was criticized in the analysis of the citizen as well as the solitary being therefore is dispensed in favour of a flexible and hybrid self that is prompted by otherness, but that also takes a meaningful engagement with the otherness of the other. This entails what Georg Simmel later would call a "subjective objectivity" (Simmel 1908, 404). Analogously, what Rousseau in my opinion wants to argue for is an ethics of variety while still not giving up local ties.

Yet it is not surprising that Rousseau is often blamed for defending what in hindsight appears to be a "nationalistic" point of view. The sovereignty of the nation, how Hans Joas (2011, 36) depicts it, as well as the defence of republican city states are of course main clues for this interpretation. And indeed, when thinking of the insula of Clarens in *Julie or the New Heloise* (1761), the dedication to Geneva that has to be freed from despotism as Rousseau expresses it in the *Discourse on the Origin and Foundation of Inequality Among Men* (1755), or his *Considerations on the Government of Poland* (1772) where he suggested a federal system, much of Rousseau's philosophy is precisely about erecting barriers, isolation, and even encapsulation. Yet the reason for his preference of small and exclusive societies must not necessarily be seen as a defence of a "nationalistic" ideology or dogmatic patriotism, but as a plea for an *authentic* cosmopolitanism. What scholars like Tzvetan Todorov, Timothy O'Hagan, Helena Rosenblatt or Jason Neidleman stress is that Rousseau's critique of cosmopolitanism refers to an abstract theory of it. In his eyes the theoretical approach to cosmopolitanism not only fails to inspire virtue but in modern society it must also be seen as another force that undermines fulfilling the duties that lie nearest. Therefore it stands against the transparency Rousseau wants to foster in Émile, but educates hypocrites.

Accordingly, Helena Rosenblatt (2008, 64) offers us at least three arguments in favour of a cosmopolitan reading of Rousseau's seemingly republican standpoint that I want to support. In her opinion, Rousseau's depiction of patriotism and "nationalism" has to be differentiated from a dogmatic and oppressive boundary thinking. She is right in my opinion when therefore indicating that Rousseau's understanding of patriotism is closely linked to political and even personal freedom. The fundamental problem in the *Contrat Social* that Rousseau wants to solve is concerned with finding a form of association of such nature that each, uniting himself with all, may still obey only himself, and remain as free as before (cf. Rousseau 1762, 12). In understanding the citizen as being a member of the sovereign, Rousseau believed that only free men would act morally towards others. The solidarity that is demanded by any form of social association has less to do with group identification and is more an outcome of symmetrical relations of acknowledgement, given that the role and meaning of autonomy must be taken into consideration. The doctrine of autonomy which Rousseau is conceptualizing must not be confused with individualistic egoism (Nussbaum 1994). It must rather be seen as the capacity of a certain self-examination that is accessible only by the intersubjective exchange. Neuhouser (2008) reflects in his analysis of the problematic role of *amour-propre* on a complex intertwined relation between reason and intersubjectivity, or in other words, the process of internalizing norms through a certain, yet not necessarily symmetrical, mutuality. The straight self-determined independent judgement is due to reciprocity raised to a qualitative higher level. The normative context to which the notion of freedom therewith is subscribed constitutes a moral freedom which nevertheless remains a matter of negotiation. Thus, the citizen obeying a law must be understood as a person who is capable of making decisions about moral norms autonomously (cf. Honneth 1995, 110). Being recognized as such a legal subject means to be respected by others. This also contributes to the formation of an attitude of self-respect. One could now object that this might be the case regarding the citizen and the nation state, but it would not count for strangers or for other cultures or nations. But Rousseau is not arguing for an absolute norm valid for every nation or culture. In *Émile* he even criticized the Eurocentric view of European travel accounts since they were full of national prejudices where the truth is tinged with false colours from the travellers own eyes (cf. Rousseau 1762/1921, 371). Regarding this, Rousseau was very critical of the idea of a general society as it is presented in Diderot's writings. Yet he is convinced of a certain common ground even though he accepts the heterogeneity of societies. Accordingly he is not attempting to assimilate or condemn the customs of other societies:

> Cast your eyes over every nation of the world; peruse every volume of its history; in the midst of all these strange and cruel forms of worship, among this amazing variety of manners and customs, you will everywhere find the same ideas of right and justice; everywhere the same principles of morality, the same ideas of good and evil. (Rousseau 1762/1921, 226)

Even if this sounds like a euphemism, Rousseau's view derives from a strong belief in genuine equality. The latter is already present in Rousseau's depiction of the *noble savage*. Of course he does not question that there might be differences in height, age and strength etc. but the abstract potentialities are intrinsic to human nature, and therefore all men have the same basic human qualities (Cohen 1997, 108). A free will, perfectibility and a natural capacity for compassion are common to all men, while the latter became more and more repressed and corrupted in the process of socialization. Regarding this, it is again the problematic role of *amour-propre* that comes into play. *Pitié* as the natural feeling of compassion due to an inflamed *amour-propre* that seeks for a vicious competition for zero sum goods like vainglory or pride, becomes in society a mere chimera. It then becomes obvious that the cosmopolitan spirit cannot be realized by simply increasing social interaction (Rosenblatt 2008, 65). With the moral individual and how it is depicted in the first section of my essay, Rousseau wants to transcend the malign role of *amour-propre* in favour of an irreducibly relational construct where the dialogical recognition of the other is the key to moral togetherness.

While this fundamental equality contains the condition of recognizing the other as an agent with similar moral significance, Rousseau is still convinced that a certain resemblance but also a kind of common understanding in the sense that one subscribes oneself to a common law, is necessary to act according to this moral significance of the other: "[...] the further we get from equality, the greater the change in our natural feelings [...]" (Rousseau 1762/1921, 330). In his opinion, a true bond of community that also vouches for moral acting can only be provided in small societies. Only then "[...] they will love their fellow citizens, and serve them with all their might [...]" (Rousseau 1762, 207). Accordingly, Rousseau preferred small communities instead of an abstract cosmopolitanism that to him seemed powerless to motivate moral action. Like I have cited above, in Rousseau's opinion there are only a few great cosmopolitan souls, like Socrates for example, whose benevolence does not diminish when they extend their effects to all humankind, but this cannot be applied to mankind in general. Yet "[i]n defending patriotism, one need not be anti-cosmopolitan" (Neidleman 2012, 79). What therefore has to be considered for example when reflecting on Rousseau's disposedness to a political concept based on nations is the defence against imperialism. Considering the case of Poland (officially the Polish-Lithuanian Commonwealth at the time) and therewith a people that was confronted with a world where cosmopolitan ideals remain an ideal but have no practical impact, Rousseau's concern, in my opinion, was mainly that the Poles would not be absorbed by the Russians. But thinking of Rousseau's own theoretical world order, he is not arguing for an imperialistic attitude. While preferring small societies with respective customs and cultures, it was not part of Rousseau's idea to expand the territory of *la patrie*. His suggestions to the Polish nation therefore must be seen in the context of the situation, where in a non-cosmopolitan world Rousseau clearly pursues a strong nation state.

Yet the same argument is not applied when taking account of the individual perspective. Instead, Émile is educated to:

> Have respect then for your species; remember that it consists essentially of the people that if all the kings and all the philosophers were removed they would scarcely be missed, and things would go on none the worse. In a word, teach your pupil to love all men, even those who fail to appreciate him; act in such way that he is not a member of any class, but takes his place in all alike: speak in his hearing of the human race with tenderness, and even with pity, but never with scorn. You are a man; do not dishonour mankind. (Rousseau 1762/1921, 171)

What this constitutes is a "rooted cosmopolitanism" (Appiah 1996, 22) that is realized from the bottom up (cf. Neidleman 2012, 89). Émile is educated to live everywhere. He learns a trade in order that it might be useful everywhere, and "Wherever there are men", he tells the tutor, "I am among my brethren" (Rousseau 1762/1921, 391).

Concluding Remarks

The internalization of the view of the other and independent, critical thought and self-awareness of the station which one occupies in society indicate the central moments which vouch for objective positioning, without however giving up a *local identity*, and fostering a rooted cosmopolitanism. The complex understanding of *amour-propre*, accessible through current receptions, shows that Rousseau is not arguing for a simple equality of the subjects, but that he allows for several strategies that superiority or a certain type of competition can pursue in a non-inflamed way, despite, or even because of, *amour-propre* being identified as the necessary condition of "rationality, morality, and freedom—indeed subjectivity itself" (Neuhouser 2008). Regarding the intersubjective sphere, Rousseau's doctrine wants to vouch for being socially recognized independently of the accumulation of luxury goods or hypocracy. With respect to the political sphere, Rousseau is aiming for a sovereign individual that is capable of an autonomous stance toward moral norms in terms of reasonable decision-making, who is independent of local loyalties but still aware of his *local identity*.[6] The mutual recognition expressed by the *volonté général* contributes to an attitude of self-respect and is therefore part of forming an individual that will not totally alienate himself from society, but devote himself to humanity.

When Rousseau founds this very universalism on the reflective judgement as thus defined, he not only conceives the entanglement of the individual and the common but also shows how the individual in being a representative of others allows for an understanding of moral acting. This doctrine provides an understanding of individuals in particular by their struggle with a desire for safety in terms of a stable identity and attraction of the unknown in terms of a level of reflection and expansion of the self. The pursuit of identity, and thus the pursuit of appropriation of culture, is thus a necessary condition for the development of what Rousseau would

6 For more on the meaning of the relation between autonomy and society in terms of the capacity of reasonable decision-making, see Honneth (1995).

consider a truly human, meaning moral, personality. What Rousseau's discussion of *amour-propre*, namely recognition, teaches us is that this openness with respect to alterity, at the end of which perspective universality is to be found, is above all the necessary condition for this purpose. In this intertwining of universality of values and plurality of cultures, the original tradition of the Enlightenment is expressed in Rousseau, which advocates neither dogmatism nor nihilism, and embodies a controversiality which has remained unfractured to this day.

References

Appiah, Kwame Anthony, 1996. "Cosmopolitan patriots". In: Martha C. Nussbaum, 1996. *For love of country: Debating the limits of patriotism*. Ed. Joshua Cohen. Boston: Beacon Press, 21–29.

Cohen, Joshua, 1997. "The natural goodness of humanity". In: Andrews Reath, Barbara Herman and Christine M. Korsgaard (eds.), 1997. *Reclaiming the history of ethics: Essays for John Rawls*. Cambridge: Cambridge University Press, 102–139.

Cooper, Laurence, 1999. *Rousseau, nature, and the problem of the good life*. Philadelphia: Pennsylvania State University Press.

Dent, Nicholas J.H., 1988. *Rousseau: An introduction to his psychological, social and political theory*. Oxford: Blackwell.

Dent, Nicholas J.H., 1998. "Rousseau on amour-propre". *Proceedings of the Aristotelian Society*, 72(1), 57–74.

Gauthier, David, 1997. "Making Jean-Jacques". In: Timothy O'Hagan (ed.), 1997. *Jean-Jacques Rousseau and the sources of the self*. Aldershot: Avebury.

Hall, Cheryl, 2005. *The trouble with passion: Political theory beyond the reign of reason*. New York: Taylor & Francis.

Honneth, Axel, 1992/1995. *The struggle for recognition: The moral grammar of social conflicts*. Trans. Joel Anderson. Cambridge, MA: The MIT Press.

Jacob, Margaret C., 2006. *Strangers nowhere in the world: The rise of cosmopolitanism in early modern Europe*. Philadelphia: University of Pennsylvania Press.

Joas, Hans, 2011. *Die Sakralität der Person: Eine neue Genealogie der Menschenrechte*. Frankfurt am Main: Suhrkamp.

Kolodny, Niko, 2010. "The explanation of amour propre". *Philosophical Review*, 119(2), 165–200.

Laertius, Diogenes, 1925. *Lives of the Eminent Philosophers*. Trans. Robert Drew Hicks, vol. 2. Harvard: Harvard University Press.

Marotta, Vince P., 2010. "The cosmopolitan stranger". In: Stan van Hooft and Wim Vandekerckhove (eds.), 2010. *Questioning cosmopolitanism*. Dordrecht: Springer, 105–120.

Melzer, Arthur, 1990. *The natural goodness of man: On the system of Rousseau's thought*. Chicago: University of Chicago Press.

Neidleman, Jason, 2012. "Rousseau's rediscovered communion des coeurs: Cosmopolitanism in the Reveries of the solitary walker". *Political Studies*, 60(1), 76–94.

Neuhouser, Frederick, 2008. *Rousseau's theodicy of self-love: Evil, rationality, and the drive for recognition*. Oxford: Oxford University Press.

Neuhouser, Frederick, 2010. "Rousseau and the conflict between the educations of 'man' and 'citizen'". In: Paul Cobben (ed.), 2010. *Institutions of education, then and today: The legacy of German idealism*. Leiden: Brill.

Neuhouser, Frederick, 2011. "Jean-Jacques Rousseau and the origins of autonomy". *Inquiry*, 54(5), 478–493.

Nussbaum, Martha C., 1994. "Patriotism and cosmopolitanism". *Boston Review*, 19(5).

O'Hagan, Timothy, 1999. *Rousseau*. London and New York: Routledge.

Rosenblatt, Helena, 2008. "Rousseau, the anticosmopolitan?". *Daedalus*, 137(3), 59–67.

Rousseau, Jean-Jacques, 1755. "A discourse on a subject proposed by the Academy of Dijon: What is the origin of inequality among men, and is it authorized by natural law?". In: Jean-Jacques Rousseau, 1923. *The Social contract and Discourses by Jean-Jacques Rousseau*. Ed. G.D.H. Cole. London and Toronto, 152–207.

Rousseau, Jean-Jacques, 1762. "The social contract". In: Rousseau, 1923. *The Social contract and Discourses by Jean-Jacques Rousseau*. Ed. G.D.H. Cole. London and Toronto, 32–134.

Rousseau, Jean-Jacques, 1762/1921, *Emile, or Education*. Trans. Barbara Foxley. New York: E.P. Dutton.

Rousseau, Jean-Jacques, 1772–1776. "Dialogues: Rousseau judge de Jean-Jacques". In: Jean-Jacques Rousseau, 1959–. *Jean-Jacques Rousseau: Oeuvres complètes*, vol. 1. Ed. Bernard Gagnebin and Marcel Raymond. Paris, 657–992.

Rousseau, Jean-Jacques, 1782. "Les rêveries du promeneur solitaire". In : Rousseau, 1959–. *Jean-Jacques Rousseau: Oeuvres complètes*, vol. 1. Ed. Bernard Gagnebin and Marcel Raymond. Paris, 993–1100.

Rousseau, Jean-Jacques, 1882. "Geneva manuscript". In: Jean-Jacques Rousseau, 1994. *Collected writings of Rousseau*, vol. 4. Ed. Rodger D. Masters and Christopher Kelly. Hanover: Dartmouth College Press.

Sen, Amartya, 2006. *Identity and violence: The illusion of destiny*. New York: W.W. Norton & Company.

Simmel, Georg, 1908. "The stranger". In: Kurt Wolff (ed. and trans.), 1964. "The sociology of Georg Simmel". New York: The Free Press, 402–408.

Starobinski, Jean, 1958/2003. *Rousseau: Eine Welt von Widerständen*. Trans. Ulrich Raulff. Frankfurt am Main: Fischer Taschenbuch Verlag.

Todorov, Tzvetan, 1985/2001. *Frail happiness: An essay on Rousseau*. Trans. John T. Scott and Robert D. Zaretsky. Philadelphia: University of Pennsylvania Press.

Velkley, Richard, 2002. *Being after Rousseau: Philosophy and culture in question*. Chicago: University of Chicago Press.

GEORG CAVALLAR

Kant and the Right of World Citizens: An Historical Interpretation

> To carry back to distant centuries the ideas of the century in which one lives is of all sources of error the most fertile.
>
> — MONTESQUIEU (*Spirit of the Laws*)

Introduction

Discourses on cosmopolitanism and cosmopolitan theories have reached unprecedented levels of intensity in recent years: conferences, special issues in journals and monographs abound (among many other publications, see Brock and Brighouse 2005; Brown and Held 2010; Lutz-Bachmann *et al.* 2010; Vertovec and Cohen 2002). Opinions are divided on what the crucial reasons are for this renewed interest in an old concept going back to ancient Greek philosophy. Among other factors, economic and cultural globalization, the rise of ethnocentric nationalism and a growing awareness of global risks are mentioned. In these discourses, Kant is often regarded as the most prominent founding father of contemporary cosmopolitan philosophies (cf. Brown 2009; Cheneval 2002; Häntsch 2008). I suppose that part of this reputation can be traced back to Kant's essays *Idea for a Universal History with a Cosmopolitan Aim* (1784a) and *Perpetual Peace* (1795) as well as to one element of Kant's philosophy of peace which he termed cosmopolitan right. This cosmopolitan right, a translation of *Weltbürgerrecht*, literally the right of world citizens, has acquired a kind of cult status in recent literature. Daniele Archibugi and David Held made a start in the 1990s, taking Kant's cosmopolitan right as a point of departure to propose the normative model of a cosmopolitan democracy, a global and democratic civil society where individuals have "a voice, input and political representation in international affairs, in parallel with and independently of their own government" (Archibugi and Held 1995, 13). Jacques Derrida's (1996; 2000; 2001) "unconditional hospitality" is frequently quoted in conjunction with Kant (see, e.g., Brown 2010; Morgan 2009, 105), and helped to raise awareness of this part of Kant's legal philosophy which had been quite neglected up to the 1990s (cf. Cavallar 1992, 236–240).

Publications which draw attention to the historical dimension of the current cosmopolitan discourses have been rare (cf. Albrecht 2005; Lettevall and Linder 2008; Cavallar 2011). In this essay, I will try to contextualize Kant's right of the world citizens, and offer an historical interpretation while avoiding the pitfalls of historical relativism. I build on a previous essay (cf. Cavallar 2012a), where I clarified the concept of cosmopolitanism, distinguished among its various forms, namely epistemological, economic or commercial, moral, theological, political and cultural versions, and argued for the compatibility of legal, moral and ethico-theological cosmopolitanisms. There is a three-part division in Kant's philosophy concerning the highest good and the future of the human species: The foundation of a cosmopolitan condition of perpetual peace, a global legal society of peaceful states, a "*cosmopolitan* whole" (Kant 1790/2000, 300), perhaps a world republic, is the highest *political* good. The establishment of a global ethical community is, secondly, the highest *moral* good in this world. Finally, the highest good proper coincides with the transcendent kingdom of God, the intelligible world, the kingdom of Heaven or a moral realm. This chapter focuses on one particular aspect of the global legal society, namely Kant's cosmopolitan right (second section). I will also try to illustrate how this right relates to other conceptions of hospitality rights developed in international legal theory from Francisco de Vitoria up to Kant's time. I will make comparisons and suggest where Kant's originality should be located (third section). Kant has distinguished between right and virtue, between external compliance with norms or legality and an inner disposition, between prudence and morality, and between the doctrine of rights and the philosophy of history. In the latter, Kant understands Nature reflectively and tentatively as a "moral facilitator" of the education of the human species. There is a tension between the human species propelled or instigated by Nature towards legal and moral ends on the one hand, and on the other hand, an understanding of human history as a collective learning process, whereby humans are seen as more or less autonomous agents not manipulated by Nature. The next section thus focuses on this very philosophy of history: on the role of the "spirit of commerce" to promote more peaceable relations among communities, on the so-called four-stage theory, *doux commerce*, global integration and mutual self-interest (fourth section). I will conclude with some general remarks on Kant's cosmopolitan right and how it can be criticized.

The highest political good in the world is a global juridical state (*Rechtszustand*) which approximates world peace. There has been an ongoing debate on whether Kant endorsed a free federation, a world republic or some sort of intermediate "cosmopolitan condition" in his writings, and on what his arguments were, and if they are convincing (see i.a. Brown 2009, 87–122; Budelacci 2003; Cavallar 2011, 64–84; Cheneval 2002, 563–610; Höffe 2006; Kleingeld 2004; Lettevall 2009; Williams 2006). I make no attempt to discuss this complex and fascinating issue here. In my view Kant's normative ideal is a "state of nations" (*Völkerstaat* or *civitas gentium*) (Kant 1795, 328), "a universal *association of states* (analogous to that by which a people becomes a state)" (Kant 1797, 487) as opposed to a universal monarchy, international anarchy or the federation of republics (cf. Byrd and Hruschka 2008, 600–635; 2010, 188, 200–205; Cheneval 2002, 572–573, 592–601; Kleingeld 2012, 40–71). The *Völkerstaat* requires states to submit themselves to "public coercive rights" (according to *Perpetual Peace*), and is a regulative idea which cannot be fully realized, but continually approximated (Kant 1797, 487). The basic thing for Kant was that this ideal should not be instituted by violence or force, but that humans should try to realize it step by step with peaceful and morally acceptable means. Kant hoped that states, even though they are reluctant to abandon their external sovereignty, might be willing to further this "continual approximation". The German phrase *sich freiwillig bequemen* (to bring oneself to do something, to find oneself compelled, to accommodate oneself) is quite telling (Kant 1795, 328): It combines free choice and the force of external circumstances. States are reluctant to cooperate, but they bring themselves to do so because under the given circumstances (e.g. threat of war, trans-border ecological problems) it is the lesser of two evils. *In thesi*, that is, according to reason, the world republic is the ideal and should be the ultimate goal; *in hypothesi*, under given circumstances and conditions, the federation or league of states establishing a permanent state congress for initiating or instituting public coercive right is the second-best option and should be an intermediate goal (Kant 1795, 328, 1797, 487–488; cf. Byrd and Hruschka 2008, 637–640, 2010, 201–205; Cheneval 2002, 599–600).

The Right of World Citizens and International Trade: Kant's Commercial Cosmopolitanism

As mentioned in the introduction, Kant's cosmopolitan right has attracted a lot of attention in recent years (see Kleingeld 1998; 2012, 72–91, 134–148; Brown 2006; 2008; Keil 2009; Marini 1998; Morgan 2009; Muthu 2000; Thompson 2008). In this section I will leave out the question of how Kant tried to justify this right (see Byrd and Hruschka 2010, 122–132; Kleingeld 2012, 72–86; Cavallar 2002, 363–366 for this aspect) and focus on one particular problem, the systematic status of this right within the doctrine of right. Various interpretations have been offered.

According to what can be termed the loophole-thesis, cosmopolitan right was designed to overcome the state of nature among states, non-state communities and individuals, thus complementing (not replacing) domestic and international right. All persons "who can mutually affect one another must belong to some civil constitution" (Kant 1795, 322), and all spheres of external freedom have to be subject to the rule of right. According to Kurt Borries, who wrote a book on Kant's politics in the 1920s, Kant feared that the predominance of the right of nations would leave a loophole for European powers to violate the rights of non-European communities which lacked essential features of modern states (Borries 1928/1973, 228;

see also Morgan 2009, 117). A more widespread contemporary interpretation stresses the "individualistic turn" of cosmopolitan right (Cheneval 2002, 610). The addressees of cosmopolitan right are individuals in their role as "citizens of the earth", and the right is read as an anticipation of contemporary developments in international right, where individuals are no longer exclusively mediated by the state, but elevated to bearers of rights they can assert on an international level (Kleingeld 1998, 83–85 and 2012, 87–89). Hospitality then coincides with international human rights, and strengthens the status of individuals vis-à-vis states and global corporations (Anderson-Gold 2001, 96, 99). Some interpreters take this a step further and claim that Kant envisioned a "cosmopolitan public space" (Anderson-Gold 2001, 100; cf. Kemp 2006, 155, 159 and 161), that he anticipated a global and democratic civil society, where, in the words of James Bohman, "[e]ach inhabitant of the planet is elevated to the position of international 'magistrate'" (Bohman 1997, 180).

I think the most convincing interpretation has recently been offered by Sharon Byrd and Joachim Hruschka. They claim that for Kant, cosmopolitan right is nothing but "the idea of a perfect World Trade Organization" (Byrd and Hruschka 2010, 7). Kant distinguished among three forms of justice in a juridical state, corresponding to the three *leges*: the *lex iusti*, the *lex iuridica* and the *lex iustitiae* (cf. Kant 1797, 450; Byrd and Hruschka 2010, 58–62). The *iustitia tutatrix* amounts to positive legislation to make rights possible. The *iustitia commutativa* "represents the public market where people can exercise their rights to external objects of choice by buying and selling them" (Byrd and Hruschka 2010, 69, cf. 36–38 and 71–74; Kant 1797, 443, 446, 447) and makes rights a reality. Finally, the *iustitia distributiva* represents the judiciary (making rights a necessity): A judge decides with binding force in cases of dispute. According to Byrd and Hruschka, cosmopolitan right refers to commutative justice, the public order for the market beyond state borders. International trade or "possible commerce" requires a legal framework, "certain universal rights" (Kant 1797, 489; cf. Byrd and Hruschka 2010, 210) to guarantee an ordered market.

Some interpreters have been surprised that Kant's cosmopolitan right is so limited. According to the Byrd-Hruschka or commercial interpretation, Kant's cosmopolitan right is distinct from a more mainstream *moral* understanding of hospitality (and therefore also different from Derrida's (cf. 2001) conception). Kant does not call for a global and democratic civil society, and if so, only for a very thin one where citizens of republics are represented indirectly via their representatives on a global level. The modern system of sovereign states is not swept "into limbo" (Bull 1995, 24), but reformed. Following this interpretation, Kant's international right refers to *iustitia tutatrix* and *iustitia distributiva*, to public legislation and to an international court with enforceable and binding decisions. By contrast, cosmopolitan right offers an ordered commutative justice in the absence of a (not yet) fully achieved international juridical state with *iustitia tutatrix* and *iustitia distributiva*.

> Consequently, an ordered *iustitia commutativa* and thus "cosmopolitan right" can exist on the international level in the absence of a *iustitia tutatrix* and a *iustitia distributiva* in a state of nation states. Cosmopolitan right is thus (logically) independent from right in a state of nation states. It requires its own *iustitia tutatrix*, meaning public right and legislation ordering the international market, the *iustitia commutativa*, and its own *iustitia distributiva,* meaning an international trade court which can reach final binding decisions under cosmopolitan right in case of trade disputes. (Byrd and Hruschka 2010, 211)

For various reasons, alternative interpretations are not convincing. To oppose this loophole-thesis, one could argue that if Kant had meant to ban or outlaw colonialism, this would have been included in the preliminary articles. For instance, he could simply have expanded the fifth preliminary article to read: "No state shall forcibly interfere in the constitution, government *or civil society* of another state or *a political community not meeting European standards of statehood*" (Kant 1795, 319 [changes in italics]). This would have taken care of the problem of colonialism. However, the three definitive articles are not meant as "rights of prohibition" (Kant 1795, 320) but as articles to establish "a condition of peace" (p. 322). Cosmopolitan right includes a legal duty to actively promote this establishment of peace, not (only) to abstain from an action. Against the widespread global-society or globalist interpretation, one might argue that it simply goes beyond Kant's express statements and does not even attempt to explain why Kant shrank back from a more daring and extensive conception of cosmopolitan right. It simply takes Kant as a starting point for one's own Kantian agenda. The interpretation moves from strict exegesis to creative reformulation or extrapolation in the spirit of Kantian philosophy and explicitly goes beyond Kant's texts (cf. Brown 2009, 20–22). This approach may be legitimate in its own right, but should clearly demarcate where a textual interpretation ends and one's own extrapolation starts.

There is a lot of truth in the interpretation that Kant initiated an individualistic turn in international legal theory. After all, *Perpetual Peace* refers to the "right of a foreigner" (Kant 1795, 328), and a footnote claims that not only states but also individuals should be regarded "as citizens of a universal state of mankind" (p. 322). However, the *Doctrine of Rights* published two years later only refers to the rights of *peoples* or of *nations* and not of individuals or states (Kant 1797, 489; cf. Byrd and Hruschka 2010, 208). Kant has apparently changed one element of his doctrine: the right of individuals to visit has become part of international right, and no longer belongs to cosmopolitan right (cf. Kant 1797, 478, 482). Only peoples and not individuals or states are entitled to engage in international trade or commerce.

Interpreters disagree about the scope of cosmopolitan right. Some argue that *Verkehr*—roughly "interaction"—has a narrow meaning in Kant's texts, and coincides with commercial trade (Byrd and Hruschka 2010, 209; Thompson 2008, 306 and 315), whereas others claim that it is "clearly not limited to trade" and also encompasses cultural and intellectual exchange (Kleingeld 2012, 75; cf. Eberl and Niesen 2011, 250–251). There is a broad and a narrow meaning in Kant (for a discussion, see Byrd and Hruschka 2010, 209). The distinction between the doctrines of virtue and right is crucial. We have a moral (not legal) duty to *interact* with each other (Kant 1797, 588).[1] As juridical persons, however, we "stand in a community of possible physical *interaction* [*Wechselwirkung*]" (p. 489). In cosmopolitan right, therefore, interaction has a narrow meaning and coincides with commercial interaction or trade (*Handelsverkehr*). In legal terms, engaging in commerce is an exchange of property through contract (cf. Kant 1795, 329;

1 Interaction, i.e., "*Verkehr zutreiben*", *officium commerci, sociabilitas*.

1797, 489). Cosmopolitan right is exclusively concerned with international trade and commerce in the narrow sense (see also Kant 1795, 334 note; 1797, 387, 434). This is also the meaning predominant in the eighteenth century, for instance in Montesquieu or Vattel (cf. Cavallar 2002, 243–244, 263–264, 314–315; 2012c).

Kant's shift from the rights of states to the rights of nations or peoples in cosmopolitan right is consistent with the role he assigns to the state in domestic right. Here, the state should not interfere in the market, but should regulate it, to make a free and just public market possible. The guiding principle is the external freedom of the citizens, not their happiness as interpreted by the sovereign (Kant 1793a, 291–292, 297–298; 1797, 461; Byrd and Hruschka 2010, 41, 209). Relevant passages are usually interpreted as an endorsement of economic libertarianism and a rejection of welfare measures for the poor. Presenting Kant as an early liberal has to be qualified, though. He is all in favour of individual initiative, competition and equality of opportunity, but he also argues for a right of the poor to be supported by the government, provided that poverty was not their own fault (Kant 1797, 468–469; see also Wood 2008, 193–205 and Kleingeld 2012, 136–145, for a discussion). By analogy, states have a duty to regulate international trade through treaties based on "certain universal rights" (Kant 1797, 489), while abstaining from interference. Since the ideal of a "state of nations" (*Völkerstaat* or *civitas gentium*), "a universal association of states" cannot fully be realized, only approximated, because, in other words, the international state of nature might not be left completely, and since a free international public market is a natural right of all nations, it has to be regulated and ordered, that is, brought under the rule of right. Free trade is therefore not an unconditional right. States are entitled to restrict or even prohibit trade if its natural right of self-preservation is at stake (cf. 1793a, 298; 1795, 329–330). As Pauline Kleingeld put it: "The positive role Kant attributes to international trade does not imply an unconditional endorsement of '*free*' trade, although a considerable liberalization of trade is compatible with Kant's views, provided that the conditions of international justice are in place" (Kleingeld 2012, 147; see also 137–148). In this way, Kant qualifies the free-trade doctrine, developed in the eighteenth century by authors such as Dietrich Hermann Hegewisch (1746–1812), who endorsed a version of free-market cosmopolitanism and whose relevant essays were probably known to Kant (cf. Kleingeld 2012, 124–134). I assume that Adam Smith, who is usually interpreted as a champion of free trade, should be positioned between Kant and Hegewisch (see below).

The Historical Context—I: International Legal Theory

In this section and the next one, I want to contextualize Kant's cosmopolitan right. Here, I argue that its topic, the right to visit and to seek commercial contact, has been controversially discussed in international legal theory since Francisco de Vitoria in the 1530s. I think we can press the positions which evolved in these debates rather brutally into three "schools" or camps in terms of hospitality rights: the imperialist school, the society of states school and the cosmopolitan school (for the following, see Cavallar 2013 and 2012c).

Representatives of the imperialist school assumed a thick conception of the good, and posited a material end of human volition, which trumped the rights of a community or state in case of conflict. Hospitality was conceived as an extensive natural right and could be enforced. The term "imperialist school" is misleading with respect to Francisco de Vitoria (1486–1546) and the Second Scholastic, because the theological dimension was dominant in their writings, and the consequences of the close cooperation with the Spanish crown (which resulted in Spanish colonialism and imperialism) were apparently unintended. Vitoria's thick conception of the good coincides with the Gospel and the teachings of Catholic Christianity. The goal of his famous lecture *De Indis* (1539) is to justify preaching the Gospel and bringing salvation to the Native Americans. The Spaniards are the ambassadors of Christ, who are therefore protected by the right of nations (*ius gentium*, roughly the basic norms of conduct shared by [almost] all [civilized] nations or *gentes*). The right to travel, to contact others, to trade and to settle, based on natural right and the right of nations in this sense, is merely a means to an end, namely the spreading of the Gospel, not an end in itself. In addition, Vitoria conceptualizes extensive hospitality as a perfect, enforceable right of the visitors, who have—in a famous passage—the consent and the sanction of "the whole world" on their side (Vitoria 1528, 40). Hugo Grotius, a more straightforward representative of the imperialist school than Vitoria, carefully hid a material end in his writings, especially in *De Jure Praede* (written in 1604–1608). This end was Dutch colonialism, in particular the interests of the United Dutch East India Company (VOC or *Vereenighde Oostindische Compagnie*). Aiming at vindicating the VOC's privateering campaign in the East Indies, Grotius employed the language of natural right and rights and various philosophical and classical sources to offer arguments for this political goal. For instance, Grotius used and abused Stoic "cosmopolitan" philosophy to defend Dutch interests in free trade and navigation (see especially Ittersum 2006 and 2010). In Grotius, commercial goals replace theological ones.

In the course of the eighteenth century, the second "camp", the society-of-states school, gradually gained the upper hand. It endorsed an international legal theory which is closest to so-called "classical" international right. It was state-centred, emphasized the sovereign right of each community to restrict or prohibit trade, and turned hospitality into an imperfect moral duty. The two crucial authors establishing this tradition were Thomas Hobbes and Samuel Pufendorf (cf. Armitage 2006; Hüning 2009; Hunter 2001 and Schröder 2001; 2010). The key and long-term changes were the following. First, a dualistic concept of right developed after 1750, where jurists now distinguished between natural right and positive right (*lex*). The latter was more and more identified with the will of the legislator and seen as quite independent of the idea of natural justice and natural right. Secondly, jurisprudence became an independent and autonomous science. A third change was the secularization of politics, or its "deconfessionalizing" or "desacralizing" (Hunter 2001); the weakening of moral theology was part of this process. The consequences of this new legal philosophy were far-reaching. It meant the end of traditional *ius gentium* as a source of right (almost) all *gentes* (peoples) had in common. This was a result of the dualistic concept of right (natural or rational versus positive), which left no room for the older version of *ius gentium* (cf. Schröder 2000 and Simons 2003). Secondly, the right of nations was assigned to the sphere of natural right and seen as a distinct field of right applying to a unique set of legal subjects, that is, to sovereign rulers or states (*civitates*) only. Pufendorf, for instance, conceptualized the sovereign state as a composite moral person (*persona moralis composita*), constituted by the union of individuals under a government. The third consequence was a state-centred political philosophy, the result of the developments just mentioned. The impact on hospitality rights was tremendous, because the perfect right of ownership became trumps. Pufendorf not only dismissed Vitoria's first just title of "natural partnership and communication" and the right to preach the Gospel, but also Grotius' arguments on behalf of Dutch commercial interests. Instead of a natural, enforceable right to trade, Pufendorf posited that hospitality was an imperfect moral duty and any trans-border contact dependent on the native communities' express permission, which could be revoked if this contact conflicted with the duty of self-preservation, defined and interpreted as the communities or the sovereign saw fit.

The rather marginal cosmopolitan school posited a formal end of international society, namely peaceful interaction and exchange, based on reciprocity and equal spheres of external freedom, and sometimes focused on individuals and their rights rather than states. Representatives went beyond the state-centred approach of the second school and emphasized natural rights of a global reach, but tried to avoid the imperialist and hegemonic implications of the first school. Hospitality, Vitoria's right to travel and to communicate, was now an end in itself or the means to peaceful interaction, trade or exchange. I consider Christian Wolff the first important representative of this school (cf. Cavallar 2004; Cheneval 2002, 132–213). He developed a new concept of right (*lex*) as a binding body of rules no longer connected with the feature of the legislator. The decisive criterion is the obligatory force of the right, with the right of nature based on the essence of man and of things (and not on God's will) (Schröder 2008, 66–67). The idea of *civitas maxima*, a hypothetical international legal commonwealth based on tacit consent, underlined the primacy of natural right, and was logically prior to the society of sovereign states. Wolff's regulative idea of *civitas maxima* did not have any bearing on the right of hospitality: Wolff refused to qualify or soften the principle of state sovereignty here, and was thus actually close to both Pufendorf and Vattel.

Most international lawyers after Wolff belonged to the mainstream society-of-states school, for instance, Achenwall and Pütter, Vattel and Martini, whereas the cosmopolitan school remained marginal. The imperialist school receded for some time into the background, to become dominant in the second half of the nineteenth century. Gottfried Achenwall (1719–1772) and Johann Stephan Pütter (1720–1807) wrote a widely used textbook on natural right, *Elementa iuris naturae* (1750), which incorporated elements of Grotius, Wolff, Thomasius and Gundling (Achenwall and Pütter 1750/1995; Schröder 1995). Achenwall later published his own treatises, namely *Ius Naturae, Iuris Naturalis pars posterior* and finally *Prolegomena Iuris Naturalis*. These subsequent books profoundly influenced Kant, who held lectures on them for more than twenty years (Byrd and Hruschka 2010, 16–18). In the *Elementa*, Pütter and Achenwall endorsed the primacy of positive legislation and of the *salus publica*, defined as the common welfare of the community as interpreted by the sovereign. The category of imperfect duties towards strangers disappeared. Emer de Vattel (1714–1767) replaced Wolff's *civitas maxima* with the moral concept of the *société humaine*, which implied that humans were only bound by conscience to assist each other, provided that this imperfect duty of mutual assistance was compatible with the perfect duties towards oneself (Kapossy and Whatmore 2008; Vattel 1758/2008, §§ 10–13 and 3.12.189). Karl Anton Freiherr von Martini (1726–1800) belonged to the "younger" natural lawyers after 1780, with a new focus on the individuals and their rights, and a new function for natural/rational right. Gradually, natural law was merely supposed to replenish or complete positive legislation. Disciplinary demarcations were set up, for instance, between political science, moral philosophy, philosophical legal theory and natural right (cf. Brockmöller 1997, 36–42; Hebeis 1996). Influenced by Wolff, but close to the society of states school, Martini claimed that there was no general (*allgemeines*) positive right of nations, only a particular, namely European, right of nations, which included the American free states, presumably because they were of European descent (Martini1791/1969, II, § 22). Martini did not even endorse the minimalist notion of a European political community of states as Vattel had done. States had no legal authority over other states, which were "by nature" independent (Martini 1791/1969, II, §§ 19–20; II § 29). Martini also closely followed the society of states school in terms of hospitality rights. Each nation had a right to refuse entry to foreigners. Martini criticized Grotius, whose opinion on duties towards strangers was, according to Martini, too "vague" (Martini1791/1969, II, § 57).

Next I am going to compare Kant's cosmopolitan right with these three schools. Kant attacked the society of states school and its emphasis on state sovereignty and incipient legal positivism with his famous description of Grotius, Pufendorf and Vattel as "sorry comforters" (Kant 1795, 326; cf. Cavallar 2011, 64–84), although he endorsed some of its key tenets, especially the secularization of politics. His legal theory focused on external actions, and jurisprudence was an autonomous discipline separate from theology, right was divided into positive and rational right, and *ius gentium*, the right of nations, was the right of sovereign states. Kant did not dismiss state sovereignty out of hand; rather, it enjoyed legitimacy, if only provisionally. However, he differed from the society of states school with his thesis of the *provisional* quality of sovereignty and its dismissal of hospitality as an imperfect *moral* duty, or its complete eclipse. Kant was close to the cosmopolitan school of authors such as Wolff, who had posited the *civitas maxima*, akin to Kant's own long-term goal or regulative idea of a limited republican world government. However, there are Kantian modifications: a clear-cut distinction between norms and facts, between the rational idea and the will of the majority, between pure practical reason and the practice of "more civilized nations". These distinctions illustrate Kant's new methodological approach, the programme of a pure practical philosophy, or "completely isolated metaphysics of morals, mixed with no anthropology, theology, physics, or hyperphysics and still less with occult qualities" (Kant 1785, 64). In *Perpetual Peace* as well as in the "Doctrine of Rights", Kant criticized European colonialism, which suggests that he rejected the imperialist school and the religious titles of theologians such as Vitoria. Scattered passages in other writings of the 1790s attacked central tenets of this school, such as the agricultural argument or titles based on the superiority of European civilization, although at times it seems that

Kant believed in this very superiority. Perhaps Kant denied that any rightful claims could be derived from it.[2]

Pufendorf had conceptualized hospitality as an imperfect moral duty. Achenwall, Pütter, Vattel and others stand for the eclipse of imperfect moral duties towards strangers, and the rise of "international morality". Kant, in contrast, claimed that we are talking about a right, not morality or philanthropy (Kant 1795, 328; 1797, 489), since right delineated external spheres of freedom and was connected with coercion. Any form of rightful/*rechtmässige* contact was based on the mutual prohibition of injury: *neminem laedere*. Kant, for instance, asserted that European colonial endeavours were so unjust and violent that Chinese and Japanese inhospitality was justified (Kant 1795, 329–330). For methodological reasons, Kant keeps legal and moral duties apart; the doctrine of right should not be confused with the doctrine of virtue. Kant's main target of criticism was probably Vattel, whose book *Droit des Gens* was available in Kant's library in a German translation (Warda 1922, 8 and 16). There is another small detail which underlines Kant's clear-cut distinction between spheres of right on the one hand and morality or virtue on the other: legal relations among communities and nations can be "peaceful", but must not necessarily be "friendly" (Kant 1797, 489; see also 1795, 329), which would be the term reserved for moral relations, as in personal friendship (cf. Kant 1797, 586–588).

In terms of content, Kant's cosmopolitan right did not differ much from what authors before him had written about the subject. Others had also criticized colonialism, defended Chinese or Japanese isolationism, or attempted to balance the rights of visitors with those of the natives (Cavallar 2002 and 2011, 17–38). I believe that Denis Diderot is especially close to Kant, though his publications were not part of his library (cf. Warda 1922) and it is unclear whether he influenced him. As a philosopher, Diderot did not explicitly contribute to international legal discourses of his time,

2 Giving a fully adequate account of this complex issue of the European civilization's putative superiority here is beyond the scope of this inquiry. See Cavallar (2002, 359–368); Hedrick (2008); Kleingeld (2007 and 2012, 92–123), for more.

and apparently had little impact on them. He can be interpreted as a creative representative of the cosmopolitan school. Though partly following familiar distinctions, Diderot added new arguments to the debate. In his contributions to *Histoire philosophique et politique des établissements et du commerce des Européens dans les deux Indes* (edited by Abbé Guillaume-Thomas Raynal; revised and enlarged edition 1780), he offered an explicit attack on European colonialism. Diderot supported familiar hospitality rights, and distinguished between a right of necessity, a right to visit, a right to be a guest and the right of settlement. If travellers wanted to settle in a foreign country, it was up to the natives to grant permission (Diderot 1780, 175). The right to visit was only a perfect one if the traveller's life was at stake. The right to be a guest, in contrast, was imperfect, and contingent upon the consent of the parties involved. Like Kant, Diderot considered the actual history of European commercial expansion as one of unmitigated moral disaster (cf. Diderot 1780, 173, 178–179, 197 and the discussion in Muthu 2003, 87–104).

The main differences between Diderot and Kant are the following: Diderot's normative ideal and goal was more extensive than Kant's, including not only trade, but also the peaceful exchange of ideas and possible intermarriages which might lead to the creation of a new people. As in Adam Smith and others (and later Ward), hospitality was historicized. Diderot tended to idealize ancient hospitality, claiming that it was universally practised in the ancient world and led to innumerable friendships—so again, hospitality is located in the sphere of morality and philanthropy. Finally, and again unlike Kant, Diderot perceived the history of hospitality as a history of decline, and the key factors were modern technology as well as a form of moral disorientation. The latter was a result of European travellers finding themselves so far away from home that they felt "outside the network of reciprocal relationships and expectations that had once given them the cultural contexts for their actions, beliefs, and values—for their *moeurs*" (Muthu 2003, 86). In addition, Diderot denied that European incursions and atrocities could be stopped.

The originality of Kant's contribution lies in his revision of the traditional argument from original ownership, his methodological distinctions (between right and virtue and between the philosophies of right and of history, for instance), his new justification of hospitality rights and the thinness of his account. In addition, his philosophy of history embedded cosmopolitan right in a teleological and tentative reconstruction of political history as continuous progress towards more peaceful trans-border interactions. Though Kant found clear words denouncing European, especially British and Dutch colonialism, Diderot's pessimism and cynicism were absent in his account, and an optimistic tone prevails. Two elements of Kant's originality deserve special attention: the goal of cosmopolitan right and the just mentioned thinness of his account.

I have argued that in Vitoria or Grotius, a material end, or a thick conception of the good, prevailed in their accounts of hospitality rights. Kant has become famous for his criticism of teleological ethics or consequentialism where the purpose is crucial, and his own theory is usually labelled "deontological" (cf. Kant 1785, 49–55). Along these lines, Kant attacked—in the context of cosmopolitan right—authors who had argued that "the good end justifies immoral means": Non-European peoples could be subjugated, expelled or exploited because it was "to the world's advantage", because those savages would "become civilized" or the home country could be "cleaned of corrupt men" (Kant 1797, 490; cf. Cavallar 1992, 232–234). Kant held that an obvious injustice remains one, even if morally acceptable (and usually unintended) consequences should follow. This criticism of consequentialism has sometimes been misunderstood as implying that any end of volition is incompatible with Kant's ethics. In fact, material ends are acceptable, provided that they do not conflict with the formal principle of morality or right. Ends and states of affairs do matter, but actors have to avoid the pitfalls of consequentialism, for instance by violating a moral principle "by the lure of some great good to be gained in the relatively near future" (Wood 2008, 260). Proper moral reasoning combines the conformity with the categorical imperative or the principle of right with aiming at a common, rationally defensible set of moral or legal aims that are compatible with this imperative or the legal principle, respectively. Kant conceptualizes these ultimate aims or goals as the highest moral or political goods (cf. Wood 2008, 266–269 and Cavallar 2012a). It is therefore not contradictory when Kant claims that cosmopolitan right *does* have a formal end, namely "the possible union of all nations" (Kant

1797, 489) under the rule of right, or the approximation of a "cosmopolitan constitution" (Kant 1795, 329), where the reciprocal spheres of freedom of all humans are respected.

The second element of Kant's originality is the thinness of his account. I have tried to show that natural hospitality rights have been interpreted in divergent ways from Vitoria to Kant. Vitoria himself argued for a very extensive right which was, in addition, enforceable and included the right to dwell in the countries or territories visited for an unspecified amount of time, the freedom to use common property, the freedom of residence, nationalization and citizenship and finally, the negation of a right of expulsion without just cause (cf. Cavallar 2002, 108–111). Kant rejected all these extensive rights. Achenwall, Pütter, Martini and Martens belong to a second group where hospitality rights have virtually vanished, usually in the name of state or community sovereignty. Kant himself was closest to a third group, which limited or qualified hospitality rights and included Pufendorf, Wolff and Diderot: hospitality is not a right to settle (cf. Kant 1797, 489), it is not a "*right to be a guest*", but only a right "to *seek* commerce" and "to present oneself to society" (Kant 1795, 329). Only this thinness guaranteed due respect for the equal spheres of external freedom of all parties involved.

It has been argued that around 1794, Kant's theoretical philosophy "was falling out of fashion" in Germany, with a younger generation moving into very different directions (Kuehn 2001, 378). This also seems to have been the case with Kant's legal philosophy. The three main trends in the late 1790s, when Kant elaborated cosmopolitan right, were legal positivism, incipient historicism and the turn to Europe. I do not find any traces of these developments in Kant's texts. I will begin here with legal positivism. A member of the younger generation was the international lawyer Georg Friedrich von Martens (1756–1821), who became well-known for his collection of treaties, the *Recueil des princip aux traités* (1791). His main work, *Précis du droit des gens moderne de l'Europe fondé sur les traités et l'usage* (1789), was edited in German under the title *Einleitung in das positive Europäische Völkerrecht* one year after Kant's essay *Perpetual Peace*, namely in 1796. Martens' work is nowadays considered the final breakthrough of legal positivism (cf. Ziegler 1994, 201–202). Martens moved from generic *ius inter gentes* to state-centred European right of nations and from natural and volitional right to positive right (Martens 1796, §§ 2–3; for a brief introduction see Cavallar 2011, 96–98). While he did not deny that there was a "pure natural right of nations" (*reines natürliches Völkerrecht*), natural and volitional rights of nations coincided with international morality or *Völkermoral* (Martens 1796, §§ 1, 5, 117, 122 and 136). Martens' paragraph on the right of immigration (now the traditional concept of hospitality was really dead) reads like a succinct summary of previous authors' key statements as well as legal practice (the only *explicit* sources here). His starting point was the perfect right of the sovereign territorial state or nation to prohibit entry, passage or permanent residence of foreigners, for whatever reasons. The only exceptions were cases of necessity such as distress at sea. These were obvious remnants of natural-right doctrine, now justified by state practice. In Marten's legal system, there is not even room for Kant's very thin natural right to offer to engage in commerce.

I continue with incipient historicism. *An Enquiry into the Foundation and History of the Right of Nations in Europe* by the thirty-year-old Robert Plumer Ward (1765–1846), published in the same year as Kant's *Perpetual Peace* in 1795, is usually considered the first historical study of the right of nations. Ward doubted that the right of nations was universal, as European codes were not. This European right became an historical phenomenon, subject to change depending on geography and historical periods (Ward 1995, vol. 1, XV, XX, XIII–XIV, 60, 130–131; for an introduction see Cavallar 2011, 98–101). Ward was obviously influenced by the "philosophical historians" of the Enlightenment such as Montesquieu, Adam Smith, David Hume, Lord Kames, Adam Ferguson, Edward Gibbon and John Millar. In Ward, their delicate balance between philosophy and history tilted towards the latter. Like Diderot, Ward historicized hospitality, noting its many examples among Germanic tribes during the migration of peoples in the fifth century AD, when hospitality was a virtue, a personal quality of individuals, and perhaps an established custom (cf. Ward 1795, I, 232–233). While Ward is not a full-blown cultural or moral relativist, his balance between moral universalism and culturally sensitive relativism or particularism is a precarious one. At any rate, Kant's claim that there are universally binding rights *a priori* is seriously challenged (cf. Ward 1795, vol. 1, 58), together with traditional forms of moral or legal cosmopolitanisms.

This has to do with Ward's turn to Europe, European culture and Christianity, the third and final trend I want to mention. The right of nations became a European phenomenon in his account, historically and culturally embedded as well as rooted in Christianity. In spite of elements of cultural relativism in his account, Ward tended to see non-European cultures as inferior, and claimed that Chinese isolationist policies demonstrated their "barbarity" and the "inferiority" of their concept of the right of nations (Ward 1795, vol. 2, 4). Forgotten were those European lawyers like Gentili, Leibniz, Wolff or Vattel who had defended Chinese isolationism as legitimate, since it was interpreted as a clear case of self-defence in the face of European aggression or threats. Authors like Martini or Martens had anticipated this turn to Europe in their respective writings. This was a general trend after 1750, when cosmopolitan elements were gradually and partly replaced by the ideas of "Europe" and "civilization" (cf. Cavallar 2011, 85–108, especially 107–108). I cannot detect traces of this trend in Kant's published writings of the 1790s.

The Historical Context—II: The Spirit of Commerce, the Four-stage Theory, *Doux Commerce*, Global Integration and Mutual Self-interest

In this section, I continue with my contextualization of Kant's cosmopolitan right, turning to the writers of what came to be called political economy, and especially to David Hume and Adam Smith. A lot of what I say about possible influences is mere conjecture. Sometimes influence is evident, for example in the case of Smith (cf. Fleischacker 1996). The books found in Kant's personal library and then sold after his death are another clue, though the list offered might be incomplete (cf. Warda 1922). I suppose that another possible source are Kant's famous dinner talks, which started at 1pm. and often lasted until the evening. Kant "liked to disregard learned matters. At times he even cut off such associations. He most loved to talk about political things. Indeed, he almost luxuriated in them" (quoted in Kuehn 2001, 325). So Kant might have learned about the investigation against Warren Hastings in the House of Commons in the late 1780s and early 1790s (see below). Another source might have been Kant's friend Christian Jacob Kraus, who was also a professor at Königsberg University and taught courses in economics (cf. Kuehn 2001, 324). Finally, Kant might have borrowed books from friends or from his publisher Friedrich Nicolovius. Thus it is possible that Kant was, for instance, familiar with some of the ideas of Johann Heinrich Gottlob von Justi (1717–1771). Be that as it may, it is obvious that Hume and Smith had some impact on Kant, and I will therefore focus on these two philosophers. In the next paragraphs, I am going to take sentences or half-sentences from Kant's section on cosmopolitan right, and try to embed them within eighteenth-century discourses. My aim is to show that the theories about the spirit of commerce, the four-stage theory, *doux-commerce* thesis, the assumption of global integration and conceptions of self-interest and (unsocial or commercial) sociability were recurrent themes in Kant's time, that Kant joined these debates, and that in many cases he integrated these theses and assumptions into his framework of a critical, namely reflective and tentative philosophy of history.[3] Kant distinguished between the doctrine of right, which focuses on the original right to external freedom, and the philosophy of history. The latter investigates the natural forces and trends in history and the possible unintended consequences and beneficial results of (possibly determined) human actions. Like the other two relations of public right, the gradual approximation of cosmopolitan right is guaranteed by "the great artist *nature*" (Kant 1795, 331) since humans know what they "*ought* to do in accordance with rights of freedom" but simply refuse to do it (p. 334).

3 Kant's critical philosophy of history is not my issue here. See, however, Rorty and Schmidt (2009) and Cavallar (2012a), for recent introductions.

The key factor Kant hoped might promote his cosmopolitan ideal of a legal world community was the spirit of commerce (*Handelsgeist*), "which sooner or later takes hold of every nation" (Kant 1795, 336–337). Here, Kant briefly hints at the so-called four-stage theory, widespread since the middle of the eighteenth century, and developed since the late seventeenth century by diverse thinkers such as Pufendorf, Bossuet, Locke, Montesquieu, Rousseau, John Dalrymple of Cranstoun, Lord Kames, Mirabeau, Ferguson, Millar and Turgot (cf. Cavallar 2002, 236–239; Hont 2005, 159–184; Morgan 2009, 109–110). The key tenet was that all communities moved naturally through various stages until they became commercial societies. One function of the stages scheme was to explain why norms differ in various societies. Smith explained these differences with the help of the economic development, offering a socialized and historicized theory of natural right and stressing natural factors as well as human efforts (Cavallar 2002, 236). Kant was definitely familiar with Smith's elaborate account. An early reference to the four-stage theory can be found in his *Conjectural Beginning of Human History*, published in 1786.[4] The passage compared the life of the hunter and herdsman with that of the farmer, offering economic and social explanations of changes (Kant 1786, 171–173; see also Kant 1795, 333, 334 and Fleischacker 1996, 389).

The four-stage theory is crucial for Kant's right of world citizens, since commercial societies tend to be more peaceful than previous stages of development (cf. Kant 1795, 333). Kant claims that the "*spirit of commerce* [...] cannot coexist with war" (p. 336). This is an obvious reference to the *doux-commerce* thesis developed since Montesquieu, who had claimed that commerce destroys prejudices, promotes gentle mores, polishes barbarous ones, unites nations, leads to peace, and "produces in men a certain feeling for exact justice" (Montesquieu 1989, 20.1–2, 338–339; cf. Cavallar 2002, 243–244 with secondary literature). Softness or *douceur* is the antonym of violence, commerce also conflicts with despotism, and in a democracy based on rights and equality commerce does not corrupt mores, but brings

4 Kant was actually an early reader in Germany of the *Wealth of Nations* (cf. Fleischacker 1996, 379–383, 390).

"the spirit of frugality, economy, moderation, work, wisdom, tranquillity, order, and rule" (Montesquieu 1748/1989, 22.14, 416–417; cf. 5.6, 48). While Montesquieu's analysis of commerce is ambiguous, as he only partially broke up the link between commerce and what the civic humanist tradition called corruption, many Enlightenment intellectuals were more enthusiastic. They offered a range of positive effects of commercial interaction: people had to learn to please and serve others, the arts and sciences might profit, and a focus on this-worldly welfare and wealth would replace uncompromising religious fanaticism. Finally, commerce might increase cross-cultural interaction and overcome parochial attitudes like patriotism and dated and potentially violent pursuits of military glory and honour (cf. Mendham 2010, 606–607; Hirschmann 59–62). Kant was particularly interested in the last two, the pacifying effects. For him, the high esteem attributed to military courage is typical of "savage" cultures, such as the European age of chivalry (Kant 1795, 334).

There is one thinker whom Kant adored and who explicitly attacked the *doux-commerce* thesis in his writings: Jean-Jacques Rousseau. "The ancient politicians forever spoke of morals and virtue; ours speak only of commerce and of money" (Rousseau 1750, 18). Rousseau, who closely followed the civic humanist tradition in this respect, criticized the thesis from a moral perspective, and also doubted that commercial interdependence would foster peaceful relations (cf. Mendham 2010 and Cavallar 2002, 287–290). The society created by mutual needs was a Hobbesian state of anarchy and instability. There was no natural order or alliance between private interests and the general good. Proponents of the *doux-commerce* thesis, Rousseau claimed, deceived us into believing that commercial society constituted a kind of moral whole, while it was not even a society. "They live together without any real union, like men grouped on the same piece of land but separated by deep ravines" (Rousseau 1887, 121).

Both Hume and Smith distanced themselves from this pessimistic assessment. Hume praised commercial society as a training ground of the arts, of improved industry, sociability, politeness and good manners (Cavallar 2002, 246–249). Smith stressed two aspects Kant was particularly interested in. First, commerce, the result of an expanding division of labour, had beneficial political effects: it undermined paternalistic and dependency-generating social institutions like slavery, feudalism or unfree labour and offered more political freedom for individuals (Hill 2010, 463–464 with references; cf. Cavallar 2002, 251 and Hont 2005, 278). There was a good chance that the paternalistic and despotic governments loathed by Kant might gradually be replaced by republican governments where the original or natural "principles of external human right", namely freedom, equality and independence, would be guaranteed, and individuals could start to overcome their immaturity (Kant 1793a, 291–292; cf. Kant 1784a, 117; 1798, 315 and Fleischacker 1996, 385, 387–388, 401–402). Secondly, Smith assumed that unhindered commerce would expand indefinitely, eventually transgressing national borders, helping to create a global society of distant strangers, "uniting [...] the most distant parts of the world [...] enabling them to relieve one another's wants", and encouraging "one another's industry" (Smith 1762–1763; 1766/1978, 4.7.c.80, 626; cf. Hill 2010, 463–465). There was a good chance that destructive "national jealousies", the irrational "jealousy of strangers" (Smith 1762–1763; 1766/1978, 6.164–165, 391–392; 1776/1976, 1.10.c.22, 142) would eventually be replaced by "habituation to foreigners", a "general attitude of restrained amity" and "forms of amicable *strangership*" in the commercial *cosmopolis* (Hill 2010, 470–471 and 473; cf. Smith 1776/1976, 4.3.c.9, 493). Kant's formulation of cosmopolitan right as the "idea of a *peaceful*, even if not friendly, thoroughgoing community of all nations" (Kant 1797, 489) suggests that he had a similar vision in mind. "*Freundschaftlich*" (translated as "friendly") belongs to the realm of virtue, not to the market, where peaceful (*friedlich*) interaction is more likely (and indispensable). Friendship, at least for Kant, is not based on mutual self-interest, but on a moral disposition, namely "equal mutual love and respect" where the other is regarded as an end in him- or herself (Kant 1797, 584, as opposed to Smith 1776/1976, 1.2.2, 27). However, friendship is not required for market relations.

So the essential advantage of commerce was global integration or economic globalization, whose beginnings Smith dated back to the 1500s (Smith 1776/1976, 4.1.33, 448–449, 4.7.c.80, 626; Hill 2010, 450–451). Kant's philosophical reconstruction of world history stresses its paradoxical elements. For instance, the European conquerors who did not distinguish between visiting and conquering a country committed injustices and brought havoc upon the natives, while at the same time these very activities opened up the trade routes between the continents, contributing to a possible cosmopolitan world order which approaches the ideal of just and peaceful relations among nations (cf. Kant 1795, 329–330). This is very close to Smith's assessment, who—like Abbé Raynal and Diderot (cf. Cavallar 2002, 257)—also praised global integration, but criticized the "savage injustice" of Europeans from a moral point of view. The discovery of America or the passage to the East Indies opened new markets, promoted the divisions of labour, and improved the arts but the Europeans spoiled what could have been "advantageous" and "beneficial" for all sides (Smith 1776/1976, 4.1.32., 447–448; cf. 4.7.b.59, 588; Hill 2010, 451–452). Apparently drawing on Smith, Kant claimed that modern history moved towards a global economy, where, for example gold and silver mines in Peru and New Mexico were inextricably linked with European manufacture of goods. Both productive industries stimulated each other, causing a mutually reinforcing process. "In this way industry [or industriousness; the German original uses the term *Fleiß*] always keeps pace with industry" (Kant 1797, 435). Humans invented money as a means to measure this industry and to facilitate trade among individuals as well as nations (p. 436).

Kant briefly mentioned in *Perpetual Peace* that the Europeans often did not even profit from the crimes committed against the natives in the colonies, and that "trading companies" were "on the verge of collapse" (Kant 1795, 330), citing some examples. Several writers before Kant had written against conquest, colonies, imperialist adventures or trading monopolies, among them Montesquieu, Bayle, Hume, Rousseau, Davenant, Rutherford, Blackstone, Raynal, Diderot, Marmontel and Justi (Adam 2006, 61–70; Cavallar 2002, 254–259; Muthu 2003). Abbé de Raynal mused about the disadvantages of the immoral behaviour of the European conquerors, colonists and slave owners: in the short run, it works and leads to prosperity, but in the long run power based on "goodness, kindness, benevolence and humanity [...] is more solid and long-lasting" (Raynal 1780, 31). Jeremy Bentham considered colonies an economic disaster, their emancipation was thus above all in the interest of the home countries. Colonial expenses by far overbalanced profits, and trade should replace colonial exploitation (cf. Cavallar 2002, 258 and Cavallar 2011, 50–51). A few years before Bentham,

Smith arrived at similar conclusions, offering moral as well as economic arguments against colonies and ensuing exclusive trading companies like the East India Company. Like others before him, Smith rejected the assertion of mercantilism, neo-Machiavellism and civic humanism that war and expansion were "the keys to national survival and *grandezza*" (Hont 2005, 75). Colonies were not only unjust but also economically self-defeating, since the mother country would eventually ruin its own finances, investments, resources and trading capacities (cf. Smith 1776/1976, 4.7.c.16–108, 594–641, 5.3.92, 946–947; Hill 2010, 452–454). Provided that the "jealousy of trade" and the fallacies of mercantilism such as monopolies were avoided, a condition of commerce was synonymous with peaceful relations (cf. Smith 1776/1976, 4.3.c.9, 493, 4.3.c.11, 494; Hill 2010, 469). Kant seemed to have subscribed to Smith's analysis. Perhaps there was some additional meta-analysis involved on Kant's side: Smith could be seen as one of the scholars who used their own reason "before the entire public of the *world of readers*" (Kant 1784b, 18) to promote enlightenment, the cultivation of reason and thus a world with more political freedom and peaceful interaction.

According to Kant's philosophy of history, the driving forces of these changes were part of the phenomenal world and mundane factors such as "mutual self-interest" (Kant 1795, 336) and "unsocial sociability" (Kant 1784a, 111). Both had been stock themes of Enlightenment moral philosophy and political economy. Theories about the sociable and unsociable character traits of the human species can be traced back to Hugo Grotius and Samuel Pufendorf (Schneewind 2009, 95–103; Cavallar 2002, 237–239), and Kant transformed this concept in new and interesting ways (cf. Hedrick 2008, 253–255; Schneewind 2009, 104–109; Wood 2009). As for self-interest, this was a recurrent theme in nascent psychological theories of Enlightenment moral philosophies, which Kant could easily find in authors he read and liked, such as Hume, Vattel, Rousseau or Smith (Cavallar 2002, 245, 251; 2012b; Stapelbroek 2008, 75–76; Schneewind 2009, 102–103). Smith in particular held that self-interest or self-love—and not benevolence—had lead to more individual liberty and justice in the legal systems in the past, and that it was natural that humans put themselves, their families and their friends first (Cavallar 2002, 251; Hill 2010,

455; Hont 2005, 397). In a manner reminiscent of Rousseau, Smith attacked the Stoic notion of universal benevolence as psychologically implausible and counter-productive (Hill 2010, 456–458). Self-love and self-interest was a more reliable motive-force than benevolence (Smith 1776/1976, 1.2, 26–27), and this also applied to the international realm. Self-interest had the potential to weaken nationalist feelings, the irrational "jealousy of strangers" mentioned above, and foster a "general attitude of restrained amity" and amicable, commercial strangership among communities (Hill 2010, 470–471, 460–461).

Kant's advocacy of a cosmopolitan society based on the natural right of hospitality should not be identified with the idea of an "ethical commonwealth" (Kant 1793b, 130–136; Cavallar 2012a). Kant keeps both types of commonwealths apart, though they are related to each other. The right to visit regions and to engage in commerce, though justified deontologically as being based on innate freedom and original collective possession, has the function to promote a possible "communion of all nations" (Kant 1797, 489). Kant apparently expected that complex interdependence and globalization as empirical phenomena would drive humans towards, and urge them to establish, a global commonwealth under the rule of right. However, this union aims at the compatibility of external actions (and is based on mutual self-interest), not at morally good dispositions. Moral progress in this respect seems to have been Kant's additional hope based on his moral theology (cf. Cavallar 2012a).

I conclude with the somewhat unclear and frequently cited claim that the "community of the nations of the earth has now gone so far that a violation of right on *one* place of the earth is felt in *all*" (Kant 1795, 330). Modern economic globalization also leads to increased interaction and migration, creates new "lines of communication". It urges people to widen their circles beyond families, friends and immediate civil society. This is the objective side, already outlined by Smith. There is another, moral or juridical dimension. As Diane Morgan puts it:

> Kant suggests that injustices in one part of the globe (such as slavery in the West Indies) send out shock waves which reverberate along these ever developing lines

> of communication, thereby gradually consolidating a public sphere which is, which should be the concern of all rational beings. (Morgan 2009, 115)

Kant seems to believe that historical developments, triggered by the aforementioned economic globalization, will eventually change people's attitudes towards distant strangers, so that an at least thin "community of the nations of the earth" (Kant 1795, 330), based on mutual-self interest, is established.

For me this passage is unclear since I am not sure how Kant arrived at this assessment. Which convincing evidence did he have in mind? Perhaps it was the recurrent criticism of European theologians, natural lawyers, philosophers and intellectuals of European overseas crimes since Francisco de Vitoria, culminating in the eighteenth century (Cavallar 2002; Muthu 2003; Cavallar 2011, 17–38, and above). It might have been Smith's criticism of European, especially British, colonialism on moral as well as economic grounds (Hill 2010, 450–455). My guess is that for Kant, additional evidence might have come from another eighteenth-century bestseller, from events in Haiti, and from Great Britain.

The book I am referring to is Abbé de Raynal's monumental *A history of the two Indies* (1770, revised and enlarged edition 1780), which became an international blockbuster with more than thirty editions (for the following see Richter 2006, 165–167). Raynal and his co-authors, among them Diderot, fiercely attacked European colonialism, the slave trade and the violation of the rights of natives in their extensive and meticulous study, with the third edition encompassing ten volumes. For instance, one passage commented on the belated British attempt to found trading posts and colonies: "They believed that it was difficult to acquire great wealth without great injustice, and that in order to surpass or even match the nations they had criticized they had to act in the same manner" (Raynal 1780, 31). The text usually—but not always—denounced slavery as immoral. Especially Diderot contrasted "savage" peoples—which were in his opinion morally superior—with the corrupt and unjust European civilized man. As Melvin Richter put it: "More than any other major work of the century the book systematically reversed prior judgements about the old world's political and moral superiority" (Richter 2006, 166).

Raynal's *Deux Indes* is said to have influenced the Haitian revolutionary leader and former black slave François-Dominique Toussaint Louverture (1743–1803). Some passages of the book indeed invited native populations to revolt (cf. Richter 2006, 167). The revolutionary events in Paris triggered social instability on Saint Domingue, which had been the most profitable French colony due to coffee and sugar exports (for the following see Bell 2008; Blackburn 2006; Césaire 2008; Dubois 2005). Initially the rebel slaves, who outnumbered the whites by a ratio of ten to one, were willing to bargain for better conditions. In the wake of the *Declaration of the Rights of Man*, Julien Raimond and other free people of colour demanded civil equality with whites. After 1791, the abolition of slavery became the goal. Though Toussaint fought the French with the help of the Spanish, he switched allegiance as soon as the French National Convention proclaimed the abolition of slavery and granted civil and political rights to black men in February 1794. In 1796, the government even held elections to choose colonial representatives for the national assembly. However, tensions between Toussaint and the French government grew when the *Directoire* was suspected of planning to reintroduce slavery on the island. Kant may have been familiar with some of these developments. Perhaps his remark that the consequences of the French Revolution would be "infinitely great and beneficial" also referred to the Haitian events (Kuehn 2001, 392).

Another political event Kant might have heard or read about could have been Edmund Burke's famous attack on Warren Hastings (1732–1818), who was the first Governor-General of India from 1773 to 1785 and was charged in the House of Commons with high crimes, corruption and misdemeanours by Members of Parliament, among them Burke, two years later. Some of Burke's arguments during the long investigation are worth to be mentioned. Against Hastings, Burke asserted that the British were not entitled to suspend their moral and legal standards when dealing with non-Europeans. Instead, as Jennifer Pitts summarizes, "the British had an obligation to extend universally the fundamental standards of respect, rightfulness, and humanity that applied at home" (Pitts 2005, 78). A way to overcome "geographical morality" limited to a certain region was to boost the moral imagination, and increase sympathy for strangers. In a manner reminiscent of Francisco de Vitoria, Burke compared India with

Germany, "not for an exact resemblance, but as a sort of middle term, by which India might be approximated to our understandings, and if possible to our feelings; in order to awaken something of sympathy for the unfortunate natives" (Burke 1783, 390). This comparison only worked—and this is the third element—if Indians and their culture and institutions were not seen as inferior. Thus Burke was at pains to show that Indian alleged inferiority and so-called oriental despotism were psychological or cognitive problems of *Europeans* in the first place: a convenient myth of Hastings and other British administrators to justify their own oppression, injustices and arbitrary rule. Burke identified with considerable historical accuracy Montesquieu as the main culprit of this distorted picture of India (see Burke 1794, 264–265; Pitts 2005, 74–80). Hastings was acquitted in 1795, but the trial probably had a moral significance for Kant. A European criticizing the "violation of right on *one* place of the earth"—far away from Europe—by another fellow-European, so that this violation might be felt by some among his European audience: episodes like this were perhaps what Kant had in mind when he wrote the passage quoted above. Note that Burke, in his attack on Hastings, implicitly relies on the key tenets of Kantian formal moral principles, namely impartiality and the universalization of maxims, on normative individualism (humans as ends in themselves), and the enlarged way of thinking. As Kant did not refer to principles or concepts but to *feelings*, it might be claimed that he saw these and similar episodes as proof of his claim that every rational person has moral feelings, which are defined as one of the four "predispositions" or "*subjective* conditions of receptiveness to the concept of duty" (Kant 1797, 528).

These three examples with their possible impact on Kant are in need of qualification: the text of Raynal's monumental work was ambiguous on the issue of slavery, for instance. On the one hand, this institution was condemned as immoral, on the other hand, the authors approved of the plantation systems even if they were based on slavery, provided that the slaves were treated in a humane way (Raynal 1780, xxvi). Against my interpretation, one might argue that Burke was not a moral cosmopolitan or anti-imperialist thinker, that he did not really care about the Indians, did not respect cultural pluralism, and that his attack on Hastings was motivated by deeply conservative and patriotic concerns, and this criticism could find support in a relatively recent article, which claims that Burke "remained firmly committed to the continuation of a providential imperial project in India throughout the course of his long political career" (O'Neill 2009, 497). This interpretation of Burke's thought sounds plausible; still, I think it is open to criticism. Be that as it may, the claim does not invalidate Kant's passage about the violation of rights in one part of the globe. What matters for Kant is the fact that colonial practices were criticized, for whatever reasons. Kant's philosophy of history does not presuppose universal benevolence or a respect for Europe's external "other", it presupposes pragmatic considerations revolving around self-interest. Finally, there are the sobering results of the Haitian revolution, which did indeed transform a society of slaves into a self-governing nation. However, after the defeat of the French forces in 1803 the mulatto descendants became the Haitian elite which ruled the country, thus creating another two-caste society. Still, the Haitian revolution tested the ideals of the French revolutionaries and their declaration that all men are born equal and free; they were forced to investigate into the meaning of their revolution. It was an opportunity, and nothing more than that, to expand one's way of thinking, or *Denkungsart*.

Conclusion

I want to finish with a few remarks on possible criticism of Kant. His hope that the spirit of commerce would guarantee cosmopolitan right was perhaps too optimistic: commercial interaction normally leads to exclusive hospitality rights, without extending to *all* humans. Implementation of cosmopolitan right currently depends on states, their interests and their power, and thus is often arbitrary and selective (cf. Kleingeld 1998, 82–83; Habermas 1997, 121–122). Kant could be defended with the argument that he saw commercial interactions based on mutual self-interests as deficient but with possible beneficial results, admittedly incomplete, but still a step in the right direction. Second, Kant's (and Smith's) enthusiastic praise of world trade seems to be outdated in our contemporary world troubled by environmental crises which are partly rooted in an excessive use of mass transportation of goods. Kant lived in an age of a relatively environmentally friendly world trade (at least if one restricts the comparison to the transportation systems), in a world of sailing ships, horses and camels (cf. Kant 1795, 329). Third, since the eighteenth century there has been an ongoing debate about restrictions on free trade and the legitimate amount of state intervention. Kant himself held that the supreme power of the state was entitled to pass rights meant as "means for *securing* a *rightful condition*", not in order to make the state's citizens happy or prosperous but in order to secure its very existence as a commonwealth, also against foreign enemies. In a footnote, Kant included "certain restrictions on imports [...] among these rights" (Kant 1793a, 298)—a provision that clearly qualified the free-trade doctrine.

"I cannot but regret the proneness of German philosophy to vague and misty abstraction", John Austin once declared. In this chapter, I tried to show how Kant's cosmopolitan right comes alive when considered within its historical setting. One major challenge for any interpreter is the briefness of Kant's account—cosmopolitan right is just one paragraph in the *Doctrine of Right*, so one is tempted to conclude that it is too vague and abstract. I hope I have somewhat managed to counter this impression.

References

Achenwall, Gottfried and Johann Stephan Pütter, 1750/1995. *Anfangsgründe des Naturrechts (Elementa iuris naturae)*. Ed. and trans. Jan Schröder. Frankfurt am Main and Leipzig: Insel.

Adam, Ulrich, 2006. *The political economy of J.H.G. Justi*. Oxford: Peter Lang.

Albrecht, Andrea, 2005. *Kosmopolitismus: Weltbürgerdiskurse in Literatur, Philosophie und Publizistik um 1800*. Berlin and New York: de Gruyter.

Anderson-Gold, Sharon, 2001. *Cosmopolitanism and human rights*. Cardiff: Wales University Press.

Archibugi, Daniele and David Held (eds.), 1995. *Cosmopolitan democracy: An agenda for a new world order*. Cambridge: Polity Press.
Armitage, David, 2006. "Hobbes and the foundations of modern international thought". In: Annabel Brett, James Tully, and Holly Hamilton Bleakley (eds.), 2006. *Rethinking the foundations of modern political thought*. Cambridge: Cambridge University Press, 219–235.
Bell, Madison Smart, 2007. *Toussaint Louverture: A biography*. New York: Pantheon.
Bielefeldt, Heiner, 2004. "Verrechtlichung als Reformprozess: Kants Konstruktion der Rechtsentwicklung". In: Herta Nagl-Docekal and Rudolf Langthaler (eds.), 2004. *Recht – Geschichte – Religion: Die Bedeutung Kants für die Gegenwart*. Berlin: Akademie-Verlag, 73–84.
Bielefeldt, Heiner, 2008. "Menschenrechte als interkulturelle Lerngeschichte". In: Hans Jörg Sandkühler (ed.), 2008. *Philosophie, wozu?* Frankfurt am Main: Suhrkamp, 289–301.
Bittner, Rüdiger, 2009. "Philosophy helps history". In: Amélie Oksenberg Rorty and James Schmidt (eds.), 2009. *Kant's* Idea for a universal history with a cosmopolitan aim*: A critical guide*. Cambridge: Cambridge University Press, 231–249.
Blackburn, Robin, 2006. "Haiti, slavery, and the age of democratic revolution". *William and Mary Quarterly*, 63(4), 633–674.
Bohman, James, 1997. "The public spheres of the world citizen". In: James Bohman and Matthias Lutz-Bachmann (eds.), 1997. *Perpetual peace: Essays on Kant's cosmopolitan ideal*. Cambridge, MA and London: MIT Press, 179–200.
Borries, Kurt, 1928/1973. *Kant als Politiker: Zur Staats- und Gesellschaftslehre des Kritizismus*. Reprint Aalen: Scientia.
Brandt, Reinhard, 2009. *Die Bestimmung des Menschen bei Kant*. 2nd ed. Hamburg: Meiner.
Brock, Gillian and Harry Brighouse (eds.), 2005. *The political philosophy of cosmopolitanism*. Cambridge: Cambridge University Press.
Brockmöller, Annette, 1997. *Die Entstehung der Rechtstheorie im 19. Jahrhundert in Deutschland*. Baden-Baden: Nomos.
Brown, Garrett Wallace, 2009. *Grounding cosmopolitanism: From Kant to the idea of a cosmopolitan constitution*. Edinburgh: Edinburgh University Press.
Brown, Garrett Wallace, 2010. "The laws of hospitality, asylum seekers and cosmopolitan right: A Kantian response to Jacques Derrida". *European Journal of Political Theory*, 9(3), 1–20.
Brown, Garrett Wallace and David Held (eds.), 2010. *The cosmopolitanism reader*. Cambridge: Polity Press.
Budelacci, Orlando, 2003. *Kants Friedensprogramm: Das politische Denken im Kontext der praktischen Philosophie*. Athena: Oberhausen.

Burke, Edmund, 1783. "Speech on Fox's India bill, December 1, 1783". In: Edmund Burke, 1981–2000. *Writings and speeches*, vol. 5. Ed. Paul Langford. Oxford: Clarendon, 378–451.
Burke, Edmund, 1794. "Speech in reply, May 28, 1794". In: Edmund Burke, 1981–2000. *Writings and speeches*, vol. 7. Ed. Paul Langford. Oxford: Clarendon, 231–281.
Byrd, Sharon and Joachim Hruschka, 2008. "From the state of nature to the juridical state of states". *Law and Philosophy*, 27(6), 599–641.
Byrd, Sharon and Joachim Hruschka, 2010. *Kant's doctrine of right: A commentary*. Cambridge: Cambridge University Press.
Cavallar, Georg, 1992. *Pax Kantiana: Systematisch-historische Untersuchung des Entwurfs "Zum ewigen Frieden" (1795) von Immanuel Kant*. Wien, Köln, Weimar: Böhlau.
Cavallar, Georg, 2002. *The rights of strangers: Theories of international hospitality, the global community, and political justice since Vitoria*. Aldershot: Ashgate.
Cavallar, Georg, 2004. "The law of nations in the age of Enlightenment: Moral and legal principles". *Annual Review of Law and Ethics*, 12, 213–229.
Cavallar, Georg, 2011. *Imperfect cosmopolis: Studies in the history of international legal theory and cosmopolitan ideas*. Cardiff: University of Wales Press.
Cavallar, Georg, 2012a. "Cosmopolitanisms in Kant's philosophy". *Ethics and Global Politics*, 5(2), 95–118. Available at: http://dx.doi.org/10.3402/egp.v5i2.14924. Accessed 1 June 2012.
Cavallar, Georg, 2012b. "Educating Émile: Jean-Jacques Rousseau on cosmopolitanism". *European Legacy*, 17(4), 485–499.
Cavallar, Georg, 2012c. "From Francisco de Vitoria to Alfred Verdross: The right to preach the gospel, the right of hospitality, and the international community". In: Matthias Lutz-Bachmann (ed.), 2012. *Recht zwischen Philosophie, Theologie und Jurisprudenz: Beiträge zur Begriffsgeschichte von Vitoria bis Suárez*. Stuttgart: frommann-holzboog, 1–35.
Cavallar, Georg, 2013 [forthcoming]. "From hospitality to the right of immigration, 18 to 20c". In: Gideon Baker (ed.), 2013 [forthcoming]. *Hospitality and globality*. Palgrave.
Césaire, Aimé, 2008. *Toussaint Louverture: La Révolution Française et le problème colonial*. Paris: Éd.
Cheneval, Francis, 2002. *Philosophie in weltbürgerlicher Bedeutung: Über die Entstehung und die philosophischen Grundlagen des supranationalen und kosmopolitischen Denkens der Moderne*. Basel: Schwabe.
Derrida, Jacques, 1996. "Die Gesetze der Gastfreundschaft". Available at: http://www.kuwi.euv-frankfurto.de/de/lehrstuhl/lw/westeuropa/Lehrstuhlinhaber/publikationen/rara/Derrida_in_FFO.pdf. Accessed 23 May 2010.

Derrida, Jacques, 2000. *Of hospitality*. Stanford, CA: Stanford University Press.
Derrida, Jacques, 2001. *On cosmopolitanism and forgiveness*. London: Routledge.
Diderot, Denise, 1780. "Extracts from the *Histoire des Deux Indes*". In: Denise Diderot, 1992. *Political writings*. Ed. and trans. John Hope Mason and Robert Wokler. Cambridge: Cambridge University Press, 165–214.
Dubois, Laurent, 2005. *Avengers of the New World: The story of the Haitian revolution*. Cambridge, MA: Belknap Press.
Eberl, Oliver and Peter Niesen (eds.), 2011. *Immanuel Kant, Zum ewigen Frieden und Auszügeaus der Rechtslehre*. Berlin: Suhrkamp.
Fleischacker, Samuel, 1996. "Values behind the market: Kant's response to the *Wealth of nations*". *History of Political Thought*, 17(3), 379–407.
Förster, Eckart, 2009. "The hidden plan of nature". In: In: Amélie Oksenberg Rorty and James Schmidt (eds.), 2009. *Kant's* Idea for a universal history with a cosmopolitan aim*: A critical guide*. Cambridge: Cambridge University Press, 187–199.
Geismann, Georg, 2009. "Sittlichkeit – Religion – Geschichte". In: Georg Geismann, 2009. *Kant und kein Ende Band 1: Studien zur Moral-, Religions- und Geschichtsphilosophie*. Würzburg: Königshausen und Neumann, 11–118.
Geismann, Georg, 2010. *Kant und kein Ende Band 2: Studien zur Rechtsphilosophie*. Würzburg: Königshausen und Neumann.
Guyer, Paul, 2009. "The crooked timber of mankind". In: In: Amélie Oksenberg Rorty and James Schmidt (eds.), 2009. *Kant's* Idea for a universal history with a cosmopolitan aim*: A critical guide*. Cambridge: Cambridge University Press, 129–149.
Habermas, Jürgen, 1997. "Kant's idea of perpetual peace, with the benefit of two hundred years' hindsight". In: James Bohman and Matthias Lutz-Bachmann (eds.), 1997. *Perpetual peace: Essays on Kant's cosmopolitan ideal*. Cambridge, MA and London: MIT Press, 113–153.
Häntsch, Carola, 2008. "The world citizen from the perspective of alien reason: Notes on Kant's category of the *Weltbürger* according to Josef Simon". In: Rebecka Lettevall and My Klockar Linder (eds.), 2008. *The idea of Kosmopolis: History, philosophy and politics of world citizenship*. Huddinge: Södertörn University, 51–63.
Heater, Derek, 2002. *World citizenship: Cosmopolitan thinking and its opponents*. London and New York: Continuum.
Hebeis, Michael, 1996. *Karl Anton von Martini (1726–1800): Leben und Werk*. Frankfurt am Main: Peter Lang.
Hedrick, Todd, 2008. "Race, difference, and anthropology in Kant's cosmopolitanism". *Journal of the History of Philosophy*, 46(2), 245–268.
Hill, Lisa, 2010. "Adam Smith's cosmopolitanism: The expanding circles of commercial strangership". *History of Political Thought*, 31(3), 449–473.

Höffe, Otfried, 2006. *Kant's cosmopolitan theory of law and peace*. Cambridge: Cambridge University Press.

Hont, Istvan, 2005. *Jealousy of trade: International competition and the nation-state in historical perspective*. Cambridge, MA: Harvard University Press.

Hüning, Dieter (ed.), 2009. *Naturrecht und Staatstheorie bei Samuel Pufendorf*. Baden-Baden: Nomos.

Hunter, Ian, 2001. *Rival enlightenments: Civil and metaphysical philosophy in early modern Germany*. Cambridge: Cambridge University Press.

Ittersum, Martine Julia van, 2006. *Profit and principle: Hugo Grotius, natural rights theories and the rise of Dutch power in the East Indies 1595–1615*. Leiden: Brill.

Ittersum, Martine Julia van, 2010. "The wise man is never merely a private citizen: The Roman Stoa in Hugo Grotius: *De Jure Praedae* (1604–1608)". *History of European Ideas,* 36(1), 1–18.

Kant, Immanuel, 1781/1998. *Critique of pure reason*. Ed. and trans. Paul Guyer and Allen W. Wood. Cambridge: Cambridge University Press.

Kant, Immanuel, 1784a. "Idea for a universal history with a cosmopolitan aim". In: Immanuel Kant, 2007. *Anthropology, history, and education*. Ed. Günter Zöller and Robert B. Louden. Cambridge: Cambridge University Press, 107–120.

Kant, Immanuel, 1784b. "An answer to the question: 'What is Enlightenment?'". In: Immanuel Kant, 1996. *Practical philosophy*. Ed. and trans. Mary J. Gregor. Cambridge: Cambridge University Press, 17–22.

Kant, Immanuel, 1785. "Groundwork of the metaphysics of morals". In: Immanuel Kant, 1996. *Practical philosophy*. Ed. and trans. Mary J. Gregor. Cambridge: Cambridge University Press, 37–108.

Kant, Immanuel, 1786. "Conjectural beginning of human history". In: Immanuel Kant, 2007. *Anthropology, history, and education*. Ed. Günter Zöller and Robert B. Louden. Cambridge: Cambridge University Press, 160–175.

Kant, Immanuel, 1790/2000. *Critique of the power of judgement*. Ed. Paul Guyer, trans. Paul Guyer and Eric Matthews. Cambridge: Cambridge University Press.

Kant, Immanuel, 1793a. "On the common saying: That may be correct in theory, but it is of no use in practice". In: Immanuel Kant, 1996. *Practical philosophy*. Ed. and trans. Mary J. Gregor. Cambridge: Cambridge University Press, 273–309.

Kant, Immanuel, 1793b. "Religion within the boundaries of mere reason". In: Immanuel Kant, 2005. *Religion and rational theology*. Ed. and trans. Allen W. Wood and George di Giovanni. Cambridge: Cambridge University Press, 39–215.

Kant, Immanuel, 1795. "Toward perpetual peace : A philosophical project". In: Immanuel Kant, 1996. *Practical philosophy*. Ed. and trans. Mary J. Gregor. Cambridge: Cambridge University Press, 315–351.

Kant, Immanuel, 1797. "The metaphysics of morals". In: Immanuel Kant, 1996. *Practical philosophy*. Ed. and trans. Mary J. Gregor. Cambridge: Cambridge University Press, 363–603.

Kant, Immanuel, 1798. "Anthropology from a pragmatic point of view". In: Immanuel Kant, 2007. *Anthropology, history, and education*. Ed. Günter Zöller and Robert B. Louden. Cambridge: Cambridge University Press, 227–429.

Kant, Immanuel, 1900. *Werke: Akademie-Textausgabe*. Berlin: de Gruyter.

Kapossy, Béla and Richard Whatmore, 2008. "Introduction". In: Emer de Vattel, 1758/2008. *The law of nations, or, Principles of the law of nature, applied to the conduct and affairs of nations and sovereigns […]*. Ed. Béla Kapossy and Richard Whatmore. Indianapolis: Liberty Fund, ix–xx.

Kater, Thomas, 1999. *Politik, Recht, Geschichte: Zur Einheit der politischen Philosophie Immanuel Kants*. Würzburg: Königshausen und Neumann.

Keil, Rainer, 2009. *Freizügigkeit, Gerechtigkeit, demokratische Autonomie: Das Weltbürgerrecht nach Immanuel Kant als Masstab der Gerechtigkeit geltenden Aufenthalts-, Einwanderungs- und Flüchtlingsrechts*. Baden-Baden: Nomos.

Kemp, Peter, 2006. "Kant the cosmopolitan". In: Hans Lenk and Reiner Wiehl (eds.) 2006. *Kant today – Kant aujourd'hui – Kant heute*. Berlin: Lit, 142–162.

Kersting, Wolfgang, 1984/1993. *Wohlgeordnete Freiheit: Immanuel Kants Rechts- und Staatsphilosophie*. New paperback ed. Frankfurt am Main: Suhrkamp.

Kersting, Wolfgang, 2004. *Kant über Recht*. Paderborn: Mentis.

Kleingeld, Pauline, 1995. *Fortschritt und Vernunft: Zur Geschichtsphilosophie Kants*. Würzburg: Königshausen und Neumann.

Kleingeld, Pauline, 1998. "Kant's cosmopolitan law: World citizenship for a global order". *Kantian Review*, 2, 72–90.

Kleingeld, Pauline. 1999. "Six varieties of cosmopolitanism in late eighteenth-century Germany". *Journal of the History of Ideas*, 60(3), 505–524.

Kleingeld, Pauline, 2004. "Approaching *Perpetual peace*: Kant's defence of a league of states and his ideal of a world federation". *European Journal of Philosophy*, 12(3), 304–325.

Kleingeld, Pauline, 2007. "Kant's second thoughts on race". *The Philosophical Quarterly*, 57, 573–92.

Kleingeld, Pauline, 2009. "Kant's changing cosmopolitanism". In: In: Amélie Oksenberg Rorty and James Schmidt (eds.), 2009. *Kant's* Idea for a universal history with a cosmopolitan aim*: A critical guide*. Cambridge: Cambridge University Press, 171–186.

Kleingeld, Pauline, 2012. *Kant and cosmopolitanism: The philosophical ideal of world citizenship*. Cambridge: Cambridge University Press.

Kuehn, Manfred, 2001. *Kant: A biography*. Cambridge: Cambridge University Press.

Lettevall, Rebecka, 2009. "Turning golden coins into loose change: Philosophical, political and popular readings of Kant's *Zum ewigen Frieden*". *Jahrbuch für Recht und Ethik*, 17, 133–150.

Lettevall, Rebecka and My Klockar Linder (eds.), 2008. *The idea of Kosmopolis: History, philosophy and politics of world citizenship*. Huddinge: Södertörn University.

Louden, Robert B., 2000. *Kant's impure ethics: From rational beings to human beings*. Oxford: Oxford University Press.

Louden, Robert B., 2008. "Anthropology from a Kantian point of view: Toward a cosmopolitan conception of human nature". *Studies in History & Philosophy of Science*, part A, 39(4), 515–522.

Lutz-Bachmann, Matthias, Andreas Niederberger and Philipp Schink (eds.), 2010. *Kosmopolitanismus: Zur Geschichte und Zukunft eines umstrittenen Ideals*. Frankfurt am Main: Velbrück Wissenschaft.

Marini, Giuliano, 1998. *Tre studi sul cosmopolitismo Kantiano*. Pisa and Rome: Istituti editoriali e poligrafici internatzionali.

Martens, Georg Friedrich von, 1796. *Einleitung in das positive europäische Völkerrecht auf Verträge und Herkommen gegründet*. Göttingen: Johann Christian Dieterich.

Martini, Karl Anton Freiherr von, 1791/1969. *Erklärung der Lehrsätzeüber das allgemeine Staats- und Völkerrecht*. Reprint Aalen: Scientia.

Mendham, Matthew D., 2010. "Enlightened gentleness as soft indifference: Rousseau's critique of cultural modernization". *History of Political Thought*, 31(4), 605–637.

Montesquieu, Charles de Secondat, baron de, 1748/1989. *The spirit of the laws*. Ed. and trans. Anne M. Cohler, Basia Carolyn Miller, and Harold Samuel Stone. Cambridge: Cambridge University Press.

Morgan, Diane, 2009. "Trading hospitality: Kant, cosmopolitics and commercium". *Paragraph*, 32, 105–122.

Muthu, Sankar, 2003. *Enlightenment against empire*. Princeton, NJ and Oxford: Princeton University Press.

Muthu, Sankar, 2000. "Justice and foreigners: Kant's cosmopolitan right". In: Sharon Byrd and Joachim Hruschka (eds.), 2006. *Kant and law*. Aldershot and Burlington: Ashgate, 449–471.

Nagl-Docekal, Herta and Rudolf Langthaler (eds.), 2004. *Recht – Geschichte – Religion: Die Bedeutung Kants für die Gegenwart*. Berlin: Akademie-Verlag.

O'Neill, Daniel, 2009. "Rethinking Burke and India." *History of Political Thought*, 30(3), 492–523.

Onuf, Nicholas, 2009. "Friendship and hospitality: Some conceptual preliminaries". *Journal of International Political Theory*, 5(1), 1–21.

Osterhammel, Jürgen, 1998. *Die Entzauberung Asiens. Europa und die asiatischen Reiche im 18. Jahrhundert*. München: Beck.

Pauen, Michael, 1999. "Teleologie und Geschichte in der 'Kritik der Urteilskraft'". In: Heiner Klemme *et al.* (eds.), 1999. *Aufklärung und Interpretation: Studien zu Kants Philosophie und ihrem Umkreis.* Würzburg: Königshausenund Neumann, 197–216.

Pollmann, Arnd, 2011. "Der Kummerder Vernunft: Zu Kants Idee einer allgemeinen Geschichtsphilosophie in therapeutischer Absicht". *Kant-Studien*, 102(1), 69–88.

Raynal, Guillaume-Thomas-Francois Abbé de, 1780. "A history of the two Indies". In: Peter Jimack (ed.), 2006. *A translated selection of writings from Raynal's Histoire philosophique et politique des établissements des européens dans les deux Indes.* Aldershot: Ashgate.

Richter, Melvin, 2006. "The comparative study of regimes and societies". In: Mark Goldie and Robert Wokler (eds.), 2006. *The Cambridge history of eighteenth-century political thought.* Cambridge: Cambridge University Press, 147–171.

Rorty, Amélie Oksenberg and James Schmidt (eds.), 2009. *Kant's Idea for a universal history with a cosmopolitan aim: A critical guide.* Cambridge: Cambridge University Press.

Rousseau, Jean-Jacques, 1750. "Discourse on the sciences and arts or first discourse". In: Jean-Jacques Rousseau, 1997. *The Discourses and other early political writings.* Ed. and trans. Victor Gourevitch. Cambridge: Cambridge University Press, 1–28.

Rousseau, Jean-Jacques, 1887. "First version of the *Social contract*". In: Stanley Hoffmann and David P. Fidler (eds.), 1991. *Rousseau on international relations.* Oxford: Clarendon Press.

Schneewind, Jerome B., 2009. "Good out of evil: Kant and the idea of unsocial sociability". In: In: Amélie Oksenberg Rorty and James Schmidt (eds.), 2009. *Kant's* Idea for a universal history with a cosmopolitan aim*: A critical guide.* Cambridge: Cambridge University Press, 94–111.

Schröder, Jan, 1995. "Gottfried Achenwall, Johann Stephan Pütter und die 'Elementa Iuris Naturae'". In: Gottfried Achenwall and Johann Stephan Pütter, 1750/1995. *Anfangsgründe des Naturrechts (Elementa iuris naturae).* Ed. and trans. Jan Schröder. Frankfurt am Main and Leipzig: Insel, 331–351.

Schröder, Jan, 2000. "Die Entstehung des modernen Völkerrechtsbegriffs im Naturrecht der frühen Neuzeit". In: Jan Schröder, 2010. *Rechtswissenschaft in der Neuzeit: Geschichte, Theorie, Methode: Ausgewählte Aufsätze 1976–2009.* Ed. Thomas Finkenauer, Claes Peterson and Michael Stolleis. Tübingen: Mohr Siebeck, 259–282.

Schröder, Jan, 2001. *Recht als Wissenschaft: Geschichte der juristischen Methode vom Humanismus bis zur historischen Schule (1500–1850).* München: Beck.

Schröder, Jan, 2008. "The concept of (natural) law in the doctrine of law and natural law of the early modern era". In: Lorraine Daston and Michael Stolleis (eds.),

2008. *Natural law and laws of nature in early modern Europe*. Aldershot: Ashgate, 57–71.

Schröder, Jan, 2010. *Rechtswissenschaft in der Neuzeit: Geschichte, Theorie, Methode: Ausgewählte Aufsätze 1976–2009*. Ed. Thomas Finkenauer, Claes Peterson and Michael Stolleis. Tübingen: Mohr Siebeck.

Simons, Penelope, 2003. "The emergence of the idea of the individualized state in the international legal system". *Journal of the History of International Law*, 5, 293–336.

Smith, Adam, 1776/1976. *An inquiry into the nature and causes of the wealth of nations*. Ed. R.H. Campbell, A.S. Skinner, and W.B. Todd. Oxford: Clarendon Press.

Smith, Adam, 1762–1763, 1766/1978. *Lectures on jurisprudence*. Ed. R.L. Meek, D.D. Raphael, and P.G. Stein. Oxford: Clarendon Press.

Stapelbroek, Koen, 2008. "Universal society, commerce and the rights of neutral trade: Martin Hübner, Emer de Vattel and Ferdinando Galiani". In: Petter Korkman and Virpi Mäkinen (eds.), 2008. *Universalism in international law and political philosophy*. Helsinki: Helsinki Collegium for Advanced Studies, 63–87.

Thompson, Kevin, 2008. "Sovereignty, Hospitality, and Commerce: Kant and Cosmopolitan Right". *Jahrbuch für Recht und Ethik*, 16, 305–319.

Vattel, Emer de, 1758/2008. *The law of nations, or, Principles of the law of nature, applied to the conduct and affairs of nations and sovereigns [...]*. Ed. Béla Kapossy and Richard Whatmore. Indianapolis: Liberty Fund.

Vertovec, Steven and Robin Cohen (eds.), 2002. *Conceiving cosmopolitanism: Theory, context, and practice*. Oxford: Oxford University Press.

Vitoria, Francisco de, 1528. "On civil power". In: Francisco de Vitoria, 1991. *Political writings*. Ed. Anthony Padgen and Jeremy Lawrance. Cambridge: Cambridge University Press, 1–44.

Ward, Robert, 1795. *An enquiry into the foundation and history of the law of nations in Europe from the time of the Greeks and the Romans to the age of Grotius*, 2 vols. London: Allen and Unwin.

Warda, Arthur, 1922. *Immanuel Kants Bücher*. Berlin: Breslauer.

Williams, Howard, 2006. "Back from the USSR: Kant, Kaliningrad and world peace". *International Relations*, 20(1), 27–48.

Wood, Allen, 2008. *Kantian ethics*. Cambridge: Cambridge University Press.

Wood, Allen, 2009. "Kant's fourth proposition: The unsociable sociability of human nature". In: In: Amélie Oksenberg Rorty and James Schmidt (eds.), 2009. *Kant's* Idea for a universal history with a cosmopolitan aim*: A critical guide*. Cambridge: Cambridge University Press, 112–128.

Ziegler, Karl-Heinz, 1994. *Völkerrechtsgeschichte: Ein Studienbuch*. München: Beck.

EVA PIIRIMÄE

Herder and Cosmopolitanism

Johann Gottfried Herder (1744–1803) is the philosopher most commonly remembered for his appreciation of the diversity of national cultures, as well as his defence of moral particularism and pluralism in general (see e.g. Berlin 1980). In recent years, this view has been complemented by an increasing emphasis on the universalist side of Herder's thought (Beiser 1992; Barnard 2003; Sikka 2012; Spencer 2012). It is now widely recognized that Herder's relationship to Enlightenment ideals is a complex one, and that his distinctive kind of moral relativism and pluralism do not exclude commitment to universal ideals (Sikka 2012). At the same time, Herder's relationship to cosmopolitanism continues to be characterized as one of straightforward rejection (Barnard 1965, xix; Barnard 2003, 40; Muthu 2003, 226; Evrigenis 2004, xx; Sikka 2012, 24, 87, 101, 120).[1] Indeed, there is much to commend this interpretation, since Herder was an outspoken critic of various forms of eighteenth-century cosmopolitanism. Yet does it do justice to Herder's own moral views? Were there perhaps also forms of cosmopolitanism which he approved of, or even appropriated for his own moral and political philosophy?

In this chapter I wish to argue that Herder does articulate an evocative version of cosmopolitanism that is based on a distinctive kind of universalism which is sensitive to moral particularism and pluralism. It is true that the best-known accounts of cosmopolitanism are based on foundations which exclude this kind of sensitivity. The original Stoic idea of cosmopolitanism, for example, holds that all human beings are (or can and

1 Michael Forster seems to be the only commentator suggesting that Herder's "fundamental position in international politics" is "a committed cosmopolitanism, in the sense of an impartial concern for *all* human beings" (Forster 2002, xxxii).

should be) citizens in a single large community (*cosmopolis*) by virtue of their common rationality (Brown and Kleingeld 2006). As rational beings, humans can cognize the laws of the general human community, and must aspire to determine themselves rationally so as to comply with these laws. First of all, this involves helping other human beings regardless of their belonging. Even if the Stoic cosmopolitanism in its moderate version allows that moral agents' responsibilities may be weighted differently, and that we may have a strong reason to prioritize helping those with special ties to us (Brown and Kleingeld 2006), the Stoic account of moral cognition as well as moral psychology are manifestly rationalist (Nussbaum 1996 and 1997). Similarly, the Kantian version of moral cosmopolitanism is based on the idea that all rational beings have insight into the basic moral principle, the *categorical imperative*, just like Kant's political cosmopolitanism is bound with his account of the fundamental *a priori* propositions of right (see Kleingeld 2012).

The rejection of moral cognitivism, rationalist moral psychology and rationally derived theories of political and international right does not, however, commit one to extreme moral particularism. As Michael Walzer has argued, we can distinguish between two kinds of universalism, the "covering-law" and "reiterative" variety of universalism (Walzer 1990, 183, 191, 194, 196). In contrast to the former, reiterative universalism accepts no single stable covering law, cognizable through reason. At the same time, it posits that different moral agents and communities can "recognize themselves and one another as moral makers" and that "from this recognition there follows the minimalist universalism of reiteration" (Walzer 1990, 199). Reiterative universalism, according to Walzer, emerges from "trial and error", giving rise to a number of universal moral demands at different levels. On the one hand, it gives rise to the demand for national self-determination (Walzer 1990, 212), on the other, it occasions such individualist demands as the expectation not to be deceived, treated with gross cruelty or murdered, tortured, oppressed, tyrannized or treated with manifest injustice. These demands of "minimal morality" can be seen as the minimal content to universal human rights (Walzer 1987, 24).

The need for a theory that would balance moral pluralism and national self-determination with a minimalist yet universal regime of international rights is widely acknowledged in contemporary thinking on human rights (Gutmann 2001, xix; cf. Ignatieff 2001). Such a theory, it is argued, should inspire a form of moral and political agency, one that could also be characterized as "weak cosmopolitanism" (cf. Miller 2012). Due to the reluctance of modern political theory to engage in any kind of "foundational thinking", however, there is little sustained analysis of what this kind of agency would involve,[2] nor is there any significant awareness of the historical examples of this kind of cosmopolitanism. Walzer's analysis of reiterative universalism also suffers from this kind of reluctance: it rejects moral cognitivism and monism, yet remains remarkably silent about what kind of account of moral cognition or psychology reiterative universalism is grounded in.

It is the contention of this essay that Herder puts forward a distinctive account of "weak cosmopolitanism" based on a form of universalism which shows remarkable affinity with Walzer's notion of reiterative universalism. In contrast to Walzer, however, Herder offers a detailed analysis of human moral cognition and psychology as developing in history. We shall see that Herder directly rejects only those varieties of cosmopolitanism that rationally posit one single universal moral and political goal for humanity, while being much more sympathetic to those that articulate the ideal of world citizenship in ethical terms, and that derive political consequences from the pursuit of this ideal by individual human beings and their self-governing political communities. Indeed, Herder himself can be seen as proposing a distinctive version of cosmopolitanism as an ethic of world citizenship. As Herder's later works reveal, he saw such classic proponents of cosmopolitanism as Marcus Aurelius, Fénelon, Shaftesbury and Lessing as his allies in defending our duties to the community of humanity.[3] Furthermore, as I will seek to show, the cosmopolitan ethic he delineates poses to different individuals *and* nations not only the demand to accept the reiterative universalism of national self-determination, but also the one to exercise

2 One notable exception in this respect is Kwame Anthony Appiah's theory of "rooted cosmopolitanism" (Appiah 2005 and 2006).

3 For references, see the magisterial commentary of Herder's *Ideas for the Philosophy of History of Mankind* by Wolfgang Proß (1987a; 1987b). Unfortunately there is no space in this essay to discuss Herder's relationship to these different authors.

a rigorous kind of self-determination and self-formation consistent with the demands of what could be called "reiterative" international justice.

In what follows, I will proceed in two steps. I begin by giving an overview of Herder's critique of cosmopolitanism. Herder rejects strong versions of cosmopolitanism, criticizing them for being based on misleading accounts of human moral cognition and motivation and for inspiring what he regards as potentially morally dangerous ideas of the overall tendency or even "goal" of human history. In the second section, I will turn to Herder's own account of cosmopolitanism and universalism, discussing its foundations in his theories of moral cognition, moral psychology and philosophy of history.

Herder's Critique of Cosmopolitanism

Herder's Critique of Enlightenment "Histories of Mankind"

Herder's critique of cosmopolitanism is harshest in his early philosophy of history. In *This Too a Philosophy of History* (1774) Herder singles out David Hume, Voltaire, William Robertson and Isaak Iselin as the primary examples of misguided modern cosmopolitanism (TTPH, 307, 312).[4] In Herder's interpretation, all these authors discuss European history from the perspective of all mankind, and in one way or other see modern civilized monarchies as the signposts of the gradual liberation and pacification process of mankind. Herder disagrees. Whether celebrating modern commerce

4 All references to Herder's works are given in the form of abbreviations from the titles of his works. Please consult the list of references at the end of the article. In all of cases in which a full English translation of a work is available, I will refer to the English edition only. If there is an English translation of excerpts only, I will refer to both an English edition and a German one. If there is a reference to a German edition only in my text, it means that the excerpts do not cover this particular section of text. All translations from these German originals are mine, unless otherwise indicated.

and politeness as conducive to domestic liberty and international peace (Hume, Voltaire, Robertson), or the high aspirations of a sociable "love of mankind" in modernity (Iselin), they have overlooked the waning of genuine sociable feelings in modernity:

> We love *all* of us, or rather no one *needs* to love the other. We *socialize with each other*, are completely each other's *like—ethically proper, polite, blissful!*; indeed have no *fatherland*, no *our-people* for whom we live, but are *friends of humanity* and *citizens of the world*. Already now all of Europe's regents do so, and soon we will *all* speak the French language! And then—bliss!—the Golden Age begins again "*when everyone in the world had one tongue and language*! *there will arise a single flock and shepherd!* National characters, what has happened to you? (TTPH, 329)

Herder's point is that the advocates of modern civilized monarchy have confused shallow metropolitan civility and sociability with genuine other-regarding human sentiments, while the expressions of these sentiments in earlier periods are despised because of their aggressive aspects. Sociable manners as such are no indication of moral progress. Furthermore, aping these manners tends to coincide with adopting the French culture as an overall model of civility, leading to an estrangement from, or even straightforward rejection of, one's native language and culture, which for Herder are the deepest foundations of human sociability (TTPH, 329; cf. Hont 2005, 503–505). As Herder later explains in *Letters for the Advancement of Humanity*, this kind of self-estrangement has serious consequences for human moral agency (*Sittlichkeit*) (BBH, 305). Language is the "common organ of the innermost feelings" of a nation as a community, one that makes possible a true "togetherness and common feeling" (*Mit- und Zusammenempfindung*) (BBH, 305). Losing a language is identical to losing oneself, that is, losing the capacity for distinctive self-formation (BBH, 305). There are serious political implications, too: cultural uniformity directly supports universal despotism (BBH, 687; LAH, 384–385; cf. Sikka 2012, 119).

Herder is also highly critical of those self-styled "friends of mankind" who share his concern about the shallow character of modern metropolitan sociability, yet seek to replace it with a true, moral and sociable "love of mankind" as an ideal of virtue and as conducive to greatest possible human happiness. In an early draft for *This Too a Philosophy* Herder writes:

> For both of these [moral virtue and human beings' happiness] we not only still lack a correct criterion, but it could even perhaps be that human nature had such a flexibility and mutability as to be able to form out [*ausbilden*] for itself in the most diverse situations of its efficacy also the most diverse ideals of its actions into what is called *virtue* and the most diverse ideals of its sensations into what is called *happiness*, and to be able to maintain itself therein until circumstances change and further formation occurs [*man weiter bildet*]. (TTPHEI, 270)

This is Herder's foundational statement of moral pluralism. As Sonia Sikka (2012, 44–83) has shown, virtue and happiness are for Herder "relative concepts" to be defined and measured only within and according to the ideals of particular societies. They are also deeply incommensurable (Sikka 2012, 35–37). Even though happiness is everywhere associated with activity, "achievement[s] of purposes" and "gentle overcoming of needs", "each nation has its center of happiness in itself" (TTPH, 296). There is no single measure for comparing these concepts of happiness (TTPH, 296–297). Virtues, too, are particular and plural; some virtues are incompatible with one another, and cannot hence be realized simultaneously in a single society (TTPH, 294). They are also accompanied by concomitant vices, which nevertheless should not prevent us from regarding them as "virtues" from the perspective of the society in which they were developed (TTPH, 294–295; Sikka 2012, 38; cf. Muthu 2003, 223–224).

At a deeper level, the problem with the moral "friends of mankind" for Herder is not just a mistakenly uniform understanding of virtue and happiness, or the fact that they mistake the moral ideal of the present European society for a universal one, but that they fail to understand that virtue and happiness are abstract notions of capacities which are expressed in specific cultural contexts and which can only be known through these cultural expressions (Heinz 1991 and 1994). Herder diagnoses the tendency to reify abstract notions such as "mankind", "virtue", "happiness" as endemic in modern thinking. In their zeal to "think purely and cognize ethereally" modern philosophers have cut off the concepts from their sensuous roots, the national *circles of sensation* and *of life* (OSC, 212, 220). They hence cherish a phantom of "universal reason", which in reality only "cover[s] for our favourite whims, idolatry, blindness, and laziness" and leads the moderns to pure "*word-mongery* and *active lies*" (OSC, 223, 224). Such abstract ideals cannot have any real impact on humans' actions. The mere spread of lofty ideals, Herder insists, is hence hardly a sign of moral progress:

> Precisely because these *first principles* are so *commonplace*, pass as *playthings* from hand to hand and as *platitudes* from *lip* to *lip*—precisely for this reason, it proves probable that they *cannot* any longer achieve *any effect*. Does one *use* what one *plays* with? (TTPH, 321)

In combination with the effects of modern technology and luxury on human minds, the proliferation of such abstract idioms would even cause direct harm to social and political life (TTPH, 350). Drawing on Adam Ferguson's critique of modern monarchies in *An Essay on the History of Civil Society* (1767), Herder identifies a specific kind of slavery emerging in the modern state. Instead of liberating man from the bonds of nature, the advancement of technology has made certain key human virtues redundant. Instead of manliness, courage and self-reliance, there is now extensive reliance on technology and guidance from superiors. The invention of the gun, for example, has turned armies into mere *puppets of movement* (TTPH, 316). The situation is aggravated by the new obsession with luxury as the source of state income and ultimately the basis for technological achievement and military prowess (TTPH, 318, 325). Far from supporting true political liberty, these developments facilitate the transformation of the entire society into a "machine" led by one. Philosophy being busy undermining the existing moral principles in the name of its lofty ideals, there is no power to resist this process: there are no citizens in modern states any longer, but only "cogs in a machine", a "forced-together pile", remaining in place "from *fear* or *habit* or *luxury*" (TTPH, 319).

Finally, Herder has no patience for the view that modern commerce in combination with an abstract morality would directly facilitate achieving peace in Europe, or indeed, the world. Throughout his *oeuvre*, Herder emphasizes that European states are grounded "in a system of military and religious conquest" (BBH, 106). Even though a certain equilibrium, called "balance of power", has been achieved in Europe, the states continue "rubbing" against each other, waging "passionless" wars (TTPH, 326; cf. BBH, 337; LAH, 379). Drawing on the abbé de Raynal's critique of the modern states system and colonialism,[5] Herder points out that a new cycle of warfare has been launched in modern times, one in which commerce, too, is becoming a reason for war. Precisely thanks to their abstract and "refined" quality, modern moral idioms can easily be used to justify new versions of Machiavellian politics (TTPH, 349).[6] Referring explicitly to Frederick the Great's Voltairean anti-Machiavellian Machiavellianism, Herder concludes: "The universal dress of *philosophy* and *love of humankind* can hide oppressions, attacks on the true, personal *freedom of human beings* and *lands*, *citizens*, and *peoples*, of just the sort Cesare Borgia would wish for" (TTPH, 351).

Herder's Critique of Kant

In his magisterial *Ideas for a Philosophy of History of Mankind* (1784–1791), Herder also directly challenges some of the key ideas of his erstwhile teacher Immanuel Kant's famous *Idea for a Universal History with a Cosmopolitan Purpose* (1784).[7] Herder passionately rejects the anthropological picture that Kant presents in this essay, particularly his argument of human "unsocial sociability". But most outrageous for Herder is not Kant's anthropology, but his contention that "a human being is an animal who needs a master":

5 Herder's engagement with Raynal is highlighted by Proß (1987b, 850, 862–863) and Dreitzel (1987, 276–277).

6 For an analysis of the appropriation of the term *friend of mankind* for war propaganda and crude power politics during the Seven Years' War, see Sonenscher (2007, 189–199).

7 Kant, in his turn, wrote two critical reviews of Herder's first and second volume of *Ideas* in 1784 and 1785 respectively, in the second one directly answering some of Herder's critique. He also elaborated his alternative anthropological view in a separate piece entitled *Conjectures about the Beginning of Human History* (1786) and delineated his own account of teleology in nature and history in his Third Critique. On Kant-Herder debate see Irmscher (1987); Zammito (1992); Reiss (2000); Proß (1987a, 155, 27–28, 1023).

> The maxim, that "man is an animal who needs a master when he lives with others of his species, so that he may attain happiness and fulfil his destiny on earth" is both facile and noxious as a fundamental principle of a philosophy of history. (IPH, 323; IPGM, 368–369)

A number of commentators have suggested that Herder's retort does not do justice to Kant's argument. First, Kant is not defending absolute monarchy, but a republican constitution guaranteeing equal freedom under external laws to all citizens (Kant 1784a, 45–46; cf. Reiss 2000, 198). Second, Kant's argument is not that a rightful master (just civil constitution) would make humans happy, but that only in such a setting would it be possible for humans to fully realize their moral potential and thereby create a "realm of ends" (Wood 1999, 226–233). Third, Kant explicitly warns in the *Idea for a Universal History* that this kind of constitution is also "the most difficult" and the last to be achieved, because it would require not only overall enlightenment and "a good will" from the rulers to implement it, but also—and this is the crucial claim of the essay—the creation of an international state with coercive powers, in order to tame the "masters" that men would necessarily have to have (Kant 1784a, 46–47; cf. Guyer 2009).

What these commentaries on Kant-Herder debate tend to neglect, however, is that there is a fundamental disagreement between these two authors on the nature of republicanism. In his critique of Kant, Herder is protesting against Kant's Hobbesian concept of a representative republic, and more specifically, against his idea of modern civilized European monarchies as necessary steps towards the realization of modern liberty and international justice. In Herder's view, it is rather the republican tradition in medieval European towns from which European traditions of political liberty and pacific emulation originate (IPGM, 854–862, 891–898). Although Herder acknowledges that modern monarchies have adopted some of the republican principles (first of all, the rule of law), they are built on military foundations, which is also reflected in their machine-like social structure which excludes citizens' participation in public life. Uniting such states into "Achaian leagues of the rulers of the world", in Herder's view, is essentially self-contradictory. Although the current balance of power in Europe may guarantee a certain longevity to states, it would ultimately be unsustainable unless the foundations of modern republics are changed (SW, 455).

Second, while it is true that Kant can hardly be accused of presenting the republican state form and peace as directly conducive to virtue and happiness, Herder has a point in insisting that neither morality nor happiness depend straightforwardly on the state form or even international condition. Virtue and happiness, as we have seen, are relative concepts for Herder. There are hence plural forms of being virtuous and happy. Although he agrees that forms of government strongly mould the subjects' character and living conditions, this influence is not absolute in his view. In principle, there is a possibility of "pursuing the human goods [of activity and affection]" in all kinds of constitutional settings. It is this pursuit, precisely, that makes it possible to be happy, and hence it is possible to be happy in all forms of government, even despotic ones. Indeed, Herder is worried that an inverse relationship might obtain; the more the states are turned into "machines", the less opportunities for pursuing virtue and happiness there are for the citizens (IPGM, 333–334, cf. 360–362, 366–368). This applies also to cosmopolitanism which in its generalized form is very likely not to have any real motivational power or efficacy: "the inundated heart of the idle cosmopolitan [...] offers shelter to nobody" (IPGM, 333; IPH, 309).

Third, Herder is highly critical of Kant's sharp contrast between the character of the ruler and the subjects. In Kant's *Idea for a Universal History* subjects are described as self-seeking animals, fundamentally unable to govern themselves. Unless contained by coercive laws enforced by an executive power, they are unable to achieve social peace, let alone cultivate morality. True, they are able to gradually "enlighten themselves" about the true foundations of political order, yet this is a rational enlightenment, unable to have any real impact on action. The rulers, by contrast, need to be able to tame themselves so as to establish a constitution that would guarantee freedom to all. For Herder, this account reveals Kant's Hobbesian leanings, according to which the representatives of the people have no other limits to their power than moral ones. In Herder's view, even though abuse of power is endemic in human history, it is no reason to give up on searching for constitutional ways of limiting the possibility for the abuse of power by those in power. Representation by a ruler, Herder maintains, is symbolic, not substantial. A ruler gives a symbolic unity to the nation, necessary in particular in external relations. Yet wise constitutions are such that also limit the possible "damage to the machine" that a bad ruler might do (SW, 453).

In contrast to Kant, Herder hence rejects the Hobbesian notion of sovereignty, supporting a classical concept of republic, in which political power is divided between different bodies. At the same time, Herder by no means holds that constitutional mechanisms alone would be able to sustain lawful government, highlighting the responsibility of the people itself for the way in which it is governed: "All in all it is worthwhile accepting as a general principle of history that it is impossible to oppress [*unterdrücken*] a people unless it is willing to let itself be oppressed" (IMPG, 367; cf. SW, 457). Nature has left it entirely up to humans themselves, Herder argues, how they construct "the finest product of their art, the state", and each nation has had to bear the consequences of their forefathers' wisdom or ignorance in doing so (IMPG, 367). At the same time, there is always also a possibility, and indeed, an obligation, to "improve things". While it is true that humans in modern Europe seem to "require a master" more than ever, it is possible also to "undo the damage" resulting from the modern social and cultural developments, using the positive means (*Hülfsmittel*) that human culture provides (SW, 456). "We are certainly tied to a chain of tradition binding so many centuries [...]", Herder insists in an unpublished early version of *Ideas for a Philosophy of History*, "yet humankind [*Menschheit*] with all its rights and duties remains eternally young [...], shakes off the old prejudices and learns, even if against its will, reason and truth" (SW, 457).

While Kant and Herder hence both view republic as the state form most conducive to human freedom and agency, they disagree about its nature, foundations and moral status. For Herder, the republican form of government is no unconditional good, since it is not necessary for achieving virtue or happiness, nor is it sustainable unless supported by moral sentiments. Herder argues that it is a historical ideal first conceived in ancient Greek city-states and transformed successfully in the conditions of medieval municipal government. He believes it has lost nothing of its appeal in modern times, and needs to adapt itself to the Christian principle of human equality (IMPGM, 854–856; LAH, 375–376). Yet although Herder makes calls for the people to assert its agency and supports abolishing all kinds of political privileges, he remains silent about the republic's precise constitutional form in modern Europe. He also shared the widespread worry about whether it can also be successfully established in a large country. Some hope in this respect came with the French Revolution. As Herder's unpublished manuscripts for *Letters on the Advancement of Humanity* reveal, in the early 1790s he followed France's attempt to create a republic with ardent sympathetic interest (BBH, 785).

Herder's rejection of Kant's mature cosmopolitanism as developed in various writings in the 1790s proceeds from the same foundations. In 1797, in the tenth collection of his *Letters for the Advancement of Humanity*, Herder responds to Kant's *Perpetual Peace* (1795) and its followers (cf. Pizer 2007; Nakhimovsky 2011, 36–37). One of the key ideas of Kant's essay is famously that the only form of government conforming to reason is the republican one, and that the latter is also inherently conducive to peace. Without directly naming Kant, Herder again takes issue with those authors who present the republican form of government as an unqualified good. First, he points out that it is impossible to imagine that the rulers—in a republican form of state, accordingly the people or their representatives—would really pursue peace unless they develop appropriate sentiments favouring peace: "the tree of peace [would] bloom [only] for the nations with firm, inextirpable roots *from within to outside*" (LAH, 403). Second, he warns against the absolutization of republicanism as an abstract ideal. "The so-called best form of government", he argues, has not and cannot be discovered, as it needs to conform itself to the national character and circumstances in which the nation finds itself. Disregarding this fact, the republican ideal would only too conveniently be misappropriated for justifying revolutionary republican imperialism. "Cosmopolitan history" seemingly introduces "a nobler yardstick of merit" than the "one of naked reason of state", but in fact calls into being a new kind of deceptive universalist "phantom", one leading to "the *calculation of undertakings towards a future better republic, towards the best form of the state, indeed of all states*" (LAH, 413; BBH, 734). In order to guard against this kind of republican imperialism, Herder suggests, it should rather be a principle that each nation must itself, "by its own hands", "pick the roses of the wreath of *freedom*" (LAH, 413; BBH, 734).

Herder's Account of Cosmopolitanism

Herder's critique of various contemporary forms of cosmopolitanism stems from his non-cognitivist, sentimental account of moral epistemology and psychology, and affirms the value of human natural sociability. It also simultaneously reveals a commitment to republicanism as the most desirable form of government in Europe, insofar as it is grounded in people's moral sentiments and pursued and developed according to local traditions. Indeed, Herder can legitimately be described as a linguistic-cultural "nationalist" and a "republican patriot" (cf. Beiser 1992; Barnard 2003; Muthu 2003; Patten 2010; Spencer 2012). Yet particularly in his later work starting from *Ideas for the Philosophy of History of Mankind* (1784–1791), he also argues that these forms of loyalty can and must be combined with a strong commitment to international justice (cf. Beiser 1992, Forster 2002; Muthu 2003; Spencer 2012; Sikka 2012). Furthermore, as I shall attempt to show, Herder lays out this commitment in terms structurally resembling moral cosmopolitanism in its early, Stoic, form. In Herder's own words, we need to become "citizens, finally, of the great city of God on earth, governed, ordered and led by only one law, one daemon, the spirit of a universal reason and humanity" (BBH, 154). Like the Stoics, whom he quotes immediately after this statement, Herder links the ideal of world citizenship to the goal of passional enlightenment and "therapy of desire" (cf. Nussbaum 1997, 46). Yet while the Stoic ideal ultimately calls for removing the passions, Herder affirms the value of sentiments. Indeed, while Herder is painfully aware of the partial nature of our sentiments, he also paradoxically makes clear that the "single law" of "universal reason and humanity" is not accessible through reason alone. He lays out this ideal not in terms of a rational cognition of a universal law, but rather as an outcome of a learning process, which combines both rational as well as sentimental elements.[8] As an ethical principle, further, it is expressed in a striving for the neutralization of

8 I hence disagree with Nussbaum, who also invokes Herder's term of "purification" for describing a "globally sensitive" variety of patriotism, but criticizes Herder for

group myopia and fanaticism so as to develop adequate cross-cultural moral judgement and dependable "dispositions of peace" (BBH, 805).

Humanität

The conceptual linchpin of Herder's ethic of cosmopolitanism is his distinctive concept of *Humanität*. According to Hans Dietrich Irmscher's often quoted apt summary, this concept comprises three key components:

1. the general nature of man as a being that determines itself;
2. the particular realization of the possibilities of this general nature in a specific historical situation;
3. the historical task of the co-evolution of nations, involving the sublation of individuality in a world community characterized by solidarity (Irmscher 1994, 294; cf. Gaier 1996, 62; Adler 2009; Sikka 2012, 20).

All these three components are interconnected. Indeed, it is important to see that self-determination is the key element in this concept recurring in different forms and at different levels. First, Herder views human beings as cultural beings that create the conditions of their own existence. In contrast to animals, humans possess reason and language, and hence bring along everything "from themselves" (IMPG, 631). Second, he argues that humans consciously aim to create or transform these conditions according to their normative ideas (IMPG, 632). In each historical situation, hence, they not only unconsciously fit into, and develop, a common culture, but also consciously transform and reform it. Third, and this is Herder's argument about moral progress, it is possible to do so *ever more* consciously, indeed, to learn from history and hence also pursue a distinctive form of ethical world citizenship conducive to peace (IMPG, 671).

In *Ideas for a Philosophy of History* and *Letters for the Advancement of Humanity* Herder attempts to combine various contemporary idioms of

---

failing to specify the "moral sentiments that a [...] purified patriotism should call to aid" (Nussbaum 2008, 4).

system theory to create a unified account of the principles underlying natural as well as social order and thereby to explicate the possibility of such a learning process (see Proß 1987b, 723–746). His central contention is that multiple diverse individuals necessarily move towards ever higher degrees of systemic organization in their interaction (IMPG, 630). The progress of order, however, is not linear, but proceeds in a quasi-dialectical way. Different subsystems try to impose themselves on other subsystems, which leads to antagonism between them. Yet through this antagonism, governed by a logic of action and reaction, a "state of balance" is ultimately reached:

> Just as our gait is a constant falling to the right and left and yet we come further with each step: so is the progress of culture among human generations and whole peoples. We often try both extremes separately, until we reach the still middle, as the pendulum strikes out to both sides (IMPG, 655 [translation from Sikka 2012, 93]).

In Herder's view, the operation of this logic is observable in European history. Most tellingly, in Europe, the "barbaric system of war and conquest" is receding, together with the aggressive dispositions supporting it (LAH, 361–365; BBH, 763–768). The increasing order expresses itself in the growing commercial and cultural interaction and emulation between different nations as well as the increase of "art", including the art of government and technological mastery over the natural environment (IMPG, 639–646; BBH, 319–329). Borrowing the Kantian term "antagonism" to characterize his own distinctive view, Herder insists that humanity must reach a state of universal brotherhood of nations "through the inner laws of this species itself and the antagonism of its forces": "Certain fevers and stupidities of humanity *must* cease their ferment with the advance of the centuries and the life-ages" (LAH, 418; BBH, 741).

Herder's positive view of the developments in Europe in his later works is certainly quite different from the tenor of his discussion of European history in *This Too a Philosophy*. Yet it does not directly contradict his earlier critique of the various kinds of optimistic scenarios of "cosmopolitan history". As we saw before, even then Herder was not denying the epochal role of commerce and technology in changing the social and political environment in Europe as well as European and global international relations.

His point was to show that modernity was not living up to its high moral standards, and instead had created its own pathologies, such as modern abstract and motivationally inert morality, reason of state politics, colonialism, etc. In his later philosophy Herder becomes more optimistic about modern Europeans' ability to withstand these tendencies and makes it the central moral demand to do so. In an early unpublished manuscript of what became *Letters for the Advancement of Humanity*, Herder summarizes his views:

> [Humans] create ever more and better instruments for themselves; they even learn to use each other ever more and better as instruments. The power of mankind accordingly increases, even if the physical forces of individual humans remain the same. The ball of those to be driven forward becomes ever larger, while the machines that do so are ever more elaborate, complex, powerful and fast. Will the self-determination of a human being also be ever more rational, honest, good? It seems to me that it must become so, even though the *brutal* nature of our species is protesting and defending itself against it. (BBH, 804)

Sympathy, Reciprocity and Reiterative Universalism

Recent commentators have pointed to the crucial role that human sympathy for Herder plays in moving towards the ideal of peaceful international co-existence. How does Herder conceive of sympathy? Michael Frazer (2010, 148–149) has rightly pointed out that Herder views human sympathy (*Theilnehmung*, *Mitgefühl*) as continuous with the animal one, yet also as "different in kind", being present in, and hence necessarily modified by, human reflective awareness (*Besonnenheit*). As such, Frazer argues, Herder's notion of sympathy "operates also through the medium of ideas, [...] or even the imaginative reconstruction of another's experience [...]" (Frazer 2010, 150). It is this kind of imaginative sympathy that also provides a chance for intercultural human communication.

It is important to emphasize, however, that for Herder sympathy both unites *and* distances humans from each other. If activated through the sense of hearing—as animal sympathy in general—human sympathy encompasses all living beings, including all humans (IMPG, 157). If activated through our sense of sight or imagination, it is already much more dependent on the "delicacy of the physical frame" of the sympathizer, as well as on the degree of proximity between the sympathizer and the person being sympathized with (IMPG, 156). The effects of imaginative sympathy on intercultural communication are particulary ambivalent, as sympathy is precisely the medium for creating cultural communities, as well as for marking them off from each other. Indeed, it creates what could be labelled (inverting Kant's famous phrase) a distinctive kind of "sociable unsociability". In *This Too a Philosophy*, Herder writes: "Everything that is still *similar* with my nature, that can be *assimilated* to it, I covet, strive for, make my own. Beyond that, kind nature has armed me with *feelinglessness, coldness and* blindness; this can even become *contempt* and *disgust*" (TTPH, 297). Sympathy also gives rise to various partial opinions (always favourable to those who hold them), such as the idea of an "innate superiority" of one people over another, or a high vocation of a specific culture (LAH, 394–397; BBH, 698–702). When Frazer hence argues that sympathy for Herder "is a matter of imaginative projection of the self into the position of the other", thus bearing greater resemblance to Adam Smith's than Hume's notion of sympathy (Frazer 2010, 154), he understates the degree to which both Smith and Herder view imaginative sympathy as reflecting and reinforcing, rather than correcting our natural partiality.[9]

At the same time, Herder holds that it is possible to extend our sympathy so as to broaden the horizon of sociability. There is a distinct term that Herder invents precisely for describing the mental process necessary for that: *Einfühlung* or "feeling into the situation of another". In anglophone literature, it is commonly translated as "empathy" or even "sympathy" (Frazer 2010, 154–155), hence collapsing Herder's two distinct notions into one. One could indeed characterize *Einfühlung* as a type of sympathy, insofar as they both involve imagination as well as imaginative sharing of an emotion of another person. Yet this neglects the fact that as Herder himself lays it out, *Einfühlung* is a highly complex mental process, consisting

9 On Adam Smith's notion of sympathy, see Forman-Barzilai (2010).

of many stages. It is opposed not only to abstract characterization, but also to natural sympathy. In contrast to the latter, it is not an "imaginative insight" or "exercise", but a conscious will and effort to understand what is different from us:

> The whole living painting of mode of life, habits, needs, peculiarities of land and climate, would have to be *added* or to have *preceded;* one would have first to *feel into* [*hineinfühlen*] a nation, in order to feel a *single one* of its *inclinations* or *actions all together*, one would have to *find* a single word, to *imagine* everything in fullness—or one reads—*a word*! (TTPH 291–292. (I have slightly modified the translation [EP].))

Instead of hence sympathizing with a situation in a foreign culture straight away (imagining from the horizon of our own life experience what it would be like to be in another's situation), we first need to prepare for that. We imaginatively make ourselves familiar with its various aspects, which Herder describes as "feel ourselves into [*hineinfühlen*] this situation" (TTPH, 291). Frazer rightly points out that in Herder's view we can only feel what we basically can recognize as a human feeling, one that we have a "disposition for [...], if only time, opportunity [would allow it to us]" (TTPH, 292; cf. Frazer 2010, 154–156). Hence it is indeed "we" whom we rediscover in an alien culture. In order to do so, however, we need to consciously bracket our own life experience and tastes, including moral sentiments, and study the actions and various kinds of cultural works of a particular nation as expressions of the distinctive kinds of sentiments, aspirations and tastes that these nations could possibly have developed in their particular natural and historical situation (LAH 396; BBH, 700; BBH, 338; TTPH, 285). It is *Einfühlung*, not sympathy, which would make us truly appreciate, and respect, moral pluralism.

Justice and Reiterative Universalism

While insisting on the need to cultivate sympathy through *Einfühlung*, Herder harbours no illusions with regard cultivated sympathy's ability to overcome our strongest selfish inclinations:

> In novels we cry for the butterfly whose wings get wetted by the rain; in conversations we bubble over with great sentimental dispositions—and for this moral corruption of which all evil arises, we have no eye. We slaughter to greed, to pride, to our slothful boredom a thousand sacrificial victims who do not cost us a single tear. [...] Or one expresses disapproval of what happened in Peru, Ismail, Warsaw, while, as soon as our prejudice, our greed for gain, finds a role in the matter, one wishes similar and worse with grim anger. (LAH, 384; BBH, 686; cf. IPGM, 159)

As Herder states in *Ideas*, "man's sympathy cannot [...] be extended to everything indiscriminately", and as such it is an "uncertain and unreliable guide for so restricted and complex a creature" as man "in matters that are more remote and less familiar to him" (IPH, 270; IMPG, 159). For this reason, he argues, "Mother Nature" has placed in human beings a separate and "safer guiding rule" (*Regel*), the one of "justice [*Billigkeit*] and truth". This rule is "written even in the breast of the human monster [*Unmensch*], for when he [the monster] eats the flesh of others, he would expect to be eaten in his turn" (IPH, 270; IMPG, 159). It is grounded in our special physical and physiological constitution (erect posture and the organization of our senses) and consists in our ability to detect relations of symmetry and identity. In the moral sphere, it draws together "[our] various interwoven tendencies under a guiding rule [...] *Do not unto others what you would not wish them to do unto you; but what you expect others to do unto you, do unto them too*" (IPH, 270; IMPG, 159).

As Wolfgang Proß has pointed out, by linking this Golden Rule to the notion of justice [*Billigkeit*], Herder restates the Ciceronian and Grotian "sense of equity [*aequitas*]" as the basis of all natural law and thereby directly responds to Rousseau's critique of natural law in the *Discourse on the Origins of Inequality* (Proß 1987b, 301–304). Indeed, while Grotius emphasized the "sense of equity" as an attribute of the will rather than of reason, Herder regards it as a fundamental rule governing both our reason and will. As such, the Golden Rule for Herder serves as the very cornerstone of "all the laws of man, as well as those of international and animal society" (*alles Menschen-, Völker- und Tierrecht*) (IMPG, 159). We can witness its operation everywhere: "the law of justice [*Billigkeit*] is foreign to no nation" (LAH, 417; BBH, 739–740).

Thus, while Herder emphasizes the irreducibly individual quality of each culture in history, he also believes that there is one basic universal rule of justice common to all nations. Does it not make him a "covering-law universalist", after all? Even if he does not derive it rationally, he views it as "written in the [human] breast" and dictated by the human constitution. Yet he also emphasizes that this rule is necessarily indeterminate. It does not say anything specific about what is valuable in life, and it is often counteracted by various kinds of opinions of the differential worth of human beings and communities. Furthermore, it refers only to the fundamental condition of reciprocity among human beings, calling for correcting our partial and biased view of intersubjective matters, and for implementing certain standards of propriety in our own conduct.

Just like reason is one and the same in all human beings, and yet "something acquired" (*etwas Vernommenes*) (IMPG, 144), so are the more substantive moral norms (*Sitten*) worked out by humans in specific natural and historical contexts. Our understandings of what is valuable in life reflect these contexts, while this connection is often hidden to us. As we have already said, virtue and happiness are relative concepts for Herder. Nevertheless, human actions conforming to all these different norms Herder views as expressions of human freedom (IPH, 265–266; IMPG, 145–146). For example, a Greek patriot sacrificing his life for his city-state would follow his "sociable inclinations" and "capacities" in their distinctive cultural forms, overcoming simultaneously certain other, more brutal forces (like fear of death). In so doing, he both "determines himself" and expresses (and thereby both affirms and transforms) the norms of his society (IPH, 267; IMPG, 148).

Throughout most of history, humans have developed these particular *morals* (*Sitten*) pre-reflectively within smaller culturally bound societies. As the history of moral philosophy reveals, it has also been possible to reflect critically on these norms in the light of their conformity to the principle of reciprocity and a generalized understanding of the fundamental moral equality of all human beings. Thanks to increased communication and interdependence between human communities, it has become particularly pertinent to do so in modern times. There is now a direct need for negotiating the relationships between human communities. Herder suggests that we become capable of doing so by engaging with philosophy, poetry and history in a reflective and sentimental way. This is precisely the aim and strategy of his later writings such as *Letters for the Advancement of Humanity* (1793–1797) or *Adrastea* (1801).

It is also here that reiterative universalism comes in. In Herder's view, in our search for more specific rules that would be binding to all of humanity, we can only proceed by generalizing from experience, moving case by case. We also have to use all our different capacities, including, prominently, sympathy, in order to do so. We notice that examples of human goodness and happiness in history bring us joy, just like examples of human cruelty bring us sorrow or make us shudder. It is because we take into account the joy and sorrow of all parties involved in an action. Indeed, in imagining the "situation" of different nations we cannot help noticing: "No human being can live *for himself alone*, much as he might wish to do so. The capacities that he attains, the virtues or vices which he acts out, to a lesser or greater degree will bring pain or joy to others" (BBH, 124; cf. LAH, 423; BBH, 750). At the same time, a sustained engagement with history would also convince us that there is a measure of "justice" in it, one that corresponds to our human understanding of just deserts as expressed in the indeterminate "rule of justice" in our breast. Herder calls this principle by the name of a Greek goddess: *Nemesis*. Nemesis, Herder explains, is the principle that demonstrates that no single act of cruelty remains unpunished, just like every act of human goodness is amply paid back (LAH, 413; BBH, 735; LAH 421–422; BBH, 747).

Modern history, for Herder, hence has to combine sympathetic understanding (*Einfühlung*) and moral judgement (LAH, 399; BBH, 708). This has implications for our understanding of international justice. Instead of rationally positing, and demanding recognition for, a certain number of abstract "rights", we should aspire to a generalized view of right and wrong, based on both our various sentimental reactions and an estimation of the overall consequences of these actions for all parties involved: "[...] we cannot cut ourselves off from *human feeling* [*Menschengefühl*] when we write or read history; history's highest *interest*, its *value* rests on this human sensibility [*Menschenempfindung*], the *rule of right and wrong*" (LAH, 411–412; BBH, 733).

This is Herder's key response against Rousseau's critique of the sense of equity as a sublime, yet motivationally inert "maxime of reasoned justice". The indeterminate rule of reciprocity acquires substantive content through reflective and sentimental engagement with empirical examples of human action. Thereby we develop not only our understanding of the rules of justice, but also a disposition to follow these very rules in our own action (BBH, 671–674; LAH, 380–383; cf. Sikka 2012, 32–33). At the same time, emphasizing the importance of human sociability and agency as well as the pluralism of human conceptions of virtue and happiness, Herder does not think we have equally strong obligations to all members of human society, or indeed, that we would need to promote the happiness of everyone everywhere. As we saw, understanding the complex ways of life in a different culture requires *Einfühlung*. This kind of "feeling into the situation or way-of-life of another", however, does not create any motivation to actively participate in or contribute to this way of life. Rather, it promotes appreciation of, and respect for, differences and cultural self-determination. In cases of manifest human unhappiness, however, our emotional responses would also be likely to prompt us to action. In Herder's view, we empathize with, and approve of, particularly the victims' resentment, as based on the rule of justice, while we also find certain satisfaction from observing the operation of *Nemesis* in history.

Indeed, Herder particularly emphasizes our responsibility with regard to contributing to removing the "causes of unhappiness". In contrast to the positive ideal of happiness, the cases of unhappiness are reiterative and hence relatively uniform in Herder's view. Wars, persecutions, cruelty, oppression and enslavement are evidently conducive to human misery. As Sonia Sikka rightly points out, it does not matter for Herder whether these acts are directed against external groups or members of one's own cultural community (Sikka 2012, 18–19). Morally condemning these cases is important in Herder's view because it supports the victims' case and cry for justice. In the final letter of *Letters for the Advancement of Humanity* Herder writes:

> We cannot be happy or entirely worthy and morally good as long as, for example, a single slave is unhappy through human beings' guilt, for the vices and bad habits that make him unhappy have effect on us as well or derive from us. (LAH, 423; BBH, 749–750)

This emphasis on the interconnectedness of humanity and human history certainly exceeds the minimalist demand of respecting national self-determination usually associated with Herder. Furthermore, although it does not directly contradict the latter, it stands in obvious tension with it. National self-determination is not an absolute value; it has to be negotiated with the demands of justice by individual victims of injustice. It acts as a barrier against direct use of force as well as grand plans of liberation, yet does not preclude international solidarity or solidarity with individuals and social groups beyond national or state borders. Herder does not provide any further guidance as to how much involvement or intervention is really possible or desirable in a foreign cultural context. What he does make clear is that there is a growing interdependence of humans in history that creates a chance for human self-determination at a new level. In contrast to early societies, the principles for international interaction now develop reflectively; thanks to humans' ever more widening scope of self-knowledge, it is possible to consciously contribute to this process. At the minimal level, hence, international justice would entail searching for "the rules of right and wrong", as derived from the victims' and our own moral reactions to historical experiences of misery caused by other human beings. At a more substantial level, it would also entail counteracting our established and necessarily partial understandings of the higher "value" of our own culture by cultivating enlarged sympathy and understanding for foreign cultures and life situations within them.

Moral Traps and Self-purification

Alongside proposing a positive view of history's vocation in promoting an understanding of the principles of justice, Herder also warns against history falling captive to various kinds of ideological self-deceptions. Essential aspects of "human sensibility", Herder maintains, are self-reflection, self-criticism and, indeed, self-purification. With all our respect for humanity, it is important to accept that humans are necessarily prone to delusion (*Wahn*) and prejudices (*Vorurteile*) (BBH, 244). Herder is well aware that the process of self-purification can only be gradual and never complete, as human inclinations will remain the same at a deeper level. He insists, however, that this is no reason to give up.

As we have seen already, our delusions are characteristically strong in the area of the things relating to ourselves—our person, rank, nation (BBH, 244). In Herder's view, there is a certain kind of reiteration in these instances of delusion. Hence he warns that what we should primarily guard against in searching for the "rules of right and wrong" is missionary patriotism. Nearly every ancient nation, Herder argues, has succumbed to a "mania of pride about the fatherland, religion, lineage and ancestors" (LAH, 375; BBH, 333). As the case of the Hebrew, Greek and Roman patriotism reveals, this mania is prone to develop particularly strong in those communities which aspire to higher moral standards and regard themselves as chosen by the god(s) (BBH, 332–333; LAH 375; BBH, 773; LAH, 412).

The same kind of tendency of self-glorification, Herder points out in one of the final letters of *Letters for the Advancement of Humanity*, exists in modern times. Modern states are engrossed in a vicious military and commercial rivalry, hence directly working against the cultivation of enlarged sympathy by their subjects. Furthermore, different types of sentiments have evolved that support this logic, rather than criticize and correct it. Modern national historiographies accept the "coldest calculations of reason of state" as an appropriate way of looking at international relations, taking a cynical view of human nature and human interaction in general. They are now often "warmed up" by an appeal to patriotism, so that patriotism, even moral patriotism, has all too often turned into a cloak for the "most tangled, most loathsome state interests, of personal presumptions and of state trickeries" (BBH, 733; LAH, 412). Unmasking and criticizing such a way of thought and view of history is paramount for spreading true "human sensibility". What is needed in modern times, in particular, Herder writes, paraphrasing and developing Gotthold Efraim Lessing's outline of freemasonic cosmopolitanism in his *Masonic Dialogues* (1776–1778), is an understanding of "when patriotism stops to be a virtue" (BBH, 137).

It is in this context, now, that we also have to place Herder's critique of Kant's account of cosmopolitanism. Even though Kant's theory involves a sharp critique of the modern reason of state thinking, it is unable to provide resources for fighting against it in Herder's view. Kant hopes to solve human problems with the help of a universal institutional solution, neglecting the fact that institutions need to be grounded in sentiments and underestimating the importance of cultural self-determination for nations. Without an adequate "human sensibility", the ideal of perpetual peace is likely to be abused in international politics. We have already seen that Herder is deeply suspicious of the humans' ability to determine themselves merely by reference to abstract universal rules or ideals (cf. BBH, 248–249). He keeps emphasizing that "the names of 'freedom', 'enlightenment', 'highest happiness of the peoples'" can deceive so as to make one disregard the distinctive concerns, experiences and perspectives of the oppressed nations, motivating misguided plans of liberation (LAH, 413; BBH, 773). As we saw above, Herder includes Kant's idea of a "perfectly just constitution" among such phantom ideas, warning against its possible abuse in the form of republican imperialism. Herder's own view is that an essential precondition of the successful application of these rules, next to enlarged sympathy, is the development of self-criticism, and the corresponding striving to reflectively purify one's beliefs and sentiments from the unwelcome impact of the human passions (*Leidenschaften*) and delusion. It is this complex kind of "sensus humanitatis [sense of humanity], *sense* [*Sinn*] *and sympathy* [*Mitgefühl*] *for the whole of humanity*" that is the best kind of bulwark against the danger of aggressive moral absolutism (LAH, 420; BBH, 742). In what is quite evidently a direct rejoinder to Kant's moral philosophy, Herder contrasts this sense with all these attempts that wish to associate moral law with only one single human moral capacity:

> [The spirit of history] knows that in human nature the principles of *sensuality*, of *imagination*, of *selfishness*, of *honor*, of *sympathy with others*, of *godliness*, of the *moral sense*, of *faith*, etc. do not dwell in separated compartments, but that in a living organization that gets stimulated from several sides, many of them, often all, cooperate in a living manner. […] Let each human being chew as he can, history treats human beings not as word-mongers or critics, but as agents of a moral law of nature which speaks in all of them, which initially warns gently, then punishes harder, and richly rewards every good disposition through itself and its consequences. Does this *spirit of human history* not appeal to you? (LAH, 415; BBH, 736–737; cf. LAH 423; BBH, 750)

Viewing Herder's opposition to Kant's political cosmopolitanism in the light of his emphasis on the human propensity to self-delusion, it becomes evident that Herder's rejection of Kant's cosmopolitanism is not a rejection of cosmopolitanism as such, but stems from his alternative theories of republicanism and cosmopolitanism, which in turn are grounded in his account of human moral psychology. In *Letters for the Advancement of Humanity* Herder elaborates his claim that purely institutional ways of resolving the problem of international antagonism are doomed to failure. Rather than enabling humans to develop moral principles, these institutions would not be able to sustain themselves, becoming vehicles of new kinds of oppression. Hence, before we can devise any substantial institutional frameworks for regulating international relations, Herder argues, we need to develop human "dispositions of peace" (*Friedens-Gesinnungen*) (LAH, 404; BBH, 720). These dispositions would follow the overlapping consensus of different nations regarding the ways in which "nations should take effect on each other" (LAH, 380; BBH, 114), while also directly informing people's moral judgement (sentiments) as well as action. They include "horror of war", "reduced respect for heroic glory", "horror of false statecraft", "purified patriotism" (including self-contained, stable feeling of national worth), a "*common feeling* so that every nation feels itself into the position of every other one", including an "indignation of all nations" against those violating the authentic "unifying spirit of commerce", and finally, "love of useful activity" in promoting human well-being (LAH, 404–409; BBH, 720–726).

Conclusion

Michael Walzer's reiterative universalism is opposed to strictly rationalist forms of universalism that affirm moral cognitivism, purely principle-based moral motivation and the existence of *transcendent* universal norms or values. Yet as a form of universalism, it is compatible with a concept of universal moral community bent on following "reiteratively" universal norms. As we have seen, Herder articulates a version of an ethic for such a community, one based on noncognitivist, sentimental moral epistemology and psychology and an account of the deeply contextual nature of morality. These foundations also ground Herder's theories of republicanism and cosmopolitanism, ruling out the veneration and pursuit of republican or cosmopolitan institutions as self-sufficient universal goals. In this article I have focused on Herder's cosmopolitan ethic in particular. I have attempted to show that its essential mental preconditions are *Einfühlung*, sympathy and an indeterminate, yet universal "rule of justice", while its core elements include self-reflective and self-critical "purification" of sentiments and the "dispositions of peace".

Herder's account of "weak cosmopolitanism" raises an array of further questions. In particular, one cannot avoid comparing Herder's diagnosis of, and proposed cure for, the modern European predicament with the historical developments after him. Herder's warnings against the rise of republican imperialism and modern military and commercial patriotism are astonishingly astute in hindsight, while he seems not to have been able to recognize what further legitimacy and appeal this form of patriotism would gain through being combined with linguistic-cultural national identity. His emphasis on the need to combine constitutional mechanisms and sentimental foundations in republican forms of government may be apposite nevertheless. Even more important, his account of the sentimental foundations or preconditions of peace seems to have materialized to a high degree in the public opinion of European countries. But is it the "dispositions of peace" which have led to peace or rather peace which has led to the cultivation of the "dispositions of peace"? How deeply engrained are, or indeed, can be, these principles? Furthermore, as we have seen, Herder also insists on a solidarity with victims of injustice with all over the world. If negative justice alone would not do, what is the appropriate global ethic for a "union for peace" such as the European Union? Emphasizing the importance of both national self-determination as well as humanitarian solidarity, Herder remains ambivalent about the ways and prospects of European, and indeed, global, atonement (LAH, 418; BBH, 740–741, 777–778). With the view to his own deep appreciation of the complexity of the human world, however, it is hardly appropriate to blame him for this ambivalence.

Acknowledgement

Research for this essay has been funded by the Estonian Science Foundation Grant No. 8887, and the Target Financed Program No. SF0180128s08 and Institutional Research Funding project IUT20-39.

References

Adler, Hans, 2009. "Herder's concept of humanity". In: Hans Adler and Wulf Koepke (eds.), 2009. *A companion to the works of Johann Gottfried Herder*. Rochester, NY: Camden House, 93–116.

Appiah, Kwame Anthony, 2007. *Cosmopolitanism: Ethics in a world of strangers*. New York: Penguin Books.

Appiah, Kwame Anthony, 2005. *The ethics of identity*. Princeton, NJ: Princeton University Press.

Barnard, F.M., 2003. *Herder on nationality, humanity, and history*. Montreal and Kingston: McGill-Queen's University Press.

Beiser, Frederick C., 1992. *Enlightenment, revolution, and romanticism: The genesis of modern German political thought, 1790–1800*. Cambridge, MA: Harvard University Press.

Berlin, Isaiah, 1980. "Vico and Herder". In: Isaiah Berlin, 2000. *Three critics of the Enlightenment: Vico, Hamann, Herder*. Ed. Henry Hardy. Princeton, NJ: Princeton University Press, 3–242.

Brown, Eric and Pauline Kleingeld, 2006. "Cosmopolitanism". *Stanford Encyclopedia of Philosophy*. 2002 winter edition, subst. rev. autumn 2006. Ed. Edward N. Zalta. Available at: http://plato.stanford.edu/entries/cosmopolitanism/. Accessed 7 October 2012.

Dreitzel, Horst, 1987. "Herders politische Konzepte". In: Gerhard Sauder (ed.), 1987. *Johann Gottfried Herder, 1744–1803*. Hamburg: Meiner, 266–298.

Eggel, Dominic, Andre Liebich and Deborah Mancini-Griffoli, 2007. "Was Herder a nationalist?". *The Review of Politics*, 69(1), 48–78.

Evrigenis, Ioannis D. and Daniel Pellerin, 2004. "Introduction". In: Johann Gottfried von Herder, 2004. *Another philosophy of history and selected political writings*.

Ed. Ioannis D. Evrigenis and Daniel Pellerin. Indianapolis and Cambridge: Hackett, ix–xxxix.

Fénelon, François de Salignac de la Mothe-, 1699/1994. *The adventures of Telemachus, son of Ulysses*. Ed. and trans. Patrick Riley. Cambridge: Cambridge University Press.

Ferguson, Adam, 1767/1995. *An essay on the history of civil society*. Ed. Fania Oz–Salzberger. Cambridge: Cambridge University Press.

Forman-Barzilai, Fonna, 2010. *Adam Smith and the circles of sympathy: Cosmopolitanism and moral theory*. Cambridge: Cambridge University Press.

Forster, Michael N., 2002. "Introduction". In: Johann Gottfried von Herder, 2002. *Philosophical writings*. Ed. Michael N. Forster. Cambridge: Cambridge University Press, vii–xxxv.

Frazer, Michael L., 2010. *The Enlightenment of sympathy: Justice and moral sentiments in the eighteenth century*. Oxford: Oxford University Press.

Gaier, Ulrich, 1996. "Von nationalen Klassik zur Humanität: Konzepte der Vollendung bei Herder". In: *Regine Otto (ed.), 1996. Nationen* und *Kulturen: Zum 250. Geburtstag Johann Gottfried Herders. Würzburg: Königshausen* and *Neumann,* 49–64.

Gutmann, Amy, 2001. "Introduction". In: Michael Ignatieff, 2001. *Human rights as politics and idolatry*. Ed. Amy Gutmann. Princeton, NJ: Princeton University Press, vii–xxviii.

Guyer, Paul, 2009. "The crooked timber of mankind". In: Amélie Oksenberg Rorty and James Schmidt (eds.), 2009. *Kant's* Idea for a universal history with a cosmopolitan aim: *A critical guide*. Cambridge: Cambridge University Press, 129–149.

Heinz, Marion 1991. "Die Bestimmung des Menschen: Herder contra Mendelssohn". In: Beate Niemeyer and Dirk Schütze (eds.), 1991. *Philosophie der Endlichkeit: Festschrift für Erich Christian Schröder zum 65. Geburtstag*. Würzburg: Königshausen and Neumann, 263–285.

Heinz, Marion, 1994. "Historismus oder Metaphysik? Zu Herders Bückeburger Geschichtsphilosophie". In: Martin Bollacher, 1994. *Johann Gottfried Herder: Geschichte und Kultur*. Würzburg: Königshausen and Neumann, 75–85.

Herder, Johann Gottfried von, 1774a. "This too a philosophy for the formation of humanity [an early introduction]". In: Johann Gottfried von Herder, 2002. *Philosophical writings*. Ed. Michael N. Forster. Cambridge: Cambridge University Press, 268–271 [quoted as TTPHEI].

Herder, Johann Gottfried von, 1774b. "This too a philosophy for the formation of humanity". In: Johann Gottfried von Herder, 2002. *Philosophical writings*. Ed. Michael N. Forster. Cambridge: Cambridge University Press, 272–358 [quoted as TTPH].

Herder, Johann Gottfried von, 1784–1791/1877. *Ideen zur Philosophie der Geschichte der Menschheit: Herders Sämmtliche Werke*, vol. 13. Ed. Bernhard Suphan *et al.* Berlin: Weidemann'sche Buchhandlung [quoted as SW].

Herder, Johann Gottfried von, 1784–1791. *Ideen zur Philosophie der Geschichte der Menschheit.* In: Martin Bollacher (ed.), 1989. *Werke in zehn Bänden,* vol. 6. Ed. Günter Arnold *et al.* Frankfurt am Main: *Deutscher Klassiker Verlag* [quoted as IPGM].

Herder, Johann Gottfried von, 1778. "On the cognition and sensation of the human soul". In: Johann Gottfried von Herder, 2002. *Philosophical writings.* Ed. Michael N. Forster. Cambridge: Cambridge University Press, 187–246 [quoted as OCS].

Herder, Johann Gottfried von, 1793–1797. *Briefe zu Beförderung der Humanität.* In: Hans Dietrich Irmscher (ed.), 1991. *Werke in zehn Bänden*, vol. 7. Ed. Günter Arnold *et al.* Frankfurt am Main: Deutscher Klassiker Verlag [quoted as BBH].

Herder, Johann Gottfried von, 1784–1791. "Ideas for a philosophy of history". In: F.M. Barnard (ed.), 1965. *Herder's social and political thought: From Enlightenment to nationalism.* Oxford: Clarendon Press [quoted as IPH].

Herder, Johann Gottfried von, 1792. "Letters concerning the progress of humanity [excerpts on European politics]". In: Johann Gottfried von Herder, 2002. *Philosophical writings.* Ed. Michael N. Forster. Cambridge: Cambridge University Press, 361–369 [quoted as LPH].

Herder, Johann Gottfried von, 1793–1797. "Letters for the advancement of humanity [excerpts]". In: Johann Gottfried von Herder, 2002. *Philosophical writings.* Ed. Michael N. Forster. Cambridge: Cambridge University Press, 370–424 [quoted as LAH].

Hont, Istvan, 2005. *Jealousy of trade: International competition and the nation-state in historical perspective.* Cambridge, MA: The Belknap Press of Harvard University Press.

Ignatieff, Michael, 2001. *Human rights as politics and idolatry.* Ed. Amy Gutmann. Princeton, New Jersey: Princeton University Press, 3–98.

Irmscher, Hans Dieter, 1987. "Die geschichtsphilosophische Kontroverse zwischen Kant und Herder". In: Bernhard Gajek (ed.), 1987. *Hamann, Kant, Herder Acta des vierten Internationalen Hamann-Kolloquiums im Herder-Institut zu Marburg 1985.* Frankfurt am Main: Peter Lang.

Irmscher, Hans Dietrich, 1991. "Herder's Verständnis von 'Humanität'". In: Johann Gottfried von Herder, 1793–1797/1991. *Briefe zu Beförderung der Humanität.* Ed. Hans Dietrich Irmscher. *Werke in zehn Bänden*, vol. 7. Ed. Günter Arnold *et al.* Frankfurt am Main: Deutscher Klassiker Verlag, 817–840.

Kant, Immanuel, 1784. "Idea for a universal history with a cosmopolitan purpose". In: Immanuel Kant, 2000. *Political writings*. Ed. H.S. Reiss and trans. H.B. Nisbet. 2nd, enlarged edition. Cambridge: Cambridge University Press, 41–53.

Kant, Immanuel, 1795. "Perpetual peace: A philosophical sketch". In: Immanuel Kant, 2000. *Political writings*. Ed. H.S. Reiss and trans. H.B. Nisbet. 2nd, enlarged edition. Cambridge: Cambridge University Press, 93–130.

Kleingeld, Pauline 2012. *Kant and cosmopolitanism: The philosophical ideal of world citizenship*. Cambridge: Cambridge University Press.

Miller, David 2007. *National responsibility and global justice*. Oxford: Oxford University Press.

Muthu, Sankar, 2003. *Enlightenment against empire*. Princeton, NJ: Princeton University Press.

Nakhimovsky, Isaac, 2011. *The closed commercial state: Perpetual peace and commercial society from Rousseau to Fichte*. Princeton, NJ: Princeton University Press.

Nussbaum, Martha, C., 1996. "Patriotism and cosmopolitanism". In: Martha C. Nussbaum, 1996. *For love of country: Debating the limits of patriotism*. Ed. Joshua Cohen. Boston: Beacon Press, 2–17.

Nussbaum, Martha, C., 1997. "Kant and *cosmopolitanism*". In: James Bohman and Matthias Lutz-Bachmann (eds.), 1997. *Perpetual peace: Essays on Kant's cosmopolitan ideal*. Cambridge: MIT, 25–57.

Nussbaum, Martha, C., 2008. "Towards a globally sensitive patriotism". *Daedalus*, 137(3), 78–93. Available at: http://www.thefreelibrary.com. Accessed 19 April 2011 [page numbers according to the online version].

Patten, Alan, 2010. "The most natural state: Herder and nationalism". *History of Political Thought*, XXXI(4), 658–689.

Pizer, John, 2007. "The German response to Kant's essay on perpetual peace: Herder contra the Romantics". *The Germanic Review: Literature, Culture, Theory*, 87(4), 343–368.

Proß, Wolfgang, 1987a. "'Natur' und 'Geschichte' in Herders 'Ideen zur Philosophie der Geschichte der Menschheit' (Nachwort)". In: Johann Gottfried von Herder, 1784–1791/1984–1987. *Ideen zur Philosophie der Geschichte der Menschheit*. Ed. Wolfgang Proß. *Werke*, vol. 3/1, 839–1040.

Proß, Wolfgang, 1987b. "Anmerkungen". In: Johann Gottfried von Herder, 1984–1987. *Ideen zur Philosophie der Geschichte der Menschheit*. Ed. Wolfgang Proß. *Werke.*, vol. 3/2.

Reiss, Hans S., 2000. "Introduction to *Reviews of Herder's Ideas on the philosophy of mankind* and *Conjectures on the beginning of human history*". In: Immanuel Kant, 2000. *Political writings*. Ed. H.S. Reiss and trans. H.B. Nisbet. 2nd, enlarged edition. Cambridge: Cambridge University Press, 250–272.

Sikka, Sonia, 2012. *Herder on humanity and cultural difference: Enlightened relativism.* Cambridge: Cambridge University Press.
Sonenscher, Michael, 2007. *Before the deluge: Public debt, inequality, and the intellectual origins of the French Revolution.* Princeton and Oxford: Princeton University Press.
Spencer, Vicki, A., 2012. *Herder's political thought: A study of language, culture, and community.* Toronto, Buffolo, London: University of Toronto Press.
Walzer, Michael, 1990. "Nation and universe". In: Michael Walzer, 2007, *Thinking politically: Essays in political theory.* Ed. David Miller. New Haven and London: Yale University Press, 183–218.
Walzer, Michael, 1994. *Thick and thin: Moral argument at home and abroad.* Notre Dame: University of Notre Dame Press.
Walzer, Michael, 1987. *Interpretation and social criticism.* Cambridge, MA: Harvard University Press.
Wood, Allen, 1999. *Kant's ethical thought.* Cambridge: Cambridge University Press.
Zammito, John H., 1992. *The genesis of Kant's* Critique of judgement. Chicago: University of Chicago Press.

PART III

East of *Cosmopolis*

GALIN TIHANOV

De-Romanticizing Exile

This essay is prompted by the need to locate a methodological tool that could assist us in addressing the open wounds of transition; the ruptures and apertures of difference channelled through the experiences of border-crossing. Equally, I would like to talk about exile as creativity, not just suffering. On either occasion, however, my ultimate goal is to ask why exile came to be so firmly associated with these two experiential fields, different as they might be at first sight, and in order to see whether this lasting inscription in narratives of suffering and creativity is not hampering attempts to rethink the concept of exile, I will re-examine its use value for our age here. For my purposes, it is necessary to confine myself to "exile" and leave aside cognate designations, such as "refugee", all the more so since within the pervasive twin discourse of suffering and creativity these two appellations have often been used synonymously.[1] At the same time, I want to probe deeper into the resilient notion that exile somehow produces cosmopolitan attitudes. The problematic aspects of "enforced cosmopolitanism", which I look at briefly in the final part, have been enshrined in the powerful liberal consensus that first came to prominence in the social sciences during the 1980s–1990s. According to this consensus, the cross-border experience of migrant workers, worshippers or writers is always a source of cultural enrichment and a display of personal energy and endurance that glosses over—or simply fails to see and acknowledge—the attendant manifestations of inequality and disempowerment. Exile, on this reading, is a dependable machine for churning out cosmopolitans who emerge from the exilic experience as reliably enriched, unfailingly energized and

1 Witness, e.g., Hannah Arendt's powerful essay, "We Refugees", as an instance of such interchangeable use (Arendt 1943, 264–274).

dependably cultivated and tolerant citizens. By adding to the arguments that interrogate this consensus, I seek to address the multiple, and often contradictory, inscriptions of exile in current debates on cosmopolitanism. Exile captures the bifurcating moment of expanding and narrowing one's life-world (*Lebenswelt*). Conceiving of exile solely as an engine for the production of cosmopolitan attitudes can, and often does, leave out its other essential aspects: the need to circumscribe one's experience in the constraints of a new cultural framework, the imperative to begin to translate that experience in languages that are often not yet one's own, and to grope one's way through the loss and trauma intrinsic in this process of transition. When this work of translating and accommodating one's experience and life-world fails, when the participation in a new *polis* proves beyond reach, the spectre of rupture, deprivation and disenfranchisement makes its numbing appearance.

These tensions are at the heart of my analysis; by considering them I wish to offer arguments that would help the ongoing work of questioning the liberal consensus that still shapes the way we think about exile today. Rather than imagining exile on the plane of individual creativity or suffering, victory or failure, and thus also binding cosmopolitanism as a project to this notion of individual accomplishment (or the lack thereof), I wish to urge the possibility of contemplating a cosmopolitanism that breaks the spell of the liberal imagination and goes beyond the idea of fixed attainment.

My three specific reference points (and also sections) in this essay are as follows. The first section deals with the history of modern literary theory and comparative literature as disciplines and the significance of exile in their rise in the interwar decades of the twentieth century. Second, I focus on what I term the "East-East exilic experience", that is, the exile of Left Central- and East-European intellectuals in Stalin's Moscow in the same period (1930s–1940s). Finally I go into the Romanticization of exile and the consequent need to de-romanticize and de-liberalize it; hence also the brief reflection, in this final section, on the recent notion of "enforced cosmopolitanism" and the framework of transnationalism regarding their relation to exile. The first reference point enables us to appreciate the creative energies of exile (much insisted upon by the liberal consensus that I am interrogating), and to project exile as an ally of cosmopolitanism; the second reference point offers a counter-perspective: exile as the generator of undesirables that the liberal imagination tends to suppress or attempts to think away; exile is here considered a site of suffering and anguish, and an enemy of cosmopolitanism. In these two sections I draw in part on my previous research; the first section, in particular, is also a self-reflective, and, in the fullness of my present argument, qualified return to my earlier fascination with the creative energies of exile. The third (final and longest) section carries a wider methodological significance in that it seeks to identify these seemingly divergent scenarios—exile as creativity and exile as suffering—as the two sides of a deeper foundational narrative of transgression and border-crossing.

I must conclude this introduction with a more general question: what does it mean to be in exile? Philosophically, this is a pointer of ambivalence revealed in questions that do not necessarily envisage the specific condition of exile but can, rather, be placed in relation to a range of basic human acts. Thus, when Hannah Arendt asks, "Where are we when we think?" (Arendt 1978, 197), this is a question that articulates the duality of our position as thinking beings: our situatedness in the moment of time and the particular environment in which the thinking occurs, but also our being-not-there, being-else-where because of our abandonment to the act of thinking. Because of the act of thinking, to put it somewhat differently, we reside in a mode of concentration that removes us from the world around us and invites us to contemplate, in Arendt's words, "universals", "invisible essences"; as we move amongst these invisible essences, we are spatially "nowhere", "homeless in an emphatic sense" (Arendt 1978, 199). What is more, we enter a form of authenticity: "the flight of one alone into one", in Plotinus' words.[2] Exile draws on this ambivalence of situatedness and non-situatedness at once, of living here and elsewhere in the same breath, or, in different terms, of being "nowhere", a no-where-ness conceived positively as a cognitively enabling "Void" (Arendt 1978, 200), or negatively as a cultural and existential gap. Similarly, Paul Virilio's question, "Where

2 On mental concentration as a form of exile, see Bartoloni (2008, 80–81); Plotinus' words are quoted there on p. 80.

are we when we travel?" (Virilio 1978, 19), articulates uncertainty vis-à-vis space and mobility; it points to the likelihood of finding ourselves located not in this or some other territory, but in what Virilio calls "the land of speed". Exile, then, is more than an indicator of shifting experiential perspectives. It is a condition of deterritorialization where presence and absence are negotiable valences; it is a withdrawal that harbours a trace from that which has been withdrawn, contemplation whose intentionality, to speak phenomenologically, is retrospective before it becomes prospective. These momentous ambivalences of exile are also reflected in the twin narratives of creativity and suffering, which I will discuss in the next two sections.

Exile as a Site of Creativity

In an article written some years ago, I set forth a working hypothesis essaying to explain the birth of modern literary theory in the twentieth century (cf. Tihanov 2004). Exile, rather than acting as an impeding factor, was right at the heart of salutary developments that promoted the growth of literary theory in the interwar period. The picture I painted then, and which I still think to be largely true, saw exile as part and parcel of a renewed cultural cosmopolitanism that transcended local encapsulation and *monoglossia*. For a number of years the activities of the Russian formalists were taking place in a climate of enhanced mobility and exchange of ideas between the metropolitan and émigré streams of Russian culture. The most gifted ambassadors of the formalists abroad were Viktor Shklovsky, during the time he spent as an émigré in Berlin, and Roman Jakobson, while in Czechoslovakia (where he arrived as a Soviet citizen, deciding eventually not to return to Moscow). Jakobson is a particularly important example. His subsequent cooperation with Pyotr Bogatyrev (another Soviet scholar who resided in Prague for nearly two decades—and for about two years also in Münster—but remained a Soviet citizen, maintaining close cooperation with his colleagues in the Soviet Union and returning in the end to Moscow in December 1938), with Nikolai Trubetzkoy, a Vienna-based émigré scholar, and with Yuri Tynianov (who stayed in Russia but was involved in the work of his Prague colleagues), were all crucial in attempts to revive the Society for the Study of Poetic Language (*Opoyaz*) in the Soviet Union. These attempts, while unsuccessful, yielded an important document in the history of literary theory, a brief set of theses titled "Problemy izucheniia literatury i iazyka" (Problems in the Study of Literature and Language), written in Prague jointly by Jakobson and Tynianov. The theses signalled the urgent need to revise the supremacy of "pure synchronism" and promoted attention to the "correlation between the literary series and other historical series."[3] Thus the work of Russian Formalism in its concluding stages, and later the formation and flourishing of the Prague Linguistic Circle, became possible through intellectual exchanges that benefited from the crossing of national boundaries, often under the duress of exile. The work of the Prague Linguistic Circle, in particular, proceeded in the situation of a veritable *polyglossia*, which rendered narrow nationalistic concerns anachronistic. Jakobson, Trubetzkoy and Bogatyrev were each writing in at least two or three languages (Russian, German, Czech); their careers invite us to consider the enormous importance of exile and emigration for the birth of modern literary theory in Eastern and Central Europe. Exile and emigration were the extreme embodiment of heterotopia triggered by drastic historical changes that brought about the traumas of dislocation but also, as part of this, the productive insecurity of having to face and make use of more than one language and culture. The work of Jakobson, Trubetzkoy and Bogatyrev came to embody the potential of what Edward Said was to term later "travelling theory": "The point of theory is [...] to travel, always to move beyond its confinements, to emigrate, to remain in a sense in exile" (Said 1994, 264). The possibility to "estrange" (to borrow Shklovsky's telling word) the sanctified naturalness of one's own literature by analysing it in another language, or by refracting it through the prism of another culture, seems to have been a factor of paramount significance

3 Quoted here from the 1977 English translation (Tynyanov and Jakobson 1928, 49). The article was originally written in December 1928 and first published in Russian in *Novyi Lef* 12, 1928—actually in early 1929.

not just in the evolution of Russian Formalism and its continuation and modification in the structuralist functionalism of the Prague Linguistic Circle, but—more importantly—for the emergence of modern literary theory in the interwar period as a whole. Appropriating literature theoretically meant after all being able to transcend its (and one's own) national embeddedness by electing to position oneself as an outsider contemplating the validity of its laws beyond a merely national framework. In Prague, in particular, one could observe in a nutshell the stupendous diversity of approaches marking émigré literary theory and scholarship between the world wars. Along with Jakobson's post-formalism and Bogatyrev's early functionalist structuralism, we can also see the unfolding of fruitful historico-philological research (centred around the Dostoevsky Seminar, 1925–1933, founded by Alfred Bem) and psychoanalytic literary scholarship, the main exponent of which was Nikolai Osipov (1877–1934) who had made Freud's acquaintance in Vienna in 1910 and had propagated his ideas in Russia before arriving in Czechoslovakia as an émigré in 1921. To this one should add the Prague wing of Eurasianism (a Russian interwar cultural and political movement which evolved entirely in exile), led by Pyotr Savitsky who had set himself the task of establishing "Eurasian literary studies" (*evraziiskoe literaturovedenie*), in which Russian literary history, both before and after 1917, was to be re-examined from the point of view of its potential to assert Russia's special geopolitical and cultural status. Savitsky acknowledged his failure in this task, but he did succeed in persuading a number of followers in Prague (Konstantin Chkheidze, Leontii Kopetskii, G.I. Rubanov) to embrace Eurasianism as an interpretative prism through which to follow the Soviet literary scene of the 1920s–1930s. Importantly, Prague was a place where some of these currents intersected, most noticeably in Jakobson's attempt to lend legitimacy to Eurasian linguistics (encouraged in part by Savitsky), in Savitsky's efforts to found a linguistic geography with structuralist ambitions, but also in Bogatyrev's (later abandoned) idea of a specifically Eurasian Russian folkloristics.[4]

4 For more on the Prague scene of exilic literary theory and criticism, see Tihanov (2011a).

This interpretation of exile as an enabling factor that unlocks creativity can be reinforced and extended by examining the birth of a related discipline in the interwar decade. In equal measure, one could argue, modern comparative literature begins life in exile, with the Istanbul works of Erich Auerbach and Leo Spitzer and their post-war continuation in the United States.[5] The qualifier "modern" is not trivial here: I mean by this a comparative literature that had moved beyond the nineteenth-century model of examining cultural bilateralisms and exchanges between nations,[6] and had instead embraced a wider perspective that focuses on larger supranational patterns: mimesis, style, genre, etc. Auerbach and Spitzer behaved, of course, differently in Istanbul: Spitzer was eager to learn Turkish and to immerse himself in the local culture; Auerbach hardly looked further than German and French in his communication with colleagues and his teaching. But despite that, he was not a total stranger either (contrary to the propensity to portray him, in the Romantic vein, as an example of creative solitude). In contradistinction to Said's apparent emphasis on the Orient as an environment shaped by Western cultural ideologies, recent research has emphasized Atatürk's indigenous—and rather proactive—revival of humanist values that marked the scene at the time of Auerbach's work in the city (see, in particular, Konuk 2010).

Be that as it may, in both cases—the birth of modern literary theory and of modern comparative literature—we witness a narrative of exile that foregrounds, and for good reasons, creativity, seminality and the desirability of cosmopolitan attitudes fostered by denaturalizing one's own cultural inheritance.[7]

5 The literature on Auerbach and Spitzer has grown substantially over the last twenty years. For a very good overview, especially with reference to the role of exile in their work, see Apter (2006, Ch. 3); see also Damrosch (2005) and Konuk (2010).

6 On this nineteenth-century model of cultural-national "bilateralism" see Tihanov (2011b, 143–144).

7 I am far from alone in drawing on this narrative of exile as creativity; see e.g. Edward Said's well-known essay "Reflections on Exile" (1984), or Leszek Kolakowski's "In Praise of Exile" (1985), in which Kolakowski states that "the position of an outsider

Exile as Affliction and Distress

Let me now dwell in more detail on the other foundational narrative of exile: that of suffering, anguish and distress—a narrative that captures exile as affliction and an incapacitating reality. To lend added persuasiveness to my argument, I will once again look at the interwar decade from which my previous narrative of exile as promoter of creativity was drawn; cosmopolitanism will once again loom large in my exposition, this time as a painfully receding, and ultimately failing, desideratum.

By now we possess considerable knowledge about emigration and exile from Eastern and Central Europe to the West, or from Soviet Russia to Central Europe, in the 1920s–1930s. Yet we have tended to under-research and under-conceptualize the alternative destination. Seemingly less glamorous and lastingly tainted by the open glorification or silent acquiescence to Stalin and the purges, Moscow as a place of emigration and exile of Left East-Central European intellectuals in the 1930s presents a uniquely important trajectory.

My protagonists in this section are a host of Hungarian and Polish Left intellectuals and literati (Georg Lukács, Belá Balázs, Ervin Sinkó, Gyula Háy, Aleksander Wat and Bruno Jasieński), all of whom found themselves in the Soviet Union at the end of the 1920s or in the 1930s. The "East-East exilic experience", as I term the complex texture of events, actions, beliefs and dispositions exhibited during the long enforced stays of Left intellectuals from Eastern and Central Europe in the Soviet Union during the 1930s, carried the deeper meaning of a tirelessly pursued, yet culturally and politically frustrated cosmopolitanism. In the *Communist Manifesto*, Marx and Engels had famously asserted the spirit of a proletarian cosmopolitanism that would envelop the awakening working class and lend its emancipatory ambitions a truly global scale. Proletarian solidarity was envisaged as a world-wide network that defeats the supremacy of a bourgeoisie profiting

offers a cognitive privilege"; it arises "from insecurity, from an exile of a sort, from the experience of homelessness".

from an equally globalized mode of production. But by the mid-1930s cosmopolitanism was becoming a word of denunciation in Moscow; it was employed to stigmatize the enemy—without and within the Party, Soviet and foreign alike—as a rootless agent who evades Party control and gives the lie to the ever more vociferous propaganda of Russianness.[8] "Cosmopolitan" was often a concealed anti-Semitic qualification, the origins of which should be sought in the revival of the mythology of Russian uniqueness, reinforced by the ongoing fight against Trotskyism. During the Second World War, this line gathered momentum (in 1943, Fadeev warned in *Pod znamenem marksizma* against the "hypocritical sermons of groundless cosmopolitanism"[9]), culminating after the end of the War in the wide-ranging 1949 campaign against cosmopolitanism.

Instead, the official Party line promoted proletarian internationalism as a discourse reflecting the more desirable world-wide co-operation between various Communist parties and movements under the indisputable leadership of the Soviet Union. Internationalism, unlike cosmopolitanism, did not erase the boundaries between nations; it preserved a core idea of belonging and left intact the assumption of alienness that informed attitudes towards foreign Communists and sympathizers of the Left in the Soviet Union. In Stalin's hands, internationalism was little more than a smoke-screen slogan concealing the tactics of maximizing the benefits of nation-building at a time when the Soviets were still the only country where the revolution had triumphed. The resulting ambiguity—openness towards supporters from without, checked at the same time by a fundamental distrust and concerted policies of control and Russification—shot through and affected profoundly the life worlds of numerous East- and Central-European Left émigrés and exiles in Moscow during the 1930s.[10]

8 From the literature on Stalin's nation-building and the process of Russification in the 1930s, see especially Terry Martin (1998).

9 Quoted in Ronen (2005, 336); the Russian reads: "khanzheskikh propovedei bespochvennogo kosmopolitizma".

10 For an alternative interpretation of "proletarian internationalism" in a more positive light, see chapter by Khader in this volume.

Ervin Sinkó arrived in 1935 from Paris (and an economically precarious existence) on the recommendations of Romain Rolland, determined to find a publisher for his ill-fated novel *The Optimists*; Béla Balázs set foot in Moscow in 1931, driven by the desire to shoot his best film yet; Gyula Háy (Julius Hay) went there in 1936 from Paris via Prague and Zurich, following an invitation from Lunacharsky (which had reached him after the latter's death).[11] None of these three intellectuals achieved their immediate goals: Sinkó's novel remained unpublished until after the Second World War; Balázs's film *The Tisza Burns*, although finished in 1934, was banned and never shown; Háy scattered his energy in journalism and commissioned work.

Unlike these three literati, others were *forced* into exile. The Polish-Jewish writer Aleksander Wat, in his youth amongst the founders of the Polish Futurist movement, fled Warsaw in 1939. In 1941, in Saratov, he converted to Christianity, referring to himself as "a Jew with a cross around his neck" (Wat 1988, 360). Another Polish-Jewish writer whose early work shaped Polish Futurism, Bruno Jasieński, was twice expelled from Paris for Left propaganda and found safe haven in Leningrad in 1929, becoming closely involved in Soviet literary and political life and enjoying huge literary success until his arrest in Moscow in 1937 (the precise year of his death in Vladivostok is still unclear).[12] Georg Lukács's Moscow exile, from March 1933 to the end of August 1945 (with a brief spell in Tashkent), was the result of persecution and insecurity; a Communist and a Jew writing in both German and Hungarian, in September 1919, following the defeat of the Hungarian Soviet Republic, he had found refuge in Vienna, returning illegally to Hungary in 1929 and then going to Moscow in 1930 (his first visit there was in 1921 when he attended the Third Congress of the

11 The individual circumstances of these arrivals in the Soviet Union are related in more detail in Sinko (1962); Zsuffa (1987) and Hay (1974). On Sinkó, see also Kantorowicz (1977).

12 For an introduction to Jasieński's life and work, see Kolesnikoff (1982); she notes (p. 9, n. 14) that Polish sources give 1939 as the year of Jasieński's death, while Russian sources usually have 1941.

Comintern); in 1931 he was already in Berlin, doing Party work until the political climate forced him to return to Moscow.

Having found himself in Moscow, Lukács, like so many of the other East-Central European exiles, was confronted with a pressing identity problem: was he Hungarian, Soviet, Russian, German, Jewish? Or did all these cultural codes interplay, shaping a multi-layered, flexible, yet vulnerable perspective on the surrounding world? With reference to language, Balázs's answer to these vexing questions was recorded in his Moscow diary in January 1940, "a poet without a people and a homeland who must write in two languages and employ both without the perfection that befits a master" (quoted in Loewy 2003, 380). Often deprived of the opportunity to write in their *Muttersprache* (mother tongue), these literati felt the loss of a more general sense of language comfort: they were bereft, to quote Jean Paul, of a *Sprachmutter* (language mother).[13] Politically, things were not any easier. Attempts to normalize one's precarious situation were not always successful. Balázs arrived on an Austrian passport, applied in 1937 for a Soviet citizenship but was rejected, and became eventually a *displaced person* (cf. Zsuffa 1987, 281). Lukács confronted the Soviet officials with even greater difficulties: a Hungarian by nationality, a Soviet citizen, and for eight out of his twelve years in the Soviet Union a member of the German Communist Party, he was a Hungarian-Jewish intellectual writing mostly in German, a person impossible to pigeonhole. Arousing suspicion all along, he could not escape being taken into custody for two months in 1941.[14]

These East-European exiles thus cut insecure and imperilled figures on the Moscow cultural and political scene. None of them ever reached the inner circles of power; often they were not trusted even within the narrow confines of their professional environments, where their work was monitored, censured and publicly attacked, not least by their Soviet peers. Eisenstein kept Balázs at a distance (cf. Loewy 2003, 381); Shklovskii, at the

13 On current debates on multilingualism and the precariousness of the idea of "mother tongue", see Yildiz (2012).

14 Lukács became a member of the German Communist Party on 1 July 1931; in April 1941 he was registered in the Hungarian Communist Party (cf. Sziklai 2001, 229–230). He was arrested in Moscow on 29 June 1941 and released on 26 August.

time himself a hostage to the regime, stopped the publication of Lukács's book *The Historical Novel* with a negative internal review (see Tihanov 2000).[15] There was a growing sense amongst these exiled intellectuals that they didn't own the project they had subscribed to. They were cosmopolitan in their beliefs and aspirations, yet they had no *polis* to apply their civic ethos to, excluded as they were from the real political process.

Yet most crippling of all was the political and moral disorientation and loss of identity that followed the signing of the Soviet-German treaty of 23 August 1939, which entailed a full relinquishing of the ideas and values of antifascism. Lukács, along with many others, was severely hit by this radical change in Stalin's foreign policy. The new line taken by the Soviet government was bewildering, offensive and bitterly disappointing to him and to all those who had fled the Nazi persecution and had found safe haven in Moscow.

Thus neither language, nor cultural inheritance or acquisition, nor indeed their political creed and commitment could lend the exiles an unassailable and self-assured identity. One was haunted by an atmosphere, as Lukács put it in hindsight, "of lasting mutual mistrust, an alertness directed towards everybody [...] and a sensation of being permanently under siege" (Lukács 1970, 184). In Moscow, "at the heart of the world", Ervin Sinkó was plagued by a sense of "loneliness and uselessness" (Sinkó 1962, 131). His Kafkaesque story of countless encounters with the institutions of Soviet cultural life reveals the frustrations of many Left-minded émigrés who had to reconcile themselves to living in a society where compliance and bureaucracy had ousted the spirit of the Revolution: "here the task of the revolutionary consists in far-reaching conformism [...] It is not easy to be a revolutionary in the country where the revolution had triumphed" (Sinkó

15 Shklovskii was a good friend of Gyula Háy's; he helped Háy, Balázs, Fridrich Wolf and others to continue their evacuation journey to Alma-Ata by securing a locomotive from Tashkent (Hay 1974, 248–253). Lukács travelled with the same group from Moscow to Tashkent; Shklovskii and Lukács no doubt met on this journey. Aleksander Wat was also helped on several occasions by Shklovskii in Alma-Ata (Wat 1988, 319–321).

1962, 116).[16] For Sinkó, and for many other communists who shared his itinerary, Moscow in the mid-1930s was a city where reality seemed to be dissolving without hope. Distrust and anonymous opposition stood in their way; "an oppressive, impervious resistance [...] a resistance so incognito that I cannot seize it", as Balázs wrote in resignation (quoted in Zsuffa 1987, 221).[17]

De-Romanticizing (and De-Liberalizing) Exile

What do these two radically divergent narratives have in common? They seem dramatically, and diametrically, opposed: the first one interprets exile as an enabling factor, a spring of creativity and an enduring materialization of cosmopolitanism as a high-minded attitude of openness to cultures transcending one's immediate background and comfort zone; the second one sees exile as a site of anguish and deprivation, the terrain of an ever receding and failing cosmopolitanism. Beneath the surface, however, these two narratives do intersect and share a substantially common ground through their conjoined origins in the metanarratives of Romanticism. Exile, I argue, is a Romantic cultural construct. The exile supplements a whole series of Romantic protagonists marked by a twofold aberration from the customary: representing either the woefully inadequate and inefficient—the mad, the morbidly impractical (the lover serenely hovering above reality)—associated with the social outcast, or the inordinate potency of the superhero. The latter group, as all readers of poetry and novels dating from the late eighteenth and the early nineteenth century would know, disintegrates

16 Lion Feuchtwanger, writing in response to André Gide's *Back from the U.S.S.R*, did his best to justify conformism by presenting it as no more than the Soviet people's "general deep love [...] for their homeland" which elsewhere "is simply called patriotism" (Feuchtwanger 1937, 58).

17 For more on the East-East exilic experience, see Tihanov (2009).

into two further groups: the creative genius (a poet, more often than not) and the monster (a Frankenstein, or, in the end of the nineteenth century, a Dracula).[18] Romanticism is, I submit, the foundational metanarrative of border-crossing and exile in modernity: what is transgressed here is the habitual norm of the everyday; creativity and suffering—given and received—go hand in hand in this spectacle of (both forced and voluntary) removal from reality. The Romantic hero is an outcast, an exile from the logic of the routine.

Romanticism is a Janus-faced discourse that thrives on an exfoliating polarity. In its responses to the defining event of the French Revolution, it is at once forward-looking and retrograde (Marxist literary criticism, notably Gorky and Lukács, thus tends to speak, somewhat crudely but not without a point, of "progressive" and "reactionary" Romanticism).[19] In Germany, Romanticism begins with an emphasis on the individual (the "early Romantics") and ends up accentuating community life and cohesion (the so called "late Romanticism"). This constitutive dualism is also present in the foundational narrative of exile. Not only does Romanticism furnish the framework in which exile is interpreted as a dramatically private affair, and the exile as an emphatically *individual* embodiment of either extraordinary suffering or creativity (or both); at the same time, Romanticism also supplies the framework that inscribes the exile in a nation-bound collectivity, without which the very phenomenon of exile becomes incomprehensible. It is precisely in the folds of Romanticism that the nexus between language and nation, and between language and national culture, is discursively produced and reinforced.[20] Fichte's praise of the German language; Central and Eastern European purism; the idea of the poet as enunciator

18 Exile as a fillip to poetic creativity is a common place in literary studies. For a controversial interpretation that casts a bridge between exile and violence/monstrosity (via nostalgia as a mental disorder), see Karl Jasper's dissertation *Heimweh und Verbrechen* (1909/1996). On the medicalization of nostalgia in the eighteenth and nineteenth centuries, see Starobinki (1966) and Boym (2001, 3–7).

19 See, above all, Löwy and Sayre (2001).

20 While recognizing the "essential association" of nationalism with exile, Said's own influential interpretation of exile stubbornly remains within the other framework

of national values and the prophet of national triumph—these are all phenomena engendered by Romantic ideology and inscribed in the metanarratives of Romanticism. And it is against this powerful and resilient nexus that the figure of the exile assumes its ambivalent prominence: either as a formidable creative genius who manages to safeguard and masterfully employ the national language in the inclement conditions of separation from the nation, or as a detractor, or rather disbeliever, who embraces another culture and language only to wither away—so the verdict of the national majority goes—in sterile suffering, torn away from his roots and his national audience. It is not by chance that the literary canons of a number of Central and Eastern European countries, particularly those who had to fight in the nineteenth century for their independence or unification, rest on works written by Romantics who were also exiles (Poland and Bulgaria are two good examples).

Significantly, the Romantic notion of exile lends wider significance to sentiments that previous epochs had thought of as enjoying but limited articulation and validity. A case in point are the changes reflected in the history of the word 'Heimweh' (nostalgia, pining after one's home place), that quintessential Romantic formula of longing *cum* grief. Friedrich Kluge tells us in an exemplary study that throughout the eighteenth century, and before that, "Heimweh" was actually a word confined to the Swiss dialects, and largely avoided in written German by poets, journalists and philosophers. Unsurprisingly, as Kluge (1902, 246–247) demonstrates, it is only in the very late eighteenth century and the first third of the nineteenth, the time of the Romantics, that "Heimweh" begins to be used in poetry and fiction and gains currency across the German-speaking realm. This migration and generalization of the word from the scattered Swiss dialects into standard German reflects the momentous transformation and broadening of the very notion of exile: from an evocation of the painful detachment from one's little home place to an indicator that could now point to the expulsion from an entire nation, its language and its culture.

---

posited by Romanticism which I have just discussed: that of individual creativity, suffering and longing (see Said 1984).

It is only within this larger framework of the Romantic metanarratives of transgression, underpinned by the duality of creativity and suffering, equally excessive, that we can begin to understand the longevity of our post-Romantic attachment to interpreting exile through the seemingly divergent, but essentially convergent, optics of extraordinary resourcefulness and creativeness, on the one hand, and overwhelming anguish, distress and affliction, on the other.

To make exile a concept fit for purpose in the twenty-first century we thus must begin to de-romanticize it, to peel away the resilient crust of Romantic ideology that still sticks to it. That is to say, we need to relax the bond between language, literature and national culture, and we need to look beyond the paradigm that captures exile as aberration—creative or destructive—from a presumed norm. Writers do not need to switch language to relax that bond (some did, perhaps most instructively Nabokov). Witold Gombrowicz, the Polish modernist in Argentine exile, continued to write in Polish, while at the same time claiming (envisaging another Polish exile, the Romantic poet Mickiewicz who was born in the Grand Duchy of Lithuania and whose *Pan Tadeusz* became a foundational text of the Polish canon): "A hundred years ago, a Lithuanian poet forged the shape of the Polish spirit and today, I, like Moses, am leading the Poles out of the slavery of that form. I am leading the Pole out of himself" (Gombrowicz 1988, 36). Form, language and spirit constitute the (un)holy trinity that exilic writing here seeks to rethink and interrogate, denaturalizing it and looking for a way out of it.

But above all we need to de-romanticize exile by removing the layers of exceptionality with which Romanticism has endowed it. Speaking of the "universality of rootlessness", Zygmunt Bauman dwells on the figure of the "universal stranger"; exile is no more, Bauman avers, because we are all now exiles in the wider sense of not fully belonging in any one subsystem of social life, according to a diagnosis of social displacement formulated by Luhmann (whom Bauman cites). Even as he keeps as his baseline the Romantic notion of belonging—and its gradual frustration in late modernity—Bauman moves beyond this baseline to invest in exile a historical rather than timeless significance. For him, exile is a meaningful category when related to our experiences in, and of, what he calls "solid" modernity;

in "liquid" modernity (postmodernity), "it has lost its particularity as human condition; with that loss, it has lost the once rebellious, potentially revolutionary, edge" (Z. Bauman 1991, 95). In other words, it has also lost its privileged status of an exceptional experience that embodies suffering or creativity of supposedly unique intensity. Here a case in point might be the semantic history of "diaspora", from a shorthand for the singular experience of Jewish life in (at first a voluntary) dispersal, with a gradually coalescing, later dominant, tenor of suffering and loss, to a more recent, now freely proliferating and largely de-semanticized, appellation of any globally scattered communities, to which distress and affliction no longer necessarily apply as markers of their existence.[21] This transformation away from the value-laden language of exile towards the descriptive, non-evaluative, "value-free" vocabulary of transnationalism is one of the most significant changes attending the waning of exile as a privileged methodological prism through which to conceptualize experiences of (enforced) border-crossing.

I have used brackets in the sentence above, for exile has persistently been interpreted as an enforced experience. This is very much consonant with the notion of exile as the repository of unique distress and anguish or of equally unique creative/destructive energies: imminent obstacles, insurmountable difficulties, unliftable barriers are all part and parcel of the semantic palette of change under duress that elicits responses of suffering and creativity beyond the customary. Indeed, the insuperable nature of these obstacles, and the enduring sense of duress and blockage that ensues—but also the colossal energy generated by the efforts to deal with these impediments—are amongst the formative components of the Romantic mythology of exile as an experience of heroic transgression. The state has been assigned the role of the arch-villain in this scenario, a reputation strengthened particularly during the Cold War era of political exile that continues to cast a long shadow on how we think of exile long after the Iron Curtain had been raised. In fact, exile had been very much a case of negotiation between the state and the individual rather than a unilateral application of force by the state. Significantly, studying the history of banishment in Roman

21 For more on "diaspora", see Vertovec (2009, 128–131).

antiquity would reveal that the discourse of exile begins as a discourse of rights, not of punishment as such. Gordon Kelly draws attention to the fact that exile, in Cicero's speech "Pro Caecina", is a "refuge from punishment", a "harbour" that shelters one from (capital) punishment (quoted in Agamben 1998, 110).[22] How should one gauge the position of the state in this negotiation over its own and the individual's rights has in turn been a matter of dispute and negotiation. Kojève went perhaps too far by suggesting that exile was a practice exposing the state as fundamentally weak (cf. his argument in Kojève 1982/2000); unable to deal resolutely with its enemies (physically destroying them), it preferred the second-best option (expulsion). Historians have tended to offer more nuanced answers: Richard Bauman emphasizes the moment of choice and sees exile as evolving from the Roman notion of humanitas (cf. R. Bauman 1996), while Gordon Kelly, in his book mentioned above, derives the practice of exile from the principle of concordia that allows for a reconfiguration of the political landscape to take place without explicit violence (Kelly 2006, 13). Exile rests on the soft techniques of an often metaphorically inscribed power that works not through direct removal but through a *pars pro toto* prohibition: *aqua et ignis interdictus* (the prohibition to use water and fire).[23]

It is this moment of exile as a process of negotiation involving the application of indirect force on the part of the state that had been obscured and left out of active consideration, especially as a result of the prevalent patterns of exile imposed by the totalitarian regimes of the twentieth century. De-romanticizing exile entails acknowledging this moment of negotiation, of complex mediation and give-and-take between the state and the citizen that often flows through the channels of a less than manifest coercion. In the figure of the exile, the clash of the individual and the state has been recast from a constant feature of political life in modernity to an embodiment of extremity: a Romantic hero or a monster, both appealing and grotesque beyond the ordinary (think of Hugo's Quasimodo or of Agamben's

22 For the historical background to exile as right, only later evolving into a doctrine of punishment, see Kelly (2006).

23 On the metaphoricity of exile, see also Zoric (2006, 30–32).

wolf-man), the exile stands for a regularity re-styled as exception. In the footsteps of Romanticism, the exile has been turned into an emblem of solitary existence, allegedly beyond networks and beyond negotiation with the state (despite the fact that Romanticism itself had elaborate networks of sociability), with the nation often serving as his only point of reference.

The final act that brings this process of de-romanticization to its logical conclusion should thus be the *de-liberalization* of exile. The idea that the exile is a fully formed, autonomous social actor is a projection of the principle of "methodological individualism", inviting us to see and explain social phenomena as shaped solely by the aspirations of individuals who set out to do better for themselves in a new environment (or, "field of competition", to use the liberal language). "Methodological individualism" is here only the reverse of the pervasive logic of "methodological nationalism", the notion that the nation and the nation-state are the only appropriate prism and unit of analysis through which to spectate and interpret social occurrences. The latter is no doubt a deeply misguided premise (and it has, for that reason, been criticized by many[24]), but going into the other extreme seems to me to be fraught with problems that are no less significant. "Methodological individualism", while endeavouring to de-romanticize the social world by exploding the centrality of the nation and the nation-state, seemingly also destroys the framework that makes exile possible in the first place: it seeks to send into oblivion the exile who becomes an exile only to the extent to which they internalize this centrality and experience its loss as tragic. Yet, as most extreme reactions, methodological individualism, too, carries the birthmarks of the body it sets out to outgrow: as it sheds the Romantic overtones of a nation-bound existence, methodological individualism smuggles in the Romantic focus on the individual, the Romantic preoccupation with solitary vigour, now recognizable in the new guise of the skilful and resourceful (but often illegal) migrant labourer who—in a context confronting him with threat, humiliation and harassment—miraculously develops the toolkit of a cosmopolitan. His survival is no longer "heroic",

24 See, e.g. Beck (2002), and for a critique of critiques of "methodological nationalism", not least Beck's own, see Chernilo (2006) and Fine (2007, 9–14).

but it is at least as much a celebration of individual strength and prowess as is any other lonely act of endurance (not to mention "victory" in the newly formed "market place", in which these border-crossers find themselves).

This bizarre extolment of inequality masked by the proliferating (especially in social anthropology and mobility studies) myth of enhanced adaptability and "enforced cosmopolitanism"[25] is indeed a post-Romantic continuation of the faith in the inexhaustible significance of the individual, this time through the philosophical and cultural resources of liberalism. De-liberalizing exile means ending this belief in man as an accomplished social agent, it means giving preference to the cold transnational logic of networks,[26] dependencies, and, yes, also creativities that are conditioned and channelled through mediated solidarities (those of long-distance belonging, those of Internet communities, etc.). It means re-inscribing the individual into collectivities that are no longer necessarily nation-bound, and, as such, produce a different border-crosser: no longer an exile (or even a refugee), nor, for that matter, a consummately proficient individual doer and getter. How this re-inscription would bear on the way we think about cosmopolitanism—a cosmopolitanism extricated from the grip of the liberal imagination—is a question that rings with unmistakeable urgency. This new cosmopolitanism would not be exclusively centred on individual agency and a humanistic recognition of uniqueness; it might even be that the new cosmopolitans, going as they do beyond the framework posited by the liberal imagination, would reject the very notion of exile, to the extent to which it rests on the liberal assumption of core experiential modes (such as self-sufficient creativity, or its negative version:

25 Ulrich Beck speaks of these effects of cosmopolitanism, from below and almost by serendipity, when praising the "transportation workers, doormen, janitors and cleaners who can successfully communicate in more languages than the graduates of the average German or French high school or American college" (Beck 2006a, 104); see also Beck (2006b, 340–341), where he evokes the spirit of an "enforced cosmopolitanism" induced by the new world risks.

26 On the transnational optic to migration, see Nina Glick Schiller's recent works (Glick Schiller 2010; the co-authored Wimmer and Glick Schiller 2003; and the co-edited Amelina *et al.* 2012).

individual suffering).[27] Crucially, this new cosmopolitanism would not be norm-orientated, nor will it be beholden to an imposing roster of context-insensitive values. Rather, I should like to imagine a cosmopolitanism that is an open-ended, reversible condition, not a normative category or fixed attainment. Its legitimations are perhaps best sought in a range of "rooted" manifestations,[28] collective or individual, that tend to retain the intensity, the colour and the often controversial charge of the historical moment in which they originate.[29]

Acknowledgement

I wish to thank my former RICC colleagues at Manchester for many good discussions.

References

Agamben, Giorgio, 1998. *Homo Sacer: Sovereign power and bare life*. Trans. Daniel Heller-Roazen. Stanford: Stanford University Press.

Amelina, Anna, Devrimsel D. Nergiz, Thomas Faist and Nina Glick Schiller (eds.), 2012. *Beyond methodological nationalism: Research methodologies for cross-border studies*. New York: Routledge.

27 Timothy Brennan has written about the rejection of the assumption that exile and cosmopolitanism are intimately linked; he has already diagnosed the imminent decline of exile as a "dominant theoretical category of twentieth-century fiction" (Brennan 1997, 38)—and of philosophy and the social sciences, I now add.

28 On "rooted cosmopolitanism", see Appiah (2005, Ch. 6).

29 See also my argument in Tihanov (2011b).

Appiah, Kwame Anthony, 2005. *The ethics of identity*. Princeton, NJ: Princeton University Press.

Apter, Emily, 2006. *The translation zone: A new comparative literature*. Princeton, NJ: Princeton University Press.

Arendt, Hannah, 1978. *The life of the mind: Thinking*, vol. 1. London: Secker & Warburg.

Arendt, Hannah, 1943. "We Refugees". In: Hannah Arendt, 2007. *The Jewish writings*. Ed. Jerome Kohn and Ron H. Feldman. New York: Shocken Books.

Bartoloni, Paolo, 2008. *On the cultures of exile, translation, and writing*. West Lafayette, IN: Purdue University Press.

Bauman, Richard, 1996. *Crime and punishment in ancient Rome*. London and New York: Routledge.

Bauman, Zygmunt, 1991. *Modernity and ambivalence*. Cambridge: Polity Press.

Beck, Ulrich, 2002. "The terrorist threat: World risk society revisited." *Theory, Culture and Society*, 19(4), 39–55.

Beck, Ulrich, 2006a. *Cosmopolitan vision*. London: Polity Press.

Beck, Ulrich, 2006b. "Living in the world risk society." *Economy and Society*, 35(3), 329–345.

Boym, Svetlana, 2001. *The future of nostalgia*. New York: Basic Books.

Brennan, Timothy, 1997. *At home in the world: Cosmopolitanism now*. Cambridge, MA: Harvard University Press.

Chernilo, Daniel, 2006. "Social theory's methodological nationalism: Myth and reality". *European Journal of Social Theory*, 9(1), 5–22.

Damrosch, David, 1995. "Auerbach in Exile". *Comparative Literature*, 47(2), 97–117.

Feuchtwanger, Lion, 1937. *Moscow 1937: My visit described for my friends*. Trans. Irene Josephy. London: Victor Gollancz.

Fine, Robert, 2007. *Cosmopolitanism*. London and New York: Routledge.

Glick Schiller, Nina, 2010. "A global perspective on transnational migration: Theorizing migration without methodological nationalism." In: Rainer Bauböck and Thomas Faist (eds.), 2010. *Diaspora and transnationalism: Concepts, theories and methods*. Amsterdam: Amsterdam University Press.

Gombrowicz, Witold, 1988. *Diary*, vol. 1. Ed. Jan Kott and trans. Lillian Vallee. London and New York: Quartet Books.

Hay, Julius, 1974. *Born 1900: Memoirs*. Trans. James Amery Underwood. London: Hutchinson.

Jaspers, Karl, 1909/1996. *Heimweh und Verbrechen*. Munich: Belleville.

Kantorowicz, Alfred, 1977. "Das Vermächtnis des Ervin Sinkó" In: Alfred Kantorowicz, 1977. *Die Geächteten der Republik*. Berlin: Verlag Europäische Ideen, 44–55.

Kelly, Gordon, 2006. *A history of exile in the Roman republic*. Cambridge: Cambridge University Press.
Kluge, Friedrich, 1902. "Heimweh". *Zeitschrift für deutsche Wortforschung*, 2(2–3), 234–251.
Kojève, Alexandre, 1982/2000. *Outline of a phenomenology of right*. Ed. Bryan-Paul Frost and trans. Bryan-Paul Frost and Robert Howse. Lanham, MD: Rowman & Littlefield.
Kolakowski, Leszek, 1985. "In praise of exile." *TLS*, 11 October.
Kolesnikoff, Nina, 1982. *Bruno Jasieński: His evolution from futurism to socialist realism*. Waterloo, Ontario: Wilfrid Laurier University Press.
Konuk, Kader, 2010. *East West mimesis: Auerbach in Turkey*. Stanford: Stanford University Press.
Loewy, Hanno, 2003. *Béla Balázs: Märchen, ritual und film*. Berlin: Vorwerk 8.
Löwy, Michael and Robert Sayre, 2001. *Romanticism against the tide of modernity*. Trans. Catherine Porter. Durham, NC: Duke University Press.
Lukács, Georg, 1970. *Marxismus und Stalinismus*. Reinbeck: Rowohlt.
Martin, Terry, 1998. "The Russification of the RSFSR." *Cahiers du Monde Russe*, 39(1–2), 99–118.
Ronen, Omry, 2005. "Kosmopolit". In: Omry Ronen, 2005. *Iz goroda Enn*. St. Petersburg: Zvezda, 321–342.
Said, Edward, 1994. "Travelling theory reconsidered." In: Robert M. Polhemus and Roger B. Henkle (eds.), 1994. *Critical reconstructions: The relationship of fiction and life*. Stanford: Stanford University Press, 251–265.
Said, Edward, 1984. "Reflections on exile". In: Edward Said, 2001. *Reflections on exile and other literary and cultural essays*. London and New York: Granta Books, 173–186.
Sinkó, Ervin, 1962. *Roman eines Romans: Moskauer Tagebuch*. Trans. Edmund Trugly Jr. Cologne: Wissenschaft und Politik.
Starobinski, Jean, 1967. "The idea of nostalgia". *Diogenes*, 54, 81–103.
Sziklai, Laszlo, 2001. "'41 bin ich doch aufgeflogen': Das Verhör Georg Lukács's in der Lubjanka". In: Frank Benseler and Werner Jung (eds.), 2001. *Lukács 2001: Jahrbuch der Internationalen Georg-Lukács-Gesellschaft*, vol. 5, 215–242.
Tihanov, Galin, 2000. "Viktor Shklovskii and Georg Lukács in the 1930s". *The Slavonic and East European Review*, 78(1), 44–65.
Tihanov, Galin, 2004. "Why did modern literary theory originate in Central and Eastern Europe? (And why is it now dead?)". *Common Knowledge*, 10(1), 61–81.
Tihanov, Galin, 2009. "Cosmopolitans without a *polis*: Towards a hermeneutics of the East-East exilic experience (1929–1945)". In: John Neubauer and Borbála

Zsuzsanna Török (eds.), 2009. *The exile and return of writers from East-Central Europe: A compendium.* Berlin and New York: Walter de Gruyter, 123–143.

Tihanov, Galin, 2011a. "Russian émigré literary criticism and theory between the world wars." In: Evgeny Dobrenko and Galin Tihanov (eds.), 2011. *A history of Russian literary theory and criticism: The Soviet age and beyond.* Pittsburgh: University of Pittsburgh Press, 144–162.

Tihanov, Galin, 2011b. "Cosmopolitanism in the discursive landscape of modernity: Two Enlightenment articulations". In: David Adams and Galin Tihanov (eds.), 2011. *Enlightenment cosmopolitanism.* London: Legenda, 133–152.

Tynyanov, Yuri and Roman Jakobson, 1928, "Problems of Research in Literature and Language". In: L.M. O'Toole and Ann Shukman (eds.), 1977. *Formalist theory: Russian poetics in translation*, vol. 4. Colchester: University of Essex, 49–51.

Vertovec, Steven, 2009. *Transnationalism.* London and New York: Routledge.

Virilio, Paul, 1978. *Fahren, fahren, fahren.* Trans. Ulrich Raulf. Berlin: Merve.

Wat, Alexander, 1988. *My Century: The odyssey of a Polish intellectual.* Trans. Richard Lourie. Berkeley: University of California Press.

Wimmer, Andreas and Nina Glick Schiller, 2003. "Methodological nationalism and the study of migration: Beyond nation-state building." *International Migration Review*, 37(3), 576–610.

Yildiz, Yasemin, 2012. *Beyond the mother tongue: The postmonolingual condition.* New York: Fordham University Press.

Zoric, Vladimir, 2006. *Metaphoric aspects of exile.* Melbourne: CERC Working Papers Series, No. 3.

Zsuffa, Joseph, 1987. *Béla Balázs: The man and the artist.* Berkeley: University of California Press.

TAMARA CARAUS

Cosmopolitanism and the Legacy of East European Dissent

Recently there has been increasing interest in the theories of cosmopolitanism, with authors being challenged by the call to identify, explore and understand "the cosmopolitan condition" (Beck and Szneider 2006, 1) in terms of the most common points of view, topics of research, lived experiences and visions. The core idea shared by all cosmopolitan views is that all human beings belong to a single community, in which the ultimate units of moral concern appear as individual human beings, not states or particular forms of human associations.

In this chapter, I intend to investigate whether East European dissent may provide any lessons for the contemporary debates on cosmopolitanism. The chapter focuses on the dissident thinking of *Charter 77*, a human rights movement in socialist Czechoslovakia, with particular focus on the writings of Jan Patočka (1907–1977), philosopher, co-founder and spokesperson of *Charter 77*.

The chapter explores two sets of interrelated questions. The first set of questions concerns the possibility and practice of dissidence. In this context, it would be relevant to examine how the dissidents' claims were formulated, in terms of what values, and if these values were local, national, international or universal. The East European dissidents questioned and contested the given/imposed meanings in their political regime, but what values legitimated such contestation is an aspect that also should be explored.

My assumption is that the *Charter 77* civil, non-violent resistance to a hegemonic ideology and to a totalizing system was possible through an appeal to universal values, that is, human rights, and to a cosmopolitan vision positing that the ultimate units of moral concern are individual human beings, not states, certain regimes, or particular forms of human associations.

The second set of questions concerns the possible contribution of East European dissident thought to a non-foundationalist cosmopolitan theory which needs to tackle several unavoidable tensions: How should a cosmopolitan project look in the alleged post-metaphysical and post-universalistic theoretical framework? Is cosmopolitanism possible without universalism? How should we conceive of cosmopolitanism after the skepticism towards the grand narratives of modern ideologies? How can one justify cosmopolitan values without falling back on certain conceptions of a fixed human nature or a shared system of belief? What does it mean to be cosmopolitan today, given the plurality of the interpretative standpoints in the contemporary world? In this context, my hypothesis is that Jan Patočka's concept of "permanent questioning" provides us with a minimalist framework for conceiving a non-totalizing and post-universalist cosmopolitanism theory, avoiding the postulation of a global "overlapping consensus" and exploring the dynamics of contestability and disagreement. In addition, given the universality of cosmopolitan principles, a shadow of totalitarianism is present in every cosmopolitan theory. Each new proposal of a cosmopolitan approach risks formulating a new legitimating narrative that will take the vacant place of previous "grand narratives" (Lyotard 1979/1984). A new grand narrative should be suspected of having, more or less voluntary, ideological intentions. From this perspective, the legacy of East European dissidence provides, once more, a valuable resource when thinking about cosmopolitan political theory.

In order to respond to these questions, the chapter is structured into two parts: in the first part I approach dissidence as a cosmopolitan practice and in the second part I present dissident thinking as a possible philosophy of cosmopolitanism.

Part I: Dissidence as a Cosmopolitan Practice

Jan Patočka (1907–1977) was a Czech philosopher, and was considered the most important and influential thinker from Eastern Europe of the twentieth century.[1] He studied philosophy with Husserl and Heidegger, in the 1930s, and his phenomenological approach, which was his main contribution to philosophy, is understood as a continuation, development and critique of what he considered to be un-thought by his masters.[2] After the Second World War, he refused to join the Communist Party and was banned from academia, with the exception of a few years after the Prague Spring of 1968. In 1977, he founded and was one of the spokespersons of the Czech human rights movement *Charter 77*. In this context, Patočka was arrested by authorities. He died after a prolonged interrogation by the secret police. His death suggests an analogy to the fate of Socrates (Tucker 2000, 3; Falk 2003, 242; Findley 2003, 132). This comparison is not out of place, because Patočka lent to the Charter the sense that it was led by a figure committed to truth, much like Socrates (cf. the chapter by Vlasak in this volume). The influence of Patočka, and through him, of

1 Among Patočka's most important works are: "Negative Platonism: Reflections Concerning the Rise, the Scope, and the Demise of Metaphysics and Whether Philosophy Can Survive it" (1952), *An Introduction to Husserl's Phenomenology* (1965), *Body, Community, Language, World* (1968), *Plato and Europe* (1973), *Europe and the Post-European Age* (1973), *Heretical Essays in the Philosophy of History* (1975), "Two Charta 77 Texts": "The Obligation to Resist Injustice" and "What We Can and Cannot Expect from Charta 77" (1977).

2 As a result of reconsidering what he considered to be un-thought by his masters, Patočka develops an original aspect of phenomenology: an a-subjective phenomenology with an ethically and politically oriented life-world. Patočka argues that the Cartesian pure consciousness and the Husserlian ego-cogito cannot be a basis for experience and knowledge. What we experience seems to be a more overwhelming process than a grasping by pure consciousness, argues Patočka, and this external appearance is something *a-subjective*. In other words, what we experience takes place in the body as well, not only in consciousness; therefore the human being is an "incarnate being" in a concrete world.

philosophy and even phenomenology on Václav Havel, on the Chartists, on the Czechoslovak dissidence, and on the Velvet Revolution of 1989 in general is considered to be decisive (Findlay 1999, 404; Tucker 2000, 3–5; Falk 2003, 242–247).

Charter 77: A Brief Presentation

The catalyst for the formation of *Charter 77* is thought to be the arrest and trial of the underground rock group *The Plastic People of the Universe* (Falk 2003, 84–92). The declaration of the Charter was published on 6 January 1977, along with the names of the first 242 signatories. That document described the *Charter 77* as a "loose, informal and open association of people [...] united by the will to strive individually and collectively for respect for human and civil rights in our country and throughout the world" (*Declaration of Charter 77* 1977, 3). *Charter 77* criticized the government for failing to implement the human rights provisions of a number of documents it had signed, mainly the Final Act of the 1975 Conference on Security and Co-operation in Europe (Part III of the Helsinki Accords), and the United Nations covenants on political, civil, economic and cultural rights.

The government's reactions to the appearance of *Charter 77* were harsh. The text was considered illegal and its dissemination was a political crime. Signatories of *Charter 77* were punished through different means characteristic of the Communist regime: dismissal from work, forced exile, loss of citizenship, forced collaboration with the Communist secret police, detention, trial and imprisonment. Repression of *Charter 77* members continued during the 1980s (Falk 2003, 88–92). Despite unrelenting harassment and arrests, however, the Charter continued to issue reports on the government's violations of human rights. The smooth and rapid transition to democracy in November–December 1989 can be ascribed to the existence of a strong opposition to communism over two decades by *Charter 77* (Tucker 2000, 133–134).

Charter 77 produced 572 documents over the decade and a half of its existence, considered to be the collective oeuvre of Chartists who monitored the injustice committed by Communist authorities in everyday life, the relations between dissident organizations in Central and Eastern Europe, and the human rights abuses around the world (Falk 2003, 251–254). There was a strong element of transnationalism in the activity of *Charter 77*, showing that human rights cannot be limited by nor exclusively protected within national borders. Chartists were writing and arguing that international mechanisms must support the domestic defence of human rights and that international human rights have to be codified in domestic law (Falk 2003, 251–256). In spite of the unifying framework of human rights, scholars notice the pluralism of the *Charter 77*: it appealed to a broad range of supporters, including leading intellectuals, former revisionists of Communist doctrines, independent socialists, religious activists, workers, etc., coming together in "a pan-societal conversation about what the ground rules of politics ought to be" (Falk 2003, 252).

Patočka's Charter 77 Texts

Not only did Jan Patočka join this Central European initiative, but he also agreed to assume the role of one of the three *Charter 77* spokespersons. In this capacity, he wrote a series of texts which—as he died shortly afterwards of a stroke suffered following prolonged police interrogations—are now regarded as a kind of political testament (Palouš 2011, 164; Crepon 2011, 176). Patočka wrote them in the midst of the most serious political struggle he had ever engaged in, and he was interrogated on a daily basis by the secret police and threatened by the state prosecutor with charges of subversion and "anti-socialist" activities. These texts reflect the events of the last weeks of Patočka's life, yet all deal with older questions of political theory and express an unmistakable cosmopolitan vision.

In my opinion, Patočka's "Charta 77 texts"[3] directly answer the first set of questions posed by the present chapter: In the name of what values were the dissidents' claims formulated? Are these values local, national,

3 The translator of Patočka's *Charter 77* texts, Erazim Kohák (1989, 340–347), maintains the original Czech word "charta", instead of using the English word "charter".

international or universal? What legitimates the dissidents' permanent questioning and contestation of the given/imposed meanings in a political regime? Patočka's *Charter 77* texts show that the values that legitimated the protest of the Charter signatories and their contestation of the political regime are universal, unconditional values. Concomitantly, without using words like "cosmopolitan" or "cosmopolitanism", these texts express a cosmopolitan viewpoint. A close reading of the *Charter 77* texts reveals the following cosmopolitan aspects, which in the following will be addressed under their respective subtitles. The first aspect is that unconditional universal morality is considered to be "higher" than the sovereignty of nation-states. The second aspect refers to the preeminence of the universality of human beings over the particularity of the state. The third aspect concerns the difference between cosmopolitanism and the sphere of international relations. Another aspect will point to the role of transparency and publicity in creating a global public sphere. Finally, the role of education in achieving the preeminence of unconditional universal values will be examined. A description of each identified aspect shows the unmistakable cosmopolitanism of Patočka's *Charter 77* texts.

Unconditional Universal Morality: Higher than the Sovereignty of the Nation-state

Patočka indirectly addressed one of the main questions of political philosophy concerning the sovereignty of states, the core meaning of which is the *supreme authority within a territory*. For Patočka, all *raison d'être* of a state—the so-called national interest, the collective well-being, the appeals to a common identity, religion or ideology as foundations of a state—are irrelevant. In Patočka's argumentation, the sovereignty of states should be subordinated to a higher sphere, above or outside of politics, and this is the realm of morality: "No society [...] can function without a moral foundation" (Patočka 1977, 341). Unlike the dominant tradition of international relations or of state-oriented political theory, in Patočka's argumentation states are not based on particularistic ethics, but on a "morality that is not mere tactical and situational, but absolute" (Patočka 1977, 340). The alleged instrumental value of states is not dismissed entirely. Nevertheless, sovereign states, having the power to enact and enforce binding laws, are obliged to respect the elementary fact that our humanity has precedence over any political role we may be assigned to or pressed to play as citizens:

> Humankind needs to be convinced of the unconditional validity of principles which are, in that sense, "scared", valid for all humans and all times and capable of setting out humanity's goals. (Patočka 1977, 340)

Patočka's texts explain that the signatories remain within the bounds of the law and that the task of the Charter is to help the Czechoslovak government implement its own laws: the Universal Declaration of Human Rights and the 1975 Final Act of the Helsinki Agreement of Human Rights. Through human rights, politics requires adherence to general principles that include respect for civil and democratic rights, irrespective of particular practices and customs:

> The idea of human rights is nothing other than the conviction that even states, even society as a whole, are subject to the sovereignty of moral sentiment: that they recognize something unconditional that is higher than they are, something that is binding even on them, sacred, inviolable. (Patočka 1977, 341)

This position expresses a cosmopolitan morality that centres on the fundamental needs and interests of all individual human beings and makes the concentration of sovereignty at the nation-state level no longer defensible. Similar argumentations are currently present in the works of authors who, without arguing for a world state, go beyond a state-centred morality of the people towards a normative framework of global justice (e.g. Mollendorf 2002; Caney 2005) or global democracy (e.g. Held 1995; Archibugi *et al.* 2011).

The Individual's Preeminence Over Collectivity and the State

States and societies recognize something unconditional that is higher than they are, and this feeling is present in individuals as well, writes Patočka. *Charter 77* is an effect of this conviction: "*Charta 77* is an outgrowth of this conviction. It is an expression of the joy of our citizens that their country, confirming the right of humans with its signature, bestowed on this act the force of a Czechoslovak law […]" (Patočka 1977, 341).

Although the Charter is viewed as an expression of citizens' willingness to do their part in the realization and fulfillment of the principles proclaimed in the Helsinki Agreement, Patočka stresses that "*Charta 77* represents no political act" (Patočka 1977, 342) and that "its basis is strictly personal and moral, and so are the obligations it entails" (Patočka 1977, 342). The citizens' protest is not political but moral, because, according to Patočka, all moral obligations are rooted in what he calls "a person's obligation to himself—which includes, among other things, the obligation to resist any injustice done to him" (Patočka 1977, 342).

The obligation to resist injustice is similar to the Kantian obligation to oneself. From a Kantian point of view, people who are oppressed have an obligation to resist their own oppression. Oppression can harm people's rational nature, and therefore resisting oppression is an instance of fulfilling the obligation to respect and protect one's rational nature (Johnson 2011). The obligation to speak out for oneself is also the person's obligation to his society, maintains Patočka. Defending moral rights is an obligation to one's self as well as to others:

> No individual who is genuinely oppressed but who is determined not to surrender his obligation to speak out for himself—which is his obligation to his society as well—should rightly feel isolated and at the mercy of overwhelming circumstances. (Patočka 1977, 342)

The signatories of *Charter 77* understand that their acts might make their condition worse, writes Patočka, and it may provide the regime with an incentive to harshly repress, but there is no justification for not speaking out for oneself: "Submissiveness has never led to relaxation, only to greater severity. The greater the fear and servility, the more have the mighty dared, the more they dare" (Patočka 1977, 340). This duty to oneself relates immediately to the duty to others based on our humanity, which is the ground for interdependence. This argument clearly alludes to the idea that humanity is an end in itself. Nevertheless, morality for Patočka is not a product of an ahistorical categorical imperative or other metaphysical framework. Here the underlying source of moral analysis is his phenomenology and philosophy of history, as Patočka's commentators have argued (Findlay 2002, 132–135).

Why is the obligation to resist injustice a cosmopolitan one? Firstly, the obligation to resist injustice stresses the importance and preeminence of the individual over the community and state, because in this case the injustice is done by the state, that is, by the authoritarian state in socialist Czechoslovakia. The obligation to resist injustice is a cosmopolitan obligation, because it does not necessarily arise out of social institutions and social relations within this concrete society and state. This obligation is part of the universal duties that we have, both to ourselves and to others, simply as human beings. The universal duties are in some sense the foundations of all our duties, within which we also acquire duties as a result of social customs, institutions and relationships. Secondly, the obligation to resist injustice, which is a personal duty and an obligation to reassert universal unconditional values, has the features of the obligation characteristic of moral cosmopolitanism, which holds that all persons stand in certain moral relations to one another, highlighting the obligations we have to those whom we do not know.[4] Cosmopolitan solidarity does not require bonds of common identity or the discourses of us/them: it is constituted as a reaction to the same risks and injustice.

The Difference Between Cosmopolitanism and the Sphere of International Relations

More than thirty years ago, Patočka explained the difference between the traditional sphere of international relations and the new realm in the world, created by the Declaration of Human Rights:

> We consider a time when it became possible to sign a Declaration of Human Rights a new historical epoch, the stage of an immense outreach, since it represents a reversal of human consciousness, of the attitude of humans to themselves and to their society. (Patočka 1977, 342)

4 Moral cosmopolitanism is characteristic especially of analytical political philosophy, discussing how much we owe to distant others. See Brock and Brighouse (2005, 3–11).

Recently scholars have argued that the *Declaration of Human Rights* from 1948 is a transition from international norms to a cosmopolitan sphere. For example, Seyla Benhabib (2006, 13–45) explains the difference as follows: norms of international laws are established through treaties and agreements and are focused on states as actors in the wider world, while a cosmopolitanism of human rights conceives individuals as moral beings in the worldwide society. Even if states should sign and adopt the human rights declaration, the *Declaration* has an unprecedented feature—it concerns individuals endowed with rights. In addition, notions like "crimes against humanity", "genocide", "war crimes" and "humanitarian intervention" stipulate that there are certain norms that states have to respect in their treatment of citizens, and that certain actions are no longer acceptable. When a sovereign state violates basic human rights within its own borders, there is a generalized moral obligation to end actions such as genocide and crimes against humanity. No matter how controversial these notions may be in application and interpretation, their use is based on a growing consensus that the sovereignty of the state to dispose of the life, freedom and property of its citizens is neither unlimited nor unconditional. Obviously, the current world order is not entirely cosmopolitan: the authors criticize it for being an international order and not a truly cosmopolitan one. Nevertheless, the claim of the Westphalian state enjoying unlimited authority over all its subjects within the circumscribed territory is not more legitimate.

"We who have signed Charta 77 are convinced that this Act is far more significant than the usual treaties among nations, which deal only with the interests of countries and powers", affirms Patočka (1977, 341). Therefore, to the extent that protection of the individual is at the heart of the cosmopolitan project, we can say that Patočka affirmed a cosmopolitan point of view while defending the necessity of the *Charter 77* movement.

The Role of Transparency and Publicity in Creating a Global Public Sphere

In Patočka's argumentation, people resisting the injustice of the regime learn to think for themselves and to make public use of their reason (as opposed to private ways of resisting the regime) and, in this manner, persons inaugurate a global and cosmopolitan public sphere.

By explaining "What we can and cannot expect from Charta 77", Patočka clarifies first of all what the expectations were of those who signed the act, on both sides. The representatives of East European countries "signed expecting that nothing will change in the way the powerful treat the public, that all will go as before" (Patočka 1977, 345), while the other side signed in hopeful expectation that there would be no repetition of the events from the 1920s and 1930s in the Soviet Union and from the 1950s in Eastern Europe. What *Charter 77* already achieved is the fact that "It has shown that carrying out the Helsinki agreements will not be as effortless as some had thought" (Patočka 1977, 345).

The repressions and so-called political trials of the 1920s and 1930s in the Soviet Union and in the 1950s throughout Eastern Europe took place in states that "swore by socialism and humanity and boasted of the freest constitutions in the world" (Patočka 1977, 345). In spite of the commitment to safeguard humanity and freedom, the Communist regimes perpetuated crimes. Therefore, the Helsinki Agreements introduced a hope that regimes would change by respecting the signed documents. From here comes the disappointment of those who expected the communist block to change after the Helsinki Agreements. Nevertheless, Patočka notices that the actions of the government and of the opponents of *Charter 77* "have won us more sympathy at home and abroad that we dare to expect" (Patočka 1977, 344). An uncontestable achievement of the *Charter 77* is that it drew attention to what happened in Eastern Europe: "the positive achievement of the Charta is that all of this has been revealed, that the world has not remained blind and unsure, as in a fog" (Patočka 1977, 345). The attention of the entire world is for Patočka a "powerful factor" in world politics and the ways of obtaining this attention point to the public use of reason by the *Charter 77* followers: "Clear conscience and decency have proved to be also a powerful factor of political reality. The legality of the presentation of the *Charta*, the fact that its entire goal is to strengthen legality, without exception and under public supervision [...]" (Patočka 1977, 344). The public supervision involved here has two dimensions: the internal dimension, that is, supervision of the government by the *Charter 77* movement; and the external one; that is, public supervision of the Czechoslovak authorities (and, in general, of Communist authorities from Eastern Europe) by the entire world.

Patočka's texts show how *Charter 77* makes the norms of publicity and transparency both real and effective in world affairs, and this aspect of his argumentation points to a cosmopolitan public sphere. To contest policies or imposed obligations on a global level does not necessarily entail the presence of a global state, but of a public sphere, which is meant to be the negative substitute for the infeasibility of the "global Leviathan", that is, the world state. Transparency conditions open institutions and regimes to outside inspection and, in this way, various actors have access to information about the regime's effectiveness and can even observe political and decision-making processes. This form of scrutiny is crucial for ensuring public accountability and it is an essential element of global democratic practice, as authors have argued recently (Bohman 1999; Linklater 1998). Furthermore, public reason and transparency norms are essential prerequisites for the emergence of meaningful notions of global citizenship and democracy, and for the promotion of new forms of solidarity in world politics.

Therefore, in Patočka's argumentation, persons speaking out for themselves, and joining *Charter 77*, taught those in power that they had to respect individual persons. Individual persons, empowered by the Declaration of Human Rights, can change the world around them and, indirectly, the entire world.

The Role of Education in Achieving the Preeminence of Unconditional Values

An interesting aspect of Patočka's argumentation in his *Charter 77* texts is the emphasis that the Charter expected nothing more than to educate citizens to act as free persons:

> Perhaps the mighty of this world will gradually come to choose our road. Perhaps they will learn at least to think in advance how to make their intended deeds conform to the letter of their agreements. Even that will be a gain. If it becomes a habit, we shall all benefit. The Charta never sought more than to educate. (Patočka 1977, 346)

And, accordingly:

> It is the hope of Charta 77 that our citizens may learn to act as free persons, self-motivated and responsible, while those in authority may realize that the sole respect worth winning comes from people confident of its worth. (Patočka 1977, 346)

The Charter's intention to educate shows its unmistakable cosmopolitan purpose when it is read from the Kantian perspective of philosophy in a cosmopolitan sense. Philosophy in a cosmopolitan sense, as a free use of reason, concerns that which necessarily interests everyone, argue Kantian researchers.[5] Kant's *Perpetual Peace* and *Idea of a Universal History with a Cosmopolitan Purpose* are texts that announce and foreshadow international institutions that appeared in the twentieth century. These institutions, just as the idea of international law or human rights that they try to implement, are based on certain values and norms that have been thought by philosophy: "These institutions, like the idea of international law that they try to implement, are already philosophemes" (Derrida 1991, 4). International institutions are philosophical acts and products not only because they have a philosophical history, but because in order to implement their purposes they imply the sharing of a culture and language, which are the effects of an education based on philosophy in a cosmopolitan sense. For Patočka the respect of human rights is also something that should be learnt and thought:

> Charta 77 introduces a new ideal orientation into our lives [...] It is a new orientation to basic human rights, to the moral dimension of political and private life. The Charta will unceasingly remind us how far we fall short of those rights belonging to our citizens by law; it will not cease to remind both our and the foreign public of it, regardless of the risks of such activity. (Patočka 1977, 347)

This account of cosmopolitan education is, to some extent, different from the topic of cosmopolitan education discussed by civic educators, for whom cosmopolitan education is either a multicultural education focused on making persons aware of the perspectives of others, or one of the attempts

5 For an interpretation of the Kantian *Weltbegriff* (or *conceptus cosmicus*) of philosophy, as a free use of reason, see Höffe (2001/2006, especially 204–229).

to create a "global citizen" with global awareness (Callan 1997; Nussbaum 1996). The *Charter 77*'s intention to educate does not necessarily deal with education of a "community of dialogue and concern" (Nussbaum 1996, 9), or of all persons regardless of race, creed, class or borders. The Charter's hope was that persons would learn to act as free and responsible agents, speaking out for themselves and rejecting injustice, and this could be considered the basis of any cosmopolitan education.

I hope that given the above-mentioned features of *Charter 77* texts, this concrete event of dissidence qualifies as a cosmopolitan practice. The dissidents' contestation of the given/imposed meanings in the concrete political regime of socialist Czechoslovakia was legitimated by values that are universal, not local nor national. *Charter 77* civil, non-violent resistance to a hegemonic ideology and to a totalizing system was possible through the appeal to unconditional universal values—human rights—and to a cosmopolitan vision that considers that individual human beings are ultimate units of moral concern, not states, specific regimes, or particular forms of human associations.

Part II: Dissidence as a Philosophy of Cosmopolitanism

Jan Patočka's *Charter 77* texts help us see the cosmopolitan aspect of a concrete historical episode of dissidence. My further hypothesis is that the entire corpus of his work might help us formulate a non-foundationalist cosmopolitan theory; dissidence as a philosophy of cosmopolitanism. Patočka's concepts of "permanent questioning" and "living in problematicity" provide a minimalist framework for conceiving a non-totalizing and post-universalist cosmopolitanism theory. In this context, I will present several aspects of Patočka's political philosophy that could outline a philosophy of cosmopolitanism as dissidence. My approach is not an interpretation of Patočka's text, but a certain "use" of his ideas, similar to a thought experiment.

Patočka's Political Philosophy: Elements of a Philosophy of Cosmopolitanism

Permanent Questioning

"Negative Platonism" is Patočka's post-metaphysical approach to foundations. In Patočka's version, the story of metaphysics begins with Socratic knowledge described as "a learned ignorance that is a question" (Patočka 1952, 180). Socrates permanently challenges his interlocutors through questioning their and his knowledge. Socrates does not formulate his new knowledge in objective, factual, positive assertions but indirectly, in the form of questioning. The essence of metaphysics, as Plato and Aristotle formulated it, consists in offering an answer to the Socratic question, an answer that philosophers seek to derive from the question itself. In this way, "Ignorance became a form of knowledge [...] more secure than anything on the earth" (Patočka 1952, 181). Philosophy started to be portrayed not only as a movement towards transcending the sensible, but also as a movement towards an ideal being. In Patočka's view, "The integrity of human life is broken. Man becomes one of the beings ruled by ideas; ethics and politics as a grand unity take on the task of discovery of the inner ideal law of a humanly perfect life" (Patočka 1952, 182). Patočka's interpretation of metaphysics reconsiders one of the common objections to Platonism: critics have found the radical separation of two worlds implausible and impossible to reconcile with the claim that ideas shape and guide the order of things and events from the empirical world. Patočka takes seriously the very possibility of thinking this separation: "The separation is identical with freedom" (Patočka 1952, 192). The experience of freedom is identical to that of questioning, in the sense of being distanced from or dissatisfied with the given. Patočka's Platonism is a negative philosophy in the sense that, instead of positing a certain positive content, it takes as point of departure "the negative character of a distance, of a remove, of an overcoming of every objectivity" (Patočka 1952, 193).[6]

6 The thesis of "Negative Platonism" is found in an article of the same name, along with several accompanying texts stemming from the 1950s (Patočka 1952). Although these

Living in Problematicity

Patočka develops an original aspect of phenomenology—*asubjective* phenomenology—that leads to a comprehensive transformation of the key phenomenological concept of the life-world into an ethically and politically oriented life-world. Asubjective phenomenology is not a phenomenology of pure consciousness and subjectivity, but of "incarnate being" in the body and the world. To perceive humans as "being in and of the world" (Patočka 1968/1998, 155), Patočka examines humans in three movements: the movement of anchoring in corporeity and in the world, the movement of self-projection and the movement of breaking-through. In this third movement, man confronts his finitude and by virtue of this confrontation politics, philosophy and history are born: "The reason for this special position of politics is that political life in its original and primordial form is nothing other than active freedom" (Patočka 1975/1996, 77). Politics is born with the experience of freedom as distancing, removing and shaking up the given meaning and should not be identified with the administrative organization of life.

Politics starts in the moment/movement of shaking the naïve/given meanings, and, concomitantly, starting the experience of meaninglessness. For Patočka the question of an absolute/final meaning of being/existence cannot be answered, because meaning does not pre-exist as a (metaphysical) origin, and meaning did not pre-exist prior to the question of its possibility: "the shaking of the naïve meaning is the genesis of a perspective on an absolute meaning" (Patočka 1975/1996, 77). Patočka argues that meaning will not be given after formulating the question, because what the entire question offers is just a perspective with the inevitability of another question. "Humans cannot live without meaning", admits Patočka (1975/1996,

articles were not published during Patočka's lifetime, they represent the philosophical grounds on which his later interpretation of Europe, history and politics was able to proceed. Long before post-modern philosophers and deconstruction, Patočka was writing about the demise of metaphysics, at the same time avoiding relativism, contingency and nihilism by keeping the enigma of Being while questioning it incessantly. For an account of Patočka's postmodern philosophy, see Petr Lom (1999).

75), but this does not mean that they should live with an unproblematic meaning. Humans have to be prepared "to give up the hope of a directly given meaning and to accept the meaning as a way" (p. 77), that is, meaning as a quest for meaning. What man fails to comprehend is that "history is nothing other than the shaken attitude of pre-given meanings. It has no other meaning or goal" (p. 118), and all of modern civilization fails to understand that "the problem of history may not be resolved; it must be preserved as a problem" (p. 118).

In his understanding of war, Patočka (1975/1996, 119–137) writes that darkness is the basic condition out of which light, that is, knowledge, first arises. Metaphysics viewed darkness and problematicity as merely an absence of light, as a condition to be overcome. The preference for light and day, the looking for absolute certainties, is that it generates wars. War is an attempt to suppress the question posed by night and darkness. Although peace, light and day are seen as virtuous aspirations, their implications are destructive. In the longing for a final eschatological peace, conflicts and contingencies are considered barriers that should be eliminated. There is an urgency to accept darkness and night as consubstantial of our condition, states Patočka. The evocation of "darkness" over "light" or "day" is an attempt to reintroduce the notions of uncertainty and problematicity as an inevitable component of human existence.

Patočka calls this perpetual struggle between light and darkness *polemos*, which, for the Czech thinker, is not only an intrinsic aspect of life, but is also "the primordial insight that makes philosophy possible" (Patočka 1975/1996, 43). The concomitant birth of politics and philosophy does not mean to elevate politics to philosophy, but it means that both emerge from (Heraclitus') *polemos*. Political life, as Patočka claims, is "a permanent uprootedness, [a] lack of foundation" (Patočka 1975/1996, 38). Politics does not permit any hope for a "happy ending". Politics should allow for, and not seek to end, a free and conflictual interaction. The conflict of light and darkness is not a destructive force. *Polemos* is constructive rather than destructive of community: "*Polemos* binds together the contending parties, not only because it stands over them but because in it they are at one" (Patočka 1975/1996, 118).

Shaken Solidarities

With the movement of shaking up naïve/given meanings begins the experience of meaninglessness, admits Patočka. For Patočka the question of the meaning of existence cannot be answered, because meaning does not pre-exist as an origin. Meaning did not pre-exist prior to the question of its possibility, and will not be given as an answer. Human beings should learn to live in problematicity. Living in problematicity might sound like living in permanent conflict, but on the contrary, living in problematicity makes possible an unprecedented solidarity: the solidarity of the shaken, which is "the solidarity of those who are capable of understanding what life and death are about, and so what history is about" (Patočka 1975/1996, 43). For some authors (Chvátik 1993, 165) the solidarity of the shaken seems like a solidarity of king-philosophers, an elitist solidarity inaccessible to most human beings. Indeed, the accusation of elitism cannot easily be refuted. Nevertheless, this unity is not a monolithic unity, a kind of solidarity which we are accustomed to seeing in the case of a nation or of ethnic groups. On the contrary, it is a solidarity of those who resist any monolithic programmes and ideologies: The solidarity of the shaken can say "no" to the measures of mobilization that makes the state of war permanent. It will not offer positive programmes, but will speak, like Socrates' *daimonion*, in warnings and prohibitions (Patočka 1975/1996, 135).

Patočka admits that "permanent questioning and living in problematicity are not easy tasks, and asks if a conversion, of historic proportions" (Patočka 1975/1996, 77), which would make humans capable of accepting responsibility for the meaninglessness, is possible. The possibility of a conversion depends essentially on the capacity to live with problematicity:

> Is the part of humanity, which is capable of understanding what was and what is the point of history, which is at the same time ever more driven by the entire positioning of present day humanity at the peak of techno-science to accept responsibility for meaninglessness, also capable of [the] discipline of self-denial demanded by the state of uprootedness in which alone a meaningfulness, both absolute and accessible to humans, because it is problematic, might be realized? (Patočka 1975/1996, 75–76)

This conversion of historic proportions, although might have the features of a "godless religion of insight" (Chvátik n.d.), is not Patočka's attempt to a new absolute meaning. It is a conversion to life in problematicity. The loss of meaning is not the descent into the meaningless but the access to a quality of meaning implied in the search itself, observes Ricœur (1996, xiii). The self-denial demanded by the state of uprootedness, as described by Patočka, means that a conversion to life in problematicity is not an easy task. Does it mean that it is easier for human beings to project fantasies of unity and harmonious meanings? For Patočka the meanings and harmonies are only received/given meanings. The appearance of new meaning is not the effect of a harmonious fantasy but an effect of breaking-through.

I select these three elements—permanent questioning, problematicity of meaning and shaken solidarities—as elements necessary for a minimalist theory of cosmopolitanism. Some of Patočka's commentators consider that Patočka's thought cannot be a guideline for political action and cannot found political science.[7] Indeed, Patočka's political thought cannot help in establishing constitutional order, but the irreducible problematicity and disagreement are necessary grounds to understanding the political existence.

Cosmopolitanism as Dissidence

Given the assumption of permanent questioning, and because the question has the capacity to destabilize harmony and authority, and therefore to exercise a critical function, the cosmopolitan perspective that I have been trying to outline here has the features of the political philosophy of

7 For example, Avizier Tucker (2000), using Patočka's participation in *Charter 77* as a baseline, describes Patočka as the author of a metaphysics of human rights and as the guiding light of the Czech dissidence in the second half of the twentieth century. When Patočka's texts on problematicity, *polemos and* permanent questioning do not confirm this humanist interpretation, Tucker criticizes him as a reactionary.

dissidence. Nevertheless, how can the assumptions of permanent questioning, problematicity and shaken solidarities help us formulate cosmopolitan theory and practice?

Disagreement as an Impossible Universalism

Cosmopolitanism as dissidence offers several suggestions for formulating a post-universalist account of cosmopolitan theory, and relates in a more adequate manner to the problems of contemporary world than the cosmopolitan visions based on the assumptions of consensus and harmony:

First, the assumption of problematicity is receptive to the differences and pluralism of the contemporary world. A political theory of cosmopolitanism should not allow the illusion that the problem of this pluralism could be dissolved through consensus. On the contrary, Patočka's notion of problematicity emphasizes the democratic potential of political contestation and the disruption of settled practices, but this does not mean celebrating a world without points of stabilization; it is to affirm the reality of perpetual contest, and to identify the positive dimension of contestation.

Second, if the nation-state assumes consensus, agreement and harmony as dominant in domestic communities, then these harmonies are implausible at the global level. The global public discourse does not appear as consensus but as a disagreement regarding the decisions taken in the so-called international sphere, and communication or solidarity might be involuntary in order to avoid risks and catastrophes (Beck 2004, 144–146). In different contexts, the inter-connection at the global level takes place as a negative event, for example global warming. Assuming the necessity of a global consensus and global harmony, political theories will not correspond to actual empirical challenges.

Third, cosmopolitanism should not offer an idealized vision of the cosmopolitan condition, as a culmination of modernity and triumph of reason. In some texts, the cosmopolitan condition is idealized through the emphasis on human rights, international law and international courts, global institutions, and the cosmopolitan moment appears as a moment of synthesis and reconciliation, overcoming previous divisions and conflicts. Cosmopolitanism as dissidence is consistent with the contemporary assumptions of contingency, historicity and finitude and avoids a totalizing grand narrative.

Fourth, there are accusations that cosmopolitanism is not real, that what is presented as cosmopolitanism are in fact certain notions that hide the power of a few states, and their imperialism, domination and violence (Beck 2002; Archibugi 2004). From this perspective, cosmopolitanism as dissidence, as living in problematicity, cannot legitimize imperialisms, because it does not give any legitimacy to any political regime.

Finally, cosmopolitanism as dissidence avoids the requirements of moral cosmopolitanism that risk reducing cosmopolitanism to philanthropy, requiring all to be emotionally involved regarding the fate of other distant persons. Opponents of cosmopolitanism maintain that cosmopolitanism does not allow one to act, making persons incapable of taking any action as world citizens. Dissidence as cosmopolitanism, through the assumption of permanent questioning and problematicity, includes everyone, even though the question, disagreement or contestation are expressed or manifested now, later or, for some persons, never. From this perspective, cosmopolitanism is a minimalist framework that includes everyone without any preconditions.

Cosmopolitan "Shaken" Solidarities

Patočka's notion of "solidarity of the shaken" offers suggestions for rethinking solidarity in a global/cosmopolitan condition. A frequent objection to cosmopolitanism is that there cannot be cosmopolitan solidarity because it is impossible to have substantial global solidarity according to the universality of human rights. Even if an abstract solidarity, corresponding to the universality of human rights, cannot be formulated, it does not mean that there is nothing that could motivate persons to act globally. It should be said that it is not necessary to conceive of cosmopolitanism as a continuation of national pride, as a sacrifice, or as other virtues familiar from the national narratives. Fraternity is irrelevant to the cosmopolitan condition (Penski 2000, 2007). In Patočka's words, instead of letting questions be addressed, and instead of accepting problematicity, the political world formulated dichotomies, "us"–"them", "we"–"the enemy", mapping the evil in "them" and in "the enemy".

In a global world the instances "us"–"them" are multiplied, and sometimes dissolved, and uncertainties are multiplied as well. Globalization can destabilize given identities and cultural affiliations, and for some people this is liberating, while for others this is a loss. In a cosmopolitan condition, a rich cultural identity might be a privilege, not a norm: "The disappearance of this privileged resource could be the condition of global democratic practices" (Penski 2000, 76).

The disappearance of cultural identities as a rich resource is similar to the shaking up of naïve given meanings, as argued by Patočka. Accordingly, it could be challenging to ask if the solidarity of the shaken is possible. The disappearance of previous compulsory national or cultural identities does not mean that persons will find themselves entirely in the loss of others' identity, and that their shaken identities will overlap and they will form a new monolithic solidarity of the shaken but undaunted.

The shaking or disappearance of previous identities is not an equalizing process; it happens differentially and solidarity will be *multiple*, *partial* (or differential) and *temporary*: Plural or multiple identities mean that in a cosmopolitan condition there cannot be a single solidarity but many (*multiple solidarities*). Further, solidarity cannot be total, an overlapping of all intentions, but only of an interest of persons that otherwise remain strange and foreign (*partial solidarity*). Finally, cosmopolitan solidarity might be temporal until, let us say, a public deliberation is started and a topic is placed on the global agenda, given the global interest affected or a common global interest (*temporary solidarity*).

Therefore, instead of a global community, monolithic and uniform, which should be governed by a despotic state, we have a plural world of plural and partial solidarities, a world that recognizes its problematicity and vulnerability.

Cosmopolitan "Conversion"

Patočka's (dissident) political thought offers plausible or at least coherent premises for a minimalist cosmopolitanism. Nevertheless, does it offer a model for practicing cosmopolitanism? The living in problematicity and the acceptance of permanent questioning seem to be activities available only to a small elite who practise a permanent critique or have a "vocation" for contestation, while for others, living in problematicity might require a full display of heroism. Patočka asks if a conversion to life in problematicity is possible, and accordingly whether a "conversion" to critical cosmopolitanism seems necessary.

However, even political, legal or economic versions of cosmopolitanism require a demanding conditionality for persons. For example, Thomas Pogge affirms that a restructuring of our vision about the world is necessary in order to be able to address the necessary questions:

> A large portion of the huge quantities of natural resources we consume is imported, much of it from repressive undemocratic countries. We deplore the lack of democracy and wonder what we might do to help. But, as good explanatory nationalists, we see no connection between the international transactions and the domestic tyranny. The former involves us, but is a fair exchange at market prices, the latter is unjust, but we, not being part of it, bear no responsibility for its injustice. Once we structure our world view in this way, it becomes very hard to address the right questions. (Pogge 2002, 141–142)

Therefore, the ability to address Pogge's "right questions", for example "How to eradicate global poverty?"; "How to organize the world in a cosmopolitan manner?" etc., is not a given ability, but an effect of a certain conversion, that is, of restructuring our worldview.

If every cosmopolitan vision requires a "conversion", then the "conversion" to cosmopolitanism as dissidence is a minimalist one, because it does not require an acceptance of a new set of harmonious values, but only the recognition of the irreducible disagreement and conflict. Nevertheless, the "conversion" supposes several ways that might facilitate the acceptance of problematicity. Firstly, we have to accept the interdependence and the mix of cultures in our lifestyle and to recognize the irreducible problematicity and disagreement in human thought and actions. Secondly, the willingness to see the constructionist nature of identities and to learn to live with "unfinished" partial identities are the other preconditions of becoming cosmopolitan, as well as the renunciation to the temptation to reiterate the "us"–"them" relation with its violence of inclusion and exclusion. Finally, we also have to be vigilant not to construct global political fantasies and utopias for overcoming problematicity. Vigilance is necessary in order to preserve disagreement and problematicity without reoccupying the place of old schemas. In the face of problematicity and conflict, there is the temptation to project ideals and utopias, but according to Patočka, the promise of positivism and harmony leads to a proliferation of negativities.

Cosmopolitanism shaped by Patočka's vision is non-ideal and non-utopian. Without an ideal, we remain without the promise of harmony. We instead have the dynamics of dissent and disagreement. The recognition of the impossibility of harmony and reconciliation does not mean silence and abandonment, but productive uncertainty, because, in Patočka's words, there is a new chance for man to "break-through".

Acknowledgement

Research for this essay was supported by a grant from the Romanian National Authority for Scientific Research, CNCS – UEFISCDI, project number PN-II-RU-TE-2011–3–0218.

References

Archibugi, Daniele, 2004. "Cosmopolitan democracy and its critics". *European Journal of International Relations*, 10(3), 437–473.

Archibugi, Daniele, Koenig-Archibugi, Mathias and Marchetti, Raffaele, 2011. *Global democracy: Normative and empirical perspectives*. Cambridge: Cambridge University Press.

Beck, Ulrich, 2002."The cosmopolitan society and its enemies". *Theory, Culture & Society*, 19(1–2), 17–44.

Beck, Ulrich and Szneider, Nathan, 2006. "Unpacking cosmopolitanism for the social sciences: A research agenda". *The British Journal of Sociology*, 57(1), 1–23.
Benhabib, Seyla, 2006. *Another cosmopolitanism (the Berkeley Tanner lectures)*. Ed. Robert Post. Oxford: Oxford University Press.
Bohman, James, 1999. "Citizenship and norms of publicity: Wide public reason in cosmopolitan societies". *Political Theory*, 27(2), 176–202.
Brock, Gillian and Harry Brighouse, 2005. "Introduction". In: Gillian Brock and Harry Brighouse (eds.), 2005. *The political philosophy of cosmopolitanism*. Cambridge: Cambridge University Press.
Callan, Eamonn, 1997. *Creating citizens: Political education and liberal democracy*. Oxford: Clarendon Press.
Caney, Simion, 2005. *Justice beyond borders: A global political theory*. Oxford: Oxford University Press.
Crepon, Marc, 2011. "Fear, courage, anger: The Socratic lesson". In: Ivan Chvátik and Erika Abrams (eds.), 2011. *Jan Patočka and the heritage of phenomenology: Centenary papers*. Dordrecht and New York: Springer, 175–187.
Chvátik, Ivan, n.d. "The heretical conception of the European legacy in the late essays of Jan Patočka". CTS paper: CTS03-14. Prague: Patočka Archive.
Declaration of Charter 77. 1977. Available at: http://libpro.cts.cuni.cz/charta/docs/declaration_ of _charter 77.pdf. Accessed 10 October 2011.
Derrida, Jacques, 1991/2002. "The right to philosophy from the cosmopolitical point of view". In: Peter Pericles Trifonas (ed. and trans.), 2002. *Ethics, institutions, and the right to philosophy*. Lanham, MD: Rowman & Littlefield, 1–18.
Falk, Barbara J., 2003. *The dilemmas of dissidence in East-Central Europe: Citizen intellectuals and philosopher kings*. Budapest: Central European University Press.
Findlay, Edward, 2002. *Caring for the soul in a postmodern age: Philosophy and politics in the thought of Jan Patočka*. Albany, NY: SUNY Press.
Findlay, Edward, 1999. "Classical ethics and postmodern critique: Political philosophy in Václav Havel and Jan Patočka". *Review of Politics*, 61(3), 403–438.
Held, David and Archibugi, Daniele (eds.), 1995. *Cosmopolitan democracy. An agenda for a new world order*. Cambridge: Polity Press.
Höffe, Otfried, 2001/2006. *Kant's cosmopolitan theory of law and peace*. Trans. Alexandra Newton. New York: Cambridge University Press.
Johnson, Robert N., 2011. *Self-improvement: An essay in Kantian ethics*. Oxford: Oxford University Press.
Kohák, Erazim (ed. and trans.), 1989. *Jan Patočka: Philosophy and selected writings*. Chicago: University of Chicago Press.
Linklater, Andrew, 1998. *The transformation of political community*. London: Polity Press.

Lom, Petr, 1999. "East meets West—Jan Patočka and Richard Rorty on freedom: A Czech philosopher brought into dialogue with American postmodernism". *Political Theory*, 27(4), 447–459.

Lyotard, Jean-François, 1979/1984. *The post-modern condition: A report on knowledge*. Trans. G. Bennington and B. Massumi. Minneapolis: University of Minnesota Press.

Mollendorf, Darrel, 2002. *Cosmopolitan justice*. Boulder, CO: Westview Press.

Nussbaum, Martha C., 1996. "Patriotism and cosmopolitanism". In: Martha C. Nussbaum and Joshua Cohen (eds.), 1996. *For love of country: Debating the limits of patriotism*. Boston: Beacon Press. 2–17.

Palouš, Martin, 2011. "Jan Patočka's Socratic message for the twenty first century: Rereading Patočka's Charter 77 texts thirty years later". In: Ivan Chvátik and Erika Abrams (eds.), 2011. *Jan Patočka and the heritage of phenomenology: Centenary papers*. Dordrecht and New York: Springer, 163–175.

Patočka, Jan, 1952. "Negative Platonism: Reflections concerning the rise, the scope, and the demise of metaphysics—and whether philosophy can survive it". In: Erazim Kohák (ed. and trans.), 1989. *Jan Patočka: Philosophy and selected writings*. Chicago: University of Chicago Press, 175–206.

Patočka, Jan, 1968/1998. *Body, community, language, world*. Ed. James Dodd and trans. Erazim Kohák. Chicago: Open Court.

Patočka, Jan, 1975/1996. *Heretical essays in the philosophy of history*. Ed. James Dodd and trans. Erazim Kohák. Chicago and La Salle, Ill: Open Court.

Patočka, Jan, 1977. "Two Charta 77 texts": "The obligation to resist injustice"; "What we can and cannot expect from Charta 77". In: Erazim Kohák (ed. and trans.), 1989. *Jan Patočka: Philosophy and selected writings*. Chicago: University of Chicago Press.

Pensky, Max, 2000. "Cosmopolitanism and solidarity problem: Habermas on national and cultural identities". *Constellations*, 7(1), 64–79.

Pensky, Max, 2007. "Two cheers for cosmopolitanism: Solidarity as second order inclusion". *Journal of Social Philosophy*, 38(1), 165–184.

Pogge, Thomas, 2002. *Global poverty and human rights*. Cambridge: Polity Press.

Ricœur, Paul, 1996. "Preface". In: Jan Patočka, 1975/1996. *Heretical essays in the philosophy of history*. Ed. James Dodd and trans. Erazim Kohák. Chicago and La Salle, Ill: Open Court, vii–xvi.

Tucker, Aviezer, 2000. *The philosophy and politics of Czech dissidence from Patočka to Havel*. Pittsburgh: University of Pittsburgh Press.

PART IV

Beyond Cosmopolitanism

JAMIL KHADER

Cosmopolitanism and the Infidelity to Internationalism: Repeating Postcoloniality and the World Revolution

> What we do know is that social progress can only result from a position that bridges the gap between the universal goals of humanity and their expression, which can only be particular. This is what internationalism is all about.
>
> — MICHAEL FORMAN

Although *cosmopolitics*[1] theorists maintain that cosmopolitanism and internationalism are neither identical nor incompatible, these theorists generally omit and erase narratives of radical internationalism from their accounts of cosmopolitanism. In their work, "cosmopoliticians" such as Daniele Archibugi, Bruce Robbins and Pheng Cheah promote the utopian possibilities of a postnational world that can presumably facilitate the subject's (usually disembodied) modes of sociability and belonging in and out of communities at will. That is, they valorize multiple and overlapping allegiances to different communities through forms of "flexible citizenship",

1 As it is used here, cosmopolitics refers to the theory that suggests that the particular inscription of the universal dimension of cosmopolitanism through an emphasis on the local and the marginal is possible. It also tends to emphasize agency and praxis. To this extent, cosmopolitics theorists may appropriate the lexicon of nationalism and ethnic particularity as well as the rhetoric of empowerment, while framing their discussion within the rhetoric of postnationalism and universalism, ignoring, it is argued here, the contradictions and logical inconsistencies in their conceptual framework.

without paying enough attention to the ways in which these postmodern forms of identity reproduce the power structures and relationships of the neoliberal, global capitalism regime. As such, cosmopoliticians usually disregard the extent to which the nation-state is still the most important site for the protection of the millions of disenfranchised communities around the world from the neoliberal encroachments of the global capitalist system.[2] Consequently, cosmopoliticians subtract the dialectical articulation of national modes of sociability from international narratives of solidarity and struggle, thus omitting and suppressing histories of oppositional narratives of anti-colonial resistance, especially national liberation struggles, decolonization projects, hemispheric indigenous solidarity, communitarian forms of alliances and resistance and, also, socialist internationalism.[3] Lacking a meaningful articulation of the social bases of long-lasting solidarities, cosmopoliticians thus transmute histories of colonial and capitalist exploitation and the struggle against it into triumphant narratives of unfettered mobility and border crossings, in a way that obfuscates the possibilities for constructing alternative forms of international politics that remain grounded in collective modalities of local difference,

2 At the heart of this debate surrounding *cosmopolitics* is the problematic of the nation-state and national sovereignty and their relevance to living in a "borderless world". Tim Brennan's phenomenal book, *At Home in the World* (1997), offers by far the most eloquent defence of national sovereignty and the best critique of the premature inauguration of postnationality in academic discourses as well. Central to Brennan's critique is the cosmopolitical complicity with neo-imperialism and the hegemony of US power in this new world order, a fact that has clearly escaped cosmopoliticians but not the large number of media pundits in the USA that promote capitalism's borderless world fantasy.

3 At stake here is an Engelsian understanding of the dialectical relationship between national consciousness and such transnational forms of solidarity—what Engels in his letter to Karl Kautsky regarding Polish independence refers to as the "basis of any common international action", an idea mirrored in Frantz Fanon's argument that "national consciousness [...] is the only thing that will give us an international dimension" (Fanon 1968, 198). For more on Engels's letter, see Talmon (1991).

especially nationalism, ethnic particularism and subalternity.[4] Instead, there is a clear cosmopolitan investment in the ethics of the fragmented multitude, one that is embodied in the ideals of transnational civil society and social movements which are mostly grounded in the abstract language of rights of the hegemonic, neoliberal regime and which are not yet available to the subjects of internationalism.[5] As such, cosmopoliticians question and elide an essential part of international political culture that can reinvigorate cosmopolitanism, by linking it with a theory that allows for mapping alternative collective technologies of subjectivization, agency and praxis, and for rethinking and transcending the dominant social relations under the neoliberal, capitalist regime.

In this chapter, I argue that cosmopolitanism can affect a meaningful change in the social relations under the neoliberal, global capitalist system only within the broad context of the history and theory of radical, essentially revolutionary, internationalism that retroactively reinscribes the postcolonial dimension of internationalism back at its centre. In what follows, I will first show that normative discourses of cosmopolitan democracy and cosmopolitics, predicated upon a neoliberal corporatist rhetoric and logic, erase *revolutionary* internationalism from their accounts of cosmopolitanism, even when references to it are made or fondness to it is feigned. Second,

4 I use subalternity here in the sense proffered by Gayatri Spivak (1999) namely, as the colonized Other, whose subjectivity is foreclosed within dominant discourses of power and knowledge at both local and international levels.

5 Michael Hardt and Antonio Negri argue for the revolutionary potential of the multitude that seeks to articulate a new revolutionary language among diverse struggles based on the "communication of singularities" (Hardt and Negri 2000, 57). In the context of this discussion, their concept of the multitude which privileges the migrant labourer as a radical political subject under dominant configurations of global capitalism inadvertently reproduces the primacy of travel and other metaphors of mobility that typify the common cosmopolitical strategy of homogenizing all forms of mobility under the category of the cosmopolitan. In his search for "Lenin beyond Lenin", moreover, Negri repeats the same gesture—that the mobility of immaterial labour, its flight and flexibility, is a "sign of political autonomy, the search for self-evaluation, and a refusal of representation" (Negri 2007, 300). See also Žižek's (2006, 53) critique of the notion of the multitude.

drawing on and extending Slavoj Žižek's exhortation to repeat Lenin, the Russian communist revolutionary,[6] I will argue for the need to recuperate revolutionary internationalism today within a revisionist, even redemptive, project that retroactively reads postcoloniality as one of the central referents of the history and theory of this form of internationalism especially then, in Lenin's writings. It is exactly a true commitment to what is here referred to as revolutionary internationalism, I contend, as it is bound to emerge from within the specific material conditions of postcoloniality—where the field of revolutionary possibilities is still open for the construction and stabilization of an alternative egalitarian world order—that can maintain the relevance and critical edge of cosmopolitics theory.

Displacing Internationalism: Cosmopolitics, Ethics, Global Civil Society

In this section, I will examine the manifestation of this strategy in different influential cosmopolitan theories namely, Daniele Archibugi's cosmopolitical democracy and Bruce Robbins' and Pheng Cheah's cosmopolitics. These theorists reject the term internationalism for its valorization (*Verwertung*) of national sovereignty, and they tend to overshadow the realities of global capitalist exploitation and class struggle with the abstract language of rights and ethics, thus substituting the exclusive concerns of global civil society and transnational solidarity movements for its comprehensively transformative programme. For Archibugi, the project of cosmopolitical democracy

6 Vladimir Lenin (originally Ulyanov) was born in Imperial Russia in 1870 and died in 1924, as the Soviet Union's original "premiere". In the late 1880s and 1890s Lenin became a revolutionary Marxist and emerged as an anti-tsarist activist and a political theorist. He played an instrumental role in the split between Social Democracy and Communism and, eventually, led his own faction, the communist "Bolsheviks", to a takeover of power in October 1917, a position from which the dictatorship of the proletariat, in reality a one-party system, could be instituted.

seeks to reconstruct democracy as a form of global governance at a planetary level, for the extension of democracy internationally today "must transcend the borders of single states and assert itself on a global level" (Archibugi 2003a, 7). This requires, as he explains, establishing transnational democratic institutions that can articulate the concerns and agendas of the world's citizens and involve them in global decision making. These world citizens, the "new social and political subjects [who] are appearing in international life" (Archibugi 2003a, 9), are none other but global civil society itself, including movements for peace, human rights and environmental protection. As such, Archibugi writes off socialist (and communist) internationalism, because it remains confined to a defunct and backward international system that regulates national relations within and between states (Archibugi 2003a, 9).

Interestingly enough, in his rejoinder to Brennan's critique of cosmopolitical democracy, Archibugi seems to hold proletarian internationalism in high regard, referring to it as that "glorious tradition" which is "still an inspiring beacon in the fight for a just global society" (Archibugi 2003b, 264). Nonetheless, he rejects the term internationalism as it was theorized by Jeremy Bentham, because it envisions an international society based on "single state governments" (Archibugi 2003b, 263). While he calls for retaining the spirit of proletarian internationalism, moreover, he urges to rethink its political programme, because proletarian internationalism, whose objective is the establishment of a classless society, falls short of ensuring that "the demands of citizens, irrespective of their class, are directly represented in global affairs" (Archibugi 2003b, 264). Resolutions, he states, must be taken "by the majority, not by a single class" (Archibugi 2003b, 264). But if proletarian internationalism calls for abolishing classes altogether, how can it reflect the interests of a single class in a hierarchy of classes? Will that single class not be the majority? What Archibugi in effect does here is a projective displacement of proletarian internationalism: While he admits that cosmopolitical democracy is predicated upon "substantial disparities [...] in access to global resources" (Archibugi 2003b, 264), Archibugi refuses to admit that only the creation of a classless society can produce the right conditions for the equitable distribution of wealth and power. Ironically, the virtue of proletarian internationalism becomes here its main vice.

Even critics of this inherent unegalitarianism of Archibugi's cosmopolitical democracy, the forms of democracy that are founded upon cosmopolitical principles, fail to recognize the significance of revolutionary internationalism, even when their analysis leads nowhere but to it. Craig Calhoun, for example, criticizes the complicity of cosmopolitan democracy with neoliberal capitalism, arguing that some form of cosmopolitanism is still needed, but does not specify which form of cosmopolitanism he has in mind. One thing his analysis makes clear, though, is that such an alternative vision of cosmopolitanism must depend on developing strong social solidarities and must be clearly distinguished from capitalism (Calhoun 2003, 110). As such, Calhoun rejects the claims of international civil society, for the language of rights upon which it is based cannot replace the need for strong social solidarities and networks that must constitute the basis for struggles for a more just and democratic world order.

Nonetheless, Calhoun comes very close to identifying proletarian internationalism as that alternative form of cosmopolitanism that is much needed today for eliminating material inequality and promoting radical change, but falls short of referring to it by name. He writes: "If there is to be a major redistribution of wealth, or a challenge to the way the means of production are controlled in global capitalism, it is not likely to be guided by cosmopolitanism as such. Of course, it may well depend on transnational—even cosmopolitan—solidarities among workers or other groups" (Calhoun 2003, 109). Calhoun then specifies that such an alternative form of cosmopolitanism must "contend with both capitalism's economic power and its powerful embeddedness in the institutional framework of global relations" (Calhoun 2003, 109). It remains unclear, however, why particularly proletarian internationalism cannot "contend" with these issues. In fact, proletarian internationalism seems to speak to all the specifications he sets for viable forms of cosmopolitanism, namely, ending the structural disparities under global capitalism, reinscribing the political over the obsession with the ethical, and establishing connection to ideas of "political action rooted in immanent contradictions of the social order" (Calhoun 2003, 102). This refusal to identify proletarian internationalism can be attributed to his conviction that there is a need for forms of solidarity "outside of political organization" (Calhoun 2003,

100).[7] Invoking Oscar Wilde's infamous phrase, that socialism requires too many evenings, Calhoun strangely enough dismisses the socialist tradition as a political ideology that, in its demand for intense commitment and fidelity, forecloses enjoyment of "a non-political life in civil society" (Calhoun 2003, 100).[8]

Like Archibugi's cosmopolitical democracy, Robbins' and Cheah's cosmopolitics is predicated upon an abrogation of the term internationalism itself and the valorization of international civil society and the ethical over radical politics. In his pursuit of a form of belonging that he refers to as "denationalized internationalism", Robbins rejects the term internationalism for its alleged inadequacy for describing "the sensibility of our moment", a sensibility that is obviously framed not only within the hegemonic renunciation of "the naïve Third Worldism of the 1960s" and anti-imperialist politics in the USA, but also within absolutist discourses of cultural relativism that preclude the possibility of any "right place to stand" (Robbins

7 The question of the efficacy and viability of the (socialist or communist) party to serve as the vanguard of the proletarian revolution constitutes one of the major debates among the neo-Communist intellectuals today, especially Žižek and Badiou. While Žižek argues for the need to re-actualize Lenin, he also recognizes the dark side of many of Lenin's practical solutions. Drawing on the relatively recent rise to power of indigenous and populist movements in Bolivia and Venezuela, nonetheless, Žižek still maintains that the only way to mobilize the masses in the current historical juncture is a reloaded version of the "dictatorship of the proletariat," or new forms of popular participation outside the formal state structures of organization that affect direct mobilization among the masses (Žižek 2008, 379). On the other end of this debate, the French Maoist philosopher Alain Badiou favours new political forms embodied in what he calls a "politics without a party", renouncing thus the party system as no longer appropriate for the actualization of the Communist Idea. In his revisionist reading of Mao's politics, Badiou goes as far as stating that "Mao's dialectical thought helps to relativize the power of the Party" (Badiou 2010, 272).

8 Compare this pleading for enjoyment of non-political life with Žižek's call for adopting "aggressive passivity" as a "proper radical political gesture" which urges the radical subjects to "withdraw into passivity, to refuse to participate". This, according to Žižek, is the "necessary first step that, as it were, clears the ground for true activity, for an act that will effectively change the coordinates of today's constellation" (2006, 223).

1993, 196).[9] More recently, Robbins went as far as stating that although cosmopolitanism is not as "politically ambitious" as internationalism, the former referent is more useful conceptually and analytically in delineating various modalities of liberal Western cosmopolitanism, including Kantian universalism and the diverse social movements, non-governmental organizations and organizations of international civil society—namely, the human rights, ecological, peace and women's international movements (Robbins 1999, 7–8). Privileging these forms of cosmopolitanism, Robbins places the specific histories and traditions of radical internationalism under erasure—he omits them from his narrative of cosmopolitanism, even when he makes explicit references to them. For example, he discusses Raymond Williams's *Culture and Society*, which he considers to be an exemplary narrative in the "genre of the allegory of vocation" that traces the emergence of the "leftist" intellectual tradition (Robbins 1993, 190). Instead of situating this leftist work within the Marxist and internationalist tradition in which it belongs, a tradition that is under constant attack and obliteration in the US academy and capitalist culture, Robbins opts for obfuscating it and privileging instead models of cosmopolitanism that reflect "our ambivalence about cosmopolitanism" (Robbins 1993, 190; cf. also the idea about a "reluctant cosmopolitanism" sketched out in the chapter by Vincent in this volume). Ironically, his efforts at reconfiguring other forms of cosmopolitanism end up purposefully disavowing the same internationalism, which he admits is potentially capable of "mobiliz[ing] cosmopolitanism differently" (Robbins 1993, 190).

9 This vision of world citizenship is grounded in what Bruce Robbins calls "overlapping allegiances", or the development of a sense of belonging to various places, to which the connection of the cosmopolitan subject may be disembodied or virtual; in short, it is predicated upon reattachment from a distance. Robbins believes that these allegiances include places to which we have never travelled or ones that we have seen only on TV. Drawing on Lefebvre, however, Meyda Yegenoglu (2005) criticizes this paradigm, which renders irrelevant the concrete and embodied locales and spaces, whose materiality are fundamental for the formation of identity, consciousness and habits.

More perplexing is Robbins's more recent applaud of "socialist internationalism" as an example of the "worldly, limited, less-than-ideal alternatives" to the normative Western forms of internationalism. Unexpectedly, Robbins endorses internationalism, arguing for a "translation or transmutation of *cosmopolitanism*, usually understood as a detached, individual view of the global, into the more collective, engaged, and empowered form of worldliness that is often called *internationalism*" (Robbins 1999, 5). Not only that now Robbins locates no necessary tension or opposition between cosmopolitanism and internationalism, on the one hand, and between both ideologies and nationalism, on the other, but he also uses these concepts interchangeably. In a surprisingly Fanonian articulation, Robbins maintains that "cosmopolitanism or internationalism", as he says, is "an extension outward of the same sorts of potent and dangerous solidarity" that typify nationalism (Robbins 1999, 6). As such, he overlooks the ways in which cosmopolitanism and internationalism are, in Brennan's words, "theoretically incompatible" (Brennan 2003, 41). His references to internationalism notwithstanding, Robbins obliterates and excludes the specific histories and traditions of radical internationalism from the rest of his book. Quoting Peter Waterman, Robbins thus states that "proletarian and socialist internationalism [...] have become embarrassments to contemporary socialists" (Robbins 1999, 7–8). Instead, and in alignment with James Clifford's inclusive definition of the cosmopolitan subject as both Western and non-Western, elitist and non-elitist, including servants, migrant workers and refugees, Robbins now cites guest workers, au pairs and metropolitan postcolonial intellectuals like Edward Said as exemplars of "cosmopolitanism from the margins" (Robbins 1999, 31, 100–101). In a sleight of hand, forced exile and the recodification of peripheral labour, especially the millions of the subjects of colonial difference and subalternity around the world and their reintegration within the global capitalist economy, are conflated with the privileged, middle-class subject of the normative claims of Western cosmopolitanism. Robbins thus obscures the extent to which cosmopolitanism has been enabled by global capitalism, which recodes the exploitation of the subject of colonial difference within the global economy as the teleological emergence of the global citizen consumer. As Gayatri Spivak has argued, "The current misuse, abuse, and overuse of the rubric *cosmopolitanism* to recode labor export" is another example of the "incessant recoding and reterritorializing of capital" (Spivak 2008, 187). Robbins's failure to engage with the impact of the restructuring of the global economy on the subject of colonial difference thus conflates leftist internationalism and the globalism of the "circuits of imperialist capital" that Aijaz Ahmad insists "must always be demarcated as rigorously as possible" (Ahmad 1992, 45).

Similarly, Pheng Cheah, Robbins's co-editor of the influential collection *Cosmopolitics: Thinking and Feeling Beyond the Nation* (1998), evacuates cosmopolitical agency from the viable narratives and political histories of revolutionary internationalism. Citing the Algerian feminist Marie-Aimée Hélie-Lucas's international "activity", not activism, for the legal reform of Islamic personal codes, for instance, Cheah downplays her belief in radical, Leftist internationalism, one that is predicated on a long history of decolonization and liberation struggle against French colonial rule and on the recognition of "all the differences of interests and in wealth and class" between Muslim feminist internationalists and their Western counterparts. Instead, he foregrounds emergent forms of ethically responsible cosmopolitical agency that reflect a "practical awareness of our structured co-implication with the world, everything that we take for granted when we begin from the claim of an existent condition of freedom that transcends the given" (Cheah 1998, 322). Cheah thus argues that the only possible articulation of this ethical responsibility to the given as a cosmopolitical practical awareness cannot be enunciated under the sign of Kantian universal cosmopolitanism, global capitalism, cultural hybridity or proletarian internationalism, but can only be embodied in international civil society, including popular women's and human-rights groups that "try to link up with international networks and seek immediate support from international aid donors" (Cheah 1998, 322). But such activity, as he recently claims, is not "political in highly organized, self-conscious sense but is instead a form of low-profile pragmatic activism within the milieu of the popular-religious and national everyday" (Cheah 2006, 114). As such, he reduces the struggle for the redistribution of resources within an internationalist politics and praxis to pragmatic transnational alliances that are grounded in forms of vernacular cosmopolitanism. More importantly,

Cheah seems to discern no contradiction between linking up with international civil society and the undermining of the sovereignty of the nation-state that the subjects of postcolonial difference and subalternity must, in his words, "lovingly inhabit" (Cheah 1998, 318). One wonders how effective these subjects can be as adherents of "unblind nationalism" (Cheah 1998, 320), when the fight for equality and greater personal autonomy among members of international civil society happens without any redistribution in wealth and power. Indeed, the achievements of global civil society have been limited to information sharing, without any actual possibility of structural change. Hence, my contention here is that only an emphasis on collective rights and redistributive mechanisms through the language of radical, that is, revolutionary, internationalism can at this historical juncture translate the empty rhetoric of empowerment into structures of political agency and transformation.

Repeating Internationalism: Going Back and Following a "Different Path"

Drawing on the Slovenian philosopher Slavoj Žižek's call to repeat Lenin, I argue that it is imperative at this historical conjuncture to recuperate and reinvent this form of revolutionary internationalism, but within a revisionist project that retroactively reads postcoloniality as one of the central nodes for the articulation of revolutionary internationalism, especially in Lenin's work. While Žižek is correct in his critique of the hegemonic, poststructural brand of postcolonial thought for its preoccupation with the "pseudo-psychoanalytic drama of the subject [who is] unable to confront its inner traumas [the Other within]" (Žižek 2002, 171), I identify postcoloniality here with the long history of anti-colonial struggles of the national liberation movements that postcolonial critics and historians locate precisely in the traditions of Marxist internationalism (Ahmad 1992; Brennan 1997; Young 2001). As such, reclaiming internationalism, as I see it, requires a re-engagement with Lenin's mediation of anti-colonialism and the national question that can retroactively redeem postcoloniality, especially the constitution of the postcolonial subject as one of the main loci of the production of no less than a revolutionary internationalist subjectivity and its world-historic mission. I will show that Lenin did not simply provide a new language and broader theoretical vocabulary for articulating the concerns of the national liberation movements in the colonies, as the standard critiques of Lenin have it, but that he located the language of hope and messianism that characterizes socialist internationalism in the postcolonial field of possibilities. This is not an attempt at assigning an *a priori* ontological privilege to the postcolonial subject today, but an effort at re-visiting and reconstructing one of the main forms that could embody the subject of revolutionary internationalism, especially in Lenin's writings, even though a wager can be made that postcolonial spaces can still provide that unique opportunity for reconstructing and reimagining alternative communities grounded in radically egalitarian politics.

Arguing against all unwritten discursive taboos (the so-called *Denkverbot*) that waste no time invoking the spectre of totalitarianism, its history of the Gulag and Third World catastrophes, Žižek makes the case for the need to re-actualize the Leninist act of the October Revolution today (Žižek 2002, 168). Elsewhere, he calls this critical confrontation with the Leninist legacy as "retrieval-through-repetition" (*Wieder-Holung*) (Žižek 2007, 95). While Žižek is more than ready to recognize the monstrous failure of the solutions that Lenin's legacy embodies (the one-party system and the dictatorship of the proletariat, and with it, if one might add, the institutionalization of terror and repression), he still believes that there is "a utopian spark in [Lenin's legacy] worth saving".[10] For Žižek, the Lenin

10 When Ernesto Laclau (2000) faults Žižek's call to repeat Lenin, he is wary that such a call risks re-implementing the one-party political system and the dictatorship of the proletariat. But, as I will argue below, Žižek's weak form of "positive Marxism" makes it almost impossible to tell *a priori* the precise substance of such a repetition; hence, the emphasis on the Badiouian event in Žižek's formulation of the act. For Žižek's response to Laclau, see his "A Leninist Gesture" (2007) and *In Defence of Lost Causes* (2008).

to be reloaded is, accordingly, the "Lenin-in-becoming", the one that has not yet become a part of the Soviet institution; this is the Lenin who is "thrown into an *open* situation" (Žižek 2002, 6). As such, the Lenin to be recovered is the Lenin full of potentialities, whose language of possibilities can be located in "what he *failed to do*, his missed opportunities" which can never be predicted or foreclosed (Žižek 2002, 310). To repeat Lenin is to recuperate, as Žižek memorably says, what was "in Lenin more than Lenin himself" (Žižek 2002, 310). Above all, this excess in Lenin represents for Žižek the freedom to think outside the common discursive prohibitions of the neocolonial, global capitalist regime. This Lenin, he writes, "stands for the compelling freedom to suspend the stale existing (post)ideological coordinates, the debilitating *Denkverbot* in which we live—it simply means that we are allowed to think again" (Žižek 2002, 11). As Adrian Johnston succinctly puts it, repeating Lenin "broadly signifies a disruptive break that makes it possible to imagine, once again, viable alternatives to liberal democratic capitalism by removing the various obstacles to thinking seriously about options forcefully foreclosed by today's reigning ideologies" (Johnston 2009, 115).

For Žižek, however, Lenin signifies more than just this freedom to think outside the box of the neocolonial, global capitalist regime. For all his talk about "passive aggressivity" (Žižek 2006b, 209–226), Žižek's invocation of Lenin's name ultimately lies in his historic act, the event of the October Revolution, precisely in his call for immediate revolution. He thus notes Lenin's anti-evolutionary conviction that there can be no waiting for the "right moment" of the revolution to mature on its own and explode, but that under certain conditions, it is legitimate, even advisable, to catalyze and force the revolution to come into existence (Žižek 2002, 8). Although he perceived the situation to be desperate, Lenin realized that it could be "creatively exploited for new political choice" (Žižek 2008, 360). In "Lacanese", therefore, Lenin's revolutionary act would "not [be] covered by the big Other"—that is, for Žižek, Lenin was neither afraid of a premature seizure of power nor did he demand full guarantees for the revolution to succeed in order for him to embark on the road to revolution (Žižek 2002, 8). In short, because Lenin was capable of looking into the "abyss of the act" in the eye, he insisted that there is no right time for the revolution.

For Žižek, therefore, these completely hopeless times clear a space for enacting Lenin's freedom of experimentation and rejection of determinism, for "there is *always* a space to be made for an act" (Žižek 2008, 361). In his implicit response to Žižek's claim, Frederic Jameson asserts that Lenin's significance can be located neither in politics nor in economics, but rather in the fusion of both together "in that Event-as-process and process-as-Event we call revolution" (Jameson 2007, 68). Jameson thus states: "The true meaning of Lenin is the perpetual injunction to keep the revolution alive, to keep it alive as a possibility even before it has happened, to keep it alive as a process at all those moments when it is threatened by defeat or worse yet, by routinization, compromise, or forgetfulness" (Jameson 2007, 68). As such, Žižek reappropriates Lenin to foreground the need for reenacting another revolution, although not necessarily a communist one since Marx's Communist society, in his opinion, is an "inherent capitalist fantasy" (Žižek 2000, 19), but a revolution in the abstract whose content still requires remapping and specification. In this sense, Žižek's rejection of a Communist utopia is indeed an example of, in Johnston's words, a "Marxism deprived of its Marxism" (Johnston 2009, 112). Nonetheless, it is precisely this weak form of "positive Marxism", embodied in his insistence on keeping the revolution alive, that constitutes the highest expression of fidelity to Marx and to the Lenin who identifies "what is decisive in Marxism" as "its revolutionary dialectics" (Lenin 1923/1969, 476–477).

Although this exhortation to repeat Lenin has radical implications for the "gesture of reinventing the revolutionary project in the conditions of imperialism and colonialism, more precisely" (Žižek 2002, 11), Žižek's turn to Lenin is an example of the kind of repetition to salvage alternative history that Žižek claims as a critical gesture for maintaining a revolutionary stance. Yet strangely enough, Žižek himself misses one of Lenin's most useful linkages for promoting the revolution on a global scale—the revolutionary potential of the postcolonial subject.[11] After the

11 Although Žižek cites the postcolonial spaces of the Brazilian *favelas* as an example of "first 'liberated territories', cells of future self-organized societies" that exist "outside the law" (Žižek 2006, 51–53), he also envisions a true revolution emerging only from a Europe-centred "Second World" (Žižek 2006, 183–208), where it becomes possible

1914 crisis and his disenchantment with the Second International, as I will show below, Lenin's writings increasingly reinscribe the subject of the national liberation movements in the colonies, not the Western working class, as one of the fundamental articulations of the "real" revolutionary subject. It is not that Lenin disavowed the proletariat and their world-historic mission altogether or that he assigned an *a priori* ontological value to the postcolonial subject as the ultimate locus of revolutionary subjectivity. Žižek is fully aware, of course, that there "*never was*" a "predestined revolutionary subject", not even the working class (Žižek 2008, 289). Rather, it must be recognized that in the years leading to the Third International and until his death, Lenin's faith in the "awakening of hundreds of millions" in the colonies became more pronounced.

"Beyond the Pale of History": Lenin, the National Question and the Postcolonial Legacy of Revolutionary Internationalism

Accounting for Lenin's faith in the power of the national liberation movements to lead the world revolution to come has radical implications for retroactively redeeming postcoloniality, especially the constitution of the

---

to put up a resistance front to the global hegemony of the US. Indeed, Žižek has been reluctant to locate the world-historic mission of socialist internationalism in the field of possibilities and potentialities that characterizes the history of postcoloniality, repudiating thus the capacity of the postcolonial subject to subjectivize the position of the proletariat and the revolutionary class that was envisioned by Lenin. In part, he represents the postcolonial as both an ideological supplement to global capitalism, specifically in the case of Tibet and Buddhism, and its excremental remainder, especially the favelas and slums of the Third World. Consequently, Žižek does not only obliterate the history of the national liberation movements in the postcolonial world, but also forecloses the possibility of the construction of the postcolonial as the subject-for-itself, or more specifically, the subject of history and revolutionary internationalism. For more on this, see Khader (2013).

postcolonial subject as one of the main sites for the production of a revolutionary internationalist subjectivity and its world-historic mission. Although Lenin did not simply abandon the potential of the proletariat for revolution, he seems to consider the subjects of the national liberation movements in the colonies more than just "one of the ferments, one of the bacilli, which help the real anti-imperialist force, the socialist proletariat, to make an appearance on the scene" (Lenin 1972, 22: 357).[12] By embracing the subject of the national liberation movements, as Kevin Anderson writes, Lenin widened "the orthodox Marxist notion of the revolutionary subject" (Anderson 2007, 143). Lenin's position on the potential of the subject of colonial difference to assume the leadership of the revolutionary movement, I maintain, developed in dialogue and debates with many Third World Marxist activists and intellectuals, most importantly the Indian M.N. Roy and the Muslim Mir Said Sultan-Galiev.[13]

It is important first to note that Lenin's uncompromising socialist internationalist position on the problematic of the subject of colonial difference was first articulated at the 1907 Stuttgart Congress of the Second International (1889) especially, at the 1899 Brunn Congress. At Brunn, the solidarity of the oppressed, the Western proletariat and the subjects of colonial difference, took centre stage over the preoccupation with intra-European colonialism that characterized the First International and the early congresses of the Second (Young 2001, 116). Here, Lenin firmly rejected the pervasive conviction in the Congress that colonialism was an integral part of the socialist movement, criticizing its underlying racist bourgeois policies for "introducing virtual slavery into the colonies and subjecting the native populations to untold indignities and violence" (Young 2001, 116–117).

12 All subsequent references to Lenin from this edition of *Collected Works* (1972) will be cited by volume and page numbers in the text.

13 This reconstructive reading of Lenin's position on the true subject of revolutionary internationalism draws on the work of John Riddell's (1991) history and documentation of the Baku Conference and the Second Congress of the Third International. See also Young (2001, 115–139), and Kevin Anderson (1995; 2003) whose important work on Lenin's position on the national question which was grounded in Hegelian dialectics has refocused attention on this neglected issue in the criticism of Lenin's work.

Lenin's understanding of this common bond of oppression between colonials and proletarians and the importance of class struggle for forging a link between them was rearticulated three years later (1910) at a world conference of colonized peoples and at the 1916 Lausanne conference. In a 1916 essay, he asserted that the struggle for national self-determination in the colonies was a leading force in the opposition to imperialist capitalism (Young 2001, 125; Anderson 2007, 129). As Kevin Anderson notes, Lenin was "the first major theorist, Marxist or non-Marxist, to grasp the importance that anti-imperialist movements would have for global politics in the twentieth century" (Anderson 2007, 128). Indeed, his references and examples in *Imperialism* (1916) and *The State and Revolution* (1917) were mostly drawn not from Russia but from anti-imperialist national liberation movements in India, Ireland, China, Turkey and Iran. In his debates about the Irish Eastern Rebellion of 1916, in particular, with leading Marxists especially, Radek and Trotsky, Lenin dissented from their Bukharinian renunciation of all forms of nationalism as obsolete, distinguishing between the chauvinist nationalism of colonial powers and the revolutionary nationalism of the national liberation movements which he described as "the dialectical opposite of global imperialism" (Young 2001, 131). In the years leading to the October Revolution, moreover, Lenin reconciled the claims of nationalism and national self-determination with the need for the proletariat to "fight in conjunction with it against colonial oppression", by anticipating the dissolution and renunciation of bourgeois nationalism in favour of the establishment of proletarian internationalism (Young 2001, 121–122).

As he began considering himself a leader of international Marxism, nonetheless, Lenin viewed the production of anti-imperialist subjectivity, one constituted through the dialectics of national struggle in the colonies, as central to his vision of world revolution and communist internationalism. Indeed, in his 1914 critique of Rosa Luxemburg's Eurocentric proletarian messianism, that only the "workers of the advanced capitalist countries [...] can lead the army of the exploited and enslaved of the five continents", Lenin forcefully argues that "the national liberation politics of the colonies will *inevitably* be continued by national wars of the colonies *against* imperialism" (Lenin 1972, 22: 307). While the First Congress of the Third International, the Communist International or the Comintern (1919), mainly reiterated Luxemburg's faith in the messianic powers of the Western urban proletariat to overthrow the European colonial states, so that "the workers and peasants not only of Annam, Algiers, and Bengal, but also of Persia and Armenia [may] gain their independence", by the time of the Second Congress Lenin was becoming very skeptical about the ability of the Western proletariat to affect an immediate revolution in Europe (Young 2001, 128). With the encouragement of Sultan-Galiev, Lenin began increasingly to "identify the countries of the east as being of more potential revolutionary significance" (Young 2001, 129). In his July 5 1921 "Tactics of the Russian Communist Party, Report to the Third Congress of the Communist International," therefore, Lenin writes: "And it should be perfectly clear that in the coming decisive battles of the world revolution, this movement of the majority of the world's population, originally aimed at national liberation, will turn against capitalism and imperialism and will, perhaps, play a more revolutionary role than we have been led to expect" (Lenin 1923/1969, 289–290).

Beginning with the Second Congress, moreover, Lenin identified his critique of imperialism with that of the Indian Marxist M.N. Roy, putting thus "colonial revolution at the forefront of the priorities of the new communist government, regarding it as a central factor in the Soviet fight against capitalism" (Young 2001, 125). Indeed, Roy was instrumental in Lenin's recognition of the subject of colonial difference as one of the main loci of revolutionary subjectivity. Drawing on and revising Marx's analysis of Ireland in his debate with Lenin on the importance of Asia in developing world revolutions, Roy argued that "because of the economic dependency of imperialist powers on their colonial structures, the fate of the revolutionary movement in Europe depends *entirely* on the course of the revolution in the East. Without the victory of the revolution in the eastern countries, the communist movement in the West would come to nothing" (quoted in Young 2001, 131–132 [my emphasis]). While Lenin thought that Roy's use of the word "entirely" was hyperbolic, Lenin in his July 1920 address to the Second Congress, nonetheless, announced: "World imperialism shall fall when the revolutionary onslaught of the exploited and oppressed workers in each country [...] merge with the revolutionary onslaught of hundreds of millions of people who have hitherto stood beyond the pale of history and have been regarded merely as the objects of history" (Lenin 1972, 31: 207–208). The power of the subjects of colonial difference is thus embedded in their rejection of that status as "objects of history" and their ability to reclaim the potential for embodying the idea of revolution. Indeed, in "On the Significance of Militant Materialism" of March 1922, Lenin stated that "the awakening to life and struggle of the new classes in the East (Japan, India, China) [...] serves as a fresh confirmation of Marxism" (Lenin 1972, 33: 234).

Lenin's radical idea from the Second Congress until his death, then, was his ability to recodify the subjects of colonial difference into the vanguard subjects of socialist internationalism, an idea that he had presciently anticipated in a 1913 article entitled "Backward Europe and advanced Asia" (Lenin 1972, 19: 99–101). This idea took full form in The First Congress of the Peoples of the East, or the Baku Congress of 1920, which convened at his own instigation to underscore the revolutionary potential of the subjects of colonial difference. Lenin's understanding of the primacy of anti-colonial struggle of the national liberation movements in the march towards socialist internationalism does not thus simply mean that he bracketed the potential of the proletariat to lead the revolution, but rather the opposite: that above all Lenin was increasingly convinced that the national liberation movements in the colonies provided a new language of anti-imperial struggle and liberation with which to inject the stale legacy of socialist internationalism. Even in the last article he wrote in March 1923, Lenin reiterated his faith in the future role of the subject of colonial difference in the envisaged world revolution, stating that the mobilization of the national liberation movements in the colonies will ensure socialist victory (Lenin 1972, 45: 416–417). Such a position would not be far from Lenin's dialectical "concrete analysis of concrete situations" which, as Etienne Balibar maintains, "assumed incorporating into the concept of revolutionary process the *plurality of forms* of proletarian political struggle ("peaceful" and "violent"), and the *transition* from one form to another (hence the question of the specific duration and successive contradictions of the revolutionary transition [...])" (Balibar 2007, 211). This is not only to acknowledge that the socialist revolution is inconceivable without a diverse and international insurgency, as Kevin Anderson (1995, 135–141) argues, but that the idea of the revolution itself will inevitably be, and will have been, "exported" to the world from without Europe. To invert Stalin's statement on "The International Significance of the October Revolution," it could be said in regards to Lenin's position on the revolutionary potential of postcolonial subjectivity that the struggle of national liberation movements in the colonies created a "new line of revolution against world imperialism", extending from the oppressed nations of the East, through the Russian revolution, and to the "proletarians of the West" (quoted in Young 2001, 126).

The Postcolonial Hypothesis

The resurgence in 2011 and 2012 of the revolutionary ethos all over the world—spanning from the civil uprisings of the Arab Spring to the Occupy movement's protests and demonstrations on virtually every continent—bears witness to the need for rethinking the efficacy of cosmopolitanism as a viable theory of social change under the neoliberal global capitalist regime. The problem here is that *cosmopoliticians* cannot oppose the neocolonial, capitalist ideology that reproduces cosmopolitanism itself as another dominant myth that conceals the class antagonisms underpinning the social relations within neocolonial, capitalist conditions and that reframes complicity with them as inexorable. By suppressing and erasing internationalism, cosmopoliticians obscure the extent to which internationalism is, as Gayatri Spivak notes, "not only possible but necessary" for contemporary subjects, for whom the increasing hegemony of global capital and World Bank economics has made "social redistribution [...] uncertain at best" (Spivak 2008, 198). This internationalism, as I have argued in the previous pages, must retroactively be reinscribed with the postcolonial trajectory delineated above at its centre. As such, Lenin's October Revolution should be perceived only as "being one possible, and often even not the most probable, outcome of an 'open' situation" (Žižek 2010, 86), and that the postcolonial impetus of Lenin's revolutionary politics is the spectre that will continue to haunt the future of the radical left and the Western revolutionary theories and politics.

For cosmopolitanism, this reaffirmation of the postcolonial trajectory of revolutionary internationalism does not simply amount to re-enacting the troubled history of internationalism and communism in a teleological process as they are many times negatively understood in the humanities today. Rather, it could constitute a "repetitive movement, a movement of *repeating the beginning* over and over again" (Žižek 2010a, 210). As Žižek explains, to "begin from the beginning" does not simply mean to "build further upon the foundations of the revolutionary epoch of the twentieth century (which lasted from 1917 to 1989), but to 'descend' to the starting point and follow a *different* path" (Žižek 2010a, 210). Reframing cosmopolitanism within the internationalist history of postcolonial revolutionary experimentation can therefore be more productive, given a revolutionary agenda, for thinking through not only the practical difficulties of constructing a revolution, but also the ultimate end of the revolution. Despite the disparity in the success of postcolonial revolutionary practices, one cannot simply overlook the record of postcolonial revolutions that were thickly invested in reimagining extra-capitalist social totalities. As one of the major repressed points of exclusion under the hegemony of global capitalism today, postcolonial spaces indeed constitute the most important locus for exacerbating the antagonisms inherent to the capitalist system, turning them into a collective evental site that even in, or precisely because of, its failures can offer a radical challenge to the totality of the liberal-capitalist socio-symbolic order and actualize the "revolutionary explosion".

As such, cosmopolitanism could be reconfigured to facilitate, in Žižek's words, the "political mobilization of new forms of politics" which must not only be predicated upon a "practical alliance" with the "new proletarians from Africa and elsewhere", as Alain Badiou states (Badiou 2010, 99). Rather, they must be organized from the beginning at the level of the *real* by those same new postcolonial proletarians who recognize themselves in the socialist revolutionary *Event*. Indeed, under the current hegemony of neocolonialist global capitalism, in which the majority of people have been pauperized as a result of the polarization of wealth, it is the subjects of postcolonial difference that have assumed the position of Marx's "vanishing" proletariat. As Badiou correctly points out in regards to the Cultural Revolution, and by implication other postcolonial revolutionary acts, Žižek fails to understand not only the long series of postcolonial revolutionary acts that constitute the ultimate embodiment of the "principles of the Paris Commune", but also the "element of universality in [their] terrible failure" (Badiou 2010, 273, 274). As Žižek himself relatively recently noted, the subject's fidelity to a cause like the revolutionary Event can be only regulated through "incessant betrayals" (Žižek 2010b, xiv).

Despite the disparity in the history and practice of revolutionary ideology in the postcolonies, the postcolonial subject might seem to be the one best suited these days to reinvent and stabilize a radically egalitarian politics as well as alternative forms of political organization "in the immediate" (Žižek 2008, 427). The recent revolutionary developments in Tunisia, Egypt, Bahrain and Libya, and the increasing signs of social upheaval and unrest that are currently sweeping Yemen, Jordan and Syria, are the ultimate proof of the explosive, utopian potential of postcolonial emancipatory politics.[14] In Tahrir square, that is, Žižek needs to see that we were "allowed to act as if the utopian future is [...] already at hand, there to be seized" (Žižek 2002, 260). Indeed, it is this revolutionary postcolonial moment that proves beyond the shadow of doubt that "the 'right choice' is only possible the second time, after the wrong one; that is, it is only the first wrong choice which literally creates the conditions for the right choice" (Žižek 2010b, 88).

14 Indeed, Hugo Chavez's call for a Fifth International might also be indicative in this respect.

References

Ahmad, Aijaz, 1992. *In theory: Classes, nations, literatures*. London: Verso.
Anderson, Kevin B, 1995. *Lenin, Hegel, and Western Marxism: A critical study*. Champaign, IL: University of Illinois Press.
Anderson, Kevin B, 2007. "The rediscovery and persistence of the dialectic in philosophy and in world politics". In: Sebastian Budgen, Stathis Kouvelakis and Slavoj Žižek (eds.), 2007. *Lenin reloaded: Towards a politics of truth*. Durham and London: Duke University Press, 120–147.
Archibugi, Daniele, 2003a. "Cosmopolitical democracy". In: Daniele Archibugi (ed.), 2003. *Debating cosmopolitics*. London and New York: Verso, 1–15.
Archibugi, Daniele, 2003b. "Demos and cosmopolis". In: Daniele Archibugi (ed.), 2003, *Debating cosmopolitics*. London and New York: Verso, 257–272.
Badiou, Alain, 2010. *The communist hypothesis*. London and New York: Verso.
Balibar, Etienne, 2007. "The philosophical moment in politics determined by war: Lenin 1914–1916". In: Sebastian Budgen, Stathis Kouvelakis and Slavoj Žižek (eds.), 2007, *Lenin reloaded: Towards a politics of truth*. Durham and London: Duke University Press, 207–221.
Brennan, Timothy, 2003. "Cosmopolitanism and internationalism". In: Daniele Archibugi (ed.), 2007, 40–50.
Brennan, Timothy, 2007. *At home in the world*. Cambridge, MA: Harvard University Press.
Budgen, Sebastian, Stathis Kouvelakis, and Slavoj Žižek (eds.), 2007. *Lenin Reloaded: Towards a Politics of Truth*. Durham and London: Duke University Press.
Calhoun, Craig, 2008. "Cosmopolitanism in the modern social imaginary". *Daedalus*, 137(3), 105–114.
Calhoun, Craig, 2003. "The class consciousness of frequent travellers: Towards a critique of actually existing cosmopolitanism". In: Daniele Archibugi (ed.), 2003. *Debating cosmopolitics*. London and New York: Verso, 86–116.
Cheah, Pheng, 1998. "Given culture: Rethinking cosmoplitical freedom in transnationalism". In: Bruce Robins and Pheng Cheah (eds.), 1998. *Cosmopolitics: Thinking and feeling beyond the nation*. Minneapolis: Minnesota University Press, 290–328.
Cheah, Pheng, 2006. *Inhuman conditions: On cosmopolitanism and human rights*. Cambridge, MA: Harvard University Press.
Clifford, James, 1997. *Routes: Travel and translation in the late twentieth century*. Cambridge, MA: Harvard University Press.

Fanon, Frantz, 1965. *The wretched of the Earth*. Trans. Constance Farrington. London: McGibbon and Kee.

Forman, Michael, 1998. *Nationalism and the international labor movement: The idea of the nation in socialist and anarchist theory*. University Park, PA: Pennsylvania State University Press.

Hardt, Michael and Antonio Negri, 2000. *Empire*. Cambridge, MA: Harvard University Press.

Hardt, Michael and Antonio Negri, 2011. "Arabs are democracy's new pioneers". *The Guardian*, 24 Feb.

Jameson, Frederick, 2007. "Lenin and revisionism". In: Sebastian Budgen, Stathis Kouvelakis and Slavoj Žižek (eds.), 2007. *Lenin reloaded: Towards a politics of truth*. Durham and London: Duke University Press, 59–73.

Johnston, Adrian, 2009. *Badiou, Žižek, and political transformations: The cadence of change*. Evanston, IL: Northwestern University Press.

Khader, Jamil, 2013. "Žižek's infidelity: Lenin, the national question, and the Postcolonial legacy of revolutionary internationalism". In: Jamil Khader and Molly Rothenberg (eds.), 2013. *Žižek now: Current perspectives in Žižek studies*. Cambridge: Polity Press.

Laclau, Ernesto, 2000. "Structure, history, and the political". In: Judith Butler, Ernesto Laclau and Slavoj Žižek, 2000. *Contingency, hegemony, universality: Contemporary debates on the left*. London: Verso, 182–212.

Lenin, Vladimir, 1923/1969. *National-liberation movement in the East*. Moscow: Progress Publishers.

Lenin, Vladimir, 1972. *Collected works*, 45 vols. Moscow: Progress Publishers.

Negri, Antonio, 2007. "What to do today with What is to be done?, or rather: The body of the general intellect". In: Sebastian Budgen, Stathis Kouvelakis and Slavoj Žižek (eds.), 2007. *Lenin reloaded: Towards a politics of truth*. Durham and London: Duke University Press, 297–307.

Riddell, John (ed.), 1991. *Workers of the world and oppressed peoples unite! Proceedings and documents of the Second congress 1920*, 2 vols. New York: Pathfinder Press.

Riddell, John (ed.), 1993. *To see the dawn: Baku, 1920—First congress of the peoples of the East*. New York: Pathfinder Press.

Robbins, Bruce, 1993. *Secular vocations: Intellectuals, professionalism, culture*. London and New York: Verso.

Robbins, Bruce, 1999. *Feeling global: Internationalism in distress*. New York: New York University Press.

Said, Edward, 1993. *Culture and imperialism*. New York: Vintage.

Spivak, Gayatri, 1999. *A critique of postcolonial reason: Toward a history of the vanishing present*. Cambridge, MA: Harvard University Press.

Spivak, Gayatri, 2008. "Gayatri Chakravorty Spivak'sinfluences: Past, present, future". *PMLA*, 123(1), 247–248.
Talmon, Jacob Lieb, 1991. *Myth of the nation and vision of revolution*. New Brunswick, NJ: Transaction Publishers.
Yegenoglu, Meyda, 2005. "Cosmopolitanism and nationalism in a globalized world". *Ethnic and Racial Studies*, 28(1), 103–131.
Young, Robert J., 2001. *Postcolonialism: An historical introduction*. Malden, MA: Blackwell.
Žižek, Slavoj, 2006. *The universal exception: Selected writings*, vol. 2. Ed. Rex Butler and Scott Stephens. New York and London: Continuum.
Žižek, Slavoj, 2007. "A Leninist gesture today: Against the populist temptation." In: Sebastian Budgen, Stathis Kouvelakis and Slavoj Žižek (eds.), 2007. *Lenin reloaded: Towards a politics of truth*. Durham and London: Duke University Press, 74–98.
Žižek, Slavoj, 2008. *In defense of lost causes*. New York and London: Verso.
Žižek, Slavoj, 2010a. "How to begin from the beginning." In: Costas Douzinas and Slavoj Žižek (eds.), 2010b. *Living in the end times*. London and New York: Verso.
Žižek, Slavoj (ed.), 2002. *Revolution at the gate: Selected writings of Lenin from 1917*. London: Verso.
Žižek, Slavoj (ed.), 2010. *The idea of communism*. London and New York: Verso.

ANDREW VINCENT

Reflections of a Reluctant Cosmopolitan

Introduction

There is often a sense of implicit moral or legal rightness attached to the idea of cosmopolitanism in current discussions which is intellectually troubling. The critical intuition I am uneasily wending my way around in this concluding essay is that it is now usually *de rigueur* to be cosmopolitan, almost equivalent to being humanitarian, tolerant or right-minded. Alternatives to cosmopolitanism can thus be too horrible to contemplate. However, no less troubling are the wide-ranging criticisms of cosmopolitan argument, deriving from an assorted group of nationalists, statists, cultural commentators, postcolonial and identity theorists. A rough and ready collective noun for the latter arguments could be particularism; all such particularist arguments strike me as equally or even more problematic in substance than those of conventional cosmopolitans.

The structure of this essay is to briefly recapitulate the genealogy of cosmopolitanism and to comment on some of the provenance to the idea. I then consider some of the traditional core arguments for cosmopolitanism which in my interpretation coalesce—in much of the contemporary literature—around moral, institutional and legal argumentation. In critically assessing these various accounts I both outline and then raise further difficulties with many of the more standard particularist objections to cosmopolitanism. Finally, I conclude on a more neglected component of argument in cosmopolitanism, namely its political character and rendition. This latter view best encapsulates the sense of a more fragile, reluctant or hesitant understanding of cosmopolitanism.

The Provenance of Cosmopolitanism

There is a history to the term cosmopolitanism, which readers of this anthology will already be quite familiar with. In essence it is comparatively quite straightforward. Thus little time will be spent on it. Various figures and movements appear in this history—although at times one senses that for some an implicit hagiography is at work. Generally, Cynic and more predominantly Stoic writers are cited as a foundational moment. Certain figures take on an honorific status, for example from the middle Stoa Marcus Tullius Cicero, and from the later Stoa, Marcus Aurelius (see, e.g., Nussbaum 1991; 2000; Appiah 2006, xii; Fine 2007, 15). There is unquestionably a neologism here.[1] However, whether we are really encountering

1 The origins of cosmopolitanism date back to ancient Greece (cf. chapter by Vlasak in this volume). There were two prevalent conceptions of order in the Greek world: the natural (which could be observed and used, e.g., in agriculture or navigation); the other order was that found in the organizations of human beings, particularly the Hellenic idea of the *polis*. *Polis* implies city-state, *polites* a citizen. The community of the polis (*koinoneia*) is distinguished from nature by being under human control. There was always an interest in the link between cosmos and *polis* (natural and political order). It was first explored systematically by the Stoics. For Stoics, social and natural regularities both exemplified the same cosmic force. Nature reinforced the political order. There was thus a "wise" natural providence behind social existence. "Nature" was, in fact, one of the Stoic terms for the spiritual principle. To live according to nature was to live according to a spiritual principle, which, in essence, was a life controlled by "universal" reason. This was the source of both human happiness and virtue. All human beings were creatures of the same spiritual substance of reason, therefore it followed for the Stoics that there was a *universal bond* between all human beings. The whole universe as such might therefore, for the Stoics, be viewed as a "civic community of reason" in which the divine and human were linked in common world citizenship—*cosmopolis*—a city which was co-extensive with the whole cosmos. It was in this context that the Stoic, Marcus Aurelius, invited his readers to consider "Whether a man's lot be cast in this place or in that matters nothing, provided that in all places he views the world as a city and himself its citizen. Give men the chance to see and know a true man, living by Nature's law" (Aurelius 161–180 AD/1967, Book 10, No. 15, 157). *Cosmopolis* therefore implied a universal civic order (which is natural); a *cosmopolitan* is thus a world citizen. There are overlaps with

anything close to our current intuitions about cosmopolitanism is open to doubt. If anything, what we might now be thinking of as ancient or classical cosmopolitanism is a version of late Stoicism overlaid by Augustinian speculation on the City of God.[2] Yet in Cicero's or Aurelius's case, if one puts together the regularized brutality and callousness of Republican and Imperial Rome to slaves, barbarians, conquered peoples and non-citizens, with the purported cosmopolitan impulse, then ancient cosmopolitanism does not look a very welcoming or hospitable option. Cicero's well-known work on universalist Stoic natural law, in the period of the early Caesarist empire, looks particularly out of touch with existing realities. Possibly we might get more mileage out of the Roman law idea of *ius gentium*, but even this has deep limitation as a meaningful account of cosmopolitanism.

The usual next historical step—unless one mentions seventeenth- or eighteenth-century natural law and natural right arguments—involves a substantial temporal jump to Immanuel Kant, who for many still remains the kindly godfather of hospitable cosmopolitanism, human rights and indeed cosmopolitan law.[3] In this sense, despite the fact that Kant was well versed in Stoic writings, he can nonetheless still be contrasted against them, in the sense that in Kant (for some commentators) we have the first really *genuine* attempt at the cosmopolitan or universal condition. Personally, I

---

the terms universalism and globalism, although as yet, of course, we do not have a universalitan or globalitan.

2 In fact Augustine was deeply impressed by Stoicism at a certain stage of his intellectual development. Stoicism (plus a form of Augustianism) reappeared—with strength and panache—in a Christianized shape in sixteenth- and seventeenth-century Europe in a range of writers such as Justus Lipsius, Etienne La Boétie and Michel de Montaigne. Its relation to cosmopolitanism was more obscure at this latter stage. Kant, it should also be noted, was a close reader of Stoic thought; the cosmopolitan connection becomes much easier to ascertain at this point.

3 There were clearly others who were interested in the idea of cosmopolitanism, although Kant was the most well-known (see, e.g., chapter in this volume by Poulsen). However the idea that the eighteenth century had any systematically developed understanding of cosmopolitanism prior to, or even immediately post Kant, is critically (and probably successfully) challenged by Georg Cavallar (2011).

would argue that this judgement is far-fetched.[4] The Kant often referred to here is primarily a highly selective idealized image, deriving from an overly optimistic reading of essays such as *Perpetual Peace* (1795).[5] For Kant, cosmopolitanism was by no means a straightforward option. In fact, he appeared, unlike many of his current admirers, to take a rather pessimistic view of its potential (see Gallie 1977, 12). Despite this, it would still be true to say that Kant—and neo-Kantianism to the present day—still embody a highly influential, if sometimes more utopian-sounding moral understanding of cosmopolitanism.

However, from an historical perspective, there is still something distinctly unusual about the word cosmopolitanism. If one looks back at Anglo-European legal, political and moral philosophy over the last, say, one hundred years, or even more significantly, the last fifty years, it is notable that the usage of the word "cosmopolitanism" does *not* appear that much in the academic literature (even oddly in the early days of human rights discussion in the 1950s). It is noteworthy for its absence. If anything (outside of Kant scholarship) the term was regarded as more of an academic eccentricity or idiosyncrasy within the humanities and social sciences, up to the later 1980s. Words such as *international* or *internationalism* were clearly ubiquitous over the whole twentieth century, but one might legitimately hesitate to identify "internationalism" as a synonym for "cosmopolitanism". Even in the post-1989 world, the use of cosmopolitanism was still not that widespread. It is only really since the early to mid-1990s, although indeed being *conditioned* by the events of 1989, that the term has unexpectedly

4 In this light it is perhaps worth reading Kant's anthropological writings as a corrective to too much cosmopolitan enthusiasm (see Kant 1798/1974).

5 For an attempt to theorize Kant's political recommendations regarding a cosmopolitan world order in a limited and "thin" direction, see the chapter by Espinoza in this volume. Kant was obviously not alone in his interests in cosmopolitan ideas, particularly in the German context (see Kleingeld 1999). For an overview of the debates over Kant see Bohman and Lutz-Bachmann (1997); also see Gallie (1977); Nussbaum (1991); Cavallar (1999); Brown (2006) and Fine (2007). For a fine and immensely thorough collection of writings (and writers) associated with cosmopolitanism (to the present day), see Garrett Brown and David Held (2010).

formed its own highly distinctive niche in the academy. This niche has, of course, grown exponentially to the present day. This fact alone is still puzzling and calls for some explanation.

Synonyms of Cosmopolitanism

What might be the most apposite synonyms for cosmopolitanism? There are a few palpable candidates, for example, universalism, globalism, humanism or internationalism.[6] All can, in certain contexts, mistakenly or not, be employed interchangeably with cosmopolitanism. Universalism—as in universal human rights—is often taken as archetypically connected to cosmopolitanism. Modern claims to universalism in political and moral philosophy are conventionally located, for example, in mainstream neo-Kantian and utilitarian ethics.[7] These ethical doctrines are now frequently reconfigured as quintessentially cosmopolitan arguments (because of their apparent universalism and claims to impartiality).[8] Thus the extensive work, over the last couple of decades, of for example Martha C. Nussbaum, Brian Barry, Amartya Sen, Onora O'Neill, David Held, Simon Caney, Thomas Pogge, Peter Singer and many others, conventionally casts the whole debate about cosmopolitanism into universal-aspiring moral arguments (see, e.g., Brock and Brighouse 2005b).

Globalism is another prospective synonym for cosmopolitanism. However, its more dominant use in social sciences such as economics, politics, communication or demography does not straightforwardly interlace with current understandings of cosmopolitanism. There is "global ethics" (besides, to some extent, an emerging "global history" and "global

6 These are the main potential synonyms for cosmopolitanism, however, other terms are now used, for example, interculturalism, cross-culturalism and transnationalism, which allude to allied themes.

7 Although uses of the noun "universal" stretch way beyond this cosmopolitan debate, "cosmopolitan" has a much narrower applicability.

8 Whether impartialism really should be related to cosmopolitanism remains a debatable issue.

literature"), which has made some rather limited headway. However the most fashionable usage of global is usually via the term "globalization". This generally has an economic or political economy focus. In contemporary economics, particularly market-based economics, there is an unwitting tendency towards a form of realistic, or what some have called, a predatory cosmopolitanism (see Fine 2007, 21). The purported laws of free market economics and the demands of *homo economicus* clearly aspire to a universal status. Markets will, by their very nature, always run roughshod over boundaries, territories and localities. Globalization in economics therefore usually means the globalization of companies, labour, capital, finance, banking, credit, production and trade. Nothing is alien to market-based capitalism.[9] Some, of course, might find this a misuse of the term cosmopolitan. Yet even critiques of capitalist free markets, as in neo-Marxism, embody their own characteristic understandings of cosmopolitanism. In fact, in varying formats, there are a number of contemporary sceptics who have tended to see very deep-rooted capitalist and market-led motifs (amongst other components, such as military domination) embedded at the heart of the generic cosmopolitan demeanour (see, e.g., Chomsky 1999; Hardt and Negri 2001; Douzinas 2007).

Internationalism is another potential synonym. Internationalism was first coined by Jeremy Bentham in the 1780s to name a part of his legal theory which was concerned with the "law of nations". Internationalism is though a rather more polymorphous word than universalism, globalism or cosmopolitanism. It has appeared in many guises from the communist internationals, through international trade to international law, or even the arts (as in international biennales). There is though something slightly odd in the term "international". As a compound word it implies a "prior grasp" of the term *national*. It entails that a sense of the universal or cosmopolitan could only be established across (that is "inter") particular nationalities.

9 Benjamin Barber's *Jihad vs McWorld* opens with a quote from the chairman of the large American corporation Gillette, which neatly captures this perspective. The Gillette chairman commented, "I do not find foreign countries foreign". Barber adds—referring to a central thesis of his book—"welcome to McWorld" (Barber 1995, 1).

This, on one reading, does not quite catch the intent of the purer moral claimants to cosmopolitanism, who would conventionally repudiate the national and see the cosmopolitan as prior to, or exceeding, nationality.

Each of the above terms crosses over a number of areas of intellectual concern.[10] Thus, for example, in law cosmopolitanism can appear in debates about the viability of international law, international treaties and human rights. It also surfaces as part of the background setting for debates over "crimes against humanity" and international war crimes tribunals. In international relations cosmopolitanism can be observed, both implicitly and explicitly, in distinctions between, for example, "men" and "citizens" or "communitarians" and "universalists", or "nation states" and "international justice", as well as in debates about boundaries and sovereignty. There is also the more unpredictable empirical dimension of war and weaponry, which provides another bleaker perspective on cosmopolitanism. The nuclear warhead is as much a symbol of a kind of brutal realistic cosmopolitanism. Modern warfare, particularly nuclear, chemical or biological warfare—like environmental issues—forces a "melancholy cosmopolitanism" upon us. Boundaries become unimportant in these settings.

10 It is worth noting—*en passant*—that monotheistic world religions also embody claims to universalism. This would include the recent spate of religious fundamentalisms. It might sound odd to describe such votaries as cosmopolitans. However if one thinks of this in terms of the older use of cosmopolitan—then the religious believer has no city (that is no *polis*—other than the City of God or the world wide *Ummah*), she is a citizen of the cosmos, beyond any localities, states or nations. What better self-description could there be for a monotheistic believer than cosmopolitan? Consider, by way of illustration, the descriptive sense of the word *catholic*—that is implying universality. Another domain of fretful theorizing about cosmopolitanism is contemporary anthropology. The anxiety stems here from a challenge to the very roots of the discipline of anthropology, as developed from the nineteenth century. It is concerned essentially with the status and capacity of Western social science disciplines to objectively study the particular and local. In other words, is Western anthropology a genuinely cosmopolitan mode of objective rational discourse and observation, or is it just another indirect form of Western colonialism, imperialism or particularism? (see Marcus and Fischer 1986). Sociology has, comparatively recently, also developed a significant literature on cosmopolitanism, see, e.g., Beck (2006) or Fine (2007).

In sum, it is not at all clear that cosmopolitanism, internationalism or globalism can be seen as synonyms. There are undoubtedly considerable overlaps, but there are also divergences. One might believe in international cosmopolitan law or globalized communications, but have no sympathy whatsoever with any moral cosmopolitanism.[11] One could argue, conversely, for moral cosmopolitanism, but have no truck with international law or global markets, and so forth. It is therefore worth noting that such concepts historically shift, interweave and occasionally contradict each other, depending upon context and circumstances—in as much as the conceptual change itself to a certain extent can redefine the context and release new experiences, however encouraging or troubling (see Koselleck 1986).

Domains of Cosmopolitan Argument

In the last two decades—outside of the unrelenting postcolonial critiques—cosmopolitan argument has usually been received fairly positively in the academy.[12] It has tended to settle most frequently upon three domains, that

11 Universalism could, in one reading, appear more antiquated (as in an association with traditional Stoic or Christian natural law), whereas cosmopolitanism might be seen as a product of modernity. Rational universalism might thus assert a traditional authority over thought. This *can* be (although it does not have to be) distinguished from cosmopolitanism, which in certain modern shapes engages creatively with other cultures, eschews imperialism, claims no unique authority and does not presume any necessary commonalities (see, e.g., Hollinger 1995 and Appaduri 1996).

12 For some of the various dimensions of postcolonial critique in the 1990s, see Cheah and Robbins (1998). A more recent example blends the postcolonial critique of cosmopolitanism with the new dimension of comparative political theory. For a recent critic, therefore, the old cosmopolitanism (which embodies the bulk of even contemporary moral and political writing on cosmopolitanism) "is rooted firmly in the works of Western thinkers and implies that the West's intellectual heritage contains the resources for a cosmopolitan theorizing" (Godrej 2011, 9). Such West-centred or Eurocentric theory (in the author's terminology) never actually looks beyond its own

is, moral, institutional and legal forms, each category being both fluid and permeable; these categories were all fairly clearly demarcated in the literature by the late 1990s. The relation between these forms however remains problematic, partly because two additional distinctions began to infuse the literature and were supervened over the institutional, legal and moral forms. This consequently made matters more complex. The first is a fairly loose distinction between thick and thin variants of cosmopolitanism, or alternatively maximal and minimal accounts. A second distinction is between old and new cosmopolitanism: more on these distinctions in a moment.

Moral Cosmopolitanism

A Brief Genealogy

It is not fortuitous that the background to the recovery of moral cosmopolitan coincides quite directly with the revival of post-1970s analytical political philosophy (see Vincent 2004, Ch. 4). Admittedly there had been within international relations—particularly within the claims of liberal internationalism—references to cosmopolitanism and a rather makeshift version of Kantianism appeared here. However, the really substantively rich literature on moral cosmopolitanism developed gradually in the context of the later Rawlsian generation of Anglo-American political philosophers, particularly in the 1990s. This was also, in part, a reaction to the growth of a sophisticated analytical literature of nationalism in the early 1990s (see Brock and Brighouse 2005a, 1; see also Vincent 2004, Ch. VI).

There are some limitations to moral philosophy as a restful bedfellow for cosmopolitanism, not least because there are a wide-range of moral

---

deeply parochial resources. Godrej however looks to a new cosmopolitanism which "moves toward a disciplinary practice in which liberalism and other Westcentric modes of thought take their place in a series of plural and coeval engagements of thinkers and texts from all traditions, moving through and past the dichotomies that ground these encounters" (Godrej 2011, 25). Compare also, in this context, the works of Chantal Mouffe (e.g. 2008).

theories—for example virtue ethics, Aristotelian ethics, particularist ethics—which are not necessarily sympathetic to the cosmopolitan mentality. Nonetheless, in the period 1970 to 2000 a large and well-populated rump of Anglo-American political philosophy became, to all intents and purposes, a form of universalist-inclined moral philosophy manqué. This was a major aspect of the Rawlsian intellectual bequest. It is unfair though to judge Rawls (or his many disciples) as wholly responsible for this bequest, since the large bulk of liberal political philosophy was moving in this direction. What is most striking here is that what we see in analytical political philosophy, in this mode, is a much pared down version of contemporary moral philosophy. It is largely assumed—if we put to one side the communitarian and nationalist arguments—that the political world is divided up into competing versions of neo-Kantianism and utilitarianism. The question then became—who had the most persuasive argument? Admittedly moral philosophy itself has often been attracted by this same substantive duality, and an incessant highly inventive industry of moral argumentation ensued. However, mainstream moral philosophy frequently (as indicated above) had other moral fish to fry. The political philosophers have though usually been more constrained than the moral philosophers. Without entering into the lists (as to who has the most successful argument), what I want to extrapolate here is the fundamental point that both neo-Kantianism and utilitarianism have one notable resemblance. They *both* aspire to universality and have an intuitive sympathy for the cosmopolitan perspective.

It is thus no surprise that, at the philosophical zenith of this Rawlsian-cum-neo-Kantian moment in the 1990s, there should have been the beginnings of a clear surge of interest in cosmopolitan ethics and law. However, it is worth noting that Rawls himself did generate a significant frisson of anxiety, shortly before he died, by offering a very lukewarm reception indeed to the cosmopolitan impulse in his *Law of Peoples* (1999). In many ways though—regardless of Rawls' cool response—a new sub-discipline was already beginning to form in this period: that is, international normative theory. It was fuelled unwittingly by themes in domestic political and moral philosophy and (given what has been argued) it is no surprise at all that Kant's cosmopolitanism and *Perpetual Peace*, in particular, should suddenly become the focus of resurgent intense interest.

Cosmopolitan Moral Argument

A distinction should be drawn between a maximal more metaphysically-based moral argument and a thinner more translucent version. Such a distinction is implicit in much of the moral literature on cosmopolitanism over the last twenty years. In the richer universalist accounts the metaphysical dimension looms large. Metaphysics usually denotes a comprehensive, perfectionist or transcendental theory, which implies some form of rich objective foundation for ethics.[13] The upshot of this, in cosmopolitan terms, would be a rich metaphysical foundational defence: an example of this could be the claims of strong Stoic or religiously-based natural law thinking. My assumption—perhaps questionable—is that natural law or strong religious assumptions would now be ruled out as a sufficient moral defence of cosmopolitanism, certainly by contemporary neo-Kantians and utilitarians. The justification that one might find in, say, the Stoics, Cicero, Thomas Aquinas, or the seventeenth-century natural law arguments of Hugo Grotius, Samuel Pufendorf or John Locke, would be viewed now as largely outmoded, except by the hardy few.[14]

This distinction between maximal and minimal or thick and thin also has loose parallels to the old/new cosmopolitan distinction. The category "old" is seen by some commentators to apply to traditionalist richer or maximal defences of cosmopolitanism (that is, late Stoic or for some even Kant's arguments), whereas the new cosmopolitanism which scholars characteristically locate in the last two or three decades, argued that we should "think with Kant against Kant" (see Fine 2007, 4; Brown

13 The attempt to examine reality as a whole can be seen to be systematically pursued, for example, in Spinoza's monism, Leibniz's monadology or Hegel's absolute idealism. The comprehensive aspect of metaphysics is identifiable in terms of its explanatory breadth.

14 There are some who still wish to use natural law argumentation and it is clearly far from dead in academic writing. However, it is not clear that the older religiously-inspired forms of it have much significant purchase any longer in international law or morality debates. Some try to make a more secular argument for natural law, but that still remains unconvincing. For a significant comparatively recent attempt to formulate a case for natural law, see Finnis (1980).

2009). In this latter sense the writings of, for example, Thomas Pogge, John Rawls or Martha C. Nussbaum (in their different ways) are seen to recover, adapt and modify aspects of Kantian arguments to modern conditions of human rights and international law. Not all agree in this usage of old and new. Farah Godrej, for example, has recently categorized the likes of Nussbaum as part of what she calls the "old" cosmopolitanism. The new cosmopolitanism—in line with her idiosyncratic adaptation of postcolonial argument—repudiates the prioritizing of any Eurocentric theory and argues instead for a complex, ecumenical and plural intercultural dialogue (Godrej 2011, 10). In this context the categories of old/new become a site of philosophical contestation.

Given the old/new and maximal/minimal distinctions, it is no surprise that many late twentieth-century cosmopolitans have tried to jettison metaphysical and religious arguments. For such thinkers we are, in fact, *post-metaphysical.* There could be many illustrations of this point, for example, as the neo-Kantian Onora O'Neill puts it, modern cosmopolitanism wants a "rigorous conception of reasoning about action [...] without the need to establish any metaphysics of the person, or of the Good" (O'Neill 1996; 6). This minimalist account can also be found in most modern Kantian contractualists and indeed contemporary consequentialists and utilitarians of all shades. In this perspective, the common task is to seek for a non-metaphysical "view from nowhere". This is where we frequently find the idea of *practical reason* taking on an extra heavy philosophical load.[15] In fact, some variation of a thin universal practical reason usually fills the void left by the decline of traditional religious and metaphysical argument.

For neo-Kantians the term constructivism often figures at this point. In essence, it is a form of foundational self-recovery kit. Constructivism implies that one reasons "with all possible solidity from available beginnings, using available and followable methods to reach attainable and sustainable conclusions for relevant audiences" (O'Neill 1996, 63). Constructivism does not simply invent; it rather builds upon what is present in actual practical

15 Such a view on practical reason could be found in the writings of O'Neill, Jürgen Habermas, Brian Barry, Martha Nussbaum, Simon Caney, David Held, Alan Gewirth, Peter Singer and Thomas Pogge, amongst many others.

reason. O'Neill's conception of constructed practical reason, is thus, in her view, neither end-orientated nor norm-orientated. Reason co-ordinates in the sense of providing a negative internal authority. It must account and allow for a variety of agents—all human agents in fact—and also be able to guide action and discriminate between categories. Thus, for O'Neill, "practical reasoning begins by requiring us to reject principles which we cannot view as principles for those for whom the reasoning is to count". In other words, reason must be truly universal—universalizability implying "holding for all cases". This conception of universalizability is the essence of practical reasoning. Practical reason is neither purely formalistic nor idealized. Further, it neither assumes any idealized (metaphysical) conceptions of persons, reason or action, nor roots itself in any particular human lives. Yet, for O'Neill, although abstract, this conception of reason always begins with the "gritty realities of human life" (O'Neill 1996, 61).[16] The end result may be abstract, but it is *not* an idealized view of what ought to be.

Something very similar is at work in Jürgen Habermas' writings, although orientated differently. For Habermas genuine philosophical thought "originates in reflection on the *reason* embodied in cognition, speech, and action" (Habermas 1984, 1 [my emphasis]; see also Vincent 2004, Ch. 9). He is thus concerned to reconstruct the universal (cosmopolitan) conditions which are presupposed in all reasonable communicative action. Habermas is trying essentially to develop a universalism from what is *immanent* in human reasoning. However, this is not metaphysics; it no longer claims to be the final arbiter. Philosophy is more fallibilist, interacting with the various natural and human sciences. However, he still argues that immanent within all communicative action there is a type of interaction that is orientated to reaching understanding. Habermas keeps this distinct from what he calls "nonsocial instrumental action" and "social strategic action".

16 O'Neill comments later: "Principles indeed abstract from differences: but it does not follow that they must assume idealized accounts of human agents that not only bracket but deny human particularities and differences. Universal principles indeed apply across a plurality of differing cases, but need not prescribe or proscribe, recommend or reject uniformity of action or entitlement" (O'Neill 1996, 77). The argument tries to draw out, from the principles embodied in the ordinary "real" processes of reasoning, a basic normative pattern.

This fundamental interactive discourse consists of the type of elucidation and argumentation in which we suspend immediate action and in which participants, as Habermas puts it, seek to redeem the validity of claims which have been challenged. Essentially he wants to redeem the universalistic (cosmopolitan) conditions of understanding. Thus, implicit within the pluralism of forms of communication there are general, but stubborn, claims to reason that point to the possibility of argumentative emancipation through mutual practical reason-based dialogue.[17] There is, in other words, a reason-based universalism implicit within our communicative actions that is orientated to mutual understanding. It transcends all systematically distorting communication. It can potentially therefore critically orientate our collective political practices. This is often categorized as discourse ethics and is directly applied to cosmopolitan issues (see Bohman 2004). Habermas sees, for example, a direct connection between these accounts of reason and the justification of cosmopolitan human rights and indeed the constitutionalization of international law (see also Kumm 2004 and Habermas 2001, 2008).[18]

Legal Cosmopolitanism

The concept and practice of international law developed in embryo from the seventeenth and eighteenth centuries—although it does have older antecedents. Up to the early nineteenth century, it had links with the older idea of the "law of nations" (vis-à-vis *ius gentium*). By the end of the

17 "To gain some distance from one's own traditions and to broaden limited perspectives is one of the advantages of occidental rationalism. The European history of the interpretation and realizations of human rights is the history of such a decentering of our way of viewing things." (Habermas 2001, 119)

18 Habermas thus argues that "reflection on the starting point of a human rights discourse among participants of different cultures draws attention to normative contents that are present in the tacit presuppositions of any discourse whose goal is mutual understanding. That is, independently of their cultural backgrounds all the participants intuitively know quite well that a consensus based on conviction cannot come about as long as symmetrical relations do not exist among them—relations of mutual recognition, mutual role-taking, a shared willingness to consider one's own tradition with the eyes of the stranger and to learn from one another, and so forth" (Habermas 2001, 129).

nineteenth century, it became closely associated with the public law and constitutional law of nation-states. In fact, most European international legal theories during this period became completely focused on "the power of the state" (see Hueck 2001, 204). Thus prior to 1945, as one scholar has noted, "the only active subjects of international law were states" (Jørgensen 2000, 139).[19] International law, *per se*, could not be applied to a state unless it had expressly consented to it. The really significant shift in the outlook of international law was from the pre- to the post-1945 conceptions. Previously international law had largely regulated the relation of states; post-1945 both states *and* human individuals could be seen as significant international legal actors. This formed the backdrop to the Nuremberg Trials (1945–1946), the Genocide Convention (1948) and the Universal Declaration of Human Rights (1948).

Without entering into the complex reasons for this changing conception of international law, suffice it to say that one major consequence of this was a fresh conception which stood in a more complex nuanced relation with states. There were two very broad ways to view this phenomenon. One was to see a broad consensus on normative universal moral principles, which stood above and beyond states in some manner. The second way was to see long standing customary inter-state behaviour building up over time, which, with hindsight, begins to take the shape of accepted international rules, particularly via the catalyst of the Jewish holocaust post-1945. Some see these rules therefore constituting part of a "dense thicket" of already extant quotidian rules and practices of states over many years (see Waldron 2008). It is virtually a common law approach to international law. Such rules can have considerable longevity, although for some they lack coherence. These two outlined dimensions can of course be brought together, although

19 Although dominating the nineteenth century, this older understanding was still reflected firmly in the early twentieth century, for example, in the principles of the Lotus judgment of the 1920s. In this latter case the Permanent Court of International Justice (Lotus Case September 7th 1927) envisaged international law as solely governing the formal *relation* between states, with sovereignty taken as the central core axiom; further states were seen in this case to *make* international law. See *Lotus Judgment* (1927, 18).

there might still be some contest as to which dimension predominates in any possible disagreement. My surmise would be that the more customary approach is not that much part of contemporary discussion of legal cosmopolitanism—although there is no overriding reason why it should not be.

Another distinction occurs here on the theme of overt normative principles. Some will try to hold international rules to account, arguing, in effect, that international law needs to fulfil cosmopolitan moral principles of fairness and justice.[20] In other words, there should be a continuous moral audit of extant international laws. Another related (although more optimistic) argument suggests an extra tier of positive cosmopolitan law above states, to which states should be subject. Some renditions of human rights law could be said to be already moving in this direction (Vizard 2006).[21] This second stratagem does though contain an ambiguity in relation to moral principles. One could envisage an extra layer of cosmopolitan law above states from a legal positivist standpoint, thus without having to invoke any moral principles.[22] Other intractable problems arise here concerning enforcement and authority of such law. With no centralized world authority or enforcement practices, how could such cosmopolitan laws have any efficacy?[23] Laws, as the legal positivists frequently insist, require remedies.

20 A tiny but representative example of this large network of theorists would include Barry (1993; 1995; 1998; 1999); Beitz (1995); Brock and Brighouse (2005a); Brock (2009); Buchanan (2005); Cabrera (2004; 2010); Caney (2001; 2005); Held (2004; 2005; 2006); Mackinnon (2005); Moellendorf (2002; 2005); Nussbaum (1991; 1997; 2000; 2002; 2005); Pogge (1994; 2005a; 2005b; 2008); Sypnowich (2005); and Tan (2004; 2005).

21 For Vizard "The major international human rights treaties create legally binding international obligations on state parties progressively to implement the human rights to life, to adequate food and nutrition, to safe water and sanitation, to adequate health care facilities, and to education, both individually and collectively" (Vizard 2006, 153).

22 The legal positivist position is largely being premised on the separation between law and morality.

23 This argument is, however, not decisive, given that the establishment of the International Criminal Court (ICC) in 2002 and humanitarian interventions in Kosovo 1998–1999, and so forth, do show some sense of international efficacy;

No states are going to go to war or engage in an intervention in order to enforce a human right to say education or basic nutrition.

Let me return to the core question of this section: where does legal cosmopolitanism stand in relation to the latter sketch? My reading of this would be as follows: the establishment of "legal cosmopolitanism" is a late twentieth-century addition to the vocabulary of international law. In fact, it would still not be accepted as a description by a large majority of practicing international lawyers to the present day. It is though a form of re-description of an extant post-1945 process in international law. As in the discussion of moral cosmopolitanism, it appeared largely in the 1990s as an inferred consequence of debates in political and moral philosophy. The key figure in such debates is undoubtedly Kant. As Habermas puts unequivocally, it was Kant who "took a decisive step beyond international law centred exclusively on states" (Habermas 2006, 115). Although, as Habermas continues (correctly in my view), this process initiated by Kant, did not come to fruition as "cosmopolitan law" till after 1945. However, it is unquestionably the case that the intellectual vigour for the present interest in cosmopolitan law derives largely from an updated interest in neo-Kantianism and the themes of perpetual peace (Bohman and Lutz-Bachmann 1997).

Essentially the core legal cosmopolitan arguments dominating much of the literature are the following ones: First, the insistence that international law should be constrained, audited or designed by normative principles, that is, normative principles drawn from a conception of practical reason. Second, all such legal cosmopolitan arguments imply the rejection of the older classical conception of international law (often associated with the Westphalian state idea), that is, as largely regulating the external relations of sovereign states. Thirdly, it is usually marked out by a formal commitment

although it is clear that these are not examples of cosmopolitan normative arguments on fairness or justice. Such interventions and court processes still require the conscious political consent of collections of states to participate and enforce such rules. There are a limited number of more extreme cases in which this has taken place since 1945. Thus, efficacy will still only be achieved via the prior consent of certain powerful sovereign states.

to a more robust sense of global justice and fairness, which *for some* should have an institutional focus. There are clearly though a number of possible positions that can be taken on the latter argument. Fourthly, modern legal cosmopolitanism tends to be impatient with customary approaches to international law, seeing such arguments as lacking strength and coherence and ultimately being too piecemeal. Legal cosmopolitanism needs, in this interpretation, a more robust form of rational justification via strong consensual and universal moral principles.

At this point I make another distinction within legal cosmopolitanism. This distinction is between an optimistic and robust view, set against a more cautious or modest understanding of international law. In some ways this parallels the thin and thick distinction made under moral cosmopolitanism. There are undoubtedly enthusiasts for stronger robust cosmopolitan principles informing international law in a very substantive manner. It is however worth reminding ourselves that Kant is neither optimistic nor radical. If anything, we now live in a kind of rough and ready approximation to a Kantian international reality. There is, post-1945, a rough and ready federation of like-minded liberal-minded or democratic states, where hospitality and basic respect are accorded. Kant is much more cautious about the relation between moral beliefs and legal enactments. He is also accommodating to sovereignty. What Kant aimed at—with regard to legal cosmopolitanism—was not a rigorous moral audit of international law. His views are more modest, namely, to develop a minimal legal constitutional frame to establish conditions of something called public right, that is, laws governing individuals in relation with each other and with other states (see Brown 2009). The latter was founded on ideas of basic respect for commerce, communications and most significantly, hospitality. This scenario was distinct from law governing individuals within a state (constitutional law) and laws between states (international right). Some recent fairly intense scholarly attention has been given to Kant's views on hospitality. Hospitality can clearly be interpreted in different ways. Minimally, for Kant, if individuals travel between two or more *republican* states, they should be able to expect security of their person and should be allowed to trade (see Cavallar 2002; Brown 2006 and 2009). Some more recent scholars (including unexpectedly Jacques Derrida) want to make a lot more of this. They build more into the frail concept of hospitality than one might initially be led to expect (see Derrida 2002; Benhabib 2006).

Someone who uses the Kantian legal cosmopolitan position more modestly (and is thus distinct from the highly optimistic ethicized interpretations) is Habermas. In this context Habermas updates Kant's legal cosmopolitanism in terms of a constitutionalization of international law. International law in this latter context becomes what Habermas calls "a crucible in which quasi-natural power relations could be dissolved" (Habermas 2006, 149; see also 2008). Constitutionalization is a form of self-binding by certain kinds of states. Kant, as we know, thought that the only states really capable of such self-binding were republican. Law is, in this interpretation, no longer simply at the beck and call of state executive power; rather the reverse. Habermas is thus clear that in thinking about international law and constitutionalization, we should keep the constitution process distinct from the state. Thus the "completion of the process of constitutionalization sets the seal on the reversal of the [...] situation in which law serves as an instrument of power" (Habermas 2006, 132). For Habermas this argument would tie in closely with his understanding of *constitutional patriotism*. It is also, in this same context, that Habermas remarks on the United States invasion of Iraq in 2003 as not only destroying the US role as a "pacemaker for cosmopolitanism", but, "it's violation of international law sets a disastrous precedent for the future superpowers [...]". "Make no mistake [he continues], the normative authority of the United States of America lies in ruins" (Habermas 2006, 28–29). The USA thus moved the international legal scene back into a Schmittian world of power, invoking the state of exception through their Iraq escapade (e.g. Schmitt 1932/1996).

Institutional Cosmopolitanism

There is one important facet missing from many the above arguments on cosmopolitan law. In the various enthused debates about stronger claims to cosmopolitan law and morality one can find appeals for a new institutional authority. For example, David Held and Daniele Archibugi have indicated that cosmopolitan democracy clearly has a bright future. This portends a new world political commonwealth where democratic participation will move well beyond the borders of nation-states. In some writers, such as the slightly eccentric Alexander Wendt, it presages a full-blown world state—or for others a parliament (see Wendt 2003; also Falk and Strauss 2001). This would also entail democratic reforms to be instituted globally, applying both to the Unites Nations and organizations such as the World Trade Organization, as much as states and local, national and regional institutions (see, e.g., Archibugi and Held 1995; Archibugi 2004 and 2009; Held 2004; 2005 and 2006). For scholars, such as Held, the result would be that:

> Rightful authority or sovereignty can be stripped away from the idea of fixed borders and territories and thought of as, in principle, an attribute of basic democratic law which can be drawn upon and enacted in diverse realms, from local associations and cities to states and wider global networks [...] In this conception the nation-state "withers away" [...] states would no longer be regarded as the sole centres of legitimate power within their borders. (Held 2005, 26)

For others again this new order would entail a complex set of consensual global obligations with strong institutional implications. Thus, the neo-Kantian thinker Onora O'Neill argues that this new cosmopolitan order would entail substantial obligations to help the needy (the poor) on a global scale. She notes that "Human beings begin by being physically vulnerable. They are damaged by hunger, disease and cold, and coerced by their prospect" (O'Neill 1986, 149). If material needs are not met then there has been a systemic global institutional failure. Surprisingly, given the thinness of her conception of practical reason (outlined earlier), she argues that

> A just global economic and political order would [...] have to be one designed to meet material needs [...] It would be embodied in economic and political structures which do not institutionalise coercion or deception and so respect rationality and autonomy *in the vulnerable form in which they are actually found.* (O'Neill 1986, 149)

Thus, she argues that a just global order "would have to consist of institutions and policies whose underlying principles do not neglect human, including material, needs under actual conditions" (O'Neill 1986, 149). She describes this as a Kantian just world. It would be one "whose economic, social and political structures were based on universalizable principles" (O'Neill 1986, 159). The general tenor of O'Neill's work on poverty and its institutional implications is fleshed out in immense and impressive detail in more recent scholars such as Pogge and Nussbaum (see Pogge 1994; 2005a; 2005b; 2007; 2008; Nussbaum 1991; 1997; 2000; 2002; 2005; 2011; also Shue 1980; Copp 2004; Gewirth 2005; Bertram 2005; Vizard 2006; Caney 2007).[24]

This latter idea of extended global institutional obligations of course is light-years away from anything Kant said or actually suggested. These lines of reasoning have also moved into something more distinctively political (and occasionally utopian) rather than legal. The basic question underlying this form of institutional-orientated argument is: what is the institutional or political *authority* that is being invoked here and how could its rules be maintained and enforced? One straightforward answer is a world state or global sovereign. This strikes me as a distinctly *political* solution—indeed a very fanciful one at that. Neither Kant nor Habermas (nor Pogge or Nussbaum), it should be noted, advocate this solution. Even those such as Held and Archibugi, who write about cosmopolitan democracy in a very buoyant manner, do not suggest any highly centralized sovereign world state. It is usually a complex multi-layered federation of institutions and associations, mediated by multifaceted processes of democracy.[25] However, this question about authority (and enforcement) still remains a nagging and unresolved issue in the whole body of this institutional argument.

24 It should though be noted that there are also philosophical differences between the latter two theorists. Nussbaum has developed her own unique capabilities-based cosmopolitan approach, although it still owes a great deal to a background Kantian argumentation.

25 Some pursue a cosmopolitan vision of social movements (rather than any centralized structure), technologically networked in a utopian vision of global civil society. There is thus now a kind of libertarian romanticism for the networked global civil society (see, e.g., Castells 2009).

Particularism and Cosmopolitanism

Why might one consider contemporary cosmopolitanism(s) problematic? There is one extensive area of criticism which can only be glossed, but it highlights some of the more general issues which arise with cosmopolitan argument. We might entitle this "particularist reasoning". Nussbaum has contested fiercely against it in various writings (see, e.g., Nussbaum 2002). However more committed neo-Kantians, such as O'Neill, are clearly fully aware of its ramifications. The core argument for O'Neill of all particularisms is to "orient ethical reasoning without appeal to universal principles". Consequently, they try to anchor ethics (and law) in particular localized practices (see O'Neill 1996, 13). The real division between cosmopolitans and particularists is thus "over the *extent of the domains* across which certain principles hold, over the *content of ethical principles* and over the *degree to which* they prescribe uniform or differentiated action within their domains" (O'Neill 1996, 77).[26] However, all particularisms express a critical unease with the refusal of cosmopolitanism to engage with the situatedness or boundedness of individuals. Cosmopolitanism consequently is seen to contain an implausible account of the person. Further, it overlooks cultural difference for the sake of practical reason and such ideas of reason are too thin to bear the weight put upon them. The core question is then: is cosmopolitanism simply the expression of a Westernized culture?—leaving aside the insuperable difficulty of saying anything sensible about the term "Western".[27]

Cosmopolitans, responding to this critique, point out the inherent dangers of irresponsibility and relativism implicit in all forms of particularity.

26 O'Neill does, however, draw a further distinction between "moderate historicizing particularists" (Hans Georg Gadamer and Alisdair MacIntyre) and "radical particularists" (which she unexpectedly associates with Ludwig Wittgenstein). Historicist particularists are interested in the particularity of tradition, community and social practices.

27 This profligate use of vague terms such as "Western" or "Eurocentric" is highly characteristic of much postcolonial inspired writing (see, e.g., Godrej 2011).

Particularists make themselves intellectually redundant in terms of trying to formulate *any* general statements about other cultures or belief systems. Cross-cultural reasoning can indeed become logically insurmountable for strong particularist argument. If communal norms are constitutive of identity, then one cannot go behind or beyond them.[28] Even if particular communities embody internal modes of criticism, the basic problems are not solved, but only put back one step. Cosmopolitans do have a point here. If meaning and value lie *totally* in particular groups, nations, cultures or states, there would literally be no possibility of communication. This latter argument flies in the face of what we do know. Communication can be very difficult, but not impossible. Further, even to try to communicate the meaning of the strong particularism commits one to the assumption that others will understand your reasoning. This is a classic logical dilemma of trying to assert the universal truth of relativism.

Some particularists have responded to these arguments by arguing that there are stronger and weaker particularisms (paralleling stronger and weaker or maximalist and minimalist cosmopolitanisms). In fact a lot of the literature over the last decade in both cosmopolitanism and particularism has been dedicated to this elusive *via media*—for example situated cosmopolitanism, cosmopolitan patriotism or civic nationalism. In this sense, minimalist cosmopolitans share a great deal with weaker particularists (see, e.g., Appiah 1996 and 2006). To take an example of the weaker rendition of particularism: Michael Walzer drew a well-known but still useful distinction between thick and thin moralities, or reiterative and covering law universalisms. The reiterative universal is a minimalist universal code, constituting cross-cultural requirements which have become commonly accepted by all groups and states (Walzer 1988, 22). Walzer suggests that this "minimal morality consists in the rules of engagement that binds all the speakers" (Walzer 1994, 12). Minimal (reiterative) claims are, he argues, ultimately distilled down from maximal moralities (via covering law universalism) (Walzer 1994, 13). He identifies these minimums as: *the expectation*

28 Further, if there is a consensus in a community, there is no guarantee that it will not be a wholly iniquitous one.

not to be deceived, treated with gross cruelty or murdered, tortured, grossly oppressed, tyrannized over, or treated with manifest injustice. These might be thought of as "limit conditions"—concerning conditions of birth, death, child rearing and the like—which every human culture must engage with. He consequently posits these as a minimal content for universal human rights (Walzer 1992, 136). For Walzer, "minimalism makes for a certain limited, though important and heartening solidarity"; however, he adds that "It does not make for a full-blooded universal doctrine" (Walzer 1994, 11). There are parallels here with formulations, from a different direction, of for example situated or patriotic cosmopolitanism.[29]

The minimum is therefore distinct from the rich maximal moralities of different cultures. Walzer sees the "thicker" morality embedded in all communities. The thin universalism, as reiterative, acknowledges that, subject to these minimal universal constraints, there are many different and valuable ways of life that have equal rights to flourish in their respective locations, and deserve equal respect (Walzer 1988, 22). Walzer therefore essentially holds onto the particularist claim of cultural difference, while at the same time adhering to a "thin universalism", which upholds universal human rights. The effect of this argument on cosmopolitanism is to accommodate a much thinner version. If one translated that into say human rights terms it would be to accept the most minimal set of civil rights (but no more); thus, at a push, the first twenty-one articles of the 1948 Declaration on Human Rights.

Problems with Particularist Reasoning

If the harder-edged or stronger particularist position is self-refuting, the softer or thinner position also has some awkward problems. Thus, if basic

29 Paul Rabinow, for example, in this spirit, defines cosmopolitanism as "an ethos of macro-interdependencies, with an acute consciousness (often forced upon people) of the inescapabilities and particularities of places, character, historical trajectories, and fates" (Rabinow 1986, 258; cf. also chapter by Piirimäe in this volume).

minimums are exempted and regarded as universal, then it implies that there are apparently non-particularist universal truths about humanity, which all cultures acknowledge. If this is the case, what is the non-particularist *justification* for such rights for particularist critics? The problem here is that the potential candidates for justification of human rights—utilitarianism, neo-Kantianism and contractualism—are all rejected at the outset. The problem then for weaker particularists is that in acknowledging that the most basic cosmopolitan minimums are exempt from particularist logic, they appear then to be admitting that some universal claims have validity. However, the key question is: where do they go next to find an authoritative justification for why, for example, we abhor cruelty, or find starvation, extreme racial discrimination and torture universally unacceptable? This remains unclear.

In sum, the particularist case is caught in a dilemma. If it holds to a strong particularism, it is self-refuting. On the other hand, if it is prepared (vis-à-vis thinner particularism) to accept the minimal claim that torture or starvation, and the like, are universally unacceptable, then the question arises as to the *relation* between particularist argument and the actual justification of the universal minimums. Thus, the concept of the minimum cosmopolitan law or morals opens up a rift in the weaker particularist position. Particularist critics who exempt minimal cosmopolitan values or laws are committed to an apparent contradiction. They assume (that is the cosmopolitan minimum) what they appear to deny (via their particularist argument).[30]

30 There are also further ambiguities concerning what is minimal in, for example human rights discourse. In other words, there is a general conceptual confusion about what is precisely understood to be a minimal universal. Paradoxically, despite any intuitions we might have about basic minimums, in practice there are four contenders for minimums. First, there are (what might be called) *absolute or material minimums*, that is to say, the biological (dietary and shelter) conditions of human functioning. These correspond with the idea of basic human needs. They also fit into the sphere of extreme poverty. The conclusion would be that human rights minimums address the most basic issues of human need and extreme poverty. Second, there are the traditional broad claims to life and basic liberties. These might be called generic *civil minimums*. This appears to be what underlies the general acknowledgment, by soft

A Stock-take on Cosmopolitan Arguments

What is common to modern cosmopolitanism? First there is a sense in which moral, legal and institutional cosmopolitanism are all comparatively recent phenomena, which have arisen largely in the last two decades, that is, to the extent that they have become an accepted part of the academic *lingua franca*. Second, the manner in which this sudden advance has been achieved has been largely via a re-description of existing practices of internationalism (and specific changes in international law) in the post-1945 period. The debate on cosmopolitanism enables theorists to bring together a lot of apparently distinct debates in morality, politics and law. Third, if there is a core cosmopolitan argument, it is that a normative universal standard is needed to either audit or construct international law, institutions or political processes. Fourth, interpretations of Kant figure strongly in a large number of recent cosmopolitan accounts. It is not Kant exclusively, but he does have a large role to play. I would also contend that it is not Kant as

---

particularist critics of human rights, when they accept minimums such as prohibitions against slavery, genocide, murder, torture, prolonged arbitrary detention and systematic racial discrimination. Minimum thus refer to basic civil rights to life, liberty and freedom from oppression. Third, there are *economic and social minimums*. In this sense, many particularist critics (for example Asian values proponents) have argued that economic and social well-being are far more important than civil or political rights. Generic civil human rights are all very well, but if one is living in an insecure developing economy, subject to the vicissitudes of a global capitalist market, then basic economic and social (human) rights are far more important than the generic civil or political rights. This is also often seen in the context of a move from a *general* to a *special* conception of human rights, and can generate anger and consternation amongst some civil and political rights proponents. Fourth, human beings can be seen to function solely through cultures. What is important, minimally, is that human rights should embody the deeply-held values of these particular cultures. Human rights should thus accord with, for example, the moral and religious beliefs of diverse cultures. Thus, areas like criminal law, family law, women's and children's rights and the rights of indigenous groups, are all customary and culturally specific. These might be seen as *cultural minimums*.

such, but a manipulated and modernized Kantianism. Fifthly, traditional sources of authority—such as religion and strong metaphysics—are usually bypassed in modern accounts, despite the fact they did figure prominently in all earlier arguments in Stoicism and natural law theory. Sixthly the idea of practical reason or just reason (via Kant) is fairly continuously invoked as the key authority in cosmopolitan argument. Seventh, amongst a large swathe of modern cosmopolitans there is a variable yearning for the juridification and institutionalization of the international sphere. Finally, cosmopolitanism fragments into what I have called more maximalist and minimalist accounts. This latter distinction cross-cuts legal, moral and political cosmopolitanism.

A Reluctant Cosmopolitanism

In concluding, I want to offer some final, rather thin, reflections on cosmopolitanism which underpin the reluctant stance taken in this chapter. First, I am not convinced that cosmopolitanism has got morality right. My own sense is that some version of thinner particularism (or possibly a more situated cosmopolitanism) gives a more persuasive view of ethics. The idea of a set of strong universal moral principles, in this sense, is a form of "consoling myth" of the modern post-1945 era.[31] Thus, as John McDowell has argued (in a rather Hegelian manner), the question how we ought to live or act is not achieved by applying universal rational principles, but rather by being a certain kind of person, with a certain form of sensitivity, in a particular situation. Reason is not an external validating tool, rather it manifests itself "from within the practice whose status is in question" (McDowell 1998, 70). A view of how we should live or ought to act is not,

31 We need to "give up the idea that philosophical thought, about the sorts of practice in question, should be undertaken at some external standpoint, outside our immersion in our familiar forms of life" (McDowell 1998, 63–64).

as such, codifiable or fully rationalizable into universal rules. As McDowell argues "A conception of how to live shows itself [...] in one's seeing, or being able to be brought to see, one fact rather than another as salient. And our understanding of such a conception enters into our understanding of actions [...] by enabling us to share, or at least comprehend, the agent's perception of saliences." The thought of what is right needs in this reading a "more subtle construal than the deductive paradigm allows". Knowledge of how to live always "interacts with particular knowledge" (quotes from McDowell 1998, 69). Moral virtue is thus largely a perceptual capacity, and trying to reduce it to deductive principle of universal rules is a problem.[32] The latter strikes me personally as a more believable account of moral conduct, but it does lead to skepticism with regards to some of the optimistic cosmopolitan moral claims.

Second, there is a problem with all versions of cosmopolitanism (regardless of particularist critics) and that is *authority*. Basically, what is the nature of the authority that allows, facilitates and legitimates cosmopolitan claims? Contemporary cosmopolitans do not seem to take this problem as seriously as they should. As Hannah Arendt commented, "Authority as we once knew it, which grew out of the Roman experience of foundation and was understood in the light of Greek political philosophy, has nowhere been re-established [...]", either through revolutions or through the even less promising means of restoration, and least of all through conservative moods:

> For to live in a political realm with neither authority nor the concomitant awareness that the source of authority transcends power and those who are in power, means to be confronted anew, without the religious trust in a sacred beginning and without the protection of traditional and therefore self-evident standards of behaviour, by the elementary problems of human living-together. (Arendt 1968, 141)

Arendt's point is as true of our domestic political situation, as (even more so) of our international situation. Prior to the modern era the authority

32 Moral virtue is an ability to "recognize requirements that situations impose on one's behaviour" (McDowell 1998, 53).

of, say, religion and the sacred largely sufficed for acceptable justification, but no longer, even for those who subsist in modern theocracies such as Iran. Yet, even democracy has no concluding authoritative answer here (although I would still argue that it is better to have democracy than not to have it); all democracy does is amplify our present dilemma of authority. Secular practical reason does not really fill this vacuum of authority. It is too vague and implicitly contestable to suffice as a secure or acceptable argument. Overall this loss of the "authoritative" helps neither cosmopolitans nor their particularist critics.

This leads me to a third connected point which is both large and unwieldy. It focuses on institutional and legal cosmopolitanism and underpins my reluctant stance. Law—whether state based or cosmopolitan—needs both authority and some form of enforcement. As already argued, morality and practical reason do not provide an uncontested authority. However, what of law itself? Surely cosmopolitan law can fulfill the need for authority? Indeed there is one facet of legal and institutional cosmopolitanism which has an answer of sorts—that is a world state. A world state would provide both clear authority and enforcement. But this, in turn, is minimally slightly insane and completely unachievable under present conditions. Nonetheless, is there anything else that is redeemable in the institutional and legal cosmopolitan argument?

Rather than use the term institutional, I want to refocus on the concept of politics and its relation to law. Simply put, my argument is that *there is no law which creates a rule of law*. As one legal scholar has observed, there is a continuous tension in law "which arises from the conflict between our commitment to the 'rule of law'—a commitment that requires law to transcend mere interests and partisan ideologies—and our knowledge that in fact law does not and cannot actually be what we need it to be" (Duncan Kennedy quoted in Smith 2004, 162). He continues:

> Judges resolve this conflict by presenting decisions as deductive, and by half-believing that law in fact has this character […] They do not engage in "conscious, deliberate, strategic misrepresentation" […] Instead, the denial of the ideological character of

> legal decisions is half-conscious, or conscious and unconscious at the same time. (Quoted in Smith 2004, 162)[33]

In this sense, the relation between law and politics is underpinned by a form of noble lie—a necessary lie for the sake of judges and the judged. The upshot is that lawyers and judges continuously search for authoritative voices. Such authoritative voices indicate an "informing spirit" beyond the individual author or legislation (Smith 2004, 172–173).[34] Yet law still persists in an "ontological gap"; much of what we say about law thus "makes little sense". Law in the end is therefore "just words" (Smith 2004, 169).[35] Something is missing here.

The apparent autonomy of law with regards to politics is overdone. The constitutionalization of cosmopolitan law that, for example, Habermas advocates—as distinct from states and power—is thus a problem. There is no clear immutable distinction between "law" and "politics". Law and

33 This "ideological element [in law]" is thus described as "a kind of secret, like a family secret—the incestuous relationship between a grandfather and mother—that affects all the generations as something that is both known and denied". It is not an intentional deception, rather "judges keep the secret, even from themselves, in part because participants in legal culture and in general political culture want them to. Everyone wants it to be true that it is not only possible but common for judges to judge non-ideologically. But everyone is aware of the critique, and everyone knows that the naïve theory of the rule of law is a fairy tale" (Duncan Kennedy quoted in Smith 2004, 162–163).

34 "Western legal science is a secular theology [...] which often makes no sense because its theological presuppositions are no longer accepted" (Harold Berman quoted in Smith 2004, 158). Even precedent in the common law embodies this same sense of "holding of the case". It is no wonder that Roberto M. Unger speaks of the legal profession as "a priesthood that had lost their faith and kept their jobs" (see Unger 1983, 674–675).

35 What is happening in current discourse is that "practitioners profess *not to believe* in something—'the law', or the law's metaphysical presuppositions—that their discourse and practice would suggest they in fact *do* at some level believe in. And since their practice—or, more generally, the 'rule of law'—is something that they evidently value, their dissonant professions of unbelief in the presuppositions of law are not self-serving in any straightforward sense" (Smith 2004, 164). Assumptions are disavowed which actually are adhered to.

politics are blended at both the domestic and international levels. What we think of as law is in fact habituated and institutionalized political judgment. However, at the same time, against Carl Schmitt's rather monotonous notion of politics as implying antagonism (see Schmitt 1932/1996), there is no reason not to see a subtle form of rightness implicit in political judgment. Politics does situate and uphold the *authority* of the rule of law in certain circumstances. Politics therefore does not *exclusively* equate with antagonism, power, arbitrariness and self-interest, although such ideas are not absent from politics. To equate politics wholly with power and self-interest is, in point, a modernized and somewhat romanticized Augustinianism. Politics is a realm of plurality; but it can also be a realm of constructive engagement with plurality. Within certain kinds of state this is a constitutive (if continuously contested) feature of life.

Thus, the positive dimension of my interpretation of political cosmopolitanism is not to emphasize the "world state", but rather to focus on the *customary* vernaculars of the civil constitutional state tradition as providing a fragile authority. The civil state—where the comparative rarity of an enriched sense of politics exists—institutionalizes and authorizes the procedures of civil mediation. The civil *political* state is therefore envisaged as a formal procedural structure which engages with the condition of human plurality, that is, the inevitable range of interests and demands over resources which appears in the public sphere of politics.[36] In my interpretation therefore the shift in international law, post-1945, which formed the groundwork to cosmopolitan re-descriptions in the 1990s, was due largely to a fortuitous grouping of similar-minded constitutional and civil-orientated states, under certain unique historical circumstances. We are still living (at this moment) within the effects of this historical circumstance. This is central to understanding how modern international law comes about authoritatively. It is thus the collection of overlapping civil constitutional

36 Politics is not something which necessarily exists in all human association. When it does exist—as a tried mode of activity—it is premised on human plurality and competition, but it also focuses on ways to mediate this plurality. Part of this mediating process is through critical deliberation and negotiation.

states themselves who provide the crucial authoritative setting for the idea of a cosmopolitan rule of law. This is essentially a political setting, connected irrevocably to an understanding of political judgment.

Cosmopolitanism is thus possible, but it is something that grows very tentatively out of a particular conception of politics; something pursued by a like-minded association of civil-minded states. Cosmopolitanism is largely the outcome of a series of political judgments, made under the aegis of a concatenation of historical circumstances. This I would describe as a reluctant, bottom up version of cosmopolitanism, which grows from the occasionally piecemeal and often unenthusiastic self-binding judgments of certain types of political associations. Cosmopolitanism is not therefore a moral or legal movement in itself (although it has legal and moral ramifications), but is better understood as a somewhat belated (occasionally almost pessimistic) political attempt to assemble firewalls against the rapaciousness and destructiveness built into other historical facets of the state tradition and the human species.

References

Appadurai, Arjun, 1996. *Modernity at large.* Minneapolis: University of Minnesota Press.

Appiah, Kwame Anthony, 1996. "Cosmopolitan patriots". In: Martha C. Nussbaum, 1996. *For love of country: Debating the limits of patriotism.* Ed. Joshua Cohen. Boston: Beacon, 21–29.

Appiah, Kwame Anthony, 2006. *Cosmopolitanism: Ethics is in a world of strangers.* Middlesex: Penguin.

Archibugi, Daniele and David Held (eds.), 1995. *Cosmopolitan democracy.* Cambridge: Polity.

Archibugi, Daniele, 2004. *Cosmopolis.* London: Verso.

Archibugi, Daniele, 2009. *The global commonwealth of citizens: Toward cosmopolitan democracy.* Princeton, NJ: Princeton University Press.

Arendt, Hannah, 1968. "What is authority?". In Hannah Arendt, 1968. *Between past and future.* Middlesex: Penguin.

Aurelius, Marcus, 161–180 AD/1967. *Meditations*. Trans. M. Staniforth. Middlesex: Penguin.

Barber, Benjamin, 1995. *Jihad vs McWorld: How globalism and tribalism are reshaping the world*. New York: Ballantine.

Barry, Brian, 1993. "Humanity in global perspective". In: Bob Goodin and Philip Pettit (eds.), 1993. *A companion to contemporary political philosophy*. Oxford: Blackwell.

Barry, Brian, 1995. "Spherical justice and global justice". In David Miller and Michael Walzer (eds.), 1995. *Pluralism, justice and equality*. Oxford: Clarendon Press.

Barry, Brian, 1998. "International society from a cosmopolitan perspective". In: David Mapel and Terry Nardin (eds.), 1998. *International society: Diverse ethical perspectives*. Princeton, NJ: Princeton University Press.

Barry, Brian, 1999. "Statism and nationalism: A cosmopolitan critique". In: Ian Shapiro and Lea Brilmayer (eds.), 1999. *Global Justice: Nomos XLI*. New York: New York University Press, 12–66.

Beck, Ulrich, 2006. *The cosmopolital vision*. Cambridge: Polity.

Beitz, Charles, 2005. "Cosmopolitanism and global justice". *Journal of Ethics*, 9(1–2), 11–27.

Benhabib, Seyla, 2006. *Another cosmopolitanism (the Berkeley Tanner lectures)*. Ed. Robert Post. Oxford: Oxford University Press.

Bertram, Chris, 2005. "Global justice, moral development, and democracy." In: Gillian Brock and Harry Brighouse (eds.), 2005. *The political philosophy of cosmopolitanism*. Cambridge: Cambridge University Press, 75–91.

Bohman, James and M. Lutz-Bachmann (eds.), 1997. *Perpetual peace: Essays on Kant's Cosmopolitan ideal*. Cambridge, Mass: MIT Press.

Bohman, James, 2004 "Republican Cosmopolitanism", *Journal of Political Philosophy*, 12, 3, 336–352.

Brock, Gillian, 2009. *Global Justice: A Cosmopolitan Account*. Oxford: Oxford University Press.

Brock, Gillian and Harry Brighouse, 2005a. "Introduction". In: Gillian Brock and Harry Brighouse (eds.), 2005. *The political philosophy of cosmopolitanism*. Cambridge: Cambridge University Press, 1–9.

Brock, Gillian and Harry Brighouse (eds.), 2005b. *The political philosophy of cosmopolitanism*. Cambridge: Cambridge University Press.

Brown, G.W. 2006. "Kantian cosmopolitan law and the idea of a cosmopolitan constitution". *History of Political Thought*, 27(4), 662–684.

Brown, G.W. 2009. *Grounding cosmopolitanism: From Kant to the idea of a cosmopolitan constitution*. Edinburgh: Edinburgh University Press.

Brown, G.W. and David Held (eds.), 2010. *The cosmopolitan reader*. Cambridge: Polity.

Buchanan, Allen, 2005. "In the national interest". In: Gillian Brock and Harry Brighouse (eds.), 2005. *The political philosophy of cosmopolitanism*. Cambridge: Cambridge University Press 2005, 110–126.
Cabrera, Luis, 2004. *Political theory of global justice: A cosmopolitan case for the world state*. London: Routledge.
Cabrera, Luis, 2010. *The practice of global citizenship*. Cambridge: Cambridge University Press.
Caney, Simon, 2001. "Cosmopolitan justice and equalizing opportunities". In Thomas Pogge (ed.), 2001. *Global justice*. Oxford: Blackwell, 123–144.
Caney, Simon, 2005. *Justice beyond borders: A global political theory*. Oxford: Oxford University Press.
Caney, Simon, 2007. "Global poverty and human rights: The case for positive duties". In: Thomas Pogge (ed.), 2007. *Freedom from poverty as a human right: Who owes what to the very poor?* Oxford: Oxford University Press, 273–302.
Carter, April, 2001. *Political theory of global citizenship*. London: Routledge.
Castells, Manuel, 2009. *The rise of the network society*, 2nd ed. Oxford: Wiley-Blackwell.
Cavallar, Georg, 1999. *Kant and the theory and practice of international right*. Cardiff: University of Wales Press.
Cavallar, Georg, 2002. *The rights of strangers*. Farnham: Ashgate Publishers.
Cavallar, Georg, 2011. *Imperfect cosmopolis*. Cardiff: University of Wales Press.
Cheah, Pheng and Bruce Robbins (eds.), 1998. *Cosmopolitics*. Minneapolis: University of Minnesota.
Chomsky, Noam, 1999. *The new military humanism: Lessons from Kosovo*. London: Pluto.
Copp, David, 2005. "International justice and the basic needs principle". In: Gillian Brock and Harry Brighouse (eds.), 2005. *The political philosophy of cosmopolitanism*. Cambridge: Cambridge University Press, 39–54.
Derrida, Jacques, 2002. *Cosmopolitanism and forgiveness*. Trans. Mark Dooley and M. Hughes. London: Routledge.
Douzinas, Costas, 2007. *Human rights and empire: The political philosophy of cosmopolitanism*. London: Routledge.
Falk, Richard and Andrew Strauss, 2001. "Towards global parliament". *Foreign Affairs*, 80(1), 212–220.
Fine, Robert, 2007. *Cosmopolitanism*. London: Routledge.
Finnis, John, 1980. *Natural law and natural rights*. Oxford: Clarendon Press.
Gallie, W.B. 1977. *Philosophers of war and peace*. Cambridge: Cambridge University Press.
Gewirth, Alan, 1982. *Human rights: Essays on justification and application*. Chicago: Chicago University Press.

Gewirth, Alan, 2001. "Duties to fulfil the human rights of the poor". In: Thomas Pogge (ed.), 2007. *Freedom from poverty as a human right: Who owes what to the very poor?* Oxford: Oxford University Press, 219–236.
Godrej, Farah, 2011. *Cosmopolitan political thought: Method, practice, discipline*. Oxford: Oxford University Press.
Habermas, Jürgen, 1984. *The theory of communicative action: Rationality and rationalization*, vol 1. Trans. Thomas McCarthy. Boston: Beacon Press.
Habermas, Jürgen, 2001. "Remarks on legitimation through human rights". In: Jürgen Habermas, 2001. *The postnational constellation: Political essays*. Cambridge: Polity.
Habermas, Jürgen, 2006. *The divided West*. Trans. Ciaran Cronion. Cambridge: Polity.
Habermas, Jürgen, 2008. "The constitutionalization of international law and the legitimation problems of a constitution for world society". *Constellations*, 15(4), 444–455.
Hardt, Michael and Antonio Negri, 2001. *Empire*. Cambridge, MA: Harvard University Press.
Held, David, 2004. *Global covenant*. Cambridge: Polity.
Held, David, 2005. "Principles of cosmopolitan order". In: Gillian Brock and Harry Brighouse (eds.), 2005. *The political philosophy of cosmopolitanism*. Cambridge: Cambridge University Press, 10–27.
Held, David, 2006. *Cosmopolitanism: A defence*. Cambridge: Polity.
Hollinger, David, 1995. *Postethnic America*. New York: Basic Books.
Hueck, Ingo J., 2001. "The discipline of the history of international law: New trends and methods on the history of international law". *Journal of the History of International Law*, 3, 194–217.
Hutchings, Kimberly and Roland Dannreuether (eds.), 1999. *Cosmopolitan citizenship*. Houndsmill: Macmillan.
Jørgensen, Nina, H.B., 2000. *The responsibility of states for international crimes*. Oxford: Oxford University Press.
Kant, Immanuel, 1795. "Perpetual peace: A philosophical sketch". In: Hans Reiss (ed.), 1991. *Kant's political writings*. Cambridge: Cambridge University Press.
Kant, Immanuel, 1798/1974. *Anthropology from a pragmatic view*. Trans. Mary J. Gregor. The Hague: Martinus Nijhoff.
Kleingeld, Pauline, 1999. "Six varieties of cosmopolitanism in late eighteenth century Germany". *Journal of History of Ideas*, 60(3), 505–524.
Koselleck, Reinhart, 1986. "Social history and conceptual history". In: Reinhart Koselleck, 2002. *The practice of conceptual history: Timing history, spacing concepts*. Trans. Todd Samuel Presner *et al.* Stanford, CA: Stanford University Press, 20–37.
Kumm, Mattias, 2004. "The legitimacy of international law: A constitutionalist framework of analysis". *European Journal of International Law*, 15(5), 907–931.

Lotus Judgment, SS "Lotus" (France vs Turkey) (Judgment), 1927, Permanent Court of International Justice [PCIJ], (ser A) No 9, 18.
Mackinnon, Catriona, 2005. "Cosmopolitan hope". In: Gillian Brock and Harry Brighouse (eds.), 2005. *The political philosophy of cosmopolitanism*. Cambridge: Cambridge University Press, 234–249.
Marcus, George and M.M.J. Fischer, 1986. *Anthropology as cultural critique*. Chicago, Chicago University Press.
McDowell, John, 1998. *Mind value and reality*. Cambridge, MA: Harvard University Press.
Moellendorf, Darrel, 2002. *Cosmopolitan justice*. Boulder Colorado: Westview Press.
Moellendorf, Darrel, 2005. "Persons' interests, states' duties, and global governance". In: Gillian Brock and Harry Brighouse (eds.), 2005. *The political philosophy of cosmopolitanism*. Cambridge: Cambridge University Press, 148–163.
Mouffe, Chantal, 2008. "Which world order: cosmopolitan or multipolar?". *Ethical Perspectives*, 15(4), 453–467.
Nussbaum, Martha C., 1991. "Kant and stoic cosmopolitanism". *Journal of Political Philosophy*, 1, 1–25.
Nussbaum, Martha C., 1997. "Human rights theory: Capabilities and human rights". *Fordham Law Review*, 66, 273–300.
Nussbaum, Martha C., 2000. "Duties of material aid: Cicero's problematic legacy". *Journal of Political Philosophy*, 8, 176–206.
Nussbaum, Martha, 1996. "Patriotism and cosmopolitanism". In: Martha C. Nussbaum, 1996. *For love of country: Debating the limits of patriotism*. Ed. Joshua Cohen. Boston: Beacon, 2–17.
Nussbaum, Martha C., 2005. "Beyond the social contract: capabilities and global justice." In: Gillian Brock and Harry Brighouse (eds.), 2005. *The political philosophy of cosmopolitanism*. Cambridge: Cambridge University Press, 196–218.
Nussbaum, Martha C., 2011. *Creating capabilities: The human development approach*. Cambridge, MA: Harvard University Press.
O'Neill, Onora. 1986. *Faces of hunger*. London: George Allen and Unwin.
O'Neill, Onora, 1996. *Towards justice and virtue: A constructive account of practical reasoning*. Cambridge: Cambridge University Press.
O'Neill, Onora, 2000. *Bounds of justice*. Cambridge: Cambridge University Press.
Pogge, Thomas, 1994. "Cosmopolitanism and sovereignty". In: Chris Brown (ed.), 1994. *Political Restructuring in Europe: Ethical perspectives*. London: Routledge, 85–118.
Pogge, Thomas, 2005a. "Human rights and global health: A research program". *Metaphilosophy*, 36(1–2), 182–209.

Pogge, Thomas, 2005b. "A cosmopolitan perspective on the global economic order". In: Gillian Brock and Harry Brighouse (eds.), 2005. *The political philosophy of cosmopolitanism*. Cambridge: Cambridge University Press, 92–109.

Pogge, Thomas, 2008. *World poverty and human rights: Cosmopolitan responsibilities and reforms*, 2nd ed. Cambridge: Polity Press.

Pogge, Thomas (ed.), 2007. *Freedom from poverty as a human Right: Who owes what to the very poor?* Oxford: Oxford University Press.

Rabinow, Paul, 1986. "Representations are social facts". In: J. Clifford and G.E. Marcus (eds.), 1986. *Writing culture: The poetics and politics of ethnography*. Berkeley: University of California Press.

Rawls, J. 1999. *Law of peoples*. Cambridge, MA: Harvard University Press.

Schmitt, Carl, 1932/1996. *The concept of the political*. Trans. George Schwab. Chicago: Chicago University Press.

Shue, H. 1980. *Basic rights*. Princeton, NJ: Princeton University Press.

Smith, Steven, 2004. *Law's quandary*. Cambridge, Mass: Harvard University Press.

Sypnowich, Christine, 2005. "Cosmopolitans, cosmopolitanism, and human flourishing". In: Gillian Brock and Harry Brighouse (eds.), 2005. *The political philosophy of cosmopolitanism*. Cambridge: Cambridge University Press, 55–74.

Tan, Kok-Chor, 2004. *Justice without borders*. Cambridge: Cambridge University Press.

Tan, Kok-Chor, 2005. "The demands of justice and national allegiances". In: Gillian Brock and Harry Brighouse (eds.), 2005. *The political philosophy of cosmopolitanism*. Cambridge: Cambridge University Press, 164–179.

Unger, Roberto M., 1983. "The critical legal studies movement". *Harvard Law Review*, 96(3), 561–675.

Vincent, Andrew, 2004. *The nature of political theory*. Oxford: Oxford University Press.

Vizard, Polly, 2006. *Poverty and human rights: Sen's "capability perspective" explored*. Oxford: Oxford University Press.

Waldron, Jeremy, 2006. "Cosmopolitan norms". In: Seyla Benhabib, 2006. *Another cosmopolitanism (the Berkeley Tanner lectures)*. Ed. Robert Post. Oxford: Oxford University Press, 83–101.

Walzer, Michael, 1988. "Interpretation and social criticism". In: S.M. McMurrin (ed.), 1988. *The Tanner lectures on human values*, vol. 7. Salt Lake City: University of Utah Press.

Walzer, Michael, 1992. *Just and unjust wars: A moral argument with historical illustrations*, 2nd ed. New York: Basic Books.

Walzer, Michael, 1994. *Thick and thin: Moral argument at home and abroad*. Notre Dame and London: Notre Dame University Press.

Wendt, Alexander, 2003. "Why a world state is inevitable". *European Journal of International Relations*, 9(4), 491–542.

Notes on Contributors

TAMARA CARAUS holds a PhD in political philosophy and is a researcher at the Institute for Advanced Studies, New Europe College in Bucharest.

GEORG CAVALLAR is Universitätsdozent of Modern History and a lecturer in the Faculty of Philosophy and Educational Sciences at the University of Vienna.

TANIA ESPINOZA holds a PhD in French and is currently a visiting lecturer in the Department of Literature at the Universidad Mayor de San Andrés in La Paz.

JAMIL KHADER is Professor of English Literature in the English Department at Stetson University in DeLand, FL.

REBECKA LETTEVALL is Associate Professor of Intellectual History and a senior lecturer in the School of Historical and Contemporary Studies, as well as Director of the Centre for Baltic and East European Studies, at Södertörn University, Stockholm.

NINA LEX is a Marie Curie PhD Fellow in Enlightenment and Global History at the Spanish National Research Council, Madrid and Berlin.

KRISTIAN PETROV is Associate Professor of Intellectual History and a senior lecturer in the School of Historical and Contemporary Studies at Södertörn University, Stockholm.

EVA PIIRIMÄE is Associate Professor of Political Theory at the Institute of Government and Politics at the University of Tartu.

FRANK EJBY POULSEN is a PhD researcher in the history of political thought at the European University Institute in Florence.

GALIN TIHANOV is Professor of Comparative Literature and Intellectual History and holder of the George Steiner Chair of Comparative Literature at Queen Mary, University of London.

ANDREW VINCENT is Emeritus Professor of Political Theory at Sheffield University and Research Professor at Cardiff University.

AARON VLASAK holds a PhD in philosophy and is a Humanities Faculty Fellow at Syracuse University in Syracuse, NY.

Index of Names

Index of Terms

New Visions of the Cosmopolitan

Series Editors: Patrick O'Mahony and Tracey Skillington

New Visions of the Cosmopolitan explores how the forces of contemporary social change release a cosmopolitan energy that dilutes the relevance of the nation-state. The 'transnational turn' creates tendencies toward greater world openness. A more pluralist, multi-perspectivist late modernity requires a cosmopolitan research framework capable of illustrating how world histories and futures are intricately connected under these new conditions. This series offers a body of work exploring how cosmopolitan ideas, emerging from encounters between local and global currents, generate impulses towards social, cultural, legal, political and economic transformation.

The series invites contributions that focalize this contemporary situation using theories, perspectives and methodologies drawn from multiple disciplines. Of particular, although not exclusive, interest are proposals exploring: transnational visions of justice and solidarity; cosmopolitan publics; researching cosmopolitan worlds; cosmopolitan memory; the cosmopolitics of contemporary global capitalism; borders of the cosmopolitan; cosmopolitanism in the non-western world; security, war and peace in a cosmopolitan age; multiple modernities; divergence and convergence; political culture and multi-level governance.

This peer-reviewed series publishes monographs and edited collections.

Vol. 1 Patrick O'Mahony
The Contemporary Theory of the Public Sphere
2013. ISBN 978-3-0343-0146-6

Vol. 2 Rebecka Lettevall and Kristian Petrov (eds)
Critique of Cosmopolitan Reason: Timing and Spacing the Concept of World Citizenship
2014. ISBN 978-3-0343-0898-4

www.ingramcontent.com/pod-product-compliance
Ingram Content Group UK Ltd.
Pitfield, Milton Keynes, MK11 3LW, UK
UKHW021827100926
8556IPUK00003B/197

9 783034 308984